Culture in American Education:

Anthropological Approaches to Minority and Dominant Groups in the Schools

Books by Ruth Landes:

Ojibwa Sociology. New York: Columbia University Press, 1937.

The Ojibwa Woman. New York: Columbia University Press, 1938.

The City of Women. New York: The Macmillan Company, 1947.

Latin-Americans of the Southwest. St. Louis: Webster Division, McGraw-Hill Book Company, 1965.

Chapters contributed to other books:

"Ojibwa Indians" in Margaret Mead (ed.), *Cooperation and Competition among Primitive Peoples.* New York: McGraw-Hill Book Company, 1937 and Boston: Beacon Press, 1962.

"Culture and Education" in George F. Kneller (ed.), *Foundations of Education.* New York: John Wiley and Sons, Inc., 1963.

Culture in American Education:

Anthropological Approaches to Minority and
Dominant Groups in the Schools

RUTH LANDES
Professor of Anthropology
McMaster University
Hamilton, Ontario
Canada

JOHN WILEY & SONS, INC.
New York · London · Sydney

SECOND PRINTING, MARCH, 1967

Preface

This book describes a teacher-training experiment that paired cultural anthropology and education. My acknowledgments of aid extend back through decades to old and new relationships and experiences.

First and always, I owe my philosophy to my idealistic parents, Anna and Joseph Schlossberg. In their lively, intellectual New York home, and through careers in organized labor and public education, they devoted themselves wholly to struggling men and their dreams. These interests guided me to professional social work, first, and finally to anthropology, which I adopted soon after finishing college.

Thus in my early twenties, I joined the dozen-and-a-half students pursuing graduate anthropology studies at Columbia University. Through my father I had met the great anthropologist, Franz Boas; he in turn presented me to his great disciple, Ruth F. Benedict. The inspiring force of these two was irresistible to a young person seeking a path among the social turmoils gathering in the 1930's.

Boas introduced me to the late Zora Neale Hurston, his student and "the first Negro" (as people commented) graduated from Barnard College. This vivacious, eloquently articulate daughter of a Florida preacher brought to me in a phrase her people's complex fate, shadowed, she said, in "eyes of Africa looking out of the face of Europe." From her field studies and life among Negro workers and peasants she created vivid stories and essays. My father introduced me to the late Abram L. Harris, after the Second World War a University of Chicago professor but then "the first Negro" to secure a Ph.D. in economics from Columbia University. His first book, done with Sterling

v

D. Spero, was *The Black Worker*. My father also introduced me to Walter White, the late secretary of the National Association for the Advancement of Colored People, who also wrote novels about Negro sufferings. White's Nordic blondness, indistinguishable in looks from any "cracker" in his home state of Georgia, gave perplexing dimensions to his Negro identity. *Time's* cover carried his picture on the eve of the Second World War along with a friendly story that mentioned his residence in an elegant "white" Washington hotel near the White House. This stirred far-flung scandals among Southerners and others, a challenge to Jim Crow that White thought long overdue.

Now I was set for years of intercultural experiences and responsibilities (which are sometimes also called "interracial") that eventually led me from 1959 through 1961 to the experimental anthropology and education program described in this book. The program was initiated and designed by Claremont's education faculty and was supported generously, in finances and spirit, by the Rosenberg Foundation of San Francisco. Cordial appreciation is due Professor Donald McNassor and the late Dean Luther J. Lee, Jr. for establishing the program and for continual encouragement. Great appreciation is due Mrs. Jackson Chance, Executive Director of the Rosenberg Foundation, for her unfailing and delicate sympathy.

Public-school faculties in California invariably have been helpful. Miss Ethel M. Johnson, Director of Elementary Instruction, San Bernardino City Schools, arranged unique opportunities for the experiment during its existence. Miss B. Irene Hobbs, Supervisor, Area 6, Child Welfare and Attendance Branch, Los Angeles City School districts, guided my understanding of social work in schools. To Professor Seaton Manning, San Francisco State College, I am indebted for important discussions of race relations in California. Mr. Will Maslow, Executive Director, American Jewish Congress, was my guide to an indispensable knowledge of new developments in New York City. Ignacio L. López introduced me to many aspects of the Mexican-American life that is now approaching fulfillment in the United States, and provided invaluable insights gained from his years as a Spanish-language newspaper editor and publisher in Southern California. To my students I owe the exhilaration of a fine enterprise; their contributions swell the following pages.

RUTH LANDES

June, 1965

Contents

Prologue:

Path to an Experiment

The teacher-training experiment described in this book rested on years of studying culture as a research anthropologist and of applying the knowledge acquired to many kinds of practical operations. In North and South America, in Britain and Western Europe, through teaching, government service, and research, I lived among peoples as diverse as any to be found on earth. There were Negroes of the western nations and of Africa, American Indians of three tribes in Canada and the United States, Mexicans in the Southwest and in Mexico, Mexican-Americans of California and other southwestern states, European Jews in New York and their American descendants, upper-class and so-called "poor whites" of the old South, and the locally ruling groups we call "white."

Born and educated in cosmopolitan New York City, I have always known people of varied religions, nationalities, cultural heritages, and races. Relatives and friends spoke, read, and composed literature in several languages and expected no less of their children. This was an internationally minded group that unlike many present educators considered bilingualism a precious asset. My parents' colleagues experimented then with utopian plans for social progress as we experiment today with space explorations. They achieved their goals while still youthfully vigorous in public education, fine arts, women's rights, trade unionism, civil liberties, and nation building.

In the 1930's, during the great economic depression and the rising threats of Nazi terror, I studied anthropology with America's leading scholars. In Franz Boas, the aged titan of anthropology, and in Ruth

1

Benedict, the poetic woman, profound learning strengthened their compassion for man and fired convictions of human salvation through free inquiry. Driven by fascism, nazism, communism, race prejudices, and war, they departed the ivory tower to assert scholars' truths in the market place. Braving venomous personal attacks, these two evidenced the true scientist's care for society. No student of theirs remained unaware that our anthropological discipline committed us to humanism.

I first met Professor Boas in the early 1930's when I consulted him about my thesis for the master's degree in social work. I had come upon a new sect of Negro Jews in Harlem and was studying them. To most white New Yorkers of the time, the Negro migrants to Harlem were chiefly a pool of transient, unskilled labor. But a few of my friends enthusiastically followed the intellectual and artistic activities of the Negro "Racial Manhood Movement" and the "New Negro Renaissance," in the phrases of Alain Locke. Gifted and upper-class Negroes denounced the nascent Negro Jewish proletariat as sham, including the tiny, then-called "store-front," churches of West Indians I was studying.

These West Indians had been followers of Marcus Garvey, the West Indian black nationalist leader, before our federal government jailed him, charging him with mail fraud, and later deported him. Having lost their extraordinary leader, some of the West Indians, headed by a choir leader of Garvey's Universal Negro Improvement Association, continued to challenge white Christian supremacy and to exalt themselves by claiming an African Hebrew heritage, including ancestral bonds with the Biblical queen of Sheba, the Falashas of Abyssinia, and some tribes of West Africa. German refugees from Hitler, including some famous writers like Ernst Toller, visited them sympathetically as fellow victims of persecution, while Jews of Harlem taught them Hebrew and doctrine. A few children of these Garveyite Jews attended a synagogue school in Harlem and finished their studies with honors. When I met the Polish archaeologist, Dr. Jacques Fait-lovich, who had rediscovered the contemporary Falashas at the turn of this century, he admitted no historic grounds to the Negroes' Jewish claims but respected their brave struggle for race dignity.

It was then I sought Boas for enlightenment, and he answered that he thought proper understanding lay in my studying anthropology. Later he sent my study of the Negro Jews to Germany for publication, but the Nazi rulers of Germany had begun the burnings of books. The world learned that Boas' great works—such as *The Mind of Primitive Man, Changes in Bodily Form of Descendants of Immigrants,* and many others—constituted the first pyre at Heidelberg University where Boas had received an honorary degree the previous year, 1933. My manuscript, sponsored by him, also disappeared when the scientific journal which had accepted it was shut down. After the Second World War, I prepared a summary of the lost manuscript for the American Jewish Committee in New York.

During 1933 to 1937, I studied Ojibwa, Santee Dakota, and Potawatomi Indian tribes on reservations in Ontario (Canada), Minnesota, and Kansas, finding strange cultural traditions and conflicts, and the terrible misery of social degradation and poverty. In the Canadian and midwestern woodlands, undergoing my first separations from family and metropolis, I quaked at distant tribal drums and at somber tribesmen. But during those years on four Indian reservations, I met remarkable, gifted individuals who taught me their ancient cultures and also showed me familiar human kindness. Surmounting brutal conquest, alienation from the dominant American society and civilization, poverty, prejudice, and the reservation system, which inevitably was compared to the Nazi system of concentrations camps, these Indian personalities bore marvelous witness to the temper of man. Also at Columbia, two handsome and brilliant Indians were assisting Boas in ethnological and linguistic research. One, Archie Finney of the Nez Percé tribe, received a doctorate, worked professionally some years in Russia, then returned to his people, and died prematurely. The other, Ella Deloria of the Dakota tribe, continues to report on her people's culture and language.

My ideas about comparative mental and school performances of Indians and others received clear direction from Dr. Otto Klineberg. As a young psychologist who was also a disciple of Boas in the 1930s, Klineberg made pioneering studies of "race differences" in school learning and motivation among American Indians, Negro, and European peoples. These revealed the overdeterminism of sociocultural influences, which Klineberg showed in his Columbia lectures and in his distinguished book, Race Differences.

After conferring a doctorate in anthropology, Columbia sent me to study the life of Negroes in Brazil. This was a period of American Negro unrest, and scholars were struck by the relative lack of race discrimination in our great sister republic. Brazil even boasted of her multiracial unity, a view that amazed North Americans.

But first I spent a year teaching at Fisk University, a segregated Negro institution in Nashville, Tennessee. This was on the advice of Robert E. Park, the University of Chicago's celebrated Professor-emeritus of Sociology, then a scholar-in-residence at Fisk. Park believed that any Northerner needed a stay in the South to experience the pressures in Negro segregation and prejudice. At Fisk, too, I would meet Negroes of distinguished intellects such as James Weldon Johnson, also a scholar-in-residence, a poet, and first secretary of the National Association for the Advancement of Colored People. The physicist Elmer S. Imes and the painter Aaron Douglass were Fisk professors. Dr. Park collaborated with Dr. Charles S. Johnson, head of the university's social science program and later Fisk's first Negro president. Both men felt that I could better appraise Brazil's interracial scene if I knew our own Southern one at first hand. Tennessee's segregation laws, passed at the turn of this century, allowed only Negro students at Fisk; but the faculty was Negro and white, dating from Fisk's Abolitionist beginnings to its (then) Jim Crow present. Some Negro professors had studied at Fisk when the student body included whites, usually children of American Missionary Society founders and faculty. Professor Park's advice to spend the year on Fisk's campus stemmed from his own midwest origins and youthful experiences as secretary to Booker T. Washington, the great Negro leader and educator of the South's Reconstruction and later years.

I was entrusted with a graduate course in "culture and personality" at Fisk, following lines being developed by Edward Sapir, Ruth Benedict, and others. However, no one dreamt of instructing me in the South's crucial "etiquette of race relations" (in Bertram W. Doyle's famous phrase), though even innocent violations could provoke extreme punishment. Future events showed that my interracial missteps were totted up as shocking by blacks and whites of town and gown, by people off-campus in Nashville, and on-campus, too. Untrained and uncautioned in the habits and logic of race discrimination, I drank at any public water fountain and entered streetcars by any door, sitting down in any seat, unaware of signs restricting "colored" and "white." I greeted Negro colleagues I met in Nashville shops and sometimes wondered that they did not reply. As Park had anticipated, I was snubbed and attacked, often through anonymous phone calls. But no one ever explained the errors to me. From the heights of his repute and fifty-odd years of seniority, Park advised me to accept everything as field data. He marveled at Dr. Charles S. Johnson's perfect, often daring manipulation of the South's "peculiar" ways. Dr. Park never mentioned the toll of heartaches, possibly because he considered them obvious and hopeless.

I reached Brazil during the dictatorship of Getulio Vargas and spent sixteen hard months, until the brink of the Second World War, in Rio de Janeiro and in the great northern port city of Bahía (also called Bahía de Todos os Santos and San Salvador). Both cities have large Negro populations, dating from centuries of slavery in the plantation economy. Instead of our country's daily racist occurrences, I found life ordered by an aristocratic class structure, an impoverished plantation economy, and networks of severely intimidating police and military espionage. Unschooled in these ways, too, I found my difficulties complicated by the impropriety of being a young woman alone in a fiercely conservative Latin society. Since I traveled continually from my Bahía residence into the outlying jungle (or *mato*) to visit Negroes where they lived and worked, northern police and military supposed, or pretended to suppose, that I was a Communist spy. The fact that I was accredited from Columbia University, the Rockefeller Foundation, and the president of Brazil seemed to aggravate both local anti-Americanism and hostility to Brazil's own federal government. Even an American Negro stevedore in Bahía snarled at me for greeting him with reminders of home. "What's good about Chicago?" he demanded bitterly. "I like it here."

As far as the research assignment went, I found that Brazil largely absorbed her race differences into her class distinctions. In a traditional saying, riches made any man white and poverty made him black. Yet black women of Bahía, those glamorized in the songs of Carmen Miranda, wielded great influence. Their leaders, as priestesses of recognized cults, customarily governed religious practices of their own people and of many whites with the approval of Catholic clergy. Their covert strength among all classes allowed them to shelter cult members and friends from army, police, and other foes.

I left Brazil to join Gunnar Myrdal's study, in New York, of the American Negro, described in his famous book, *An American Dilemma*. In October 1941, Walter White, the secretary of the National Association for the Advancement of Colored People, offered me work on President Roosevelt's newly created Fair Employment Practices Committee, known as the FEPC. For the next three years my job in wartime Washington was to examine complaints by Negroes of discrimination in federal employment. Then I accepted an invitation from a private group in Louisiana to observe traditional Negro-white relationships in a conservative white stronghold. As on the Indian reservations, at Fisk, and in Brazil, I had the startling problem of organizing my identity afresh in the deep South's alien and occasionally frightening surroundings. I had to discover how to survive socially and yet retain my old self. Dr. Harry Stack Sullivan, Selective Service Chief of Mental Hygiene before the Second World War, told me that such problems of personal identity were endemic in centers of social change; he called war-anxious Washington, for example, "an enclave of personality disorders." His powerful concept of "interpersonal relationships" has become a prime key for understanding and influencing emotional disorder.

After nearly a year in Louisiana, seeing the start of open strain between white employers and newly organizing Negro workers, I returned to the Fair Employment Practices Committee. Reports reached Washington of extremely unfair discrimination against Mexican-Americans working in the Southwest's nonferrous metals industries. Because it seemed that these "Mexicans" were the only minority never to complain against unfairness, I requested assignments to study how they were being harassed and how they reacted.

After the war, I was engaged to direct a small FEPC-type program in New York City, created by Pearl S. Buck and interdenominational clergy, pending New York State legislation against discrimination. During 1949–1951, I directed a study of Jewish families in New York for the American Jewish Committee. Then Dr. Charles S. Johnson, who had become president of Fisk University and a White House adviser, invited me to study the new mounting migration of "colored colonials" to Britain, on a Fulbright Senior Research grant; the proposal was sponsored also by the Anthropology department of Edinburgh University and its head, Dr. Kenneth L. Little. In Britain it became clear that our concepts of race relationships were being adopted uncritically by British intellectuals; evolved in the United States, they seemed largely irrelevant to the British scene with its different history and social system. Notable among these concepts is the historic American assumption that Negroes "belong" though in their subordinate "place." In Britain, no one "belongs" except those recognized by conduct and appearance to be native-born. In practice, this confines recognition to whites identifiable by accepted class indicators, such as modes of speech, dress, and body carriage.

My family had been interested in Mexicans and their social revolution since at least 1924. Then the Mexican Federation of Labor, called CROM (the initials stand for Confederación Revolucionaria Obrera Mexicana or, Confederation of Revolutionary Mexican Labor), invited Samuel Gompers and other American labor leaders, including my father, to attend the inauguration of President Plutarco Elías Calles. During the Second World War, I, too, met and worked with Mexicans, first in Washington, D. C. while affiliated with Nelson Rockefeller's Office of InterAmerican Affairs, then in the Southwest while investigating FEPC violations under war contracts, and later on a private visit to Mexico City and neighboring towns. In Texas, New

Mexico, and Arizona, I saw the extraordinary three-part segregation from whites of "Mexicans," Indians, and Negroes. This was patterned as Mexican or Indian, or both; as Mexican or Negro, or both; as Negro; and whites, who were always separate. Mexican-American workers were cruelly handicapped by the usual, so-called "Anglo-Mex wage differential." This "differential" meant that "Mexicans" were paid a significant proportion less than Anglos for the same job, solely because of their "race."

Provoked still by the apparent docility of the Mexican-Americans, by their seemingly quiet acceptance of discrimination, I flew to Los Angeles in 1946 to examine it and so studied teen-age Mexican-American gangs (called *pachucos* in the Southwest's Spanish slang) of the east side slums for the Los Angeles Metropolitan Welfare Council. I met Mexican-American men and women in business, college, and professions, who had begun to develop legislative, political, and trade union techniques for the betterment of their people. Despite their personal qualities and even considerable success in their fields, they all had endured segregation and discrimination as "Mexicans."

While teaching at Fisk University, I applied cultural insights systematically to social relationships. Negro colleagues and students and white colleagues struggled for decent definitions. Dr. Park was the adept whom many followed, having served his apprenticeship with Booker T. Washington and successfully tested it with Charles S. Johnson. My second deliberate application of systematic cultural insights was at the Federal FEPC, when working with Negro colleagues and with clients of various origins. This was never simple, but always interesting. Occasionally federal rules set reason aside. An extreme instance arose when Iroquois tribesmen complained that they were refused hire on war contracts because they could not produce documents of American birth or citizenship.

Further applications of cultural knowledge proved useful in 1953 when I taught psychiatrists, psychoanalysts, social workers, and clergy at New York's William Alanson White Psychiatric Institute, and when I taught at New York's New School for Social Research. These students wanted to know how different societies handled the same life situations of, for example, sexual desire and marriage, particular neuroses and psychoses, or formal recognitions of success and failure in careers. They wanted to compare them to see where particular cultures set up differing boundaries for acceptable conduct, and to see wherein all cultures behaved similarly, and to see how cultures changed.

In 1957–1958, when training graduate students in "cultural factors" and culture research at the University of Southern California's School of Social Work, there were opportunities to extend cultural applications in many new directions, and this continued during subsequent years at workshops and lectures for social workers, public-health physicians and nurses, police, and corrections officers. From this work arose the opportunity during 1959–1961 at Claremont Graduate School, California, to conduct the Anthropology and Education program for training teachers and some social workers, as described in this book. The form and purposes of the program evolved from such cultural knowledge and applications as I had tested elsewhere, from New York to California, in different professional circles. The principles embodied in the program, and the practical recommendations that resulted can be applied anywhere, having been brought to California from everywhere. It is a truism that now, in these postwar decades, the Golden State manifests America in its mixtures and movements of peoples, its booming numbers and living standards, the irresistible spread of its megalopolis, the soaring hopes of minorities, the wealth and poverty, and its very symbolism as a station in the westerly trend of our tradition.

What happens in California happens to people in all our states, for the people carry over the continent their ways of life from the East, the Midwest, and Far West, the old South and the Southwest, from all the cities and the countryside. People journey hoping to re-establish the best they have known and to further it in California's still open land and society. In this spirit they sent children to be schooled, they expect teachers to educate, and expect public agencies to uphold standards.

But even in California this American dream must be corrected by hard realities. They are known best by minorities and the poor, and social workers are more familiar with the evil in them than are other professional groups. The Claremont program was conceived to train public-school educators to understand the social complexities of their tasks and to adapt goals and techniques accordingly. Responsibilities for many pupils, of every origin, are shared by educators and social workers. Hence, in Chapter 7 I describe as well how social workers were trained to apply cultural insights.

1

Cultures Clash
in the Schools

For some years now, public education has been served hard judgments by all sectors of the community. The people who pay mounting school taxes, pupils who suffer from inadequate learning, business and science interests which demand keener abilities in greater quantities, teachers who strain traditional simple skills to accommodate urgent, varied, and elaborate demands—all declare repeatedly that public education is gravely wanting.

These pressures constitute a crisis. Survival of mankind and civilization, and progress both depend on cultivating all minds to the fullest. Universal education is our national goal; no individual or group, for any reason whatsoever, is to be barred from equal access to standard opportunities. In 1954 the Supreme Court of the United States ordered an end to school segregation, our harshest social determinant of unequal and inadequate education. Simultaneously, the Court's decision created unprecedented dilemmas for teachers and pupils, parents and school boards, because it transferred great human problems of handicapped groups from the dark of segregation to the light of desegregation and equality. The implications embrace changed obligations of our whole society.

In California, since the Second World War, desegregation and integration of schools have been taking place gradually, though incompletely, through state laws and local practices. The floods of newcomers to the state, attracted from everywhere by the basic war and defense industries, strengthen demands for universal education but also contribute to the traditional stock of prejudicial ideas and habits

9

concerning race, culture, and society. This confuses educators who must try to guide and teach pupils of every ethnic origin and every social level, gathered in desegregated classes.

Hoping to better the myriad difficult classroom situations, the education faculty at Claremont Graduate School proposed to test a new way of training teachers. As anthropology is the science of human culture, Claremont proposed to train teachers in culture concepts and methods affecting public education; and it entitled the project Anthropology and Education. I was appointed to direct it. For two years, including summers, I presented data, theories, and skills of cultural anthropology to graduate classes of public-school teachers, counselors, and administrators who struggled with multifarious stocks of pupils.

Three chief avenues led educators to the Anthropology and Education program. One was the graduate courses in which teachers, largely employed in Southern California schools, were enrolled. I developed three different seminars in anthropology for them and joined education professors in a fourth seminar. A second avenue was the numerous elementary and secondary schools and some junior and four-year colleges of the Pomona, San Gabriel, and San Bernardino valleys. School administrators invited me to observe classrooms in action and to discuss with faculties the problems they described. The third avenue of approach was provided by the curriculum director of elementary schools in a large city when she invited me to develop a two-year program for principals and teachers. Accordingly, the school people and I met monthly to clarify cultural difficulties with Mexican-Americans, Negroes, and others.

Anthropology was new to school people, as public education was new to me; now each party proceeded to learn from the other. To understand the universe of California's public schooling, I became the field researcher even in the act of lecturing, watching all reactions carefully. In this sense, no graduate student or difficulty was ever wrong or boring, every question was valuable, every success was a provisional test until the successes were predictable. I had to learn the language and the values of the public-school world in order to select, phrase, and adapt the anthropological materials. It was a constant process of listening, asking, reading, sensing flows and halts of interest, and following them through experiments and watching reactions to lectures. Education students observed through new eyes the human creatures in their care at school and surrounding them in unfamiliar neighborhoods.

To do research in cultural anthropology, ignorance of the specific problem or group under study can have the advantage of allowing fresh slants. My own ignorance of education left me sensitive to the special use school people make of some ordinary words, particularly "frustration" and "achievement." Such words, continually repeated, proved to be significant technicalities. Some words were even reduced to alphabet codes, meaningful to teachers (as alphabet formulas are to chemists) though the mother words themselves might be lost. The special usages indicated a prevalent condition in California's melting-pot schools—a condition where efforts to communicate are blocked among faculty, between faculty and pupils, and pupils' families, and between faculty and the larger community.

The state of California was new to very many. Most pupils and their families, faculties of schools, members of school boards and chambers of commerce, employees of giant new industries, and the civil and political authorities had migrated from a distance and then continued to move frequently within the state. Particularly in its southern half, California reflects the world's startling, unprecedented daily increase in human numbers and movement.

In April 1960, according to the United States Census, California's population was 15,717,204, a rise of 48.5 per cent over the preceding ten years.[1] A year later the count had risen by almost a million.[2] To this growth, the southern counties contributed 70 per cent, or over ten million, suddenly making California the second most populous state in the Union.[1] Since then it has become the most populous state. Numbers in the fourteen southernmost counties tripled the national percentage increase in the ten years, averaging nearly 1,000 persons a day[3] but totaling some 1,500 a day for the state.[2] Population in the Los Angeles-Long Beach metropolitan area became the second largest in the nation after the New York area; its census of 6,742,696 in April 1960, marked an increase of 54 per cent over the decade. Increases in the southern counties soared from Inyo's fraction of a per cent to Orange's 226 per cent.[4] Most of the schools served by the Anthropology and Education program were situated in the populous, highly mobile and transient southern counties of Los Angeles, San Bernardino, Riverside, and Orange.

From 1915 to 1943, arrivals from other states totaled over 90 per cent of the population increase in the Los Angeles-Long Beach metropolitan area.[4] California authorities refer to them as an "in-migration"; those who remained are now called "newcomers." But "newcomers" is also the label officials apply to minority groups, even the ones whose ancestors, as among Mexican-Americans and Indians, have occupied the region for generations and centuries. Natural increase of the resident population reached a peak during 1945–1949 and has since been variable.⁴ In the years right after the Second World War, a high proportion of adults in the Los Angeles urban area came from "the East"; today they are as likely to be Westerners.

California's attractions lie in the state's expanding industries, new giant prosperity, general opportunities, mood of boundless hope and energy, spaciousness, and fine climate. The westering tide brings chiefly Americans, of every racial, cultural, and regional stock. The minorities are so-called Mexicans or Mexican-Americans, Negroes, "Okies" or "Arkies" or "poor whites," Nisei, Chinese, Filipinos and other Orientals, and American Indians. Of these minorities, Mexican-Americans are the best known and possibly the best liked, certainly the most discussed in the populous South. Notions about them are steeped in stereotypes about their differences from so-called Caucasians or whites. The few Indians in general schools are identified only vaguely; usually they are confused with Mexicans, partly because of Spanish surnames. Even college teachers declare, "Aren't Mexicans Indians!" and find it hard to credit that the two peoples consider themselves distinct from each other. Concepts of the Negro follow nationwide hostile stereotypes; easterners find no such warm interest focused on the Negro as is traditional in the Atlantic states. In Southern California it is frequently remarked, on the authority of the 1960 Census, that the Negro population of Los Angeles increased 500 per cent from 1940 to 1960; and it continues to soar. Jews, Catholics, Irish, and Italians receive less invidious notice than in the East, partly perhaps because Jews have long been prominent in the film industry and because Los Angeles and the Southwest generally are centers of Catholic prestige.

The ordinary white American in California variously identifies himself as white, Caucasian, or Anglo-American; some qualify the label with Okie, Irish, Jewish, or another distinction. The first term, white, seems to refer to our history of Negro-white relations, but it is equally employed by the speaker to distinguish himself from Mexican-Americans. Mexicans themselves care little how "gringos" (meaning literally, "strangers") choose to describe people. The second term, Caucasian, seems to refer to our separatist relationships with Orientals, especially in Northern California. The third term, Anglo-American, is taken from the speech of Latins in Europe and the Americas, where it is used to refer chiefly to culture. Anglo-Americans are usually startled to learn that Mexican-Americans include Negroes among Anglos, for Negroes inherit English speech and Anglo-American culture.

The different minorities in California hardly know one another, being separated by great distances that are only now being filled and narrowed with the postwar migrations. Sectors of the dominant white population hardly know one another or the minorities. Until after the Second World War, custom and law supported racist discriminations against Mexican-Americans, Indians, Negroes, and Oriental-Americans, in employment, recreation, public service, schooling, housing, and burial. Official restraints have loosened markedly through municipal, state, and federal legislation; the Supreme Court's 1954 decision against public-school segregation is the most widely known measure. However, customary prejudice endures, as at public schools where Mexicans and Mexican-Americans are scolded and humiliated for speaking Spanish among themselves on the school grounds.

California's postwar prosperity has profited even the poorest Mexican-Americans and Negroes, including those so destitute as to have lived, until well after the Second World War, in packing cases for shelters on the east side of Los Angeles. For the southern half of the state in 1960, personal income was estimated at 27.3 billion dollars, a gain of 6 per cent over that in 1959, the previous record year.[5] Rising tax rates support the vast, expanding school systems and youth protection agencies, such as the California Youth Authority and juvenile courts; pay the salaries of increasing numbers of public officials; and maintain the tremendous networks of freeways that serve automobiles, owned at the rate, in Los Angeles, of almost one for every two residents.[6] On December 17, 1963, the *New York Times* Western Edition said that California had more cars than any other state.

Horizontal space beckons in California, allowing dwellings, towns, and counties to spread out thinly since the Second World War. Before the admission of Alaska to the Union, Southern California's San Bernardino county was said to be the most extensive administrative unit in the United States. Californians have a truism that distance means nothing. Their phalanxes of machines speed on the freeways in numbers so vast and unwieldy as to create daily traffic dangers. A person usually travels alone in his car even on long trips, his radio chattering. By 1961 the horizontal spread gave Los Angeles county's six million persons their seventy-one incorporated cities, sixteen unincorporated areas of a thousand persons or more,[7] and hundreds of school districts.[8]

With spiraling incomes and hopes, people acquire numerous goods and services. But it is widely observed and deplored that they fail to create personal ties with a local community because they move elsewhere, continually, lured by job opportunities usually, by the chance to get a new "tract house" in real estate developments that wipe out the vernal countryside and the vast fragrant citrus groves, by the sheer love of moving on wheels, by the conviction that better things lie beyond. California's burgeoning opportunities do not ease people's acute awareness of personal isolation and drift. Individuals express this in casual encounters at supermarkets and in therapeutic sessions with counselors and doctors. In private talk and public meetings, people blame their vague, nagging dissatisfactions on the general mobility and restlessness. Various psychoanalysts in Los Angeles have remarked that the want of personal ties induces loneliness and depression in old and young newcomers. One psychiatrist privately generalized that a newcomer required ten years to conquer emotional depressions resulting from "loss of status" in moving to Southern California's jungle of anonymous faces.

In 1961, 3,600,000 pupils were attending California's primary and secondary schools, the largest public-school enrollment in the nation.[9] The figure includes about 97 per cent of all Californians of school age. In addition, in 1960, there were 700,000 at junior colleges, in adult education, and attending special schools such as those for the blind. This total body of 4,300,000, constituting 10 per cent of the nation's schoolgoers, was served by about 130,000 teachers.[10] These received the highest average teacher salary reported in 1961.[9] Classrooms frequently served double sessions and held more than 40 children, although 25 were considered the desirable maximum. Despite some opposition or inertia on the part of local taxpayers, school buildings are continually erected to accommodate the soaring numbers in accordance with highest standards; the planners' ideal of providing a building a day must, of course, remain a dream.

Schoolteachers travel to California from stabler regions to work in an atmosphere of high challenge with colleagues and pupils of unfamiliar backgrounds. Uniform school standards are promulgated by the state Department of Education and by the teaching profession. In fact, however, the general social changes and the heterogeneous human materials are considerably unknown to the authorities and are not regulated by the uniform standards or by any knowledgeable authority.

The constant movement of people affects schoolchildren directly. According to the 1960 Report of the White House Conference on Children and Youth, "The average family in the United States moves eight times, and half of American children are now living in a different community from the one where they were born."[11] Another estimate says that "Every day, some twenty thousand families in the United States move—in twelve months (1957–1958) about one million children were moved from one main geographic area in the United States to another; two millions moved across county lines; and at least twelve millions moved from one house to another. These children were all under 17 years." [12] That is, they were of school age.

In California's seventeen hundred (in 1961) school districts, school attendance is enforced by law [13] for children aged eight to sixteen years; California labor and education codes require employed minors under eighteen years to secure working papers; this can be arranged at high schools.[14] California children, even those in the earliest grades, may have attended several schools; some remain less than a month in one when parents transfer them elsewhere.

The Claremont project in Anthropology and Education was designed to approach educators' great difficulties with pupils, parents, and communities of heterogeneous social or ethnic natures and high mobility by showing some of the social and cultural aspects in the relationships of all parties and in the abilities of pupils to learn at school. This meant showing educators what culture is, its particular manifestations in different traditions (whether the manifestations be different languages and religions or different modes of treating a mother), how one recognizes specific cultural factors influencing individual and group conduct, how families pass on their ancestral cultures, even when they seem assimilated to another, how a pupil might manifest his special heritage in the classroom, and how a teacher might unwittingly do the same. Using an immense variety of details observed daily in the home, community, and school, including the operations of prejudice, the writer drew up generalizations to enable educators to appraise and meet new problems in dealing with unfamiliar ethnic groups.

The small family of parents and young children is the one stable social unit in Southern California. Its few members come to know one another well, disciplining one another's emotions and interests. The families, like the schools, look increasingly to machines for further companionship and stimulation: the machines are movies, television, cars, teaching aids. In California's social flux, it is questionable whether machines foster a person's sense of roots in the world, of fulfillment or direction, or whether they foster sensitivity to other people. Man's history shows that only other people have accomplished this, working through traditional bonds.

The most vital public bond in Southern California towns, repeatedly stressed in discussions, is the family's ties with the neighborhood elementary school. This rests on the legal obligation to send youngsters to school. The bond does not foster close ties with teach-

ers as individuals, especially in cities. Urban educators' customary
aloofness, many teachers' own frequent moves, and their unfamiliarity
with particular California schools and neighborhoods, the general
confusion about special groups, like Orientals, the clear estrangement
of Mexican-Americans and Indians from school, the tiring distances
teachers cover between home and school—all these keep teachers outside their pupils' worlds.

School faculties are given no organized comprehension of the new
and divisive social forces. But they are expected to "find themselves,"
as one college official easily assumed. This does not happen and there
is, rather, a prevailing atmosphere of "frustration" among public-
school teachers over common difficulties with pupils. Hence some
worthy teachers leave the profession, others sag below standards,
some search unhappily, and some asked Claremont College for help.

Notes

1. According to "Monthly Summary of Business Conditions in Southern California," Los Angeles: Security First National Bank Research Department,
   November 1960 (Vol. 39, No. 11, no paging).
2. Bruce Bliven, "East Coast or West—Which?" *New York Times Sunday Magazine,* March 12, 1961.
3. "Monthly Summary," December 1960, No. 12.
4. *Ibid.*
5. "Monthly Summary," January 1961 (Vol. 40, No. 1).
6. *New York Times,* April 10, 1960. According to the *New York Times,* June 18,
   1961, the World Health Organization reports 3,000,000 automobiles in Los
   Angeles.
7. "Monthly Summary," December 1960, No. 12.
8. *Claremont Courier,* March 30, 1961.
9. *New York Times,* February 12, 1961. The *New York Times* Western Edition
   reported March 4, 1963, that California paid the highest average teacher
   salary of $7,500 leading New York's average of $7,250 and the nation's of
   $5,940.
10. R. J. Bernard, "How Good are Our Schools?" Address delivered December
    20, 1960, as one of the California Citizens Commission on Public Education.
    The *New York Times,* June 24, 1962, reported that California school enroll-
    ments had risen to 4,212,000, including adult night schools and children in
    special classes. There were 1,650 school districts, 6,000 schools, 129,000
    teachers. "California's public-school system is larger than New York's de-
    spite its lesser population because there are fewer private schools and more
    children a family," Bill Becker reported, *idem.,* p. 48. (The phrase "lesser
    population" became invalid when California's population exceeded. New
    York's around late December 1962.) In Los Angeles, "Between 1951 and
    1961 enrollment increased from 421,239 to 671,250 pupils . . . ," according

to *Point of View: Educational Purposes, Policies, Practises* (Los Angeles City Schools, Publication No. 470. 1961 Revision), p. 45.

The new and disturbing presence of Negroes in California is discussed in all news media. The pressures can be surmised from these figures: Between 1950–1960, "The Los Angeles County Negro population soared from 217,000 to 461,000, most of them confined to the heart of the city" of Los Angeles, according to *Newsweek*, September 3, 1962. Such local rises all over the state, accompanied by residential segregation of Negroes, result in innumerable elementary and intermediate schools that are predominantly or almost entirely attended by Negro children. However educators in a northern California city referred casually to one of their high schools as "the Negro school" because 20 per cent of the pupils were Negro.

11. J. B. Sisk, quoted in *What's New*, February–March, 1961 (No. 222), p. 2, and Winter 1960 (No. 221).
12. *Ibid.*
13. (Compiled by) A. C. Morrison, *Education Code*, Vol. 1, Chapter 6, Article 1, paragraph 12101 (Sacramento: State of California Documents Section, Printing Division, 1961), p. 483.
14. (Mimeographed) *Annual Report of the Child Welfare and Attendance Branch*, Los Angeles City Schools, 1960–1961 school year, p. 33.

2

Teachers Ask about Society and Culture

When discussing their work, educators stress particular issues and techniques. These chiefly concern school curricula, grading the achievements of pupils, a teacher's mastery of his subject, the length of the school day and year. Listening to these, the anthropologist then asks about the *behavior* of all parties. He wants to discover the cultural traits of pupils and their families, the cultural traits of each teacher and of the local teaching body, and how the cultural traits of all parties mesh or clash at school. The anthropologist believes that adults teach and pupils learn in keeping with habits absorbed from their cultural backgrounds. Hence, apparently stupid behavior may actually reflect irreconcilable culture *differences* felt by the "stupid" person, whereas success may testify to cultural *harmony* between a person and his environment. To discover what happens in particular situations at school, the anthropologist must observe the teachers' actual procedures, become steeped in them, and then address the ideas about culture to teachers' daily experiences. This translates anecdotal occurrences, scoldings, and gossip into cultural terms of conditioned habits. Teachers can be trained to apply these anthropological methods and concepts to their work and personal conduct.

My field of cultural study lay wherever teachers worked and met: in classrooms and school cafeterias, at their college seminars and workshops, at all their public and informal gatherings. I questioned people, looked at their dealings, made tentative interpretations, checked on these, probed continually, and encouraged colleagues and students also to question, interpret, and experiment. This procedure kept the teachers and me bound to the schools' urgent practical demands. We applied cultural methods and concepts to specific problems the teachers faced in their schools, such as absenteeism or tardiness, which teachers called "classroom situations." This approach helped shape the courses of study developed for educators at Claremont and at their places of work.

This chapter reports the questions educators asked about pupils of different origins. I always asked them to describe the problems as they would if they were talking among themselves. In this way, teachers voiced their special language, preconceptions, goals, values, and logic. These belonged to their profession, and also to the middle-class American culture supporting it, a culture dominated by urban, college-trained whites. Thus, the educators revealed a great universe of ideas in whose terms they guided the young of all origins, and so helped to determine the forms and purposes of American society. This chapter also reports some other reflections of school officials about pupils' cultural variety and the problems this variety raises at school.

Educators in all grades through junior college ponder their professional identities. They worry continually about what "we" think of "ourselves" and what "they" think of "us." The "they" refers to anyone in the teaching profession, to pupils and parents, to community leaders, and to businessmen. Teachers also asked me for an opinion of their professional status. In a doctoral seminar, male educators devoted weeks to examining, as one stated, "the significant question of the existence and the nature of a public stereotype of the teacher . . . (which is) distinctly unfavorable . . . (and is) properly the cause of much concern to the teaching profession." In another seminar, a brilliant young woman self-consciously read her study showing that teachers she interviewed disparaged themselves severely. Some of their opinions were: "I wouldn't admit to being a teacher." "I am only a teacher." "He dresses like a teacher (meaning poorly)." Colleagues listened in spellbound recognition, except for a young Mexican-American who observed in tart surprise that he felt proud of being a high-school teacher for this meant much to one, like himself, who had had to overcome poverty, prejudice, and parental illiteracy.

Many graduate studies, often published in education and sociology journals, concern the "status" of teachers and of school administrators. I observed such an inquiry being drafted by the teacher-principal of an elementary school and a junior-college teacher. The two men asked first their colleagues and then their pupils to select traits, from a list of thirty they offered, that affected faculty prestige in their eyes, and to weigh them on a three-point scale. The two men had assembled the list intuitively, naming items as disparate as "manner of dress," professional competence, and "use of vacation time."

Public educators habitually separate themselves. Students consistently often select a research project entitled, "Are Teachers Part of the Community?" Rarely do they analyze the concept of "community." Some professors of education feel driven to remind student teachers that parents are people and members of the community, while teachers are parents, too, and that pupils belong to families and are future voters and parents.

Even experienced educators refer to parents and to other citizens outside the profession as "laymen . . . naïve and uninformed" about schooling. School social workers, who are accredited teachers with graduate social work training assigned in some school systems to handle difficult pupils, complain that educators barely tolerate them in the schools, considering them "outsiders," partly because their duties carry them beyond school walls into pupils' homes and neighborhoods.

The strange apartness of teachers from the communities they serve waxes in California's new cities. It contrasts with the ways in older farming sections where teachers live and even marry among their pupils' families. Authorities of California's new towns and school districts often encourage or even require teachers to live elsewhere. Hence, only in the farming areas does school staff know parents as well as other neighbors, and does it want to know them so. In the prevailing atmosphere of estrangement, teachers suffer from feelings of "frustration" caused by newcomers and once-segregated minorities who ignore their messages about school business, such as requests, which often sound like demands, for teacher-parent conferences, and who criticize school. Teachers label such parents "bad" and "uncooperative."

Teachers realize that the taxpaying community provides their jobs, funds, and rating and promotion systems. Yet "community" remains an academic abstraction in the face of mushrooming transient neighborhoods and annual turnovers of 25 to 100 per cent among school staff and pupils. Within eight years, the number of pupils in one elementary school district soared from 2,000 to 13,000 and its three schools grew to nineteen; the next eight years were expected to more than double the peak number of children and nearly to double the peak number of schools.

Not only do educators separate themselves from others, but splits also appear within their own professional structure. These splits set teachers apart from administrators, who supposedly are more highly regarded. Administrators include principals, supervisors, superintendents, and, at times, counselors. Teachers rank themselves in a progression through the grades of elementary school, then by grander distinctions between elementary and secondary schools, between junior and senior high schools, and between high schools and junior colleges. These notions about rankings are not reflected in salaries. When educators plan meetings, they ponder "whether teachers and administrators should be mixed," suggesting that teachers might not "feel free to express themselves" in the presence of administrators; but they never prevent actual mixing.

Educators are exceedingly aware of their responsibilities to pupils and want to make a good showing. Constant fears of inadequate teaching appear in self-harassing questions. A child who does not learn from schoolwork is felt by teachers to act unfairly toward them, almost by deliberate intent. Educators seldom know of the myriad social factors that constitute a child's world at home. Teachers' separateness from the families they serve is dramatized by the teachers' confinement to school grounds. Here educators part company with other helping professions, notably medicine, social work, and the religious ministry.

In their questions, teachers appraised their work from two chief aspects. One was: Why do I fall short in my best efforts to teach? The other was: Why can't he learn, or learn better what I teach? Actually, the two aspects are inseparable. A teacher's performance is reflected in the pupil's response, and classroom learning is a fine mesh of teachers' efforts with pupils'. As this relationship became understood during the Claremont project, teachers insistently asked about the cultural nature and ties of pupils and families. They asked about major trends in minority subcultures and about specific standards of particular foreign and underprivileged groups—standards they called "the Negro matriarchate," "tolerance of illegitimacy" in slum populations, and physical violence in slums.

Educators assemble a typology of pupils which purports to describe ability but also carries along certain obscure and confusing interests. These interests should be singled out and examined for their relevance to teaching. Then it appears that professional concern with tutelary programs is embedded in prejudicial stereotypes which are barely masked by pretentious labels. The labels group certain pupils by their "deficient motivation," others as the "slow learner," some in accelerated or "remedial reading" classes, others as evidencing "bilingualism," a supposed handicap which is noticed predominantly among "underachieving" Mexican-Americans. Individualities are blanketed under easy generalizations about "problem children" and "transients," racial or "ethnic" differences, "remedials" or R, mentally retarded or MR and "exceptionals," low IQ's or Specials, the unsuccessful in academic high school or Generals, the hostile or apathetic. Further classifications label children as "basic," meaning stupid; "regular," meaning average or better; "more creative" or MC; "less creative" or LC; "capable nonachievers" or CNA; and "overachievers." There are varieties of "motivation," also. There are attempts to categorize pupils' futures as "lesser college material" or XY, and "will have a struggle in college" or YZ. All classifications supposedly imply a related reading ability, keyed to over-all assumptions that whites read better than Negroes, Anglos (Caucasians, whites) better than Mexicans or "bilinguals."

In view of present legislation and opinion against segregation and other discrimination, the labels perturb some administrators. These educators ask how school integration can be effected, given pupils' differences of ability, which many teachers firmly regard as race linked. Often a grade is divided into five or six reading groups, paced from slow to accelerated readers. In a school whose pupils are 33 per cent (low income) Mexican, 5 per cent (low income) Negro, and 62 per cent (mixed income) Anglo or white, the slower reading groups are almost solely Mexican and Negro, the advanced group entirely Anglo-white. The principal interprets the groups as phenomena determined biologically by race and asks, "How then do we balance the races? How avoid race boundaries? How maintain ethnic ratios?" Such administrators fear the letter of the antisegregation law and do not grasp, apparently, its fair intent.

Still concerned with educators' visual impressions of race differences, in physical types and in selected classroom behavior, schools seek to avoid racist language by using the word "ethnic" to describe peoples who suffer civil inequities because of race, color, creed, nationality, or language. In California, the "ethnic groups" are usually Negro, Mexican-American, Nisei, American Indian, and Anglo-American "poor white." But "ethnic" does not clarify for teachers the issue of racial determinants of schoolwork. Some science teachers insist that their experiences with Negro pupils confirm ideas of inherent race inferiorities. Consequently teachers ask if "innate" differences of race should not influence curriculum. A junior high school pursued the idea. One of the teachers reported to a seminar how the school conducted a More Capable Learner (or MCL) project. The project was financed by a national foundation to develop opportunities for "ethnics," meaning, as the project's description said, "overly aggressive and sensitive to authority" Negroes and "the bilingual Mexicans . . .

often shy and less aggressive than the average school student." When working with such difficult children, teachers ask why they experience "fatigue and exhaustion"; they say they yearn for the "satisfaction" of seeing good results with easier pupils.

They debate also whether to conceal from a child his or her "problem," of any nature. This includes, absurdly, procedure with visibly pregnant high-school girls, even when these are married. The concern expresses educators' versions of psychiatric doctrines about "permissiveness" and "trauma," which challenged older standards of sexuality in minors.

Some "permissive" teachers ask, "Are we right to impose our middle-class values on everyone?" Worried over pupils' academic failures, a high-school principal asked: "How can the anthropologist aid teachers in working with pupils of different value patterns? How do middle-class values of a teacher differ from those of the pupil representing a lower social class? Teachers seem unwilling and unable to accept pupils with a different value pattern, [only] tolerating them. These conflicting values are evidenced in discipline problems . . . in lack of motivation and a positive attitude toward education. Perhaps 'class' status may not be correlated to economic status?"

Whatever their original origins, school people assume that all in their profession belong to the middle class. Certainly by the time they complete professional training, they possess substantially the same standards, ways, language, and appearance. Education and sociology research describe teachers as middle class; but some teachers stated that their occupation and earnings placed them in the "upper class." Over the years, social research has discovered that most Americans describe themselves as being middle class.

All teachers feel it necessary and helpful to place "ethnics" in society according to current theories of class difference and rank. They believe that "other-ethnics," meaning chiefly colored and Spanish-speaking peoples, are "lower class." A principal offered a variation during a seminar discussion by asking, "Isn't it true that the higher your social class, the richer you are?" His colleagues hotly denied this. Educators resort to the language of class theory to help them contain the social sprawl of humanity entering public schools.

It is an effort for teachers to consider the occasional "ethnic" colleague as a member of their class; the "middle-class" standard person has come to mean the White Anglo-Saxon Protestant, called WASP by some social workers. Educators regard so-called Okies and Arkies in California as "lower class," if not "minority," because they raise great problems of discipline and inferior achievement. Besides, tradition recalls this group's desperate economic plight in the 1930's and the westward trek for survival.

In central California, Okies are an "ethnic" minority, as shown in dramatizations repeatedly staged at annual conferences of regional educators. Three "sociodramas" prepared by local educators presented "values and drives of different cultural groups" caught in school difficulties. One drama, entitled "Left Out," centers on a Negro boy; another, called "No Ambition," centers on a Mexican-American boy and girl; the third, centering on an Okie girl and boy, is named elliptically "Incident for Dramatization." The Okie boy says, "Any time anyone calls me an old 'Okie,' I'll give it to them." Teacher then queries a pupil, "James, did you call John an 'Okie'?" James answers, "I guess I did. But that is what he is." Teacher rebukes, "We mustn't say things like that. Johnny can't help being what he is. Say you are sorry, James." James obeys; teacher demands the same of the Okie child who complies, saying fiercely, 'I'm sorry I hit you but just remember what I said." Returning to class, teacher puts her arm around James while the Okie "shuffles in." Clearly, Okie status is dubious.

In the first drama, a Negro boy asks his white teacher, "Is it because I am a negro [1] that they don't want to dance with me?" She evades, saying, "Everyone in this classroom likes you . . . aren't you our class president and the best baseball player the school ever had?" He persists, "Yes . . . but is that why they don't dance with me?" She evades again, "We will talk about it later."

In the second drama, a teacher says to a Mexican-American boy, "Guadalupe, doesn't your father want you to do good work at school?" The boy answers, "He don't care. As long as I can work good for him in the fields on Saturday. He tells me I am a big boy and I should work, not go to school." Teacher addresses the class, "Ready for our spelling test. I asked you to get your parents to help you." Guadalupe exclaims, "I forgot to study. Oh, well, maybe I'll pass. Last night my uncle got married and we had a fiesta!" Teacher exclaims, "What's the matter with you, Guadalupe? Haven't you got any ambition?" He answers, "I don't know, teacher."

In these vivid scripts, the imaginary teachers assume no responsibility for understanding and solving the pupils' dilemmas. They are little more than gently permissive. They might have in mind the notion real teachers often voice as, "Isn't it enough to love our minority children?" Actually, teachers assert themselves more decisively; they set school norms and maintain them. But usually they barely possess an inkling of knowledge of the minorities' special backgrounds and of their own faulty adaptations to them. Teachers are largely unaware that they create or worsen the pupils' dilemmas by their unfamiliar demands. Staging the sociodramas educators asserted themselves in a remarkable way: instead of securing "ethnics" for the Negro and Mexican roles, they trained three white Anglo children to enact Negroes, Mexicans, and Okies as local WASPs supposed them to be. The same children played the parts in successive years. The scripts merely voiced the teachers' "frustrations" with minority pupils, even caricaturing them, but they threw no light on the "values and drives" of the minority cultures.

Throughout history, educated classes have struggled to master additional languages, to become bilingual or multilingual. Yet public-school teachers, as monolingual as most Americans, speak of "bilingualism" uncritically as causing school failures even when research challenges the assumption.[2] Nor do they realize that they use the word to attack the Spanish-speaking group almost exclusively, especially individuals with poor school records and a poor command of either Spanish or English.

High-school faculties ask repeatedly, "Should we consider that pupils of Mexican descent have a reading problem if they speak Spanish? How does this affect their handling of the English language? Should we consider a student bilingual when he is of Mexican descent? What is the bilingual problem in such a student? Who can be considered a bilingual student?"

These questions carry a load of feelings. In elementary and secondary schools, teachers sharply rebuke pupils who speak Spanish among themselves; they even scold kindergartners and detain them after school.[3] New families migrating from Mexico, who know only Spanish, send young children to school speaking the offensive mother tongue. Teachers reported seeing Spanish-speaking kindergartners fall silent, shamefaced under the teachers' criticisms though they could not understand them. When asked why they prohibited the children from speaking their family tongue during free periods, teachers answered, "Because we don't know what they are saying! They might be talking about us!" Some teachers take up Spanish as a hobby but this does not alter the dogma of "bilingualism."

So challenged and confused do teachers feel by Mexican-Americans that they curiously eye every act. These are some of their written questions: "Spanish [a euphemism for Mexican] children start off and do well for a short time, then fade away academically. Why?" "We have a small, light-skinned child of Mexican parents, aged six years three months. She is very shy, her feelings are easily hurt, she bursts into tears on slight provocation, apparently is too nervous to hold pencils or crayons. But she seems to have a happy family life. Explain her behavior." "We have a Mexican pupil with a white mother and a Mexican father. But the girl does not want to be called a Mexican. Why?" "We have a little Mexican girl from a broken home, living with her paraplegic father and an older brother and sister who are bad influences. Our pupil seems sweet and well-mannered and tries to do acceptable work. How explain this?" "You wouldn't let your daughter marry a Mexican, would you? Their skins are so dark." "How is it that Mexicans are so poor in culture and that whites lead?" "Why do Mexican pupils say that their teachers, or gringos, are prejudiced against them? We like our brown-eyed friends and worry over their behavior problems." "Why don't Mexicans go in for athletics? Their boy gangs bring weapons to school so they can fight later. Their girls fight also, though in pairs; they grab each other by the hair and scratch and claw. We teachers recognize scratch marks on the girls' faces. I almost cheered when our [school's] girl finished her last fight without receiving marks on her face." "Until a few years ago, Mexicans wouldn't shower at school. We wondered if it was because they weren't used to them. So we offered them scented soap. Well, since then they've been showering!" "Our school was 40 per cent Negro and Mexican. Now it's 95 per cent so. How do we help teachers to adjust to the change? There is this great class gap between teachers and pupils. Our pupil absenteeism rate is 10 per cent, the population is transient, families move here from East Los Angeles [slums], the Mexican and Negro boys are fighters and TV-viewers. What should we do?" "Why are there so many dropouts?" "I try to show my Mexican pupils good examples. For instance, I say, look at this teacher, how far he's gone even though he is a Mexican. He's the same race as you but look at him. You can do the same."

Similar questions are raised about Negroes but less frequently. One teacher puzzled over "a boy of negro [1] race who prefers the company of little blond-haired girls and resents his own female race. This boy attends a white church. Why?" A principal observed that within a year the enrollment of his school had shifted from almost all white to 60 per cent Negro. Teachers thought Negro parents behaved "strangely," perhaps meaning severely. Teachers said they found themselves trying to protect Negro pupils against their habitual physical violence toward one another; necessarily the teachers used force with the pupils. "Was this correct?" One teacher decided that "the low-priced housing element" of any race "plays by a different rule book" from the school's; this automatically breeds trouble. One rare teacher blamed not pupils but pedagogy, especially in reading. Her classes included dull whites, slow to read; she said her own young sons were slow readers. She demanded, "Can't reading be taught properly?"

Questions about physical training recur almost as often as about bilingualism: "Why don't Mexican boys and girls try out for school teams?" "Why do they avoid the school swimming pool?" Unlike newcomer teachers, Mexicans remember the California practice (prohibited after the Second World War) of closing public pools to Mexicans except on the day before the water was changed. Less often are there such questions about Negroes, Orientals, and Indians.[4] Mexican-Americans girls often refuse to undress for gymnasium, as required of pupils by state law; teachers say the girls "cover up [their resistance] with horseplay and belligerency." Pressed for an explanation, girls may say that they "don't feel at home in the school dressing room or shower"; teachers do not know that the girls omit mentioning that preparation for physical training classes violates parental and clerical prohibitions against undressing in public. The pupils' opposition upsets teachers, who show resentment. Principals report, "At times it appears that the job is almost more than teachers can stand. Fatigue and frustrations cause high turnovers; new teachers come with only inadequate experience."

Educators also want to know, with a peculiar blindness to their own habits, "Why do Latin-American [a euphemism for Mexican] students take such excessive care of the hair?" They describe how youngsters cut, oil, comb, dress their waves and pompadours, and shield them during exercise. The school makes no comments on the other groups except to prohibit peroxiding and ducktail styling of boys' hair.

Educators regularly ask why teenage Mexican-American boys gather in public places, ogle teenage girls, and flirt. They do not ask this about boys of other origins. They add that the Mexican boys are generally polite and confine their attentions to Mexican girls. Mentally, teachers censure Anglo girls who, at school dances, "pursue" Mexican boys, often considered "handsome." Teachers justify themselves on grounds that Anglo parents would object. This is often so, but one asks why the teachers make this unusual effort to align themselves with Anglo parents.

Mexican-American boys disturb teachers of both sexes more than girls. Teachers ask, "What happens to Mexican-American boys at adolescence? They resent authority, especially of school people. They act as if all authority is against them. They gang and dress alike. Why? At present, they wear khaki pants. This makes the racial thing stand out as a real issue. Does the school do it to them? Mexican girls also group together, especially the slow learners; sometimes you see a blond girl with them."

Educators ask how to rouse the dynamic interest on the part of pupils which they call "motivation." The word is used as though it identified something concrete or exact. Its import roughly resembles that of "ambition" and that of the social scientists' technical term, "goal-directed." The word, in fact, refers to educators' standards of schoolroom achievement, however dubiously critics may speak of them. Absorbed in their occupational grievances instead of in their pupils' special traits and home backgrounds, educators complain:

Motivation is our problem. Doesn't this have to do with the parents? Parents are our real problem since they should give children proper values. But they don't cooperate. Mexican parents are polite, promising what we want—but they don't come through. Their excuse is of the order of *mañana*, or that they don't speak English, or that a relative is sick, visiting, working, getting married, doesn't have shoes—anything. Often they simply don't care. Otherwise they'd come to parent-teacher conferences to discuss discipline, and to the PTA meetings, and they'd help their children with homework. How do they actually feel about school achievement? Children whose parents have gone to high school are more manageable because the parents know what school is about. . . . Now, what does it mean [that is, what should we do?] when a Mexican father of a first-grade boy tells the teacher, "if he doesn't behave, beat him!" Youngsters bring all their parents' dubious notions to school. When our city withdrew a promise to compensate Mexicans in slum dwellings torn down for redevelopment, a Mexican boy in class cried out, "This is race prejudice against Mexicans!" How do they get these strange ideas about race prejudice? . . .

How does the belief that racial discrimination exists in our society affect classroom attitudes and conduct of Mexican-American pupils? Why do Mexicans hesitate to join in class discussions? They also isolate themselves from extracurricular activities.

White (or Anglo) teachers ask important questions about Negro parents, pupils, and colleagues; but Negro, Oriental, and Mexican teachers rarely speak up even when prodded. The questions concern the Negroes who have been pouring into California since the Second World War, advantaged by antidiscriminatory legislation. The Supreme Court's 1954 decision against school segregation, and the associated militancy of American Negroes encouraged by world unrest, promote far more questions about Negro-white relationships than about Mexican-Anglo ones or Oriental-Caucasian ones; and no questions are asked about relationships of American Indians with ruling groups. This is because Negroes are the historic challenge to our racial unity, unique among other minorities; indeed, other minorities can be more or less absorbed into the general population whereas Negroes must remain singled out until they "pass" for white in appearance. Negroes are among the oldest of American stocks; their singular cultural role now symbolizes traditional struggles for liberty and fraternity.

To whites in California, the tide of incoming Negroes seems threatening. However, in the present liberalized atmosphere, despite social instability, the language and stereotypes of prejudice are being carefully controlled. Many questions from educators in different cities fall into a sequence conveying a report of earnest puzzlement over desegregation and integration. They read:

Must not the negro [1] carry great hostility that is passively expressed? How does the negro principal feel in an elementary school with white and negro teachers? The negro principal of one school has such a need to control that she finds it hard to let a counselor or social worker take over a child with problems. Teachers have poor attitudes toward negroes in some schools, which principals blame on negroes' failure to meet academic standards and establish good attitudes toward authority. Other teachers become real indulgent, expecting nothing for "these are just little colored kids." A negro teacher seems to reject a negro child in her class who does poor academic work, and she generally condescends to negro children in her class. How do we handle these problems? . . .

In our city, we have two kinds of negro [1] families. One has lived here for generations, the men working in construction and agriculture and the women in white homes. The other kind, newcomers from Oklahoma, live in segregated neighborhoods definitely substandard, mostly because of low income. Children of the latter are commonly truant and tardy. When we approach the parents for help, they tell us to give corporal punishment. Of course, schools find it hard to establish authority without this, yet they do not use it as much with other youngsters. . . .

How do we help a negro [1] mother of low socio-economic status to become less punitive toward her children and use less "whupping"? In an ambitious, upward-mobile negro family, the young son has average ability and works to capacity but he is tutored and punished at home to enable him to get all E's. Another [Negro] mother says, "I whip Junior every day for getting home later than his brother." But Junior is in an upper grade and is dismissed later! . . .

I left a note in the door of a negro [1] home, asking the parents to come to school about their boy. When there was no response, I returned. The negro mother treated me nicely but couldn't settle down to details about how school and home might join to help the child. I had the impression that the mother could not actually read, because she was vague about the note. . . . Many negro parents think education has little more to offer than penalties for truancy, tardiness, and low achievement. Others think education will solve all. . . .

I find that negro [1] parents, especially the many deserted mothers with large families and financial hardships, are overwhelmed by social and personal problems. They live in substandard housing, with broken homes, and observe different customs, like accepting the illegitimate child and love-mother or love-brother. These facts alarm strictly middle-class teachers; they fail to realize it is difficult or impossible for the mothers to pay attention to the child's problems at school. What can we do? we seem unable to help such parents put pressure on youngsters to achieve beyond their rated ability level. When underachieving youngsters feel like it, they stay home to baby-sit or for less important reasons. Perhaps school people don't really understand how the youngsters feel. We want help in knowing how they do feel, and what schools can do. . . .

Many families "pay extra" for being poor and on relief. That is, they never have sufficient funds for cash repairs, so when the TV breaks—and TV brings them life and enlarged horizons—the best they can do is squeeze out another down payment and then pay high interest. The same happens with washing machines. Visiting teachers and school social workers put in late hours and night work around these neighborhoods. What is the answer here? . . .

How does a negro child [1] feel in the classroom . . . where most, including the teacher, are white? What effect does white rejection have on negro motivation to learn in the classroom? Counselors and social workers often find that negro youngsters score 70 to 80 IQ on the group tests given all children at public school. Is this a true representation of ability or is there some reason for failing to do well? . . .

What actually is the white man afraid of in regard to the negro? [1] What need we beware of within ourselves as we work with these people? What about a negro teacher who hears white teachers at school talk disdainfully of their "discouraging" negro pupils? . . . Colored families who move into a predominantly white neighborhood are resented but this does not appear in the behavior of negro [1] youngsters at school. Family problems are reflected in difficult behavior at school, but little appears as race prejudice among the children. They do show defiance of teachers and lack of respect. Does this grow from race persecution? Disrespect and defiance worsen when, as in my district, 38 per cent of the teachers are new, as are 30 per cent of the pupils. Secondary school teachers find that adolescent rebellion aggravates all problems [of Negroes]. The girls don't find anything they want at school. They want only to be married. They don't consider Home Economics practical because they already have experience in homemaking. Boys have unrealistic job goals, lack ability to achieve academically, and resent the school's expectations. Our Guidance Department cannot serve these minority areas adequately. We need a new imaginative approach. . . .

Certain areas grow congested as large families replace smaller ones [who are] displaced from [their homes as these] houses are torn down for [construction of] freeways; families [then] double up in available units. Friction and insecurity grow. Small apartments formerly for childless couples become occupied by families with children. Shacks are thrown up alongside the few respectable dwelling units. Guidance personnel find critical social and emotional problems among youngsters who lack the home experiences needed for success in primary grades. Classrooms built for 30 pupils now hold 37 to 39. Teachers, principals, and superintendents need special instructional materials, and also special guidance for their morale. . . .

We have a school district where various racial groups live together harmoniously. Economic standards are good. Families long resident assume leadership, especially the Mexicans. They accept both colored and Anglo-American families, and show pride in the school. In a poorer mixed neighborhood, however, Mexican parents have almost no control over their children, and school can't get them to relate. There seems to be no strong masculine figure with which the children identify. What are the relationships in these Mexican homes? . . .

Can counseling and casework help a child change aggressive behavior he has learned in the home and street? A superior colored family, arrived here a year ago from Texas, is distressed to find its two daughters receiving treatment from their own race that would be less surprising from an antagonistic race. A small group of colored girls dominates their neighborhood with threats, fights, and shows of knives. They mooch from white girls and forbid colored girls to associate with white. In another area, colored boys behave the same way toward white and colored schoolmates. Yet after the murder of Emmett Till [young Negro boy visiting from Chicago] in Money, Mississippi, when colored boys there got very restless, they fought only among themselves. They didn't struggle with other races. How do you explain this? . . .

These children need to learn skills that would make them employable in more than a marginal job market. They need to acquire social attitudes of helpfulness and cooperation; they need to drop surliness and suspicion. Their parents need the same. . . .

How does the [Negro] minority-group parent feel about PTA in a predominantly white school? One mother says she would like to attend PTA but fears being called to stand up and make a speech. She says, "*I* may think I'm as good as you but I know *you* don't." A middle-aged negro[1] grandmother said, "Lots of folks know that whites don't really care about teaching little colored kids anything. They might even drop the atomic bomb on school."

Teachers also say they are "frustrated" by others than "ethnics." Troublesome youngsters may come from families respectfully labeled "upper middle class" because of the fathers' income and profession. Like most teachers these are white Anglo-Americans, who are Protestants, Christian Scientists, Mormons, Jews, and Catholics of European descent. A counselor wanted help with the "crises these ordinary American adolescents bring into the classroom." Asked for details, he cited, "Foul language a girl throws at a teacher, rocks hurled through school windows, physical assault a boy threatens on a teacher," children's spoken lies and insolence, their forged notes excusing absence, smooching in halls and at classroom doors. Defacement and damage to school property is so common that school budgets regularly provide for it.

An elementary school principal marveled:

After every weekend, we find the school has been broken into and turf destroyed. Our school is in a wealthy bedroom town [residential suburb] outside of Los Angeles, all Caucasian. The income level surpasses that of Beverly Hills or Bel Air. Restlessness and insecurity fill the air, more evident in parents than in children, among both professional men and skilled workers. I wouldn't want to live in that town, and I advise my teachers against it. In fact, none of us live there. The families come and go, from all over the country. They drink, commit adultery, go into debt, perform violent crimes. We had the daughter of X [a professional man, involved in a protracted sensational murder trial] in our school: she was a sweet child. The trouble is that these newcomers don't know even their neighbors, nor what their neighbors stand for, though their homes are all jammed together. Out of loneliness, they join the country club but that doesn't seem to stabilize values. X and his wife belonged to the club. People like myself, born here and living generations in the area, find it shocking.

[However, the parents] all want college for their children. I think every parent has completed college, and many of the children are academically talented. Only a few of our pupils have an IQ of 80; some reach a 170 IQ, and the average is 117 IQ. The children *want* what we can give them. They offend rarely, and then it's simple violations of teachers' rules.

I think there is too much parent pressure on all of us. This is partly because school is the one community activity the newcomers care about. They just don't know anything else about the town. They urge the children to ask teachers for homework! Pupils and mothers hang around school for more work, and on Friday afternoons they hold up my teachers for assignments to last over the weekend! They buy out those books [5] to check up on us! So homelife becomes an extension of school. I think it's partly that the mothers don't have enough to occupy them, what with their money, servants and leisure.

[The principal said] many pupils reflected parental ambitions and anxieties in such psychosomatic forms as facial tics, nail biting, and digestive ailments. [She also spoke of] pupils' "emotional immaturity" which led them to throw rocks at the school. "They're really hostile," she repeated, and they practiced rock-throwing even in the fifth and sixth grades. [She thought] it was because they were surrounded by wealthy indulgences and people always doing for them. [But she concluded] that "on the whole, really, it's fun for us teachers. We're happy and secure, accomplishing all we want with the children. But it's frustrating trying to keep up with parents' demands! Parents insist on their children learning the fundamentals, getting rated on competitive report cards, and at the same time being happy!"

Young teachers, all obviously white Anglo, at large high schools serving children of white, small-income families, reported uneasily on these teenagers' insolences, saying that their "students do not know how to behave." A physical-education teacher demanded to know, tacitly referring to herself, "Why do girls resent a fairly young, attractive teacher who dresses well?" She did not forgive one girl, whom she sent to the dean for "combing her hair in class and attracting attention," who protested that it was the teacher who really distracted attention by sitting on the desk before the boys and girls and crossing her legs. Women teachers complained that "boys and girls never address a married woman as Mrs. but always as Miss. They refer to other teachers by surname without the courtesy title. It doesn't help to correct them." "At lunch hour they mill around so that teachers can't pass through them to the cafeteria—unless we elbowed, which we don't want—and the students make love on campus! in public! They kiss, right in front of us." [A middle-aged man declared] I feel like saying, "Go hire a hotel room." (Young teachers indignantly added) "They lay arms on each others' shoulders. They hold hands."

One principal spoke for others, "We don't say anything to pupils in public about their poor behavior, even if we're standing next to them. That's against school policy. We don't want to traumatize them, so we do no more than stare. We think it less traumatic to send the offenders to the dean's office for a private talk. But this doesn't help either. Where should we turn for help?"

When asked why they did not act more openly, teachers said in concert, "We want to be liked. We want rapport. We don't like to feel rejected. Maybe it's a sort of popularity contest but pupils do influence the powers-that-be against teachers they dislike. The lower-class [whites] frankly resent us. So they ignore commands, for example, to stop smoking. Or they get around them. Boys and girls say, 'My parents bought me the cigarettes.' What can we do? How do we raise their standards? Do we lack something personally? Or is it a lack of the school's?" A principal echoed, "We want to understand students, not punish them. We have our middle-class school pattern. What should we do?"

Principals could identify teachers who added to the strain of relationships with these Anglo pupils. A young English teacher, according to his principal, showed off to classes with adolescent-type sauciness, and classes responded accordingly. On the other hand, "My art teacher and science teacher set too high standards, and this also discourages achievement. We don't know how to control these personal quirks."

Often, teachers are under fire by Anglo parents and school boards for seeming to threaten fundamental religious and moral beliefs with their courses in biological evolution, sex hygiene, and comparative religion. Minority-group parents rarely enter this curricular fray. Curriculum directors asked, "Is it really necessary to drop these subjects or are there alternative approaches?" They felt they understood the Anglo parents and knew the key words giving offense. The staff of one high school therefore experimented with rephrasing the titles of disputed courses, and this proved a workable alternative. Thus, the staff converted "Evolution" into "Human Growth and Development" and "Sex Hygiene" into "Family Management." This illustrates the advantage of sharing a cultural background, so that educators' knowledge of pupils' lives helps to remove school difficulties.

Teachers in high school and junior college asked anxiously, "Why can't we interest [usually Anglo] students in reading good literature? Does the school culture oppose Shakespeare, Sophocles, Faulkner, Galsworthy?" A junior-college teacher of English literature asserted:

We don't really communicate with our students. They live only in the present, so only the contemporary, the latest, interests them. My students won't read anything more than once, nor carefully. They read everything in the same way that they read the comic strips and the sports pages. They want only easy reading—so they avoid Galsworthy, for instance. Above all, they wish to conform, so they avoid controversy and thinking. They want to play it safe, to disturb no one. I can't get them to care about *Oedipus Rex*. They want only knowledge that is utilitarian, that will help them make money. They don't have imagination. They sit in class bored or indifferent. They're negativistic, seem to feel I have nothing to teach them! They're in love with science, science fiction, and the so-called scientific approach. I think they have too much too soon—for instance, sex. College students don't value the teacher. You remember what Shaw said, about teaching: "Those who can, do; those who cannot, teach." When I interpret a work of literature, there are always numerous claims that I am reading in what really isn't there. They aren't interested in the truths about human nature or insights about the human condition that great literature reveals. These attitudes are rather prevalent. It seems to me most English teachers of literature in required courses feel Anglo students' responses are not what they want. We try to understand our students, find out what they are like, why they respond as they do. I and my fellow teachers regularly reexamine ourselves, our methods and the content of our courses. We don't yet know the answers.

Some teachers were more hopeful than this conscientious spokesman.

Educators from every level of public schooling asked the same kinds of questions. They were uneasy about their professional capacities, about the methods and content of their work and sometimes about their goals, about the responses of pupils from the dominant Anglo and several minority backgrounds, and about the approval or wishes of the communities served. It appeared that the principal applications of anthropology to education were to elucidate for teachers the sociocultural aspects of the Anglo and minority worlds in which they lived and worked; to clarify the purposes of the public school with its uniform standards; to illuminate teachers' professional and personal interests on the job; to interpret the diverse goals bred into pupils and educators by their respective cultures and thus to indicate how conflicts could be harmonized; and to design means for training teachers accordingly.

Notes

1. The small "n" that appears throughout is reproduced from the original text. Properly it should be capitalized.

2. *Cf.* for example, Frank Farner, "Comparative Achievement and Bilingualism of Matched Groups of Nisei, Mexican-American and Anglo High School Students." Manuscript at Claremont Graduate School. Presented at the Conference of the California Educational Research Association, March 11–12, 1960.

3. A fourth-grade teacher studying in the project passed a Mexican pupil talking Spanish to friends during a recess. She reported he was dumfounded when she greeted him in Spanish and teasingly encouraged him to speak Spanish in class if that would bring him to recite. Her dean was also very interested in developing Spanish.

4. Compared with present interest in Mexicans and Negroes, and earlier interest in Orientals, American Indians today are generally overlooked. When a few appear in schools, they are likely to be seen as inferior Mexicans. Since neither Mexicans nor Indians protest publicly, the confusions are not challenged.

5. Text books widely favored over others provided free by the State Department of Education.

3

Culture Concepts and Methods for Teachers

Man is human only when he is civilized, as we commonly say, or when he is acculturated and enculturated, as the anthropologist says.[1] He becomes civilized only through education, the disciplining in systematic relationships with others according to the rules, habits, and beliefs of society. Most of the established relationships and beliefs are traditional, handed down from forebears long deceased. They are passed along from generation to generation through the myriad systems of society. School is one such system, the family is another, and so are reasoned speech, the church, employment, friendship and marriage, homesteading, slum life, and segregation. Education triggers and guides the individual flowerings we call intelligence and personality. The traditional patterns and ethos of a society permit or compel creativity from some, and frustration and disorder from others. Individual adaptability is enormous for man accommodates to extraordinary changes in short or long time spans. But the limits, favoring conditions and potentialities for human adaptation and learning, remain to be tested for useful generalizations. Appropriate learning is measured by prevailing cultural standards; it involves the factor now termed "motivation," an apparently delicate plant which responds well or ill to many individual, social, accidental, or unforeseen circumstances.

When teachers talk about pupils' performances, particularly about their difficulties, they stress the words culture, race, class, language, minority, and prejudice. These are powerfully charged words in the news of today and in science; and teachers hope the words are keys to solutions of their problems. But the words deteriorate into jargon unless applied knowingly to education.

The most important word is culture, used in the generic sense that includes the limited meaning of polished or standardized conduct. Most people think of a generic culture chiefly as a strange group manifesting social peculiarities. This impression also carries popular judgments about the superiority or inferiority of the groups. Among ourselves, "other" groups are identified with the lower or middle class, have a minority or dominant status, are composed of a white or colored race (English-speaking peoples everywhere consider all non-European types "colored" and the British are inclined to extend the label also to Mediterranean groups), descend from specific nationalities, follow chiefly a Christian or Jewish or Oriental faith, may speak a European or an Amerindian or an Asiatic language at home. A favorite omnibus term for them employed by educators and social scientists is "ethnics."

Anthropologists regard culture as the universal condition of human beings living in society. Men's minds, meeting socially, cooperate to create culture, inventing and changing it, and teaching it to new generations. A man is always born into the environment of culture and placed, even before actual birth, into the accustomed relationships of the local civilization. Thus, he is delivered by a doctor, nursed by a mother, legitimized by a father, baptized by a priest, bathed by a relative or nurse; if American white, he has been directed to control Negroes; if American black, he has been taught to submit to whites. People are taught carefully how and what to hate and love in heaven and on earth. The culture of a group is its standardized behavior, values, and products. These have evolved through time and have been sanctified as tradition. All aspects of personal and group behavior, whether pulse rate, styles of war and burial, alimentary disease, inventions, poetry, marriage rites, divine worship are shaped by culture.[2] So fundamental is culture to man that the biologist Julian Huxley regards the human stage of evolution as a subordination of biological mechanisms (meaning physical heredity and natural selection) to cultural ones.[3]

Versions of culture vary enormously among civilizations. The variations command allegiances of prime or ultimate significance from the men trained in them. Men have died and killed for impermanent convictions about divinity, love, hereditary and elected rulers, scientific truths, race differences. At other times such men have adopted the same disputed convictions. Culture is continually pooled in tides that swirl over the earth as men migrate and communicate, passing on technologies (gunpowder, printing press), ideas (monotheism, justice), values (individual liberty and salvation), and social systems (industrialization, political democracy), along with their genes. Humanity's stocks of accumulated learnings, or cultures, are forever being toyed with and altered. The lustiness of Elizabethan England does not resemble the sobriety of the contemporary period; the family system of Confucian China is crippled by the political system of contemporary Communism; the violent measures imperial Spain employed while colonizing are now more frequent in Central and South America than in contemporary Iberia. Words shift meanings to their opposites, or to include opposite or other aspects. An essay on "the common vocabulary of Americans," especially some current idioms of Negroes,[4] shows that "fox" means a beautiful girl, "cat" means a man, "gray" means white people, "member" means a Negro. But not long ago, "kitten" (and the idea of fondling) preceded "fox" (and the idea of baying hounds in pursuit), "cat" denoted a malicious woman, "pink" connoted whites, and "blue" connoted blacks. People learn the changes; they can also learn another language and another culture but the adequacy of learning depends on the adequacy of teaching.

California's subcultures startle educators with their variety. California is now a microcosm of the world's races, languages, and social conditions; in the millions, youngsters are processed through the public schools. Each culture affects man's physical appearance, physiology, thoughts, and conduct. Some theorists say that a culture's collective ideas and trends obey regularities of a separate order. Physical anthropologists define human races according to selected criteria of measurements of individual physiques that represent local populations of family lines. The anthropologists measure variations of skin color, dimensions of head length and width, ratio of length of limbs to torso, blood groups, and other traits. Physical trait measurements are found to be inconstant. These inconstancies or variations are understood to reflect both genetic heredity and adaptations to specific environments (of physical localities and of societies), as when stature increases, head and facial proportions alter, color of skin and hair darken.[5] Stanley M. Garn believes that races are always changing, partly by adapting traits to particular circumstances.[6] Decades ago, Franz Boas described changes of the supposed immutable head forms among thousands of immigrants and their descendants, measuring Puerto Ricans and six different European national (and religious or ethnic) groups who settled in the United States. He found, for example, that "the average cephalic index of immigrating East European Jews is 83.0, that of their children born in America 81.4, and that of their grandchildren 78.7." [7] But "the South Italian, who in Italy has an exceedingly long head, becomes more short-headed; so that in this country both approach a uniform type." [8] In general, "Races . . . show evidences of change due to domestication, environmental influences, selections, and perhaps mutation." [9] Body measurements, or racial traits, do not of themselves produce, acquire, or transmit a particular culture; but through the general modes of culture, mankind adapts to the environment.

Especially in the United States, Germany, and the Union of South Africa, Western civilization weights the race concept powerfully and threateningly with declarations about levels of social worth. The declarations are embodied in all social, economic, and political relationships. Scientists today, however, show that men of all stocks are alike by the biological criterion of universal fertility in all crossings and by the psychosocial criteria of creating, acquiring or learning, and transmitting culture. [3]

Those attempting to classify human races have proposed from three (such as Negro, Mongoloid, Caucasian) to three hundred physical types, depending upon the taxonomic criteria. Some former classifications included now discredited social evaluations of traits, comparable to Cesare Lombroso's attribution of "criminal" stigmata to certain head-forms and racial groups. Because populations look dissimilar, older taxonomists tried to standardize the unfamiliar impressions of human color, shape, size, and smell; they assumed that a group's social ways were rooted genetically in these and were unalterable. Today, human biologists and physical anthropologists study instead the unceasing changes in the races of man, as these adapt to the environment in continual evolution. [5]

The distinctness of race and culture can be documented by layman and scientist. Each knows that a Chinese bred in Boston is culturally a Bostonian, and may or may not speak the ancestral tongue. Conversely, many Chinese flourish in America by cooking Chinese dishes for customers of white, Negro, Oriental, and other racial stocks. Scientists find that whereas one anthropometric variety or race of man may possess traits, abilities, and liabilities foreign to another—roughly on the analogy of traits bred differentially in the milch cow and the beef cow—these have not been proven significant for society and acculturation. On the contrary, overwhelming evidence shows that any physical type of man can learn the culture of any society if he is given the proper opportunity. In addition to scholarly proof, evidences are everywhere: the American-born and -reared children of Africans, Asiatics, and Europeans are *American* in conduct and in altered physical type, no longer Congolese, Tibetan, or Albanian; they lose the parental languages and must attend school to recover them, though recovery is limited in an English-speaking country.

Language is a universal characteristic of human groups, though the local forms vary enormously. Subhuman mammalian types on land and in the sea, and many bird types make noises and some imitate human speech but only man has the gift and tool of true speech. Language is universally and primarily verbal, though gestures and facial expressions play a large additional part. Groups who speak mutually unintelligible languages (like tribesmen of the North American plains) occasionally cultivate manual forms of communication as a *lingua franca*. Particular languages, each with its special grammar, idioms, and phonetics, are not determined by the bodily forms of speakers nor by the patterns of a local culture. Men of any race and culture learn any language when suitably exposed, as is evidenced by African tribesmen at Oxford and the Sorbonne, by Americans at Peking, by scholars and immigrants everywhere. Custom, however, attaches linguistic labels—like the politically exploited Semitic, Aryan, and Spanish ones—to physical types that are more properly designated Caucasian, European, and Mediterranean.[10]

Human beings live in organized groups, which we call society. Their minds flower best in company. The so-called backward or primitive cultures and societies have often lain off the main highways of culture contacts and exchanges. The potentialities of man, as an individual and as a group, are bound to opportunities and limitations of the local culture.[11] Massive scientific evidence to this point influenced the U. S. Supreme Court, when in 1954 it ordered the end of segregation in public schools, to assure children an equal opportunity to realize their potentials.

However, discriminatory institutions (such as our southern regions' Jim Crow which segregates by custom and law) and individual race prejudices cannot be ordered erased by single public enactments. Nothing in a personal life or a culture can be removed simply, so meshed and balanced are human functions in the continual practice of traditional relationships.[12] The anthropologist therefore studies social events holistically, as rooted in and ramifying the whole of a society. He follows each event through all of its ramifications to construct outlines of the total "pattern" which expresses its meaning. Each member of society is trained to respond according to the patterns of his tradition and becomes irrevocably involved with them, even if he criticizes or tries to destroy them. Older people are more deeply and intricately involved than younger ones because responses to the patterns have become habitual. Also, older people are likely to have stronger and wider commitments to social institutions of property, power, and friendship. Many Negroes in the old segregated South failed to support the Supreme Court's school order to desegregate, as is noted occasionally in news and magazine stories; often Negroes failed to aid Federal fair employment practices programs in the South because these orders threatened their precarious security of life and property.

Segregation had brought some monopolistic advantages to the Negro élite. On the other hand, liberal Northern whites moving South find that regional race "etiquette" guides them implacably along the traditionally "peculiar" course of "keeping the black man in his place" —and, inevitably, keeping the white in his. Traditionally, the races cannot associate equally in each other's homes and churches nor in stores, streets, and graveyards. Often it is local Negroes who prod the newcomer white into the locally accepted ways. In the old South, by custom, a white's aberrations inflict punishment on Negroes. Custom aligns conduct with ideas; it offers formulas of orientation and procedure whose tested survival and simplicity handicap the dreams of innovators. Biracial customs of Southern life are ingrained in the blacks and whites who leave the South. Often not until the next generation do the different customs of the new regions replace the old ways.

Hence, discrimination cannot be removed by schools' formal compliance alone; its conditionings persist in memory and habit of private persons and officials, of teachers and pupils, of parents and community. That Americans are all given to weighted discrimination is clear from an instant glance at a social situation. For only we, besides South African Boers, note inevitably the fact of human color; if color is not noted, the American assumes that no Negroes are present; or Orientals, if he belongs to the western coast; or Mexicans, if he belongs to the Southwest. A Briton or a continental perceives instead indicators of social class or of foreignness in bearing and dress. When the Briton singles out those we call Negroes, he stresses their social placement, which is "foreign," calling the Negroes by their (foreign) nationality designations: "black Yank," Nigerian, Jamaican, (colored) "colonial." Even Britain's derogatory terms pivot on social deficiencies, not on race complexion; these include the terms stowaway, half-caste, Fuzzy-Wuzzies (unkempt bushy hair), Wog, Kaffir. We *incorporate* Negroes and other similarly handicapped groups in our society and "place" them by physical type.

Through race rankings we justify the low statuses accorded the minorities. We say that Negroes, American Indians, and others are of different, and thus, of lesser races. To say "different from white" implies "inferior to white." About other minorities, we say or signify it. These other minorities have been every people under the sun who migrate to our shores. Those categorized unfavorably at any one time have been labeled according to pressures of politics, the economy, wars, and other kinds of competition. Besides Negroes, but less extremely penalized, the great minorities have been Jews and Catholics. These groups entered, lacking strength to manipulate our society, and were held back by restrictive practices in employment, education, housing, and recreation. Conspicuous were the Irish Catholics who streamed to America, depopulating their homeland to escape cruel British rule and their own potato famines. Only in 1960 did one, John F. Kennedy, become a president of the United States. Jews fled here from persecutions, first in Western Europe, then in Eastern Europe.

By the 1960's, some Negroes joined white minorities in high appointments to national and international services. Dr. Ralph Bunche, a United Nations Undersecretary, had already made history as a Negro awarded the Nobel peace prize. More often than his predecessors, President Kennedy appointed Negroes to high positions in the federal administration and courts. In 1965, the Negro leader, Dr. Martin Luther King, also received the Nobel peace award.

These developments mean that minorities are pacing the socially esteemed "dominant group," that the concept of minority must soon die out (as has that of "miscegenation" in recent decades), and that associated language idioms must change. American life will alter to accommodate additional holders of power. In our country, the singular minority group has always been Negroes, defined in law by discriminatory enactments and by some favorable ones (notably Lincoln's Emancipation Proclamation, Freedmen's legislation and Constitutional amendments, Roosevelt's Fair Employment Practices Committee, the Supreme Court's 1954 decision); in custom by discriminatory practices; in language by special terms including some now illegal to use in public; in ideology by stereotypes so compelling that millions of dollars have been spent studying them. A vast body of fictional works about Negroes and whites has been created by black and white Southerners. One southern author, William Faulkner, received the Nobel prize for his novels of the race-hagged South; others won Pulitzer prizes; many are best sellers, a number are literary classics. The special relations of whites with Negroes are so inseparable from our national history and culture that they monopolize the designation of race relations.

The catchall term, minorities, is a racist euphemism that has been growing on us since the Second World War. This war was occasioned partly over racist doctrines and acts: the Nazis releasing traditional German racism in an atmosphere of economic depression against Jews and practicing Christians as "inferior" races; the Japanese against us for our Oriental Exclusion Act, our Alien Land Law, and extensive discriminations in employment, housing, schooling, and recreation. Nowadays, minorities are not only groups to be regulated at large, they are also a growing number of equals at work, play, and school, and in residential areas.

Minority communities watch anxiously for the measure of their members joining the life and work of the dominant groups. Consequently, Negroes and Mexicans, unaccustomed until lately to responsibilities and privileges of authority, may seem overzealous about standards, especially with regard to their own people. They are goaded in part by continuing racist stereotypes and by the unfair weighting of words like Negro-colored, Spanish-Mexican, Oriental-Japanese, Indian-primitive, Okie "poor-white," white-superior. Reasoning follows stereotypes when teachers expect "bilingualism" to mean a minority's school retardation, or Negro and Mexican to imply lower class and academically deficient.

Educators choose to obey the new laws of desegregation and integration. But no American of our time escapes racist indoctrination, whatever his status, because culture influences thought on subconscious levels. Besides, prejudice is profoundly intertwined with major interests. Race prejudice supports the dominant group's prior claim to *every* advantage. It asserts the dominant's claims to jobs, dwellings, women; opposition was punishable, until recently in the old South, by death or torture, and punishment was sanctioned by Southerners' traditionally sacred beliefs about white people's virtue (notably in women's sexual chastity, regardless of individual prostitutes and other exceptions) and sweeping privileges.

Situations involving prejudice become more complex and confused when alien (or subordinate) cultural elements enter, in the persons of, say, Mexicans and Puerto Ricans, or of Indian tribesmen from isolated reservations. Handicapped groups preserve or foster social peculiarities when they are prevented from free and easy association with standard practices. Known thus for exceptional customs are "poor-white" Kentucky mountaineers, Louisiana Cajuns, New Mexico Hispanos, Southwestern Mexican-Americans, Poles and Italians in slums. That is, to differing degrees, minorities are incompletely Americanized in language, culture, and pride. As Americans, they are taught to despise their physical or other differences from the dominant group. Therefore, some of each group do what Negroes call "passing." All's fair in war—therefore, a Negro who seems white, a Jew who seems gentile, a Mexican who seems European or "Spanish" may trade on these high market values. Rhinoplasty has made WASPs (White Anglo-Saxon Protestants) of Jew, Italian, Armenian, Negro.[13] Name change may do this, by Jew, Irishman, Italian, Pole, Russian, German, by commoner and king. Cleveland Amory cites changes in Boston's "social folk song," as he terms it, after a Polish Jew legally changed his name, Kabotznik, to Cabot. The song had been: "And this is good old Boston / The home of the bean and the cod / Where the Lowells talk to the Cabots / And the Cabots talk only to God." The song's last two lines became, he says, "Where the Lowells have no one to talk to / 'Cause the Cabots talk Yiddish, by God!"[14]

Few men can live despising themselves, as minorities are often expected to do. The Negro taught to defer to whites, the Jew taught to defer to Christians, the Catholic obliged to defer to Protestants, does not wholly accept the mandates but incorporates them along with fears and rebellions. Richard Wright described this in his autobiography, *Black Boy:* "The white South said that it knew 'niggers.' . . . Well, the white South had never known me . . . what I thought [and] . . . felt . . . [M]y deepest instincts have always made me reject the 'place' to which the white South had assigned me. . . . But in what other ways had the South allowed me to . . . be myself, except in rejection, rebellion, and aggression?"[15] In this and other literary works, the complex reactions of particular minorities to the dominant society are detailed. It is instructive to read the books by the Santee Dakota Indian, Charles A. Eastman, who acquired an M.D. in the late 1880s, after his Santee father (held captive by the U. S. government for his part in Minnesota's "Sioux Massacre") took him from "wild" tribal life. Dr. Eastman, or Ohiyesa (meaning The Winner in Dakota), shows how a proud man, told all his life that he belongs to a despicable race, turns some hate away from himself and against the aggressors.[16] The sociologist Robert E. Park gave a related picture in the dilemma of the "marginal man," a conceptualized person descended from a subordinate family culture, say Mexican, but reared also in schools and streets of the dominant American society. Such a man, according to Park, was at home in neither culture or group.[17]

Social science now finds Park's picture too simple. We must realize that protracted poverty worsens discrimination in all functions of living and dying. Again, people who expect no rewards but only punishment, solely because of their race, color, religion, language, or defeat in war, have few incentives to honor or follow dominant regulations. The punishing discriminations bar minorities from joining people who act in approved American ways. Consequently, Mexican-Americans attending segregated classes speak with the accent ridiculed in jokes and the movies; they have little chance to hear and practice the correct accent. Western educators often consider this outcome solely a consequence of "bilingualism." Jews in ghettos retain accents and locutions; however, these now enrich our stock of dialect humor. The late President Kennedy's speech retained the provincial intonation and accent we call "Boston Irish." We recognize "Negro speech" in the voice use, enunciation, and speech melodies of the old South, practiced also by whites, especially those who never ventured North (or "East," as they say) to Princeton and Harvard, but who retain habits of forebears from Ireland, Scotland, Wales, and the South of England. Provincialisms may be regarded as retarded learning and poor motivation; they should be regarded as evidencing in part boomerang effects of prejudice.

Prejudice is often expressed in sentimental clichés. A popular one singles out the "happy" humor in Negro life; another stresses the love of music and dance among Negroes and Mexicans; another makes much of the cleverness of Jews. Psychoanalysts stress instead that such qualities are mankind's safety valves under pressure. In the biologist's language, they help ensure survival of the fittest. Yet they have been learned under specific social conditions, including police threats, unemployment, lynching, and pogroms. The dominant group has disciplined minorities to survive under abuse, fostering behavior that is now being brought home to the desegregated public schools. The sentimental clichés refer to selected cultural traits which the dominant group tolerates as being not unduly competitive; and they also reveal minority man's immense neurological plasticity—that is, his immense ability to adapt by learning. A famous zoologist is quoted as saying recently, "Heredity is only a 'predisposition' which can be molded by environment. The potent genetic trait of educability . . . is the common property of all mankind, on a par with walking upright or the nine-month pregnancy term.'" [18]

Minorities and newcomers of cultural origins unlike those of the standard "middle-class American" consciously struggle to meet requirements and persons of the dominant society across cultural gaps and blocks. There is a constant exchange of cues—in words, voice tones, body bearing, dress, silences. On both sides, these are often misunderstood, some are penalized, some go lost. The dominant representative (teacher, social worker, police officer, nurse, physician) conveys threats by his presence, threats of power and of strangeness, which obscure and distort cues. Dimensions of some gaps and blocks can be gauged roughly from a *New York Times* statement, May 27, 1962, "that 11,000,000 adult Americans are at present considered illiterate . . . [meaning that] they have less than 5 years of elementary education. The adult illiteracy rate ranges from a low of 2.8 per cent of the population above age 25 in Utah to a high of 21.3 in Louisiana." Illiterates, like other deviants from standard American modes, live by customs of their special subgroups, though their origins are often genetically and culturally akin to those composing the dominant American class. The problem, of making mutually intelligible the behavior and attitudes of different groups, grows.

This requires provisions based on knowledge of the conduct of minorities. Sources of information are at hand in the families of minority ghettos, in their leaders and neighborhood institutions such as fraternal orders, churches, and foreign-language newspapers, among specialists staffing minority agencies, and in the great literature about minorities' problems. These sources must be reached through the hostilities which prejudice induces on all sides and which custom perpetuates. Furthermore, minorities' heritages differ tremendously, except for their similar experiences of American prejudice and American equality. Therefore, teachers and other public authorities must know the specific cultures of pupils and clients as well as their own; they must also know how each group views relationships with authority and opportunities for betterment. Nothing can be learned about Mexican practices or their reactions to prejudice, for example, by studying Jews, Irish, Negroes, or any group except Mexicans themselves. Governed by their separate heritages, Mexicans in the United States show resistance through apathy, southern Negroes through violence, Jews through organized legal recourse.

Often minorities are punished for offenses and deviations that seem mysterious to them because they are defined only by the dominant group. This confusion means that public authorities, including teachers and police, must explain standard obligations and privileges, such as those pertaining to school, public order, and the political franchise. This must be a continuing function, performed in each minority's own community. Fear is not erased by one conversation nor retrained in one session. Public authorities must work in ways comprehensible to each minority; the ways need to be linked convincingly to each group's own best standards.

The educator, or other authority, can advance his inquiries and explanations by taking the position that he represents one culture talking to another. This minimizes personal and emotional involvements by focusing on the grand designs of each tradition, known to individuals, families, and others bearing the tradition in question. Unless members of the dominant group in positions of authority observe minorities attentively, the best intentioned can remain blind to the issues.[19] Authority cannot teach or regulate effectively without knowing how the minority comprehends its purposes.

In impoverished, prejudicially handicapped families, injury to male prestige is inevitable, a disaster for the whole minority group. To effect this injury is a prime object of the prejudices against the foreign, colored, conquered, poor, and ignorant. Britain's class society provides cushions, for, while honoring "exceptions," it admits most outsiders only provisionally, either for brief periods or as relegated to bottom ranks of the kingdom's social scale. Those we incorporate as minorities have been handled by Britain preferably in overseas colonies.[20] Our minority patriarchates, for example, the Mexican, find their ancestral authority systems undermined by freedoms we allow women and children, instead of restricting these freedoms to men; by our legal demand that parents submit minors for public schooling instead of deferring to the family's male head; by the extensive employment opportunities in industry for women and teenage children, which can match or outstrip opportunities for minority men. In Western society, no men exercise power without economic resources. Friction between unreconciled principles of civil equality and discrimination erodes controls geared to male command when adult males are prejudicially barred from employment. Thus so-called "matriarchates" can arise in slums, among American Negroes, Liverpool Irish, any deserted mothers on ANC (Aid to Needy Children) or ADC (Aid to Dependent Children) relief when the social instability of penalized men obliges mothers to support and govern families. In the absence of stable family men, delinquencies, as defined by the ruling society, soar.

The child brings to school the "enculturated" patterns and disorders of home. Usually these are classified by teachers' anxious assumptions into stereotypes about "poor-whites," Negroes, Mexicans, Japanese, Indians, and others.[21] Some stereotypes are more precise than others. In California, Negroes are considered "aggressive" (the old South would say "impudent"); Mexicans are considered to be of two classes, one "aristocratic," the other undesirably common; American Indians are at the bottom of the minorities' heap, and Japanese are close to the top; "poor-whites" are alarmingly "uncooperative." Struggling to impart middle-class goals, the teacher actually deals with the responses of pupils to their social horizons. Among "facts" taught in the earliest grades are hidden valuations of clean fashionable mothers, of successful fraternal fathers, of healthy happy blondish children, of a prosperous kindly English-speaking America. These valuations are lost on minority children, and with them the "facts." These children possess their own home values and associated standards. Then teachers call such pupils "retarded . . . apathetic . . . underachieving . . . truant"; they find the parents "indifferent . . . uncooperative . . . nonreaders"; and they hold parents and pupils accountable for the lack of accomplishments as if the teaching job were the latters'. Many older pupils say they find school boring and teachers unfair; they plan to drop out when possible in order to get to the real business of living.

Teachers act according to their own culture patterns, familial and professional, ordered and disordered. They are barely aware of these, unless they themselves are emerging from difficult minority sources. The educators' world, however, differs from that of the poorer minorities in wealth and status, evidenced by the relative strength of the position of men, in the linked stability of positions of women and children, and in the power or "freedom" allowed women and children by the governing men.

Teachers' family cultures, like the minorities', vary greatly. Systematic understanding of their traditional backgrounds, familial and professional, enables teachers to grasp the values that move them. They require sufficient training in cultural analysis to follow how these values accord with pupils' backgrounds, how they affect their teaching and other communication at school and in the homes served, and how they have been influenced by prejudices.

The "frustration" that teachers bewail, when serving transient and diverse populations, resembles that of minorities. It should be welcomed as a diagnostic cry for help in cultural orientations, not deplored as a cry of despair. Expressed in terms of dynamics, teachers fail to sense some preferred responses from pupils and parents (as, awaiting vigorous participation of pupils, teachers find that the Mexicans remain quiet or "apathetic," unaware that in this way Mexicans show respect for their elders, or sit out confusion), while the latter reject some cues received from teachers (as when teachers demand of the Mexican child that he initiate decisions though he is trained to accept elders' decisions and evade punitive confrontations). Then neither party feels that the other acts responsibly. Thus, Mexicans expect teachers to take strong initiatives, as do their own family heads, whereas educators expect parents to understand the permissive code that delegates to them some authority or initiative in school matters.

Smaller homogeneous societies having limited immigration, such as Britain and France, possess tremendous advantages in their old pervasive understandings, codified beyond words during centuries within the same politico-geographic boundaries. These national societies traditionally organize populations into three ranked classes. Each native-born child becomes at birth a member of his parents' class, though he may move up from a lower class through personal effort. Traditionally the classes perform distinct functions in work and government; each class bears its imprint in speech, gait, dress, education, occupation, behavior between sexes and generations, commitment to honor, and so on. Each class furthers an aspect or subculture of the national life which is as much a source of pride as is the national whole. The subculture endows carriers with convictions of their worthy identity, through immediate personal ties of kinship, marriage, work, recreation, and neighborhood.

In our country, only the old South (in the Southeast) retains a similar class organization; however, it is differentiated strongly by polarization around the segregated class (some scholars say "caste") of Negroes. This biracial system substitutes for Europe's class-linked pride the "superiority" of white class, called race, and the "shame" of Negro class, called race. This system has involved the nation and the world in its class-race confusions for about two centuries.

Yet American traditions present our national society as "classless," all men being "equal" before the law, that is, the Constitution and the legislation of many states. Civil rights are guaranteed by our Constitution and amendments, and reaffirmed in federal, state, and local legislation. This explicitness clearly does not have the force of traditional understandings, such as are expressed in anti-Negro customs and in proverbs (thus, "Honesty is the best policy"). But it is a minimum need in a mobile, young, ruthless, polyglot nation where understandings derive from many social sources and clash; and where all human types are admitted and processed similarly, especially in urban centers. Institutionalized prejudice helps order the welter of social differences, stressing shame rather than pride, as in anti-Semitic and anti-Catholic customs; the discriminatory arrangement allows the subcultures to survive, though incompletely.

In the present antidiscriminatory atmosphere, substandard ways of the minorities who are discriminated against point up lacks in public schooling. In the absence of knowledge about the cultures of their pupils, educators fall back on the supposed explicitness of their professional vocabularies. But handicapped groups suspect the words of the dominant group, even considering them cues to be followed in reverse. A Negro novelist says that "A few Negroes guard [their] idiom so fervently they will consciously invent a new term as soon as they hear the existing one coming from a white's lips." [4] During the two world wars, Negroes mistrusted government promises of equal treatment, and in the Second World War they openly threatened revolt against empty assurances of equal opportunities in military services, government, and industry. Their demands led President Roosevelt to issue Executive Order 8802 establishing his Committee on Fair Employment Practices. Minorities attend to their own leaders, whose words, silences, and gestures they can appraise through shared backgrounds.

Teachers will find cultural clues to their pupils' responses by asking themselves, "What do my pupils expect?" An Oriental expects different modes and content of instruction from a Mexican, and both differ from expectations of English-speaking Negro and white Americans. When women teachers, policemen, and social workers fail to conduct themselves with the sober responsibility defined by the concerned minority, their authority is resisted. Thus, a teacher's coquetry is resented by Mexican-American and "poor-white" high-school students because it taps sex-linked interests and subverts the structure of authority. Except for "matriarchal" Negroes and "poor-whites," minorities suspect younger women who wield public authority unless convinced that they are accountable to seniors.

A basic assumption of psychotherapy is that individuals can be led from old and inadequate learning modes into new and improved ones. The psychotherapist expects people to mislearn, strives to discover how this happens in individuals, and applies psychological and social science theory and experiment to his treatments. The educator should prepare himself for similar obligations, stressing knowledge of cultures, since his function is to teach American traditions to populations of diverse origins. Thus, in encouraging "motivation," he should proceed with pupils reared in a heavily shame-sanctioned culture, like the Japanese,[22] differently from the way he can proceed with pupils reared in our own heavily guilt-sanctioned culture. The former suffer from "loss of face" through real or fantasied ridicule or scorn by other people, visualizing themselves in situations of public exposure. The latter suffer from self-reproach based on internalized parental values, as each one harasses his individual conscience. Many rewards are enjoyed by similar modes. Thus, the Mexican child is loved and fondled for his quiet docility with elders (see Appendix 1). The middle-class Anglo child is rewarded with presents and praise for showing off skills honored at school, such as reading and writing.

Again, to understand why a child's IQ registers high or low, and to appraise its potentials, social forces beyond school must be grasped. Otto Klineberg reveals this through his psychological research of the 1930's, which singled out preeminent cultural influences on learning and on test ratings.[23] Klineberg found that girls of some Plains Indian tribes, skilled at traditional beadwork, regularly scored high on mental tests of ability to reproduce geometrical forms of varying complexity; but boys and girls refused to voice responses in class. Study of their cultures supported the children's withdrawn silences as proper expressions under traditional codes of courtesy and self-respect in public situations where voiced declarations, like boasts, would shame others. Such withdrawals the teachers could not rate. Klineberg further discovered that IQ ratings and school grades of Negro pupils rose steadily with pupils' length of residence in urban centers. Negroes in schools of Southern cities scored better than whites in schools of the rural South; Negroes in schools of Northern cities scored better than whites in Southern cities but were inferior to Northern white pupils if the whites had lived North longer than they. As Northern urban residence of Negroes and whites approached equivalence, IQ ratings tended to approach equivalence.

Since cultural considerations are intrinsic to human processes of communication and learning, educators must choose materials, modes, and paces of instruction in accordance with pupils' backgrounds. These include presenting models of responsible, successful conduct in the persons of teachers and nurses, and of the pupils and parents whom the faculty admires. Need for an authoritative American figure was strangely and strongly illustrated by a Mexican-American father who marched his teenage son to the police station for a whipping, to cure him of "pachuco" ducktail hairdo, stylized suiting, and gang friends. Schoolteachers proving helpless, the father turned to this male authority in uniform, only to be referred back to the school. Upon reaching military age, young Mexican-Americans of the California slums frequently enlist in the army, glad to join a definitively stated authority which promises them honorable scope, limits, rewards, and punishment.

Immigrants and other newcomers struggle, through their traditional modes, to keep up with obligations. When their conduct seems strange, the cultural origins and social pressures [24] should be checked for meanings. However, the obligation a teacher has to respect other cultures does not mean that he should alter his own best values or professional goals; it does mean that he should communicate them and broaden his understanding by relating them to symbols and processes of the other cultures.

When a teacher acts on the conviction that the mistakenness of other-ethnic ways is remediable and incidental, and that the ways also merit respect in their proper settings, guilt and confusion are lightened. Harry Stack Sullivan said that cultural perspectives eased his psychiatric patients. He showed them that private struggles were with the values of this culture-moment, with which they could compromise, for no one was committed to eternal damnation. This opinion, calmly stated and well documented, relaxed certain tense individuals and impelled them to make useful adjustments. The patients came to believe that culture is man-made, man always alters it, and they would join in the process knowingly.

As motivations and goals vary in different cultures, any selected ones are inculcated at different rates. Such comparisons are now only impressions, gauged best, though roughly, by American norms. Thus, it is an educator's truism that Jewish children of European backgrounds are easier to teach than most, meaning that the children are familiar with the teaching materials, like them, and readily produce the desired results. This is less attributable to genetic traits than to traditional stress on the sacred worth and beauty of booklearning.[25] Jewish refugees from Nazi Europe, studying in American universities, often achieved record successes by hallowed "cram" techniques of concentration and memory, learned in orthodox Talmudic schools. Orientals also reach school with a reverence for teaching and learning; often they know appropriate techniques of learning. On the other hand, Italian immigrants in the slums sent children to school who were difficult to teach because they lacked intellectual background. The same is reported of certain other Europeans and of Mexicans, who, in addition, are uneasy with public authorities; it is reported also of Negroes who migrate from the old South, pulled between scorn for poor whites and uneasy regard for upper-class ones.

The teacher's deep-rooted attitudes are powerful cues for responses. Dramatic evidence of this was provided by a woman whose fourteen-year-old son attended a Los Angeles school which had suddenly become predominantly Negro. The boy's father taught in a nearby college; the child was the sole white in class. Absorbed with study, the boy was troubled by nothing until gangs of overage, delinquent Negro boys jumped him. They ordered him to clip his heavy smooth hair, and to turn over his money. Complaining now about "jungle boys . . . oogla-booglas," the boy begged his parents to arrange a school transfer. In the meantime, Parents' Day came and the boy asked his mother to meet the homeroom teacher, whom he considered lovely. The boy led his mother to the teacher, whispering, "Isn't she beautiful?" The mother, prepared to admire her son's taste, only stared; the teacher's complexion was chocolate brown. Finally the boy said, "I didn't realize . . . she is colored, isn't she?" The fact was, and the mother understood it, that the boy had not generalized from his experience with the "jungle boys"; the teacher was different because she behaved differently, indeed admirably and beautifully. The mother believed that her son regarded only certain teenagers as objectionable Negroes; others were normal people.

Our monster society is competitive and discriminatory. People continually move geographically and advance materially. All of this pulverizes older functions and values assigned by subordinate cultures to the two sexes and to significant age groups of youngsters, parents, and others, leaving many individuals without social incentives and skills for survival. Psychiatrists and jailers see some of the declared failures. The Los Angeles "jungle boys," the pachucos, and the postwar Nisei delinquents pursue lives injured by degraded concepts of male and female identities. For them it is imperative to ground responsible authority on esteemed patternings of identity which derive from the dominant and the minority cultures.

Old standards linger among oppressed or subcultural groups. Even when determined to assimilate and speak English, these groups retain old meanings and sentiments, old gestures,[6] and patternings of personal ties. American descendants of European Jews retain love and honor for education and community work, though the sacred Hebrew words are no longer habitual. Mexicans retain love and devotion for their inherited esthetics of maleness—called *machismo* in Spanish and celebrated in the bullfight or *fiesta brava*—and in stylized emotional displays. If reached through principles of his home culture, a person can be led to adapt to another culture and society, for one's first-learned ways are the social paradigm to which subsequent experiences are referred.

Adolescents of dominant status also are confused by our monster society, for their parents no longer know the world in which we live. When Vassar College ex-President Sarah Gibson Blanding announced that drinking and premarital sex would not be tolerated on campus, parents and women students, who had requested clarification, were grateful that someone in authority had enunciated standards. Otherwise, adolescents evolve the so-called "teen culture," where they set and remove norms; and parents study books whose information they value for newsiness. Both desire community-based cues for orienting behavior. Neither parents nor school yet fully realize that rising families want educators in the new towns and cities to state basic values (such as the importance of study) and to develop proper skills (such as participation of parents in school and community programs.[26]

Teachers gain cultural insights from moving easily among individuals, families, and social functions of the communities they serve. This means returning to the simpler neighborhood ways of a less mobile epoch, when people knew one another.[27] One school principal in highly transient Southern California requires teachers to visit each pupil's home every November. At other schools, teachers say they would consider the obligation unusual and onerous. To the anthropologist it seems more onerous for teaching to proceed without it.

Upon entering a pupil's home, the visiting teacher keenly senses the special life there. She (or he) detects it from the atmosphere, the furnishings and color schemes, the reading matter, music, and pictures, from the signs and smells of cooking and cleaning, of illness, poverty, and sumptuousness, from the voices, words, and faces. The pupil's family sees the visiting teacher in a fresh light, as a kindlier human being—even if she is still an alarming representative of the law. The teacher-training sequence in individual child growth and development provides inadequate keys to these social factors.

The policing authority of the schools, supervising attendance and other compliance under threat of legal reprisal, may disturb home visits intended only for social research. Possibly a special staff, drawn from school counselors, nurses, and social workers, should concentrate on this.

The present separateness of teachers from the community, physically on school grounds, and symbolically in status, encourages professional defensiveness and distorts educators' complaints about pupil "frustrations." Conferences at school with parents cannot replace home visits, for parents reveal themselves best on their own grounds. Some teachers said at conferences that their visits even to bleak slum homes eased chronic sullenness among Mexicans and Negroes as readily as did their get-acquainted visits to upper-class homes where children suffered only from failing to achieve an A-plus on report cards.

Confrontations of individuals and families, observing them enact their different cultures, including confusion about American dominant situations, make teachers "more sensitive and imaginative about the needs of others," visiting teachers said. Like the minorities, teachers may worry over recastings of cultural roles (as when the American "buddy-father" becomes the Mexican domineering one) and over the irrelevance of stereotypes (that all Mexicans live by *siesta* and *mañana*, not by industrious routine). Soon the reaction of bewilderment is converted into a research indicator, guiding teachers to hunt for hidden meanings, instead of leaving them to denounce or neglect unfavored conduct. Thus a young Greek-American elementary teacher, new to California, came to appraise the puzzling ways of his Mexican and Negro pupils and of Anglo-American families in the community. First he searched out Greek-Americans to refresh his self-awareness, reviving family memories and customs. Then, he said, he gauged how the behavior of his pupils differed from that of his own group, and he tried to adapt teaching methods and materials accordingly. Quickly he discarded the educator's concept of bilingualism, with its routine expectancy of retardation, for his own first language had been Greek. He had read the Bible first in Greek, his parents also spoke Turkish at home, and he had heard no English before entering the first grade of school; nor did he ever hear English at home during his school years. Like other American-born and -reared Greeks, he had complete command of English and spoke with no trace of accent. The faulty English of California Mexicans was not, he believed, caused by bilingualism.

Some Mexican-American teachers in California proceed similarly, comparing two cultures for clues about better teaching and counseling. This suggests that Americanized or acculturated teachers of minority and foreign backgrounds should assume responsibility for interpreting the cultural phases they know. Teacher training should incorporate these capacities. Minority origins can thus be recognized as sources of strength rather than embarrassment. Such cultural permissiveness does not weaken standards of instruction, but strengthens them with new insights.

When two cultures are blocked out for comparisons, the variations can illuminate an individual personality, and often dignify it with historic purposes. Harsh inferences often then become apparent as actually prejudicial and ignorant. Thus, after a Southern Negro woman was reported to school for "whupping" her child, the visiting teacher learned that everyone in the neighborhood believed that the mother was acting for the child's good. This was the group's standard of discipline, which also released emotions, cleared the air, and even conveyed affection through the physical intimacy. The mother, it seemed, was not cruel· but conscientious; sparing the rod meant spoiling the child. The teacher had to square these goals, values, and practices with her own indoctrinated preferences for rational discussion and avoidances of self-exposure and physical intimacies.

Truancy, serious disobedience, and weak "motivations" should lead the teacher to examine their possible sources in culture conflicts and in race prejudice. Questioning Mexican and Negro adolescents about their "resistance to high-school physical education (in refusing to undress for showers and gym uniforms) brought this vital clue from a seventeen-year-old Mexican-American boy, "The Mexicans 'resist' because they feel like outsiders! When the fellows *can* get into sports, *can get on the team,* they change clothes and shower like anybody else." The situation is simple from the minorities' point of view: youths are stripped naked in the hostile camp of the Anglo or white, at the age of sexual burgeoning. These children find adolescence sufficiently punishing without gym requirements that punish further.

In brief, educators must know *what* to communicate and *how* to convey this to pupils and parents who present more than one culture or social condition. Individual psychological behavior, such as that occasioned by the need for approval, is always adapted to the ways of a culture, as a horse's gait is conditioned to the English or Spanish riding tradition. A group's social behavior, such as formally chaperoning girls, and training boys to sow "wild oats," is always guided by the norms of a culture. From these norms evolve the world views of personalities and groups in a culture. The educator's part is a threefold performance that keeps track of teaching goals; that communicates in accord with general American changes and with persisting subcultures, despite minority resentments; and that arouses trust and enthusiasm in pupils.

Teachers cannot influence the whole world but they can sharpen their sense of responsibility and their alertness. A California junior high-school principal proposed the novel possibility that Mexican-Americans liked their heritage. Faced with the need to teach Spanish to his largely Anglo-American pupils, in 1957 he asked Mexican-American pupils to volunteer as aids. "Your pronunciation will be good," he said, "and the Spanish teachers will train you in grammar." These "cadet teachers" conducted conversational Spanish classes in seventh-grade homerooms; morale of the whole student body soared; the program received a national award. Within two years, gang fights disappeared; Anglo and Mexican parents contributed ideas and materials to the language program; some Anglo parents learned Spanish; at last the local newspaper reported achievements of Mexican pupils and not their violations.[28]

Few educators have devised so constructive a use of a minority's widely bruited liability. The program aligned education with other major goals of society, in serving and rewarding fairly the varieties of pupils, meeting the population's abilities to comprehend, and in producing useful graduates. The pupils were reached in school, their parents were reached at home through them, and teachers felt a community spirit emerge. Certainly schools can help elicit constructive behavior even in booming, indifferent neighborhoods by adapting the social materials to current needs.

Notes

1. "Acculturation" labels the new learnings by alien individuals and groups about the strange society they enter. Thus, an acculturated foreigner is one who has learned to behave "correctly," measured by the standards of the new society receiving him. Anthropologists also think of acculturation as "culture contact." The social learnings of a native-born, however, are labeled "enculturation," meaning that the ancestral culture is "built into" the native from birth. The sociological term "assimilation" stresses the host society's acceptance of the acculturated foreigner, who has learned correct behavior.
2. There are famous definitions of culture. See E. B. Tylor, *Primitive Culture* (London: John Murray, 1871, 2 vols.; seventh edition, New York, 1924), p. 1: "Culture or civilization . . . is that complex whole which includes knowledge, belief, art, morals, law, custom, and any other capabilities and habits acquired by man as a member of society." See Franz Boas, "Anthropology," in (eds.) Edwin R. A. Seligman and Alvin Johnson, *Encyclopedia of the Social Sciences* (New York: Macmillan Company, 1934, 1954), Vol. II, p. 79: "Culture embraces all the manifestations of social habits of a community, the reactions of the individual as affected by the habits of the group in which he lives, and the products of human activities as determined by these habits." See Julian Huxley, "Evolution, Cultural and Biological," in *Current Anthropology*, W. L. Thomas, Jr. (ed.) (Chicago: University of Chicago Press, 1956), p. 11: "Culture in the broadest objective view appears . . . as a self-maintaining system or organization of intercommunicating human beings and their products, or . . . the results of the intercommunication of the minds of human individuals in society."
3. Julian Huxley sees culture as the "human phase of evolution . . . the psychosocial sector" and notes "the general tendency of the past few centuries . . . to intensify" blendings of all cultures and race genes so that "we can already see the inevitable outline of the future—the emergence of a single world community." In Julian Huxley, *Evolution in Action* (New York: Mentor Books, 1957), pp. 13, 122. See also Theodosius Dobzhansky, *The Biological Bases of Human Freedom* (New York: Columbia University Press, 1956), p. 80: Man's ability to transmit culture is "a new, non-biological heredity . . ." and Theodosius Dobzhansky, *Mankind Evolving* (New Haven and London: Yale University Press, 1962).
4. William Melvin Kelley, "If You're Woke You Dig It," *New York Times Magazine*, May 20, 1962.

5. See the pioneer study by Franz Boas, *Changes in Bodily Form of Descendants of Immigrants* (New York: Columbia University Press, 1912); also in the *American Anthropologist*, n.s. (Vol. 14, 1912), pp. 530–562. This appeared first in 1911 as Senate Document 208, 61st Congress, 2nd session, Washington, D. C.: Government Printing Office. Cf. also Franz Boas, *Race, Language and Culture* (New York: The Macmillan Company, 1940) and Franz Boas, "Race," in *Encyclopedia of the Social Sciences*.

   Biologists find the concept of race inadequate for explaining human variability. See "On the Non-Existence of Human Races" by Frank Livingstone and "With Comment" by Theodosius Dobzhansky in *Current Anthropology,* June 1962 (Vol. 3, No. 3), pp. 279–281.

6. Stanley M. Garn discusses race change in "Race and Evolution," *American Anthropologist*, April 1957 (Vol. 59, No. 2), pp. 218–221, 223: "If races do not change, how did races come to be? . . . there is every reason to believe that many human differences have adaptive value in climatic extremes . . . (like the) degree of melanin deposition in man. . . . (The) blood group gene frequencies as we know them now may be purely temporary . . . There is now excellent evidence that under our noses . . . often without outward signs . . . races have been changing . . . (The) criteria that . . . temporarily . . . distinguish one race from another are only temporarily suited to that purpose . . . The older, static, unchanging concept of race was essentially self-limiting . . . With changing race and adaptive traits, we have our (research) job cut out for generations to come." See also S. M. Garn, *Human Races* (Springfield, Illinois: Charles C Thomas, 1961). Also *The Race Question in Modern Science, A Symposium* (New York: United Nations, distributed by William Morrow, 1956).

7. Franz Boas and Others, *General Anthropology* (New York: D. C. Heath and Company, 1938), p. 115.

8. In J. M. Tanner, "Boas' Contributions to Knowledge of Human Growth and Form," p. 100 (in Walter Goldschmidt (ed.), *The Anthropology of Franz Boas*. Memoir No. 89, American Anthropological Association, Vol. 61, No. 5, Part 2, October 1959).

9. Leslie Spier, "Some Central Elements in the Legacy," p. 147, in Goldschmidt, *op. cit.*

10. All peoples accompany speech with traditional gestures, of varying patterns and symbolic content, learned like any other cultural item, and independent of race. See David Efron, *Gesture and Environment* (New York: King's Crown Press, 1941). Also W. D. Brewer, "Patterns of Gesture Among the Levantine Arabs," *American Anthropologist*, April–June, 1951 (Vol. 53, No. 2), pp. 232–237.

    Scientific publications describe conjectures about and experimental evidence of wide communication by extra-sensory means, especially evidence of telepathy and clairvoyance. However western civilization has not developed such communication systematically and often voices scorn of it.

11. A richly documented discussion is Alfred L. Kroeber, *Configurations of Culture Growth* (Berkeley: University of California, 1944).

12. A classic formulation of the view is by Ruth F. Benedict, *Patterns of Culture* (Boston: Houghton Mifflin, 1934).

13. See Frances Cooke Macgregor and Others, *Facial Deformities and Plastic Surgery: A Psychosocial Study* (Springfield, Illinois: Charles C Thomas, 1953).

14. Cleveland Amory, *The Proper Bostonians* (New York: E. P. Dutton and Company, 1947), pp. 14, 35.
15. Richard Wright, *Black Boy*, A Record of Childhood and Youth (New York and London: Harper and Brothers, 1937, 1945), p. 227.
16. Charles A. Eastman is discussed in Appendix 3, pp. 417–418. He lived from 1858 to 1939. He tells in *Indian Child Life* (Boston: Little, Brown and Company, 1913, 1930, pp. v–vii, Second Edition, that he was "(b)orn in a wigwam . . . When he was four years old, war broke out between his people and the United States Government. The Indians were defeated . . . Some fled northward into Canada . . . (for) refuge under an uncle. His father was captured by the whites.

"After ten years of that wild life . . . his father, whom the good President Lincoln had pardoned and released from the military prison, made the long and dangerous journey to Canada to find . . . his youngest son. The Sioux were beginning to learn that the old life must go.

"Ohiyesa, the Winner, as the boy was called, came home with his father to what was then Dakota Territory . . . Everything about the new life was strange . . . He had thoughts of running away . . . back to Canada. But his father, Many Lightnings, who had been baptised a Christian under the name of Jacob Eastman, told him that he too must take a new name, and he chose that of Charles Alexander Eastman. He was told to cut off his long hair and put on citizen's clothing. Then his father made him choose between going to school and working at the plow.

". . . He decided to try school. Rather to his surprise, he liked it . . . His teachers were pleased with his progress . . . He was sent farther east to a better school . . . In the long summer vacations he worked, on farms, in shops and offices; and in winter he studied and played football . . . until after about fifteen or sixteen years he found himself with the diplomas of a famous college and a great university, a Bachelor of Science, a Doctor of Medicine, and a doubly educated man—educated in the lore of the wilderness as well as in some of the deepest secrets of civilization.

"Since that day, a good many more years have passed. Ohiyesa, known as Doctor Charles A. Eastman, has now a home and six children of his own among the New England hills. He has hundreds of devoted friends of both races. He is the author of five books which have been widely read . . . and he speaks . . . to thousands of people every year."

In this book, Eastman describes the tribal rearing of Santee Dakota boys and girls, with an eye cocked to white American ways, as on pages 18, 24, 38–102, 132–144. He was an exceptional character who rose above any local environment. He had gone so far that the Santee Dakota whom I studied in 1935, in the Red Wing, Minnesota village to which they had returned from the Canadian exile, had only a vague recollection of him. The Red Wing group were then living on welfare funds and memories.

17. Everett V. Stonequist, *The Marginal Man, A Study in Personality and Culture Conflict* (New York, Chicago: Charles Scribner's Sons, 1937) acknowledges his debt to this concept of Park's, page vii. In Park's Introduction to this book, he says, "The marginal man, as here conceived, is one whom fate has condemned to live in two societies and in two, not merely different but antagonistic, cultures" (p. xv). Further, "The marginal man is a personality type that arises at a time and place where, out of the conflict of races and cultures,

new societies, new peoples and cultures are coming into existence. The fate which condemns him to live in two worlds . . . compels him to assume, in relation to the worlds in which he lives, the role of a cosmopolitan and a stranger. Inevitably he becomes, relatively to his cultural milieu, the individual with the wider horizon, the keener intelligence . . . The marginal man is always relatively the more civilized human being. He occupies the position which has been, historically, that of the Jew in the Diaspora. The Jew . . . has everywhere and always been the most civilized of human creatures" (pp. xvii–xviii).

Park discussed the concept in his article, "Migration and the Marginal Man," the *American Journal of Sociology*, May 1928. Park regarded Marginal Man as a "personality type" expressing "a social process . . . of acculturation" (Stonequist, *ibid.*, p. xviii).

18. Theodosius Dobzhansky, in *Newsweek*, p. 62, January 8, 1962, during a discussion at the 128th annual meeting, January 1962, of the American Association for the Advancement of Science. A news story about arctic Eskimos shows how readily Stone Age hunters learn Space Age techniques, *New York Times*, May 27, 1962: "19 young Eskimo members of the Alaska Army National Guard are learning to send and receive radio messages in Morse code to act as the eyes and ears of the Regular Army in the Far North. . . . One of the Eskimo trainees . . . (lives on) Barter Island in the Beaufort Sea at the top of the world . . . almost within snowballing distance of the Canadian Arctic . . . (He) lives by fishing and hunting whales and wildfowl when he is not soldiering, is very pleased with the Morse code system which, he says, will ensure for his village 'year-round communication with the outside world.' " © 1962 by The New York Times Company. Reprinted by permission.

19. This was clear in 1962 when a California college tried to produce a blackface minstrel show. Local Negroes objected strongly, strove fruitlessly to negotiate with the college, threatened to picket and sue. College authorities retorted that they were preserving an American folk tradition, from which "intimidation" would not deter them. A member of the local Friends' Meeting then sent this open letter to the editor of a college students' paper, who accepted and printed it: "Many comments centered on the question, 'Why should anyone be offended at holding a black face minstrel show?' Years ago . . . I too asked . . . when some . . . Negro friends . . . asked my support in protesting the annual minstrel show given by a service club . . . I was surprised to learn most Negroes DO resent such shows, and that no other issue facing the city's Negroes—inability to get better jobs and better housing, and any service at all in most barber and beauty shops—served to unite them so well. In fact, the local branch of the NAACP was organized as the result of a minstrel show . . .

"If we cannot always explain it . . . we have to accept the fact that handicapped people are often sensitive to their situation. We do this . . . in the presence of someone . . . crippled. . . . Mimicking him in a public show would be offensive in the extreme.

"To the shame of us Caucasians, colored people in America today are handicapped persons. . . . (whose complexion). . . . interferes with getting certain employment just as surely as . . . being born without use of a

limb. Fortunately, the color handicap will not always be with us, and someday the Negro, like the traditional Scotsman, will be able to enjoy a joke at his own expense.
"Pleas that minstrel shows are 'traditional' and part of our 'heritage' . . . have to be balanced against the fact that not all traditions are good ones." (Permission for this printing given by the letter writer.)

20. Such traditional exclusion is being strongly assailed by (the former British) West Indians who, as subjects of the Crown until 1963 and then as Commonwealth citizens of independent nations, have been migrating to England, Scotland, and Wales since early this century but especially since the Second World War. The interpretation rests on the writer's study of the migrations, when a Fulbright Senior Research Scholar to the United Kingdom, 1951–1952. See Ruth Landes, "Biracialism in American Society: A Comparative View," *American Anthropologist*, December 1955 (Vol. 57, No. 6), pp. 1253–1263.

21. See Appendices 1, 2, 3 of this volume for culture summaries about Mexicans, Negroes, and American Indians.

22. See Ruth F. Benedict, *The Chrysanthemum and the Sword: Patterns of Japanese Culture* (Boston: Houghton Mifflin, 1946), especially pp. 222 *ff*. "True shame cultures rely on external sanctions for good behavior, not, as true guilt cultures do, on an internalized conviction of sin. Shame is a reaction to other people's criticism . . . it requires an audience or at least a man's fantasy of an audience. Guilt does not. In a nation where honor means living up to one's own picture of oneself, a man may suffer from guilt though no man knows of his misdeed and a man's feeling of guilt may actually be relieved by confessing his sin . . . But shame is an increasingly heavy burden in the United States and guilt is less extremely felt than in earlier generations. In the United States this is interpreted as a relaxation of morals . . . because we do not expect shame to do the heavy work of morality. We do not harness the acute personal chagrin which accompanies shame to our fundamental system of morality."
"The Japanese do" (pp. 223–234).
In our society, shame and guilt are not opposed but "involve different focuses, modes, and stresses. Often they overlap. . . ." Helen Merrell Lynd, *On Shame and the Search for Identity* (New York: Harcourt, Brace and Company, 1958). See also Gerhart Piers and Milton B. Singer, *Shame and Guilt, A Psychoanalytic and a Cultural Study* (Springfield, Illinois: Charles C Thomas, 1953).
A dynamic picture of Italian upper-class behavior sanctioned by *shame*, involved with American behavior sanctioned by *guilt*, the first paired with honor, the second paired with innocence, is in Marcia Davenport's novel, *The Constant Image* (New York: Charles Scribner's Sons, 1960).

23. Otto Klineberg, *Race Differences* (New York: Harper and Brothers, 1934, and all later editions). Otto Klineberg, *Negro Intelligence and Selective Migration* (New York: Columbia University Press, 1935).

24. Social pressures are illustrated in this 1962 report to the writer from a Negro authority (whose name is withheld):
"When this (Northern California) city's police . . . speak of 'minorities,' they usually mean Negroes in spite of the fact that there are in the city

sizeable groups of Orientals, Jews and Spanish-speaking peoples. The police fixation on Negroes as *the* minority stems, I believe, from the following causes:

"1. The dramatic increase in the Negro population from less than 5,000 in 1940 to 74,000 in 1960.

"2. The civil rights battles here have been fought largely by Negroes and Negro organizations. The leadership has been articulate and expressive, equally so when wrong as when right. Thus to the factor of high visibility has been added the element of high audibility. The other minority groups have been less noisy and pushy about their rights and so have attained to less public notice, including the official organs of local government.

"3. The Police Department is highly sensitive to charges of brutality made by Negroes taken into custody. . . . The local Negro weekly and the NAACP have given the Department a bad time on this issue.

"4. The Department's statistics on arrests indicate that Negroes are arrested and convicted of major crimes far out of proportion to their representation in the population. The feeling is strong in the Department that the Negro is a congenital criminal. . . .

"5. The Police feel that Negroes are hostile to them, uncooperative and resistant. This is true. There is a deep reservoir of mutual suspicion and hostility. The police cannot understand, for example, why Negroes resent being called boys. On the more deliberate side, the usual derogatory names —nigger, shine, jazzbo—are in common use among officers . . .

"6. There are less than 20 Negro officers on the police force. . . . Two of them are assigned to the Juvenile Bureau and most of the others are assigned to traffic duties. As far as I have been able to observe, these Negro officers get along O.K. with their colleagues. A few of them complain privately that they do not get the same promotional breaks as white officers. It is difficult, of course, to assess the validity of the complaint but the fact is there are no Negro sergeants, lieutenants or captains.

"7. Relations between the Police Department and the Negro community are touchy. If one can safely generalize about such matters, I would say that Negroes regard the police not as impartial protectors but as the enemy—the instrument for the enforcement of white domination. Consequently, they withhold cooperation with the police in instances when it would be to the group interest to extend it."

25. See Mark Zborowski, "The Place of Book-Learning in Traditional Jewish Culture," *Harvard Educational Review*, 1949 (Vol. 19, pp. 97–109).

26. See related views in Frank Riessman, *The Culturally Deprived Child* (New York: Harper and Brothers, 1962).

27. Teaching young New Zealand Maori children, by taking cues from their actual lives, is described by Sylvia Ashton-Warner in her book *Teacher* (New York: Simon and Schuster, 1963).

28. The total pupil population of 1,350 included 225 Mexicans and 25 Negroes. The faculty "felt that if the Anglo-American students would become acquainted with the background, customs and language of the Mexican-American students, a more wholesome relationship might be established between the two groups. As far as faculty . . . knew, using bilingual students to teach a foreign language to other students had never before been intro-

duced in another school." Anglo-American pupils were "eager to learn," asked questions of the Mexicans, "little groups formed occasionally on the campus to ask about Spanish words. . . . (As) Anglo-American students learned it was not so easy to pronounce strange words, . . . mimicking of the Spanish-accented English stopped. . . . Mexican-American and Anglo-American students, having something in common, began working together on committees and exchanging ideas freely." In the program's first year, "fights between racial groups on the campus dropped 75 per cent" and then practically disappeared. In 1959 the school received the principal Freedoms Foundation Award for the program. Quotes are from the unpublished Master's thesis in Education by Virginia H. DuPrez (Riverside, California), "A Technique for Integration of a Minority Bilingual Group," describing the program, in which she participated as a teacher. The principal regarded his program as a first step in guiding Mexican-American youngsters toward adult participation in an integrated community. His faculty declared that, "Far surpassing the most ambitious expectation, these defensive, rebellious, insecure . . . rejected (Mexicans) . . . have become confident, capable, enthusiastic, helpful student teachers." DuPrez, *op. cit.*

4

The Courses

Teaching in multicultural public schools depends on words of the English language and proceeds chiefly by means of speaking, reading, and writing them. Some Asiatic peoples have instilled knowledge by high-pitched chanting, as orthodox religious Jews still do; some Siberian tribes have learned to the noisy accompaniment of drums.

In American schools, emphasis is laid primarily on words to represent all the reality comprehended by men: ideas, values, skills, creations, details of knowledge, teachers, and the beneficiaries of teaching —that is, the pupils and the community. But heavy use of this prime tool can fail educators in their goal of attuning instruction to actual processes of learning. This happens when educators talk more *about* pupils than *with* them and their families. Separateness from the objects of discussion forfeits the experiences words should mirror. Separation and verbal misconceptions are institutionalized when educators submit children to standardized tests, interviews, and ratings after removing the youngsters from familial settings to the school building. Standards of testing and interpretation are those of the teaching profession, which match those of the dominant social group, otherwise called the "middle class." Often these standards are entirely foreign to the particular tradition by whose norms the behavior of a given child has been cultivated, or, "socialized," as behavorial scientists say. This is readily apparent in underprivileged and even in dominant groups of our deep South and in immigrants bringing family traditions from Italy, Mexico, India, and Japan, as well as from European regions close to us historically but remote socially.

Words must be guarded with extreme awareness of all parties' experiential referents lest they go the way of each party's preference. Educators tend to use them didactically, reflecting the assumptions of their own group. Such use limits or throttles free or exploratory responses between teacher and pupils of different origins where word and other meanings diverge or are unrelated. Even within a common culture, a word can have an omnibus of meanings, requiring qualification by word, gesture, intonation, or emotion. In a multicultural class, the teacher must know how to provide for differences or mutuality of meanings. The problem is aggravated by the mandatory use of English for instruction in the schools, though pupils may come from many linguistic backgrounds. There are two exceptions to the exclusive use of English in the public schools, one the additional Spanish used in New Mexico until recently (and still used in legal affairs), the other the additional French found in Louisiana private schools (and also in the state's legal affairs).

As a first step in the Anthropology and Education project, teachers were led to discover how words act. To provide intuitions usually absent from professional and scientific reports and to encourage teachers to sense that they develop ties to pupils by emotions as well as by official duties, novels, autobiographies, and news stories about the social groups studied were recommended. Human nature was presented as the potentialities that become greatly actualized through culture and that enact known cultures. Educators' problems, phrased in the words of teachers participating in the project, guided the choice of cultures studied and the particular aspects examined.

In the three courses developed, education and problems of learning were discussed in a framework of basic concepts about human evolution, including the space frontier, and about cultural and racial diversities. These were the basic concepts stated:

1. All contemporary physical types of man are comparable in biological evolution.

2. Men do not live without society and specific cultural traditions.

3. Cultures are compared by scientists in order to learn what happens universally and what occurs in specific local or historic forms, leading to generalizations about man's social nature. Individuals of a group are compared to learn what is peculiar or original in personalities and what is absorbed from the group's tradition. (Thus male Plains Indians sought the "power visions" demanded of them traditionally, but many individuals failed to win this "blessing" and some faked having had the great experience.) Comparing individuals from different groups is useful only when the different traditional norms are reconciled by some standardizing formulation.

4. Any human society includes structures or institutions essential for serving human needs, such as an institution of the family, economic work, or religious activity. The particular form of the institution belongs to the local or historic tradition and tends to be consistent with other forms and aspects of the tradition. A particular form of economic structure is inheritance of property by male primogeniture. A particularly styled family structure is the ranking of a man's plural wives by marital seniority and by the fact of giving birth to sons.

5. Each structure serves specific functions whose details vary in tradition but always meet the need of the human group for survival. Thus every family must rear a younger generation to carry on; besides, the family stresses other locally varying interests, such as arranging marriages for wealth, power, or romantic love. A structure can survive great changes in details of functions, as have monarchial and democratic structures of government in the western world.

6. New members of human society so thoroughly learn proper behavior from culturally adept elders (important are parents, kinsmen, teachers, and clergy) that they perform predictably in conventional situations. Predictable behavior falls in the range traditionally normal or deviant for a particular role and generation, such as the paternal role, viewed differently by senior and junior generations.

7. Values are a group's traditional or prevailing attitudes about life and often include goals of effort. Some values are expressed philosophically, as are liberty, existentialism, altruism, truth, success, female virginity, male vigor, spiritual afterlife, and reincarnation. Values state norms and ranges of expected behavior in qualitative or nonstatistical terms.

8. In each of the earth's approximately 3,500 societies, a standardized communication exists, preeminently by symbolic language, and functions on several levels of awareness. Modes of behavior and thought are both manifest and covert, as words, silences, intuitions, acts (including gestures), and emotions. Under favorable conditions, humans learn at any age.

9. Culture seems to follow collective or "superorganic" laws of its own, according to certain scholars. Some laws are evidenced in: (a) the diffusion of traits (material ones like tobacco and the potato, spiritual ones like monotheism and representative government); (b) independent invention (such as the Eskimo keystone arch and tailored garments, the Arabic and Mayan zero); (c) regionalisms or "culture areas" (the cattle cultures of our Southwest, of Argentina, of primitive Africa); (d) patterns of culture (the elaborate social hierarchies of Europe and Asia, the egalitarian structures of the United

States and the Union of South Africa); and (e) cyclic rhythms (the rise and fall of civilizations, of religious trends and dress fashions in a tradition).

10. Personality and culture interact inseparably, since culture is carried by personalities, and personalities evolve in society through culture. The interaction partly explains social change. At public schools in California slums, changing phenomena of personality and culture were grossly evident among the Mexicans where certain families produced both pachuco-style gang youngsters and successful college students.

11. Life in present American society raises great questions of status, personal identity, minority cultures, and the responsibilities of the dominant groups.

Small work projects carried teachers *out* of school and college confines and *into* homes and streets of pupils. There teachers had to catch the other modes of communication and borrow from them. The mingling stirred teachers' preprofessional recollections, which illuminated many actions of their pupils. These projects marked stages of a year-long basic course; [1] only one project was conducted in each of two other courses.[2] The human societies confronting us, ready made by history, serve anthropologists as field laboratories where human behavior and attending conditions can be observed in multicultural perspective to yield hypotheses about the regularities of man's life in society and to permit checks on predictions and errors. These work projects were designed to introduce teachers to practical uses of anthropological methods. Fulfilling them, teachers sought out people they otherwise talked about in stereotypes, such as ". . . So many Mexicans are moving in, they'll lower standards. How do we get them to cooperate?" "So many Negroes are moving in, they're new to this area, the school will be full of colored children, and the white parents threaten to move across the street so they can send their youngsters to the all-white school. How can we possibly integrate?" Stereotypes and related fears lessened when teachers met and enjoyed parents, pupils, and neighbors in their own surroundings. The field projects dramatized anthropological generalizations about culture and personality and about some social processes; they took form through efforts to link the generalizations to educators' questions.

As participating educators grew in their understanding of how to apply cultural concepts [3] to their teaching and counseling, the projects grew in range and intricacy.

Because many students were novices at research, they were given simple guides to show them how to observe, record, and interpret field data. Research procedures were demonstrated continually in lectures and discussions. Each student worked independently on the projects owing to the distances between homes and the college and the fact that nearly all students held full-time jobs. Each person read his finished reports to the group so that his methods and findings could be analyzed by all.

The numerous student accounts reiterated certain tag-words and stereotypes. For example, "bilingualism" regularly characterized Mexican-American "underachievers." [4] No one associated bilingualism with successful Mexicans and Mexican-Americans. Rather these pupils were glamorized as "exceptions" which, of course, begged the question of their achievements. Nor was bilingualism associated with other "low achievers" of foreign-language background, such as Italians, or American Indians, or Greeks; it functioned as a prejudicial tag for Mexicans. Yet research exposes the fallacy of this concept, and scholars infer that "underachievers" are to be described more properly as bored and as uneducated in both Spanish and English.[5]

The first two projects in the basic course tested word usages that masked or confused meanings. Education students were discouraged from using the word "culture" loosely but encouraged to become aware of its reality in specific forms and operations. They were shown how particular traditions of the United States, Britain, a Latin country, Russia, and an American Indian tribe manifest themselves in distinctive, carefully taught body gaits, tones of voice, gestures, silences and laughs, grammatical structures and linguistic idioms, fashions of attire and hair style, overt and covert ties among individuals and groups, in specialized recognition and care of illness, and so on. The first project assigned to the students was to observe strangers in some public place without speaking to them, and then record the details of appearance, action, and speech, and describe what these conveyed.

New students reacted uneasily to the instructions to observe only passively and silently, and then systematize cultural inferences. Some protested, "This isn't factual!" Asked, "How do you define a fact?" they answered, "Our supervisors tell us to write down answers as facts, exactly as we hear them." The present object, they were told, was for them to perceive what others imparted through their social skills; that watching quietly and uncritically yielded a stream of impressions and ideas, flowing beyond the spoken word and enriching it, for persons are more than words.

The assignment consumed a week in the field. As each one read his paper aloud, listeners were gripped by the data and inferences.

With successive reports interest mounted, and after some months students had evolved a fellowship that reached beyond circumscribed tasks to studies of scope and substance.

The second project stressed the prime cultural concept that man's social behavior was *learned* from older generations and from contemporaries. The effectiveness of instruction was shown to be limited and often corrupted by such isolating social forces as unfair discrimination, great poverty, and caste restrictions. This developed implications of the first project that a person "carried" the culture taught him and functioned according to its directions. The teachers questioned intelligence tests in this light, supported by their work on the first project.

The purpose of the second project was to show that the usefulness of words depended on exact knowledge of their contexts by all parties; the unrecognized presence of outside social influences often disrupts verbal communication. Words seem more sensitive to such injury than does empathic communication by other avenues. Each student was to collect meanings of seven words commonly used, listing them orally in free interviews with men and women of at least three different professions and with two or more laymen. They were not to write, spell, or explain the words; the range of age, sex, occupation, and social status was expected to influence the meanings supplied by informants. These were the words chosen: delinquent, crisis, diagnosis, interaction, prevention, role, deviation. These words are heard regularly at meetings of educators, social workers, psychologists, social scientists, public health workers, police; various significances are attached to them among colleagues in any one group and among the different groups. A few students added words of their own, for instance, race and achievement. Results were presented on charts stating places and durations of interviews and the sex, age, and occupation of each informant. Definitions of the words given by each informant were followed on the chart by the normative definitions found in a standard dictionary. In conclusion each paper related uniformities and variations among informants' definitions to social traits of the informants, using each dictionary definition as the norm.

Students found that informants' responses were so involved with and qualified by social factors that they gave supposedly familiar words the puzzling quality of foreign languages. Thus, an Anglo-American stenographer defined the spoken word "role" as "roll that you eat, meaning bread," whereas others meant "roll of bills" or of fat, or even "a turn on the sand." Similarly "race" connoted a physical type, a national group, a competition of horses, cars, or dogs. Each respondent projected his own interests: a bookkeeper spoke of delinquent accounts, a mother referred to delinquent boys, an engineer spoke of a delinquent angle; only one informant made "prevention" synonymous with "contraception"; and one informant made "deviation" synonymous with "homosexuality." At times these identifications coincided with the questioner's definitions and at times differed drastically from them.

When the class interviewed an English-speaking Persian youth of Zoroastrian faith, many made wild surmises and interruptions of meanings soared. The young man could not respond to questions women students addressed to him about his countrywomen's pursuits of marriage and career. It never occurred to the teachers that the young Oriental might be deeply abashed by their questions, since women were situated apart in his world, young women being quite subordinate socially. When a teacher interviewed a Mexican-American school custodian, confusion followed from the Mexican's transfer of Spanish sibilants to English: for he heard "race" as though in English it meant to "raise" something. Students now saw that outsiders could confuse cultural and linguistic disorientations with stupidity or "bilingualism."

A Mexican-American teacher elicited English poetry from an eleventh-grade remedial reading class of teenage Mexicans, a few Anglos, and a few Negroes; all of the children had severe behavior problems, all had parents earning little at unskilled labor.[6] Writing poetry was unprecedented in such a class. The ideas, images, and forms of the poems were so arresting that educators at conferences repeatedly called for them; some Anglo listeners even had tears fill their eyes.

How much of this creativity—never anticipated from the test scores—was facilitated by a largely shared culture? The teacher herself could not guess. Its appearance, however, cancels out the sad phrases of *bilingualism* and *academic retardation*. These wholly retarded readers and writers responded to their teacher's confident assertion that "anybody with feelings could express them in verse when taught how." The teacher assured her remedial readers, "You are just as human as the poets." She described the lives of English and Spanish writers and musicians, not omitting their sins; she read her own verse; she directed the boys and girls to read books of poetry and copy out verses "so they would get the feel of writing." With these pupils she explored the meanings and uses of words, synonyms, antonyms, meter, rhythm, music. She told the pupils she had no interest in their prior school ratings, nor in their minority race and status, but only in their ability of expression. Finally she told them to write something of their own, in ink, in the classroom, if they wished to. One poem was submitted, then more, until nearly everyone participated; the exception was a boy who chose to write an essay on Michaelangelo derived from his own library study. The teacher read each poem aloud, discussed it, and exhibited all poems at school when for the first time these youngsters proudly brought their parents to visit.[7]

Teachers who communicate emphatically can set precedents. A new school principal in an East Los Angeles slum was confronted with the old complaint that Mexican and Negro adolescents refused to undress and shower for gym work. Thereupon she replaced the open showers with single stalls. There were no further occasions for complaint. The children appreciated the principal's concern. She had put herself in their place and imagined that she, too, might not have cared to undress publicly.

The object of the third project was to show that social "facts" are not self-evident but can be understood through probing the expected systematized relationships among individuals and groups sharing a common tradition. After discussion, students in the basic course agreed that they would like to learn about intermarriage. This is an explosive complex of supposed "facts," involving American ideas of racial and religious separateness, ideas of individual rights to happiness and self-determination, the primacy of romantic love, and the trend toward integration generally. Educators observe considerable intermarriage in California,[8] discuss it unofficially at integrated schools,[9] and some are mindful of Southern racist dreads of the mixed family. Student educators knew pupils of mixed parentage, pupils of unlike heritages who "went steady" with the occasional consequence of pregnancy, and a few such pupils who actually married. Students were interested in forecasting seriously, without resort to stereotypes, the interplay of cultures in mixed unions.

Consequently each student was asked to interview several persons at length about intermarriage, allowing each informant to provide his own understanding of the subject. The student carried interviews as far as he could, then charted responses as before and provided a summary and interpretations. Reading novels and professional studies about mixed marriages in Europe and America, students used them as aids in conducting interviews.

The chief preparation for the project was to study systematically the traditional roles of male and female in various social classes and cultures, comparing them with one another and then with their manifestations under the destructiveness of war, migration, prejudice, poverty, and general ignorance.[10] As personality develops first at home, students were drilled to interpret responses in the light of knowledge about the informant's family. To everyone, especially to younger people, his own family is standard; the pupil enacts and represents his family's standards at school, perceiving teachers and others accordingly. Teachers came to realize that such behavior is also true of themselves.

Knowledge of a family was to be assembled by diagramming relationships of the informant's parents, children, brothers, sisters, in-laws, and other significant kin according to age, birthplace, seniority, authority and responsibility, education, work, income and expenditure, marriage, religion, race, striking experiences of war, and prejudice. Students also charted the life goals traditional in different groups. Some such goals were pursuits of power (through wealth, rank, occupation, marriage ties), learning, happiness, and virtue. Goals were observed and defined according to age, sex, seniority of individuals in the family and generation, and according to rank, responsibility, special function in the home or in public life, religion, and other established conditions.

Every culture patterns identities for male and female, with varying specializations and extents of these, directing expression through duties, privileges, penalties, goals, styles of dress, speech, gesture, and emotion. Students referred strivings of individuals to such norms of the family and of the larger group, whether the strivings were conventional, rebellious, or disturbed. The discussions included occasional reports from a school social worker, a school attendance officer, and school nurses about behavioral differences among Nisei, Mexican-American, Negro, and Okie school children.

Such considerations entered the project on intermarriage. In many mixed unions, one partner is of superior social position to the other, and the community then questions the status of the union and of the offspring. This is always true of Negro-white marriages, and often true of Oriental-white and of Indian-white marriages. The mixed offspring are labeled by race, religion, nationality, language, and, in the old South as in England, social class. The children may carry a double label, such as Italian-American, resembling the British Anglo-Irish, though we assign to racially mixed children the status of the lower-ranked race. Consequently, Negro-white children are always considered Negro unless they happen to be taken for, or "pass" for, white by visual inspection; in either case they run the risk of punishment by the knowledgeable observer, who in the South may be even the always illegal white father. The same is true of American Indian-white mixtures, though recognition of the American-Indian-Negro mixture depends on where he is found and how he looks.

A counselor in junior college and another in high school discovered from interviewing colleagues that counselors were "handicapped for their job" by their racist prejudices and by their ignorance of cultures. A young woman teacher interviewed Mexicans and Jews about intermarriage but avoided Negroes fearing that "the Negro issue might be too much for me to handle." Another woman expressed elation at now "understanding the aloneness" of mixed couples she interviewed.

Most informants spontaneously commented about Negro-white unions. Even when bitterly prejudiced, white informants put questions carefully: How is the mixed couple to be fitted into the neighborhood? Their children into our school? Who is head of the family when the wife is white?

Informants linked intermarriage with integration, noting that fiery problems would center on differing values, customs, and prestige. Some informants noted hopefully that certain married couples "got along" when they had complementary cultural preferences, especially American men and compliant Mexican wives, and American soldiers with submissive European or Japanese wives. Informants supplied evidence that the mixed family suffered from discriminatory acts in the community and from expectations of them. The head of a welfare agency, functioning as an informant, described the biracial residential area in the agency's community, "where Negro-white marriages last an average of five or six years, when they disintegrate and the children become wards of the state."

The fourth project signaled the readiness of students to handle personal disturbances while gathering data about their own cultures from acts, materials, and memories of their families. They knew now that teacher-pupil relationships were not created freshly by the schooling institution but were fed from the traditional roots of the personalities involved. It became possible to rephrase "frustrations" in teaching as semantic blocks traceable to confusions of social origin.

Specific cultural principles, like the public deference of Oriental women to men of status, became clues to guide the behavior of educators. An unmarried school social worker modified her conduct accordingly with a Korean father who for two years ignored Attendance Office demands for consultations about his young son who was repeatedly "excluded" from school by "medical exemption" (words in quotes from this school system's terminology). The social worker played successfully on the traditional facts that a Korean father demands his son to excel in school, show obedience and respect to elders and teachers, and realize that failure in these shames the family. However, a Mexican-American father cares relatively little about his child's academic achievements, but will demand entire obedience to authority, congruent with the stylistically differentiated manners of males and females. In American Negro families of the rural South, it is the mother and grandmother who demand respect and compliance for themselves. Traditionally, they also train the child to comply with all white authority, voicing threats of heavy punishment from whites which may even include death.

Frustration over misunderstood cues results from the disjoined American comprehension of, for example, the Mexican concept called *mañana*. The dictionary gives the meaning of *mañana* as "morning" or "tomorrow"; Americans convert it into a label, as does a popular song, for Mexican unreliability and laziness. However, Mexicans also use *mañana* idiomatically to convey the philosophy that a man is master of his own time, of his energy, and of himself. This philosophy, exercised in defiance of American routines, especially impersonal ones, often produces acts that resemble unreliability and laziness.[11] Misunderstood cues again figure when teachers practice undue permissiveness or covertly compete with adolescents in class. Children attuned to strong command, such as Okie, Mexican, and Negro groups, are dismayed, responding with chaotic behavior that is insolent, violent, untruthful, and delinquent.

As preparation for this project, civilizations were compared in terms of such social structures as the patriarchial family or plantation system; of such basic values as social progress or individual reincarnation; of such social roles as male initiative and primogeniture or class-linked female virginity and subordination; and of the conduct of individuals, recorded or observed, and appraised by prevailing norms. Behavior was studied in its traditional details, such as the mannerisms that mark a Mexican male's daredeviltry, whether in bullfights, romancing, or the home. Behavior was also studied in the light of comprehensive patterns, such as the love of personalism in Mexican culture, which dictates specific acts. Evidences of tradition were sought in all conduct and the meanings found in them were systematically pursued.

For the fourth project, each student was to reconstruct the cultural ways of his family in the three immediate generations of parents, children, and grandparents on both sides, gleaning information from interviews and other sources; alternatively, a student could study a family of a different culture. No one accepted the alternative, despite the emotional hazards of laying bare one's own family. Details were required about each family's home, education, work, marriages, births, kinship terms and obligations, religion, ailments, offenses, crises, decisions, prejudices, honors, and geographic movements.[12] For over two months students worked at assembling data.

Students intently followed the careful analyses of family modes around the globe, primitive and modern. I provided my own studies [13] of American subcultural families and trained a young Moslem Turkish woman, married to an American and educated in a United States college, to tell the students about family patterns in Turkey. Teachers had to know that men and women frequently must function in separate areas of their culture (public activities most often being male, domestic ones often being female), but that, increasingly in America, the sexes function similarly in many areas, though women are usually outranked. The American condition of lessened social separateness and differentiation between the sexes deeply confuses those of conservative European, Latin-American, and Oriental backgrounds.

Whatever the individual origins of teachers, their adult selves become stamped by the so-called "middle-class culture" (which teachers occasionally consider "upper middle-class") through college and professional training. Ways and values of this class—cleanliness, neatness, promptness, progress, puritanism—rule public education and clash with divergent standards of minorities and of the American "upper class." Comparing families in distinct cultures helped each teacher to conceptualize the boundaries of his own inherited culture; then he could surmise cultural limits in his dealings with "ethnics." Students discussed this with our Turkish informant who, having an excellent command of English, described how she sensed culture blocks in the hardships and heartaches she experienced at the American high school and college. Through this work, minorities became understood and changed from threatening human riddles (as the idea of Moslems was to some teachers) into enjoyable elements of society, charming indeed because still "different," but now amenable to insights, and with cultures worthy of esteem. Study of his own family showed each teacher the impossibility of escaping hereditary teachings, heightened his regard for them, and promoted greater ease with himself. At the same time, the teacher's humiliation and guilt over "poor achievers" abated, for such youngsters could now be seen as "poorly acculturated."

Before the family study, students fretfully debated their "identity" and that of minorities. To know and to preserve his worthy "identity" was as vital to a Mexican-American social worker who had struggled free of the Los Angeles slums as to an Anglo-American teacher reared in an ambitious Los Angeles family of means. The first man feared loss of identity through "gringo assimilation." The second dreaded losing the family's cherished citrus groves both practically and symbolically as tract housing and shopping centers erupted for masses on the grove sites. The family study offered each of these men a clear design of the world that shaped him, of his place in it, and of his present world and place.

The yearning for personal identity, or socially oriented personal awareness, was expressed in urgent terms by all teachers. This was easy to relate to the vast, constant change and movement. Most teachers had come to California since the Second World War and witnessed the newness and transiency of populations, and the rapid gains in wealth. With rare exceptions, family histories of these students (several constituting bulky manuscripts) showed gaps and queries about ancestors' religions, occupations, birthplaces (even in America), and given names. Such losses accompanied great shifts of locality and status, and the mixing of traditions. Unplaced peoples like American Indians, some Orientals, some Europeans, and displaced ones, like Negroes and Mexicans, are usually called minorities; increasingly they move west to advance their status. The advanced status seems acknowledged when, in California's fierce climate of equality, social agencies call erstwhile minorities "newcomers," [14] thus cleansing the atmosphere of harshness. Negroes, historically among the oldest of Americans, and among the oldest displaced, are "newcomers" in California. Mexicans, the longest residents of California after the Indians, are "newcomers," too. The terminological change is facilitated by postwar Anglo California's lack of tradition. Groups who have lived in more established localities—Negroes and Arkies, reservation Indians, Mexicans, and Orientals—know, however, that social identity has always been cast by genealogy and rank, by education, residence, occupation, and religion.

Students became eager to reduce social unknowns in teaching starting with unknown factors in their own backgrounds, going on to compare their heritages with pupils' cultures. They were prepared to weigh afresh the silence and docility of young Mexican children and their mothers, and to relate these to family disciplines reinforced by terrors of discrimination and ignorance of the school world. When a Mexican girl was elected class president by efforts of young Mexican boys, the teachers abandoned the old carpings about gangs to interpret this event as evidence of the traditionally maternal role of the Mexican elder sister, who often indeed is called *mamacita,* or "little mother." When a Mexican high-school girl, invited by teachers to transfer to an "enriched" course whose rapid progress would leave her friends behind, failed to press her father for the needed permission, the student teachers recognized that the girl was staying within the bounds of her family-defined station. Students realized that a child of this patriarchial tradition could, by adopting school goals, alienate himself from family and friends. The teachers therefore considered how to draw parents into the school orbit, both for the purposes of friendship and for mutual information.[15]

Each student invested enormous feeling in his family study. Some students reflected aloud, "I haven't written everything, that would be too revealing, and I don't want to hurt my family and friends." "This is the basis of all understanding. Why haven't we done it years ago?" Students listened carefully to all of the presentations, noting parallels and differences, finding the family portraits "fascinating." Although each mentioned guilt or shame over supposed betrayals of family, listeners never sensed any offense in readers' accounts. Principally, each one felt he had created something most dear in reconstructing his family's life. The professional goal of the project, to acquaint students with the cultural forces in society, now roused such empathy that students challenged the school's practice of imposing middle-class traits on pupils of other origins.

As a ruling group in public education, teachers asked how extensive were their responsibilities to the socially handicapped? Cultures transplanted by immigrants usually fail to flourish as before, whereas prejudice allows minorities only a limited absorbtion of the dominant culture. A young teacher expressed her realization of this by crying in despair that Mexican and Negro slum children in her first grade would remain deprived and handicapped because, "Their mothers don't care! So they don't learn. They don't *want* to learn!"

The students received descriptions of aspects of Mexican-American culture and social position, and anti-Mexican prejudices were presented in perspectives of European and American history.[16] Our principles of freedom and individualism encourage most minorities to fight discrimination in order to find the proper American fulfillment. Minorities who have been successful in this struggle include Jews, Catholics, Jehovah's Witnesses and Sabbatarians, Irish, Negroes, and Orientals; Mexican-Americans and American Indians have been joining them since the Second World War, the Indians (see Appendix 3) making their formal stand for civil rights in Chicago in 1961. When cultures of subordinate or minority status persist, they probably compromise with an Americanization that includes imposed and reactive prejudice.

"Race prejudice" and "discrimination" connote our traditional hostilities toward divergent religions, nationalities, and races, and also against the regionalism manifested by low-ranked whites of Southern origins. Our celebrated hostilities have centered on Indians, Orientals, Mexicans, and emancipated Negroes, the latter becoming the paradigm of American racism. Inseparable from the dominant scheme of life is the machinery of discrimination which evolved from the Reconstruction of the defeated South; it spread to other regions with modifications. Every American receives some indoctrination in prejudice against specific races, religions, or nationalities; the emphasis varies regionally, being on Negroes in the East and on Mexicans in the Southwest, for example, whereas in the last century it was still on Indians in the West and on Irish in the Northeast. Teachers in integrated schools should know that minorities are aware of the history of prejudice in their background.

Anglo-Mexican bitterness may be traced to our armed conquests of the Southwest and to frontier plundering and outlawry, especially in Texas and New Mexico, where the Spanish-speaking inhabitants were "bullied and dispossessed. . . . [E]arly Texans were hard men, fighting men . . . [who] hated Mexicans." [17] Older festerings have origins in Europe, fed on the English navy's victory over the Spanish Armada, on competitive Anglo-Spanish privateering and explorations, on rivalries between Catholic and Protestant clergy and doctrine. The Iberian peninsula had been dominated for seven centuries by cultivated Moors. England, in these centuries and during Spain's later glory, was a provincial outpost of Europe, and many English emigrants crossed the Atlantic scorning foreign nations, races, languages, and persons. In British North America, xenophobia punished indentured servants, who were victims of the Irish and Scots wars, as it punished Negro freedmen, Jews escaping pogroms, and Italians fleeing poverty.

Xenophobia directed American scorn of Indians, producing such verbal references as squaw, squaw-man, squaw-dress, blanket Indians, educated Indians return to the blanket, the only good Indian is a dead one, and others. Xenophobia directed American scorn of Mexicans as Spanish and Indian, both latter designations being heavily loaded words even now. Mexicans were also scorned as colonials, differentiated as "white" or *criollo* (American-born offspring of Spanish parents); as *mestizo* or half-caste; and as *ladino* or civilized, latinized Indian, and "wild" Indian.

Xenophobic belittlement of Mexico scored the underdeveloped condition of the country's economy and national defenses against foreign invasion, and blamed the arrogance of Mexican aristocrats for ignoring the welfare of dependent peons and of the whole nation. After the United States forced from Mexico the southwestern lands between Texas and the Pacific, financiers penetrated the defeated neighbor, exploiting her for economic profit, and were hardly deterred by Mexico's long Revolution of 1910. In this century, as North American capital moved south of the border, impoverished and ambitious Mexicans moved north. In the Southwest that once belonged to New Spain and Mexico, Mexican immigrants found a ranching economy resembling that of their pre-Revolutionary homeland. Conditioned by centuries of old Mexico's peonage, they adjusted docilely, to the satisfaction of their Anglo-American bosses, whom the Mexicans apparently confused with *patrónes* of the homeland's traditional *latifundium.* The Second World War bettered life radically for young Mexican-Americans, opening opportunities for them which are usually monopolized by the dominant group until militant minorities challenge the inequities and begin to win rights.

Study of these developments showed how two peoples, distinct in race and traditions, met in the Southwest and became a community of upper, generally Anglo, and lower, generally Mexican, classes. The class organization encouraged separate cultures or subcultures that were mutually familiar through many shared interests, and were severely tempered by the prejudices of American conquerors and of Mexican or Mexican-American oppressed. Teachers incorporated this class-subculture viewpoint when considering the problems of their pupils in Mexican *barrios,* homes, gangs, schools, and the general community.

Other minorities at the schools and the general "white" group underwent similar scrutiny. School problems among the whites showed the practical use of differentiating the Southern "poor whites," called Okies and Arkies in California, the "middle-class whites," and the "upper-class whites," especially of New England and of the old South. These labels were meant to keep alive awareness of traditional variations, besides awareness of complex social forms. If educators did not readily recognize specific cultural differences, they were, however, to anticipate their possible presences and attempt to ferret out their meanings.

A common example of a subcultural intrusion, whose own meanings are ignored and warped by our authorities, is the Spanish-speaking person's use of the double family name or the wife's additional use of her father's name. The Hispanic double family name states first the paternal, then the maternal one; the wife states first the paternal, then the husband's name prefixed by *de*. Thus, Rosa Leos married to Baca becomes Mrs. Rosa Leos de Baca; her son Jorge is Jorge Baca Leos. These uses reveal the bilateral structure of the family and elevation of the father and husband. However, educators, social workers, and police often challenge the double names, suspecting falsehood, as in the school or welfare office regarding an ANC (Aid to Needy Children) child.

Cultural confusion arises from Mexican schoolboys' *macho* flamboyance or *machismo*, displayed when, for example, they resist authority or engage in courtship, as there is no direct provision for *machismo* in our American life. Oliver LaFarge described a young New Mexico Hispano who "superimposed upon the arrogant American boy's belief that he is already a man the Spanish necessity of being and proving himself one." [18] Similar confusion of traditions in an American situation explains the Spanish speaker's incorrect use of gender in English, as when referring to his house as "she," even when he actually knows better. This confused usage is partly due to the absence of Spanish neuter and also to the culture's personalizing philosophy, which the language habits reflect.

Mankind endures sickness besides health, pain and accident, as well as comfort; and this every tradition recognizes. Moreover, every tradition specifies its own hurts and cures, related to norms of health and life. [19] Concepts of well-being and of ill-being are linked to one another and to the total life. Here, too, there is some confusion of cultural origin, as when beliefs about magical causation and treatment of disease among many folk groups (Okies, Negroes, Mexicans, Indians, Italians, Orientals, for example) clash with public health standards at school and hospital. Each culture, or regional group, seems to favor particular ailments and treatments, as if the established interests and stresses of an epoch are paid for in appropriate injuries, perils, and restoratives. In contemporary medicine, the psychosomatic theory attributes causation of specific diseases and injuries largely to environmental stress on or "insult" to certain personality or body types. According to this theory, reactive symptoms often are predictable for named patient types. Thus, duodenal ulcer probably indicates stress experienced by one type, "accident-proneness" probably indicates stress felt by a second, whereas assault upon others often reveals the stress on a third type. Culture periods can be recognized by their outstanding disorders of health. Thus, previous centuries in Europe witnessed epidemics of bubonic plague, small pox, scrofula, yellow fever, dancing and other mass hysterias, cholera, tuberculosis, syphilis. At present in the United States, we fear cancer, colds, and respiratory ailments, coronary and heart diseases, headaches, duodenal ulcer, alcoholism, neuroses and psychoses, infantile paralysis, multiple sclerosis. Cures also vary in cultures. Fifteen-century Ojibwa Indian hunters of Canadian woodlands entrusted cures to sorcerers, visionaries, and aging herbalists, chiefly male though herbalists could be female. Fifteenth-century Europeans of all ranks entrusted cure to medical nuns and monks, to witches, sorcerers, wise women, male barber-surgeons, and the king's hands.

Today school and welfare officials may accuse pupils and parents, especially when they are from unfamiliar backgrounds, of feigning illness and accident. Most people, however, succumb involuntarily or "honestly" to stress. An act, which to another culture seems disordered, may be an answer to open dictates of tradition. Such acts include honorable Japanese suicide by hari-kiri, the Christian revivalistic sects' entranced "speaking in tongues," the American Indian visionary's conversation with guardian spirits, Siberian tribesmen's and women's entering trances from which they emerge powerful sorcerers.

The fifth project was to show, therefore, that, although all mankind suffers, tradition directs the prevailing modes or symptoms of a time and place and also the approved modes of prevention and cure.[20] Disease and accident are crises that somewhat bespeak the patient's social universe, not unlike his crisis rites of marriage, baptism, and prayer. To them, as to other social strivings, are customarily linked named goals, rewards, and punishments.

Students were given the problem, "How do children of different cultures and classes react to disease and pain?" They were asked to observe and interview their pupils, pupils' families, school doctors and nurses, at classes, clinics, and homes, to extract the special cultural meanings from sickness situations.

To illustrate, Mexican-American males complain at all ages of a generalized stomach-ache called *empacho,* meaning "blockage" or "embarrassment"; like infant colic which precedes it in the child's growth, it serves to elicit tender care. An environmental setting is the emotional "uproar"—the word is used by schoolteachers and social workers in Los Angeles—attending Mexican sociability, which often explodes into violent male hostilities toward others, including children. A child receives completest indulgence until the age of two or three. Then, a new baby having come, he becomes a target for his father's arbitrary will, which is now severe, now lax or indulgent. The break in care, from absolute tenderness in infancy to blasts of harshness in childhood, seems to be recorded as *empacho* (or, adverse conditioning of the vagus nerve?), a regular symptom in child and adult histories. Mexican-Americans say, "Yes, *empacho* comes from nervous tension." In Los Angeles slums and elsewhere, the traditional Spanish-American courting custom of teenagers, called the *paseo*, meaning "the walk," is often attacked by police as delinquent "loitering." In its original form south of the border, in Southwest border towns, and still in a large interior Southern California town like San Bernardino, young men and women parade around the town square in the cool of early evening, in separate sex groups, watched by seated adult chaperones, wooed by courting music. In our Southwest, however, the young men often have no better place to hold their *paseo* than street corners in slums, without chaperones and music; then police threaten or seize the boys. *Empacho* is one result, possibly accompanied by rebellious toyings (also on the part of teenage girls) with wine, marijuana, and heroin. The numerous Mexican-American pupils in East Los Angeles schools show high rates of illness and delinquency.

Records of a public psychiatric clinic for adults reiterated the complaints of *empacho* among young Mexican-American veterans and interpreted them as malingering. But culturally the ailment seemed a harmless mode of briefly relieving individuals from family and other social pressures, starting up Mexican maternal-type care to cushion Mexican paternal-type pressure. The psychiatric records noted "irresponsibility" of most Mexicans in dropping treatment after initial services. Lacking further evidence this could just as well be interpreted to mean that the patients were satisfied with the clinic's nursing and were enabled to resume normal *macho* ways. Certainly there was a large rift in cross-cultural communication. The doctors' and social workers' charges that Mexicans malingered echo the American injunction against males' showing "weakness" and "no guts" by complaining.

Such key positions are made explicit in proverbs, which students were asked to find. All remembered or located versions of the following: "Keep a stiff upper lip." "Keep your chin up." "It's never too late to learn." "Where there's life there's hope." "God helps those who help themselves." "A stitch in time saves nine." "Women and children must be saved first, then men." "Women and children cry, men don't." Latins everywhere know versions of: "Tears are pearls" (referring especially to women's tears). "Quarrels bring people closer together." "Better to die than endure poor health." "Passion blinds reason" (and so excuses "crimes of passion"). "Death levels all." "You die as you live." "Show a good face to bad times."

Students were requested to assemble data answering four basic questions of cultural import. One was, "*What* is disease to the individual children you are studying?" Among Southern Negroes and their "poor white" neighbors, the evil eye or other witchcraft, traced by scholars to European and African origins, is both cause and cure of some diseases. To Southwest Mexicans, brown "liver spots" on a girl's face are a flag of pregnancy, which even college-educated Mexican women teachers resent as a public exposure of their condition; skin eruptions signify resented spinsterhood in the father's home. Both conditions are expected anxiously by the girl or woman and by her relatives, their appearances are much discussed, and may be submitted to medical care.

The second question was, "*Who* has told the children about diseases?" Was it mother, priest, *bruja* (Spanish for female witch, an older woman of the community), the *curandera* (Spanish for female healer, a woman of the community), the school doctor, nurse, or teacher? Mexicans in segregated *barrios* (Spanish for town section or quarter) learn from all these sources. Individuals resolve contradictions according to their isolation from, or participation in, general American life. In a Los Angeles family, ruled by an illiterate matriarchate, there was an elder daughter who had completed junior college and settled down to rear a family; and there was a younger daughter who had finished college, taught school, and continued with graduate studies, while rearing a family. The elder daughter always protected herself and family against noxious "night airs" and she cured indispositions with folk remedies like rubbing tomatoes and vinegar on the body; the younger daughter followed only her physician's advice and said, "I barely remember all that my mother did."

The third question was, "*Who* takes care of the children *when* they ail?" Is it mother, elder sister or aunt, mammy, nurse, clinic, or hospital? Fear of the impersonal, strange doctor or nurse, observed in hospitals among deprived immigrants and native Americans of all origins, may cause patient and family to vomit or produce *empacho*, to disturb menstrual flow, to raise fevers. School officials often discredit the "genuineness" of these symptoms. Yet among minorities, cultural and racial prejudices are likely pathogenic, or medically "insulting," factors.

The fourth question was, "*How* does the patient's family show sympathy and care?" Are the demonstrations noisy, stoical, succoring, avoiding? Family customs influence the patient's understanding of an unfamiliar doctor's actions. Mexicans often bring a so-called interpreter to the clinic, ward, or doctor's office, who actually provides moral support. A Mexican woman informed a student, in competent English, "I talk Spanish when I want to tell how I *feel.*" Although a deprived family seems to quietly endure nurse's scoldings, it is also secretly planning to visit the "witch," a person meriting confidence as "our's" while rating professional doctors "quacks." Such a family, of Mexican or Anglo-American folk origins, does not treat disease symptoms alone, but mainly an individual whose personal suffering involves others of the group. Therefore, the priest is also visited for healing prayer and trusted advisers are led to prepare traditional healing recipes.

Since even preschool children learn ways of sickness, one teacher directed her first-graders, of many backgrounds, to draw their memories of pain and illness, since they could not write or verbally explain a great deal. She secured eloquent colored crayon sketches of pimpled skins, indigestion, fevered bed-patients, headaches, plain fear and worry, and shyness, and some clay modelings which were accurate, ingenious depictions of male and female adult genitals by the five-year-old son of a Negro prostitute. All these she interpreted from knowledge of each child's family and personality.

Culturally unlike settings of alcoholism [21] were studied among Jews, Irish, British, Mexicans, and American Indians; also those of homosexuality.[22] Social control by "shameful" illness was illustrated in older popular judgments of Europe and America on tuberculosis, insanity, syphilis, cancer, homosexuality, anxiety neuroses, crippled conditions, and sterility. Socially acceptable disease was illustrated in allergies, fatigues, headaches, asthmas, chronic heart troubles of the "sensitive" person, where sensitive is a cultural norm. In American tradition, artists and women have been considered "sensitive" and "frail or weak," and sometimes therefore esthetically or morally superior. A Mexican-American student, a member of a prison staff, assembled male prisoners in group therapy for group interviews and learned that the Mexican-Americans considered themselves more *macho* and "strong" in character than the Anglos because they complained less about illness. Devotion to a traditional but disease-favoring diet was illustrated by European-Jewish preference for carbohydrates predisposing to a high rate of sugar diabetes. Abandonment of a traditional food that excellently supports health was illustrated when Mexicans recently began substituting refined-flour tortillas for the ancient corn-and-lime (calcium-treated corn or *maiz*) tortillas.

Students' reports observed the recommended form, in keeping with their dearth of preparation in research and writing. Generally, this form required a clear statement of the problem being investigated, a systematic account of the methods pursued (by field observation, interview, questionnaire, projective techniques, camera, library sources), a statement of findings based always on the data secured from several groups, summaries of the uniformities and variations in the data, and interpretations of the cultural influences in the problem. It was desirable also to phrase for further study questions growing out of the report. Data had to include ages and ethnic affiliations of the children studied, the education and occupations of parents and others important to the study, and relationships of the findings to selected points in the literature.

Schools hope to guide children's maturing ever more strongly. This rests on knowing the family ground plan upon which the new generation rises. Accordingly, the purpose of the sixth project was to train educators to chart the lines or channels of authority and responsibility in the family, and the directions of flow, as mirrored in pupils' opinions. Educators were instructed to ask pupils how they would rear youngsters if they were parents; also, how they would act if they were of the opposite sex, at their present age, and later as parents. The imaginative reversal of sex and generation was introduced partly to avoid seeming criticism of parents and partly to discover a pupil's whole conceptualization of the relationships. Educators were to find out who in each pupil's family made decisions, about what, when, where, how, and why; who punished and who rewarded, and in what forms and under what circumstances; how the punished individual responded; to whom authority was delegated, as to an elder brother or sister, or to an outsider, and under what conditions, and how the punished one then responded. Each pupil's exact phrasing was to be quoted, allowing implications to be pursued further about family relationships, their present functioning, and the speaker's private reflections. The educators' selection of the phrases and silences to be entered in the report was also held significant in the processes of understanding and teaching; in this sense they were also more useful than the completer versions of a tape recording or a pupil's composition. Thus, students probed some of the family conditions that helped to evoke and design the individual's sense of identity, through sex-linked and generation-linked duties, authority, rewards and privileges, and modes of speech, silence, and posture.

Some features of middle-class life, about which there was consensus in published studies and among the educators, provided norms for estimating conformity and divergence of other culture groups. These features included the devotion to time and timing, with activities scheduled to yield measurable profits; the importance of sobriety and reliability in general, with consequences in sexual prudery and associations with sin and guilt; the replacement of "corporal punishment" by "reasoned" argument; the requirements of habitual literacy, steady work, and elevated living standards; the paramount worth of romantic love and marriage, and, hence, the tolerance of divorce; the duty to love children but to control the number of births; the sacredness of national principles that promise equal opportunities to all regardless of race, creed, nationality, and, latterly, sex. Contrasts and gaps between these features and relevant ones of other subcultural groups often remain unresolved at a given time and locality, at great cost to individual and group vitality. The school must find its way among the confusions, often an ungrateful task.

An extreme but not unlikely illustration appeared in New York. The newspapers reported that a Puerto Rican teenager called his teacher a "whore" and assaulted her after she slapped him. This seemed to confirm to the boy that the slum school was indeed a "blackboard jungle," in keeping with the surrounding slum jungle, and that the teacher was only a common female like others of the slums, so that he used a familiar slum word commensurate with his low view of himself. Of course, such cultural insights do not instantly remedy great social deteriorations, although they provide clues to human meanings and social frames of reference. At the same time, features of the subordinate traditions infiltrate dominant life, in foods, music, dance, dress, slang, and humor, providing empathic bridges for communication.

Students expressed astonishment to find that their pupils' responses demanded firm and consistent punishments and rewards from parents. Pupils stated that parents' whippings or punitive deprivations should be accompanied by clear statements about where the offending child stood afterward; they preferred such punishment, generally, to disciplinary "reasoning," silences, or permissiveness, all of which they interpreted as indifference. Pupils desired their fathers to hold chief authority in the family because he was the wage earner and male head; they desired their mothers to hold delegated specific authority as female head; they desired specific sex differentiations of duties, dress and conduct of all ages, both in the home and outside. Students found that views held by pupils departed from current accounts of alleged male overdomestication in the home and community and the reported vulnerability of men to careeristic competition with women.

At the close of each year, students were asked to present questions based on their work. Some of these were: "How can a minority

assimilate to and advance in American life and yet retain its tradition?" "Must all cultural groups in America assimilate?" "Should we
impose middle-class school standards on children of all backgrounds?"
"How can we prepare for the growing population of aged?" In such
connections students occasionally reported on significant works and
news stories related to the projects, such as accounts of rural and
urban life in Mexico and Mexican sections in California,[23] theoretical
examinations of human creativity and learning in various cultures,[24]
and cultural interpretations of provocative news reports—for example,
dropping of the traditional dowry in India's Hindu marriage contracts.

In another course in the Claremont project, Minorities of Southern California, two aspects were developed. One concentrated on
minority status as a determining formal bond with the dominant
group, which channels the cultural flow of the parties, besides mutual
services and punishments. The status varies widely in content and
operations for Jews, Negroes, Mexicans, Indians, Orientals, Italians,
Catholics, Portuguese, and Okies. The strong incorporation of minorities into the dominant society distinguishes minorities from visiting foreigners, displaced persons, and prisoners-of-war; for minorities
"belong," although they are handicapped.

The second aspect concentrated on *minority traditions*. Those
traditions that survived in America were compared with intact ancestral cultures. We discussed blendings of minority status, ancestral
culture, and American culture in any one minority; and each student evolved a related field project for his own practice. Mexicans
were always a favorite area of study. In a seminar of fourteen, one
person, a white college teacher from Alabama, studied Negroes; one
boy, a local Jewish college student, studied Jews; two studied relocated Navajo Indians; the others devoted themselves to Mexicans.
Entering homes, students saw and heard things that sent stereotypes
crashing. Thus, the spokesman of a Mexican-American family in the
barrio protested to a teacher consulting its young members on her
project, "Why do the schools label us all underachievers and poorly
motivated? All my sisters and I are college graduates, and our lowest
grades were B! We're not peons! Can't you *gringos* tell the difference?"
A teacher of Danish origin was impressed by the exalted station, in
Mexican eyes, of the Mexican father. Teenagers told her, "My father
doesn't talk [freely] to me. . . . the weekends are especially bad
[i.e., severely governed] when he's home from work; he doesn't let us
out." She concluded, "The father is domineering in [her native]
Denmark, and women haven't much status there but it's not nearly as

extreme as among these Mexicans. I guess that's why I married an American though my parents thought the marriage beneath me."

A Mexican-American teacher showed how the Jewish traditional love of learning reached out to school people. A nearby Jewish congregation created "Teachers' Day," and children of members were instructed to invite their teachers for a social evening. Guests were welcomed in the temple, and each pupil escorted his teacher on the appointed evening. The rabbi's sermon concerned Jewish respect for education and educators, and urged teachers to understand their pupils' Jewish background. Then the rabbi explained the Torah and took it out of the Ark to show to the guests. The Mexican-American teacher was one of those invited. She said, "I felt honored to be there. It gave me a different outlook on Jews. Even the refreshments were choice. The rabbi offered his and the congregation's help whenever we teachers needed it."

One teacher examined the aged as an emerging minority, interviewing vigorous oldsters retired from professional activity and studying accounts of the statuses of oldsters in other cultures, in addition to current medical views and programs of "senior citizen" groups. She felt that psychological preparation for worthy aging should begin in high school. Two teachers described relocated Indians, yet no students quite appreciated the news that during the summer of 1961 American Indian tribesmen, from all over the nation, meeting in Chicago, had organized themselves into a group whose civil-rights demands indicated active entrance into full minority status.

Although minorities attracted interest because of national and world events, such as American antidiscrimination legislation, and nation-building in Israel and Africa, students also tried to learn about local ruling groups of whites. One teacher in a rich California city canvassed his coeducational senior high-school class of eighty by having them write essays on "This I believe." Most of the class were "ordinary middle-class white . . . [their] fathers in small business or employed at large plants, mothers might work off and on . . ." but the teacher was surprised to discover divergent concerns. A third of the students developed a fundamentalist theme which the teacher summarized as, "I am a child of God and will live accordingly." The next largest group developed the theme which the teacher summarized as, "I must get along with people." A third, less numerous group was classifiable as "hard realists interested in power," who saw politics as their proper avenue. The fourth group included some whites and the Negroes, all expressing rebellion against some prevailing condition;

the Negroes frankly threatened reprisals if their lot were not soon improved.

The teacher was less disconcerted by the fundamentalists than by the other three groups. He decided to decipher implications of the essays for the development of curriculum.

Notes

1. The course title was Cultural Factors in Teaching and Counseling.
2. These course titles were (1) Cultural Anthropology and Education (which systematized culture theories for educators) and (2) Cultures of Minority Groups in Southern California (which studied traditions and American roles of Mexicans, Orientals, Negroes, American Indians and European-descended whites handicapped by diverse regional, religious or national origins).
3. See Chapter 7 for discussion of students' work.
4. Nisei and Jews do so well in school, generally, that formulas of inadequacy are seldom applied to them.
5. Thus see, Frank Farner, "Comparative Achievement and Bilingualism of Matched Groups of Nisei, Mexican-American and Anglo High School Students," manuscript presented at the Conference of the California Educational Research Association, March 1960.
   Also, George I. Sánchez, "The Crux of the Dual Language Handicap," *New Mexico School Review*, March 1954, pp. 13–15, 38.
6. Selections appear in Chapter 7, by permission of the teacher, Mrs. Soledad S. C. Coronel, California State Department of Education, Foreign Language Consultant, Los Angeles (1965).
7. "These were people who had never come to school before!" the teacher exclaimed. Asked to describe her methods to our class, she answered at first with such routine generalizations as, "I followed sociological principles, I roused motivation and rapport." It took hours of prodding for her to recall her words and acts in details and in sequence, for they were spontaneous developments of work started years before at home with her own children.
8. In 1960 many publications stressed the increase of interfaith marriages in the United States, especially upon second marriage and upon rise in family income.
9. In 1959 California was reported to have 700,000 Negroes, 600,000 Mexican-Americans, over 100,000 Orientals, about as many Jews, many small religious groups, and recent migrants of poorer social origins from the southeast and southwest. Consequently, "at least 1,000,000 members of California's cultural minorities are now enrolled in . . . (public) schools," states Sociology Professor C. Wilson Record, manuscript, July 1959, Sacramento State College. In 1962 Los Angeles alone had 500,000 Negroes, according to the *Los Angeles Times*, July 6, 1962, article by Gene Sherman, Part I, p. 11.
10. See appendices to this book. Also, Ruth Landes, "Negro Slavery and Female Status," *African Affairs* (London: Journal of the Royal African Society), January 1953 (Vol. 52, No. 206), pp. 54–57; and in *Les Afro-Américains* (Mémoires de l'Institut Français d'Afrique Noire), No. 27, IFAN–Dakar, 1953, pp. 265–268. This issue No. 27 of *Les Afro-Américains* grew from the

French Institute's view that studies of African blacks in their ancestral settings must be amplified by knowing the changes undergone by these blacks and their descendants when set by slavery in the New World. Also, Ruth Landes, "Fetish Worship in Brazil," *Journal of American Folklore*, October–December 1940 (Vol. 53, No. 210), pp. 261–270; and *City of Women* (New York: The Macmillan Company, 1947). See Edison Carneiro, "The Structure of African Cults in Bahia," *Journal of American Folklore*, October–December 1940 (Vol. 53, No. 210), pp. 271–278. See Charles S. Johnson, *Shadow of the Plantation* (Chicago: University of Chicago Press, 1934); John Dollard, *Caste and Class in a Southern Town* (New Haven: Yale University Press, 1937); St. Clair Drake and Horace R. Cayton, *Black Metropolis: A Study of Negro Life in a Northern City* (New York: Harcourt, Brace and Company, 1946). See Margaret Mead, *Male and Female, A Study of the Sexes in a Changing World* (New York: William Morrow and Co., 1949). See W. I. Thomas and Florian Znaniecki, *The Polish Peasant in Europe and America* (New York: Alfred A. Knopf, 1927).

11. See Lyle Saunders, *Cultural Difference and Medical Care: The Case of the Spanish-Speaking People in the Southwest* (New York: Russell Sage Foundation, 1954), pp. 117–140.

12. Selections from the studies appear in Chapter 7.

13. A detailed model was by Ruth Landes and Mark Zborowski, "Hypotheses Concerning the Eastern European Jewish Family," *Psychiatry,* November 1950 (Vol. 13, No. 4), pp. 447–464. See also Theodore Bienenstock, "Social Life and Authority in the Eastern European Jewish Shtetl Community," *The Southwestern Journal of Anthropology,* Autumn 1950 (Vol. 6, No. 3), pp. 238–254. See also Appendix 1 to this book, The Mexican-American Family; Oscar Lewis, *Five Families: The Anthropology of Poverty* (New York: Basic Books, 1959); Oscar Lewis, *The Children of Sánchez* (New York: Random House, 1961); Ruth D. Tuck, *Not with the Fist: A Study of Mexican-Americans in a Southwest City* (New York: Harcourt, Brace and Company, 1946); Carey McWilliams, *Brothers Under the Skin* (New York: Little, Brown and Co., 1942); Manuel Gamio, *The Mexican Immigrant, His Life Story* (Chicago: University of Chicago Press, 1931).

See E. Franklin Frazier, *The Negro Family in the United States* (New York: Macmillan Co., 1957) and E. Franklin Frazier, *Black Bourgeoisie* (Glencoe, Illinois: Free Press, 1957). Also, Hylan Lewis, "The Changing Negro Family" in *The Nation's Children,* (ed.) Eli Ginzberg, Vol. 1, "The Family and Social Change" (New York: Columbia University Press, 1960), pp. 108–137. See Gunnar Myrdal, *An American Dilemma: The Negro Problem and Modern Democracy* (New York: Harper, 1944), Vol. 2, Part x, "The Negro Community."

See Willard Waller, *The Family* (New York: Cordon, 1938). Also, Harry Stack Sullivan and (eds.) H. S. Perry and M. L. Gawell, *The Interpersonal Theory of Psychiatry* (New York: Norton, 1953).

Useful articles about families of varied origins are reprinted in *Social Perspectives on Behavior,* Herman D. Stein and Richard A. Cloward (eds.) (Glencoe, Illinois: The Free Press, 1958). Some are Ruth Landes and Mark Zborowski, the Jewish family; E. Franklin Frazier, the Negro family; Paul J. Campisi, the Italian family; Margaret Mead, the American family; Talcott Parsons, kinship system of the United States, also age and sex in the social structure; Ruth Benedict, continuities and discontinuities in cultural conditioning; Allison Davis and Robert J. Havighurst, social class and color differences in child rearing.

See also Norman W. Bell and Ezra F. Vogel (eds.), *A Modern Introduction to the Family* (Glencoe, Illinois: The Free Press, 1960).

14. See Ruth Landes, "Culture and Social Work," *Social Work Papers*, The School of Social Work, University of Southern California, Vol. 9, 1962, pp. 1–8.

15. This was undertaken in an elementary school system, described in Chapter 5.

16. See Appendix 1 of this book.

17. Harvey Fergusson, *Rio Grande* (New York: William Morrow and Co., 1955), pp. 256, 253.

18. Oliver La Farge, *Behind the Mountains* (Boston: Houghton Mifflin Co., 1956), p. 37.

19. Useful studies in this field include Margaret Clark, *Health in the Mexican-American Culture* (Berkeley: University of California Press, 1959); Lyle Saunders, *Cultural Difference and Medical Care;* Mark Zborowski, "Cultural Components in Responses to Pain," reprinted in (eds.) Stein and Cloward, *Social Perspectives on Behavior*, pp. 145–156; Frances Cooke MacGregor, *Social Science and Nursing* (New York: Russell Sage Foundation, 1960).

Sufferings under race prejudice are examined psychoanalytically in Abram Kardiner and Lionel Ovesey, *The Mark of Oppression* (New York: W. W. Norton and Co., 1951); novelistically in Richard Wright, *Native Son* (New York: Harper and Brothers, 1940); and as autobiography in Richard Wright, *Black Boy, A Record of Childhood and Youth* (New York: Harper and Brothers, 1937, 1945).

See also Franz Alexander, *Psychosomatic Medicine* (New York: W. W. Norton and Co., 1950).

20. Alfred L. Kroeber, *Configurations of Culture Growth* (Berkeley: University of California Press, 1944), argues that genius flowers only in individuals attuned to concerns of the host culture; hence genius potentials alien to these cannot emerge or achieve recognition: "more individuals born with the endowment of genius have been inhibited by the cultural situations into which they are born than have been developed by other cultural situations," page 840. Ruth F. Benedict, *Patterns of Culture* (Boston: Houghton, Mifflin Co., 1934), argues that each culture's patterns provide for only a limited range of potential human interests. Implications for individuals' suffering and sickness are discussed in the last chapter, "The Individual and the Pattern of Culture."

21. *Cf.* Charles R. Snyder, *Alcohol and the Jews* (Glencoe, Illinois: The Free Press, 1958).

22. *Cf.* Ruth Landes, "A Cult Matriarchate and Male Homosexuality," *Journal of Abnormal and Social Psychology*, July 1940 (Vol. 35, No. 3), pp. 386–397. The relationships between cultural values and emotional disorders are examined closely in Ruth Landes, *Ojibwa Woman* (New York: Columbia University Press, 1938), and in Ruth Landes, "The Abnormal Among the Ojibwa Indians," *Journal of Abnormal and Social Psychology*, January 1938 (Vol. 33, No. 1), pp. 14–33. See Ruth Benedict, *Patterns of Culture*, pp. 263–265.

23. Based on works of O. Lewis, R. Tuck, M. Clark, as before, and others.

24. Works of A. L. Kroeber, R. F. Benedict, as before, and others.

5

Culture and Training in the Schools

Many public school educators in Southern California requested the Anthropology and Education project to give them practical help in their intercultural dilemmas. Often school authorities asked for a discussion of "the schools' middle-class culture as it conflicts" with the unfamiliar subcultures of lower-class Mexicans, Negroes, and Okies. Usually, this assistance was given on the scene of school education. To design courses and other training procedures for coping with immediate difficulties arising from the culture conflicts, one had to observe how the dominant culture worked in each school. This occasioned visits to many elementary and secondary schools for studying behavior of teachers, counselors, nurses, principals, and pupils by observation, interview, and certain experiments.

It quickly became clear that the Claremont project would offer educators no simple rule of thumb for teaching their multicultural classes. Instead, it showed them how to recast their views of classroom problems in terms of the diverse cultural traits and dynamics manifested by individual pupils and teachers. First, educators had to abandon or question many old generalities. Then, they had to consider pupils as individuals, each differentiated by his culture—or subculture, class, and minority affiliation—and his temperament, as these actually showed in specific behavior toward teachers and others. Further, educators were advised to interpret "frustration" not as their personal failure, but as signaling a break in communication often caused by unrecognized sociocultural factors; the break was remediable by applying cultural knowledge. Working with knowledge of the cultures represented by their pupils, teachers could control destructive effects of the cultural variety instead of just being "frustrated" by them; they could advance "motivation" and comprehension. Educators had to realize that communication, which includes teaching and learning, travels by more than verbal means and involves more people than just teacher and pupil at school.

Therefore, when a teacher asked questions about pupils, he was directed to give many social details about each pupil and his parents, and also to clarify his own social background. Thus, a Mormon teacher explained that he could not work adequately with Negroes because of his people's doctrinal condemnation of them. Similarly, school conferences were organized around particular cases, such as reports on a child's "deficient motivation," and discussed in a clinical fashion that employed nutshell versions of the Claremont courses. Ideas of evolution, race, and culture were freshened by details from the subgroups in the schools. Race prejudice was examined as a traditional value, serving certain of our social arrangements, and now becoming a censured principle of evil. Education was presented as an institution vital for survival of man and society, a major tool of civilization in continuous need of refinement. The conferences might last for hours, involving successive groups in the school hierarchy, for teachers are articulate, love their work and pupils, and are both fascinated and intimidated by cultural differences and clashes.

California educators saw differences and changes of culture as terrible forces producing "slow readers . . . [and] uncooperative and poorly motivated" pupils and parents. In their schoolroom fortresses, teachers' self-doubts rose as they were confronted with needs to handle strange physical types (Negro, Mexican, Japanese, Indian), an unfamiliar language (Spanish), unfamiliar customs (like deference to elders), and the unfamiliar proximity of Negro neighbors.

Accordingly, one elementary-school administrator organized a two-year training sequence in her city's system with cooperation of the Claremont program. This was confined to a half-dozen lower-division (kindergarten through sixth grade) schools whose pupils were almost wholly Mexican and Negro and whose staffs were almost wholly Anglo-American whites. Thirty or forty teachers met monthly at the curriculum director's informal invitation, gathering at the close of a school day for about an hour. They were led to develop projects, which they carried out under joint supervision of the administrator and Claremont. Each project expressed an urgent need, such as persuading parents to confer with teachers on schedule, and each was carried out in the month that lapsed between meetings. In the first year of the sequence, projects focused on *behavior* of teachers, pupils, and parents; in the second year, projects focused on classroom *curricula*. To illustrate the approach to behavior studies, projects examined the specific ways in which a subject, like reading, was taught at school and again in the pupil's home, if at all; and the specific ways a teacher showed authority, responsibility, prejudice, and recognition, and how pupils and parents responded. To illustrate the approach to curriculum studies, projects examined the contents of school readers to see the pertinence of details, like illustrations, to the pupil's home experiences, since Negroes, Mexicans, Orientals, and the poor are not usually depicted except by stereotypes.

By identifying variations among cultures, it was possible to show, for example, that teachers are not substitute parents, a popular misconception that confuses feelings and responsibilities. Besides, the urban school, through compulsory mass attendance and instruction, has an enormous reach, while the family, as it moves geographically and socially, shrinks to the limit of parents and children. The teacher must train the child in the ways of the larger world through the historic tradition of the total community, whereas the parent is expected to train the child only according to hereditary family tradition, and through it, in his relationships to the larger world. The school's task is often damaged by unwitting intrusions of dissimilar family cultures of teacher and pupil, as the teacher supposes that he or she is advancing the officially approved personal models and life goals. Through other projects, described subsequently, teachers came to realize unmistakably that, as one dean exclaimed, "We also have cultures, just like the minorities!" And educators came to acknowledge that no pedagogic relationships are "culture-free," as is claimed for certain ability tests.

The remarkable cultural kaleidoscope of California schools turns on the high mobility among and within communities. A teacher studying his own city in 1961, "one of the oldest areas of settlement in Los Angeles county,"[1] found "nearly 40 per cent turnover in residents within [the last] 5-year period . . . [because at least] 25 per cent have moved within the community [about] every 2 years . . . [and] 13 per cent have moved on the average once a year or more frequently. . . . [T]he total school population in grades kindergarten through sixth. . . . [showed] a change of 55 per cent in one year . . ."[2] An official of this city's Union High School district considered that "50 to 60 per cent turnover during one school year is normal"; in 1960–61, he reported "more than 70 per cent change" although three nearby high schools showed "annual turnovers only of 12 to 29 per cent."[1]

California neighborhoods also often disappear as freeways or industrial structures push through; or they change character, as when tract housing overwhelms citrus communities, and when Negroes occupy large sections that were formerly white or Japanese. Teachers remain briefly at particular schools and also in the profession. Negroes arrive from the rural South and from urban professions and industrial occupations. In July, 1962, the *Los Angeles Times* described Los Angeles as containing "the fastest-growing Negro community in the country . . .", its 500,000 members ranking fourth in population after the Negro communities of New York, Philadelphia, and Detroit, being fairly rich in individual earnings, offering a great market where virtually none had existed twenty years before.[3]

Many Negro parents place high demands on the schools. As schools lack guidance in the changed atmosphere, desegregation and integration tax their skills. Mexican-American teachers and social workers wonder how to remain themselves and yet profit from opportunities heretofore available only to persons of dominant status. Some Los Angeles Nisei wonder if the delinquency cropping out in their group means cultural breakdown or Americanization. California teachers ask, "What are the desirable values? Should we compel all children to remain in school regardless of their wishes? Should we guide all children into academic courses? Does our culture offer suitable standards for pupils in the space age?"

Similar changes and frustrations afflict the Atlantic coast. Since 1957, New York City's Board of Education has provided special teaching and social services for Negro and Puerto Rican children and their parents, both in and outside of classrooms.[4] Charges against school personnel of showing bias are investigated and the information is used in job ratings.[5] Special services for minorities include educators' use of Spanish, enriched programs in health, guidance, welfare, and after-school events, busing children out of segregated areas on school business, and work with parents individually at home and in groups at schools, clinics, and elsewhere. Teachers are recruited for training as "community coordinators," and work in liaison with wealthier groups that fringe segregated areas. Educational services are designed for the potentially gifted among the minorities, for normal pupils, and for those retarded or disturbed. The special services are viewed as a proper adaptation to a changing society. The published report on the services [4] states bluntly that residential segregation, perpetuated by real estate agreements and general prejudice, determines *de facto* segregation of schools so that the outlook promises continued "ethnic homogeneity" [6] below senior high school, except for permitted transfers. Joint planning by New York City's school officials and Housing Authority, to coordinate building of schools and homes, becomes invalidated through sudden heavy shifts of population. The report, however, expresses clearly the goal of achieving school integration through promoting teamwork among schools, minority parents, and the larger community.

In California, educators may be less aware of culture *differences* than of the conspicuous *movements* of people and the linked instability of ties and neighborhoods. Teachers speak as if cultural variety, though "frustrating," were a tangible they could name and use, whereas "transiency" means that even slight familiarities will go. In New York, government workers reinterpreted transiency to mean establishment of a new cultural element and applied themselves accordingly. On April 10, 1960, *The New York Times* reported that "City Staffs Turn to Use of Spanish; 6,000 employees learn it as second language" because one-tenth of all New Yorkers were then speaking it.

Cannot the "apathy" attributed to minorities at school also be reinterpreted as a culture-linked symptom and therefore approached differently? Louis Alexander [7] tells how prospects soared in Texas for segregated, underachieving Mexicans when, in the summer of 1960, 12,000 such youngsters of varying ages received preschool training in English so that the following year they completed the primary grade and did as well as unsegregated, English-speaking children. This made a record in Texas history; it was "change" by a new rapport between the ranked culture groups and it forecast spiraling changes in education, employment, housing, recreation. Research into college students' "apathy" finds it actually meaningful in college behavior, as "a protective reaction to the stresses of what might otherwise be a too rapid acculturation process." [8] Dorothy Barclay also seeks the dynamics masked by the word "apathy." She asks if the findings of apathy in a study covering 15,000 American high-school and college students do not mirror some prevailing state among adults. [9]

Characteristic dilemmas about the apathy of pupils were reviewed at a modern high school in Southern California during day-long meetings with successive groups of administrators, counselors, and teachers. The schools' pupils totaled 1,750, 14.4 per cent of whom were Mexicans, 3.3 per cent American Indians, and 1.2 per cent Orientals. The Orientals offered no problem and therefore received no attention. Questions centered on Mexicans—this meant on teachers' "frustrated" views of Mexicans, not on what Mexicans meant by their "apathetic" ways. Bare notice was taken of the Indians whose apathy was rated abysmal, but these pupils, who traveled to school from reservation homes, were censured for insisting on their tribal identity despite Spanish surnames. Some teachers demanded, "After all, what difference is there between Indians and Mexicans?" Two counselors described an incident supposed to reveal antagonism between the two peoples but the telling rather revealed the speakers' confusions: "Two Indian pupils were attacked by about forty Mexicans, who stole money and clothes from them because they were Indian." Questioning elicited that the mothers of the two victimized pupils were actually Mexicans of American birth and the fathers were California Indians who, in the narration, "tried to pass for Mexican [as they] . . . took Mexican family names." The counselors made their surmises without questioning the parents of the attacked pupils, though the parents had visited them to say they were moving to another town.

Few teachers actually know about life on an American Indian reservation or the changes from its backward modes when Indians moved to cities. Tribesmen occupy lowly stations both in modern Mexico and in the United States, but Mexican tradition also fosters a cultish mystique about "Indianism" (or, *indianismo*). Mexicans assert that they constitute a special physical type they call *mestizo*, which anthropologists call a "stabilized subrace," composed of Spaniards and other Europeans mixed with Mexico's aborigines. In Mexicans' speech today, belittlement of mestizos and Indians often appears; but this does not contradict the nation's traditional pride in pre-Conquest Indian cultures and personalities. American Indians in public schools come from tribes long embittered by government policies of segregation and prohibition of native speech at schools. In the Southwest, Mexicans and reservation Indians may experience similar hardships, but the cultures are distinct, and similar Spanish surnames no more indicate kinship than do English and Scottish surnames of Britons and of West African Negroes.

At the meetings, a particular dimension was given to the concept of apathy by teachers' carping against the Spanish conversations of the Mexicans among themselves, specifically during the pupils' free hours. Because teachers expressed fears of "being talked about" in the unknown tongue, they were told that a mother tongue was felt to express the speaker's true self, and for Mexican-Americans it remained a property that withstood, even defied, Anglo prejudice. A young Mexican-American teaching Spanish at the school, from which he had been graduated, rose to observe in accented words, looking around at his colleagues, "In my day, California schools were segregated. So I never learned to express myself adequately in English. Now at home I need to use Spanish with my wife and kids." The others listened quietly. He continued, "In our school we have the third generation of Mexicans. One of our graduates, Al Mendez, is police chief of Y town."

The principal interrupted to exclaim, revealing more than he knew, "Funny! He's a Mexican. And in Y they don't allow a *Negro* to stay overnight! The one Negro working there, a bootblack, must return to Monrovia every evening."

Anglo-Californians view Mexicans as likable and tractable if subordinate partners in a joint history, whereas Negroes are outsiders. Also, Mexicans are attractive culturally and racially, despite their low status, whereas Negroes are recent and alarming arrivals who are considered "aggressive" in and out of school. Similarly, the Atlantic coast prefers Negroes to Puerto Ricans, Cubans, and Indians.[10] Mexicans, like Europeans and social scientists, call American Negroes "Anglos" or Yanks. This particular school had a single Negro pupil, a mentally retarded boy of seventeeen whom the faculty called "Angel" but whom Mexicans called "Nigger" until "we made them stop." Here again, faculty members probably projected interpretations. Mexicans call their swarthy intimates by Spanish terms meaning black, Negro, Indian (*prieto, negro, indio*) just as they call fairer ones by comparable terms (*huero, colorado, blanco*). All are nicknames intended to convey strong banter. But teachers grow upset over unquiet or unapathetic conduct among Mexicans, as was the case when a Mexican-American pupil charged his city government with "race prejudice" because it withheld promised compensation to Mexican families deprived of their dwellings by urban redevelopment.

In teachers' minds, Mexicans' alleged "apathy" and "bilingualism" are linked, and the turn of talk at the high school was no exception. The strange logic was: "They can't learn English because of Spanish and they're too indifferent to abandon Spanish." But a young Anglo-American teacher of English cheerily tilted at this stereotype. Given the chance, he rose to say, even elderly Mexicans study English now and show no handicap attributable to Spanish, for success lies in the teaching. His night class for the foreign-born included thirty-two Mexicans, chiefly men, about twenty-two of them older than sixty. He found them as enthusiastic as the European immigrants Leo Rosten celebrated in stories of H*Y*M*A*N K*A*P*L*A*N. He, on the other hand, was studying Spanish. "I'm not worried that the kids might be making snide remarks," he said. "I even throw out a

Spanish word to bring them in line, and they're as pleased as if I'd given them a present."

The principal reported the discussions in a bulletin he circulated among his faculty, giving his own slants in phrasing and selection of items. Often his versions were unexpected. He reported:

The governing fact as to whether [Spanish conversation] should be permitted is whether . . . it is pertinent in a particular situation. Groups of students speaking Spanish during the lunch hour . . . are not in any way hurting the school program . . . [though this would be] completely inappropriate in physics class . . . Anglos often assume that people are talking about them when they speak low . . . or in a foreign language. This is usually a false assumption. Often students are merely repeating things from home . . . the foreign language [Spanish] holds some of the interest [for] . . . Latin-American . . . students . . . [that] pig-Latin and other codes [do for other students].

Another aspect of Mexicans' "apathy" was advanced when teachers developed familiar protests that Mexican-Americans grow "jealous" of their successful fellows. Mexicans often agree, but not because of "apathy," as will be explained. The teachers complained that "Mexican boys with superior IQs are beaten up by other Mexicans. They don't seem to want to get ahead!" Two counselors described a "stratification of cultures" between the Mexicans "going Anglo" and the "apathetic" ones who opposed them. "When a Mexican student crosses the line [toward Anglicization], there's no returning. It's a breaking point. . . . When Mexicans join athletic teams, they have gone Anglo and no longer speak Spanish, or speak very little. When Negro and Mexican students join teams, you know they are assimilated. And then their parents attend PTA meetings."

Teachers seem to fear jealousy, with its malice and loss of confidence. More important to Mexicans, there is conveyed in jealousy, besides, recognition of a man's worth, especially along defiant *macho* lines. Teachers say that Mexicans should "back up" the successful, Anglicized members of their group, meaning applaud them in ways that teachers approve of, and not try to topple them. But Mexicans have their own exemplars, in the *caudillo* (leader), as dramatized for the world by Cuba's Fidel Castro, and in the bullfighting *matador* hailed as *número uno* or *el único* (number one, the only one). Throughout the Hispanic world, "number one" struggles to maintain supremacy against rivals—a system that, to our teachers, appears based on jealousy.

The principal's bulletin gave this version of the discussions:

No Mexican thinks he is inferior. . . . The fact that the Mexican must learn the Anglo life symbolizes . . . that he has been "conquered" . . . bringing about emotional reactions that may appear unexplained and abnormal. . . . Leadership among Latin-American students tends to change very rapidly from individual to individual. They are more apt to have a group of leaders than any one outstanding leader. . . . Fighting among Mexicans is often play-acting for show, even if physical injury results. Sometimes it expresses resentment at people attempting to change their cultural patterns . . . or it may express class distinctions brought from Mexico. . . . [Jealous] criticism of the good student or the conformist among Mexicans is probably no different than among other groups.

Many teachers regarded as genetic racial traits the indifference of Mexican boys toward team sports, their frequent refusals to use the school pool, the reluctance of the Mexican girls to undress for school showers, and explanations of both sexes that they are concerned about protecting their coiffures. Such supposed racial attributes were equated with irrationality, a general disinterest in worthwhile things, and inferiority. More to the point, however, was the Southwest's historic discrimination, a bitter background to Mexicans' general mistrust of authorities.[11]

Dynamics of the supposedly apathetic behavior pattern may actually pit Mexicans' traditionally prized individualism against the schools' valued "spirit of cooperation." There seem to be ways, however, of compromising these opposing Mexican and Anglo values. Thus, the vice-principal, who offered scented soap to her junior high-school girls for bathing, won them through their recognition of her "heart" and "sympathy"—simpatía is a valued quality of "feeling with," as the vice-principal guessed from long familiarity with Mexicans. "Ever since there's been no problem," she said, "and now they use even open gang showers as well as the stalls." She had touched the stimulus to a conditioned response. Yet even she often joined other Anglo teachers in regarding Mexicans as big-eyed pets or as pathetic, strange beings out of Steinbeck tales in whose listless lives the teachers might evangelize.

Mexican pupils sensed the element of patronage; hence, some boys said they did not like her. To such teachers, Mexicans are eternal fruitpickers; the increasing number of industrial, white-collar, and professional workers are "exceptions." Teachers seemed never to have heard of even celebrated publications about Southwest Mexicans [12] and repeatedly asked why Mexicans considered teachers and other gringos to be "prejudiced against them." The few Mexican-American teachers are hardly better oriented but some seek to define for themselves their exposed position.[13]

If the teachers evinced surprise that the behavior of their Mexican pupils had meaning and worth within the ancestral experience, they were also unprepared to realize that even these Mexicans often acted the same as Anglos. To an educator's question, "Why do most Mexican boys wear khaki pants?," the response was, "Don't Anglo boys wear khaki pants?" An administrator declared, "I hadn't thought of looking at Anglos!" To the educator's regular question, "Why do Mexican-Americans isolate themselves from the rest of the student body?" meaning, why do they cluster together? the rejoinder was, "Why not?" Having lived together all their lives, these youngsters probably saw no reason to disperse. And there were reinforcing cultural factors. Besides, having all experienced segregation and other evidences of prejudice, they might well distrust *gringos*.

The principal's bulletin solemnly reported:

Many of the remarks and actions by Latin-American students, which are taken by Anglos as vulgar, like whistling at girls, are not intended to be. They are simply traditional compliments to the physical attractiveness of the girls. It was noted humorously that the only courting males who did not whistle in some way are subhuman ones who can't. . . . Procedure for handling this should be based on teaching these people what is appropriate under different circumstances, rather than a belligerent attack on the problem. . . .

Obviously Mexicans, or any other group, must be told what behavior is tabu in today's society of the "middle-class American." And teachers must be assured that the boys were not intent on misleading girls but rather on showing off as *machos*, meaning, as culturally normal males.

Teachers were concerned about the domestic relationships of Mexican-American parents and the bearing these have on pupils' "motivation," or attitudes in school. The principal's bulletin observed:

The Mexican-American family is faced with the conflict of Anglos telling [a man's] wife that she is as good as he is, and besides, that girls of the family have rights virtually equal to those of the father. This is foreign to most Latin-American families. For the Latin-American father is ruler of his family no matter how low in the social scale he might be. He has the virtual power of life or death over other members of the family. While the Mexican-American seldom engages in major premeditated crimes, there are frequent instances of fights, beatings . . . that result from emotional outburst. This is partially the result of the male's position in the family.

Women in Mexican culture . . . begin to assume some authority after middle age but until that time the man may beat his family or not, may leave his family or not, may pay the bills or not, etc. Men's erratic behavior is aggravated by the fact that in the southwestern United States a woman often gets a job when a man can't because of membership in a minority.

When a parent comes to school, he often expects to "be blasted" for something his child has done. This happens in their own dealings, especially with schools of the "old country." It is difficult for many of them to understand [the permissive] American philosophy and practice. More Latin-American parents should be encouraged to participate in school activities.

The bulletin, containing the principal's own language and understanding of the discussions, omitted some important facets. One such was the fact that teachers had agreed that the parent "expects to be blasted" at school because this *is* what happens. Another was that teachers should try instead to reward or encourage the parent with some agreeable news or activity. Parents too learn in the hard partnership with educators, particularly their place in the educators' scheme of things, whether they attend conferences or never "cooperate." What parents learn to approve, to resent, to show or conceal, children sense and pass on to teachers in all modes of conduct, including that labeled "motivation."

In all schools and education circles, teachers conceptualize "motivation" in pupils as desirable or necessary, assume that its meaning is clear, and are distressed when they think it is absent. However, adopting a "motivation" for school, like cultivating pride or self-respect, might well be an effort of supererogation, possible in fortunate circumstances. Yet, teachers measure pupils by rigid yardsticks of "over- or undermotivation," the latter charge being shameful, the former being possibly suspect. Criticizing this in 1962, the president of the Los Angeles Board of Education reportedly said, "There has been too much emphasis on motivation and not enough on results." [14]

Examining motivation as a cultural syndrome or diagnostic entity, it seems to be idealized in the schools as a self-starting mechanism or as aggressive responses of individuals to school learning, reinforced by home training in initiative, competition, persistence, and making decisions. The goals of this motivation are socially approved by home, school, and community. The syndrome flowers as a paramount commitment of the individual to strive for himself and to win community rewards, even at the cost of family and other personal ties. To soft-pedal a drive to serve oneself merely to spare a relative or a friend is belittled as "sentimental." The Anglo proverb says, "Each man for himself."

However, to a Mexican, his paramount commitments are rather to the family, to the church, and to classic personalities like the *caudillo* and *señor patrón*. No individual cares to break from his family but prefers to be accompanied by them; this favors the abuse of nepotism on the one hand, and the strength of group loyalty on the other. Some idea of spiritual and fleshly community prevails among kinsmen, so that relatives may serve for one another as needed; the concepts are so strong as to withstand exploitation. In East Los Angeles' *barrios*, siblings may call each other *mi carnal* (my flesh), and a friend is *mi cuate* (my twin) or *compadre* (godfather of my child). The services and terms show "respect" for family and religious feelings. All personal assertions must be within such group relationships. How does this match our individualistic "motivation," justified by the proverbial notion that "God helps those that help themselves"? It does not. Further, segregation denies to minorities opportunities for learning our syndrome of "motivation," and schools penalize its absence.

The cultural gap made the efforts of a young counselor incomprehensible to a twelve-year-old Mexican-American boy in a junior-high school, as the Claremont observer saw. The child's rosy, dark-eyed face, curly hair, and enchanting smile might have been a Botticelli angel's but he was a proven mischief, regularly joining an older brother and sister in fights. The counselor had summoned him to her desk to take him to task for habitual tardiness. Gently stating the case, the counselor then gave him a chance to decide to agree with her that his lateness was caused by the distant location of his locker. "Isn't that so?" she prodded. The boy looked dazed when he nodded, as though acceding blindly. The counselor pursued, "So what shall we do?" He shrugged, truly apathetic. The counselor leaned toward the child, speaking anxiously, interrupting herself frequently with "What shall we do?" She thought she was coaxing him to decide. But, eyes steadily averted, the boy met each question with only a vague shrug. Finally the young woman proposed that "we" try to be prompt for a trial period of a week. At the end she forewent the "we" and put it frankly, "Will you do it?" Thereupon he nodded smartly, leaped up, and raced through the door like a gazelle. The boy understood better than his educators what threats the "we" concealed.

The counselor asked the Claremont observer for an evaluation. Listening to it, she grew restless and finally left for home. Neither she nor the boy had understood each other until the end of the interview when she had indicated a decision. "But I wanted *him* to make it!" she had repeated, worried that he showed no purpose and that she was forced to appear "authoritarian." Yet decision making was not the duty of youngsters in a patriarchal society like that of the Mexicans; the child's duty or proper "motivation" was to obey commands and to carry on appropriately between them. Indeed, the Mexican's respectful response to a call from another, at every stage of life, is the conventional *"Mande?,"* meaning "Command me?" Coaxing the boy to offer his own plan for school to a school official was unrealistic. The counselor might better have sat back firmly, like a confident matriarch, than to have wheedled and thus raised questions in his mind about her proper role. His confusion about her redounded in confusion about himself, a state that might set in motion the *macho* drive maturing in boys of his age.

This was an illustration of "cultural factors in counseling." Further illustration was the counselor's fear that the cultural analysis held criticism of her competence. She wanted to appear "permissive, reasonable, tolerant of a minority child and his possible trauma," as she said. She did in fact appear this way to her colleagues and the Claremont observer, but her desired message could not reach the boy because he lacked the educators' background and hence their "motivation." Something else reached him which the counselor missed because *she* lacked background in Mexican experience. During the following months, the boy remained an enigma, and his teacher applied the labels of "bilingualism" and "low motivation to cooperate"; she said she was disappointed.

Many other teachers fail to see problems troubling pupils' culturally varied personalities; chiefly they formulate deductions about "the child" in general. Some believe that "children get excited at school before rain" and entrust solutions to change of weather. In the same static manner they request a formula to "handle Mexicans' fear of discrimination." It is, of course, vital to guide Mexicans and all oppressed groups toward opportunities as carefully as the physically handicapped are taught their needed skills. Some teachers resist the mental exercise required in the new viewpoint. At a high-school meeting, teachers resisted by citing the number of Mexican dropouts at the end of the junior year, which halved the number of Mexicans continuing to senior year. Yet this is a considerable increase in the number of those who remain to graduate, as is readily confirmed by comparing current graduation lists with those of ten years or five years before.[15]

At a conference of whites planning for California Negroes, university educators trapped themselves in stereotypes. A notable incident was the reaction to a suggestion to consult a local California specialist in Negro affairs, himself a Negro college professor and community leader. The chairman exclaimed, "I never thought of asking a Negro!" Nor did the suggestion go further.

At a large California high school, attended chiefly by lower-class whites, teachers yearned to enforce "our middle-class school pattern" but feared to ask "difficult" pupils to explain themselves. Teachers had observed pupils talking out of turn in class, neglecting homework, kissing on campus; and their conclusion, expressed at a meeting with the Claremont observer, was that they were helpless before "the low middle-class Anglo children who just don't know how to behave."

Fears and stereotyped notions block insights and favor rigid practices. To better this, teachers were advised by Claremont to go so far as to play-act or simulate motions of interest in pupils, practicing these until the time came when the motions would arise spontaneously. Some effective motions included asking pupils and parents, in friendship, the meanings of puzzling acts, and listening to responses carefully and without punitive intent. Though pupils' and parents' responses may begin only slowly, a teacher's concern induces an atmosphere of empathy which advances comprehension on both sides.

By permission of a high-school principal, and in his presence, the Claremont observer questioned an Okie father about the problematic teenage son on whose account he was repeatedly summoned to school, and also about each of his other children. The man snarled answers, though heretofore he had glibly evaded the school people. Now the principal and dean listened astounded to the man's picture, defensive and dull enough, of home discipline and the other children's school histories. They were taken aback less because the tales were unusual than because they came from a parental source. That is, they heard an outsider (as teachers regard parents) talk about his own world, instead of hearing themselves utter platitudes and issue scoldings.

Teachers cannot call the tune for society or hold pupils and parents culpable for shortcomings in pedagogy. They can make genuine efforts to understand, and permit those approached to feel competent and useful. Pupils, like teachers, respond only to the meanings they glean from spoken and unspoken sources. Our American love of profuse "verbalization," to use the educators' term, is not shared by all peoples, for instance, American Indians. Our folklore even stereotypes the laconic Indian; he is so depicted in Oliver LaFarge's Navajo and Apache stories. In one biting story by LaFarge, a white woman visits the family of her Apache sweetheart, a young air force veteran, on the family's reservation.[16] Introduced, she sits silently, confused and alarmed by the strangeness. Soon the Indian mother comments in Apache, and laughs lightly. Her son, pleased, explains to the visitor: "She says—well, you see, a while back one of the government women, some kind of social worker, came here, and she came in talking her head off before anybody had time to get used to her. You came in quietly, like an Indian. So she says, 'This one has good manners!'

"The [Apache] woman laughed again, 'Yess, not walk in talkin'.'"

Teachers must adapt to such switches in conduct and values. Mexicans, however, act in more familiar ways, including talkativeness, especially in their homes where a visitor automatically stirs obligations of stylized amiability. Oriental-Americans may be less talkative, but show cordiality. American Negroes respond in usual American ways, having adapted for centuries to the pulse of our national existence.

At present, teachers report that they feel happiest in school neighborhoods whose values they share.[17] They feel safe in assuming that "motivation" and "apathy" are simple, clear polar contrasts, behaviorisms tied to pupils' good or bad intentions at will. Their contentment does not always mean that teachers are most effective in such neighborhoods. The nature, structure, and consequences of teaching relationships have yet to be clarified; they are not known any better than, for example, the import of "motivation."

To illustrate, a Southern California town is admired by an elementary-school principal for being "upper-middle class, judging by the price range on homes." Besides, all parents known to this principal have finished college. Accordingly, the mothers, "with free time and not enough to do," urge children and teachers to greater motivation and achievement. The pupils are inducted early into adult habits and values, such as country-club life, cocktails, and travel abroad; they may appear worldlier than their teachers.

At school in a less pretentious middle-class town, the Claremont observer met the "hostess" of that week, a member of a seventh grade "bright" class. This poised, heavily lipsticked moppet of twelve escorted visitors around the school reciting benevolent, correct phrases about mother and stepfather, father and stepmother, her "guardians" and baby sitters, all of whom she "loved." Her teacher, a middle-aged divorcée with a handicapped daughter, later confided how "boy crazy" this hostess was, clearly motivated toward marriage. The teacher boasted of the one Jewish child in class, who impressed her with his sophistication, "always coming up with something original, humorous, or ironical." She called on him to "show" the observer, so the boy told about "neighbors owning a dog so nervous that they took him to the psychiatrist." When the teacher assigned a written exercise in "topical sentences" to the class, and called on individuals to read theirs, he read, "The sports car is the best invention since the motorcycle, and should be long, low, and red." This was certainly worldlier than other pupils' topical sentences, which emerged as, "Yo-yo is the greatest."

"School can be fun." "We will have a party on Sunday." The teacher completely ignored the one Oriental and two Mexican girls in class. It appeared that their presence was inadvertently due to school zoning. The teacher explained privately that the other children's parents would not want their youngsters to associate with them, poorly dressed as they were.

Yet schools are expected to guide all the young "equally." The smokescreen of "motivation" does not obscure the realities for all educators. The cadet Spanish teachers' program [18] was one that rose to the responsibility of sociocultural conflicts and fostered competence among recently hostile and indifferent (or "unmotivated") Mexican pupils. A California educator who observed this program said he marveled at the poise of a dark girl cadet who faced the class easily, scolded an Anglo campus hero for sloppy English, and drilled him and others in the usually censored Spanish language. The educator exclaimed, "This is the only school doing anything specifically for Mexicans!" A notable result was that the first to volunteer as a cadet, a boy, was the next year elected president of the student council; and in the program's third year, a girl cadet was elected a member of the student council. A teacher in charge of training cadets stated, "It's worked! The program has integrated the students!" The principal was confident that these young Mexican-Americans were learning "to integrate with the community" through his teachers' special work, and would prove this "when they grew up and took jobs."

But some educators admit that they are personally outraged by the divergent ways of life and feel futile and embittered by "lower-class" misconduct, for this lies beyond the values and logic of correct motivation. The principal of an elementary school in a lower middle-class town spoke bitterly to the Claremont observer of a mother who plagued him with her immoralities and ridicule of the school's efforts; he even drove the observer some distance to point out the woman's large yellow house whose new coat of paint, he complained, was paid for with welfare funds.

"This woman goes along on Public Assistance (funds) with her legitimate and illegitimate children," he said, "producing children so as not to work. When she decides to pressure Public Assistance to repair her refrigerator, she keeps the children out of school and laughs at us. Her husband serves time in a federal pen. Her admitted common-law husband, a Mexican, is in and out of the house. She has two infants by him, she's a trollop with others, and we believe she's seduced her eighteen-year-old son, now in the Navy. Two younger sons—they're called Richard and Dick—talk about her incest with their brother as 'wrestling'; and their brother boasts of it within hearing of our school people. She's a beast. She and I have it out about once a year, yelling on the telephone. I 'graduate' her children by letter, since they never attend. They'd be good kids if they did attend school. I'm sick of the mess."

The woman was unique in this principal's conventional experience. Otherwise his school did not have real problems, he guessed, only annoyances, like absences and no lunch money or shoes.

Another principal deliberately set up models for the conduct of all at his intermediate school in a low-income white community. He scheduled teachers' visits to homes each fall so that his faculty would know the backgrounds of their pupils. He thus hoped to compensate partly for confusions arising from the 25 per cent annual pupil turnover. He devised ingenious programs involving pupils' families and teachers, which "motivated" boys to join cookery classes and girls to join carpentry classes, and guests to attend both occasionally. He sought and hired as teachers a young Nisei man, a young Puerto Rican man, and a Negro couple, "without repercussions from pupils or parents!" One noon hour with the Claremont observer, he pointed to a cluster of Negro, Nisei, and Irish teachers talking gaily in a corridor and commented, "Isn't it fine for pupils to *see* this happen daily before their eyes instead of just reading about it? Now they know integration works." He also rented a house to the Negro couple in a good neighborhood which caused no complaint except one man's feeble threat to petition against it.

Some junior college teachers feel at a loss with the ordinary mass of white American students and talk about gaps of interest and values separating them, as did the teacher of English literature quoted before (see p. 34). Even at excellent four-year colleges, students themselves say they are "bored" with literature assignments, from Beowulf to Faulkner; even bright undergraduates only vaguely recall Shakespeare as a vehicle for a glamorous actor. Would this indifference have been expressed also by students from other cultures, such as the preindustrialized Latin ones? The works studied in the junior college course mentioned (p. 34) included tragedies of Aeschylus, Euripides, Shakespeare, and Ibsen; novels of Galsworthy, F. Scott Fitzgerald, and Faulkner; and science fiction. These tragedies and novels, like the life of many preindustrial societies, emphasize humanistic ideas of tragedy and sacredness, and insist on personal respect, honor, passion, obedience, forgiveness, spirituality, and leadership. Most of these values fade rapidly in industrialized middle-class America, along with the "great man" theory of history. Perhaps this suggests why some literature teachers, as well as European observers, berate Americans for emotional immaturity.

Surely it is impossible to appraise a person's interests and motivation apart from his social background and tradition. The personalities of Shakespeare's aging King Lear and tragic Prince Hamlet, besides Shakespeare's wisdom and poetry, must be nurtured by a particular style of life. In Shakespeare's England, and still in Western Europe and Latin America, this life style builds close relationships around paternal authority, elaborates them through specialized conduct in both sexes and different generations—conduct sorted as virtue, honor, and their opposites, for example—and extends them past death through divine punishment and redemption. But today's American middle-class "equality" means considerable leveling in behavior of the sexes, the generations, and many social groups, besides considerable secularizing of all life's aspects.

Do American students generally seek release from tensions of home and kin, as recorded in much of our current fiction? In the comics and sport pages and in scientific fantasy, do students feel freed from the family's demands? Our own earlier periods, like many other lands even now, have had extended and complex family units belonging to stable communities whose intimacies provided diverse emotional targets. But today our people's intimacies are confined to the small family of parents and children whose simple organization and sparse numbers offer only few emotional targets.

The lives of our minorities still retain forms of family and community life that resemble our own of earlier periods, though they are being modified by prevailing American ways. But the schools are concerned more exclusively and urgently with problems of classroom achievement raised by desegregation and integration. Thus, one session of an educators' annual regional conference in Southern California was organized for teachers of nine municipal junior high schools and three senior high schools under the title, "Cultural and Ethnic Influences in the Schools." As usual the teachers wanted to know about Mexicans and Negroes, respectively the "old-timers" and postwar "newcomers" in the region. Besides the universal complaints, teachers asked the newer, recurring questions about "What right have we to change minorities?" "What have we a right to change in educating minorities?" "Must minorities become Americanized?" Possibly there were deeper intents prompting these general questions. Some teachers inquired, in more practical phrases, "How do the Mexican and Negro really see school?" "Which of their standards are 'good' by average American criteria?" "Is conformity the same for all cultures?" "Should we press for conformity to our standards?"

No urban people, including segregated minorities, fails to be touched by the larger society. Therefore a pertinent practical question is "Does America profit from the subcultures she contains?" Our civilization follows universal processes of culture in absorbing selectively the influences at and within its boundaries. Details in the processes vary locally, and are important there. Proverbially, China converts her conquerors—Manchu, Japanese, European. Other cultural heritages, like the high Amerindian ones of Central and South America, have disintegrated under conquest. Our national life "borrows" and "acculturates," in anthropological terms, foreign styles and details of dress (kimono, pajamas), foods (sphaghetti, pizza, tamale), vocabulary (piano, kindergarten, canoe, kibitzer, luau), music and dance (opera, ballet, flamenco, samba, conga, calypso, ballads), regional names (California, Texas, New Orleans, New York), principles of law (Louisiana's Code Napoléon, the Southwest's Spanish civil law), architecture (bungalow, mansion, ranch house, Georgian residence, Spanish mission form); and in science, business, politics, and religion we share an internationally based culture. If cosmopolitan America absorbs from others, the provincial sources also change. This is inevitable, so that even worldly, educated immigrants lose skill in the foreign mother tongue after a time; correspondingly they display traits of Americanization.

Among our acculturated borrowings are modes of ordering group relationships. Although the whole Western world clearly orders groups into three social classes, we stress one "middle class" of "equal" Americans and allocate the leftovers to divers "minorities" that sit out a kind of social purgatory. Teachers' uncertainties about "changing minorities" and facilitating their "conformity to our standards" reflect the present design that ranks minorities below the middle class. Consistent with this implied class structure, teachers often conceptualize "two classes of Mexicans," as noted before, meaning the prosperous, Anglicized ones living at good addresses versus the many others who live in slum *colonias* on unskilled workers' earnings, speak Spanish, and practice folk cures and magic. These two classes, however, are still contained within the Mexican minority; and America remains explicitly and in principle a one-class society. A European or British class structure, or even the surviving, antiquated class structure of our deep South, tolerates foreigners as "outsiders" until they absorb class tags which fit them in niches defined by education, family, speech, wealth, work, and religion. But modern America lacks the social concept of "outsider" and all admitted to residence are potential Americans, "free and equal" in the promise of the Constitution. The presence of freedmen after the Civil War drew the issues of civil rights and produced the compromise status of "minority."

A class of Anglo, Mexican, and Negro high-school students asked the Claremont observer to discuss their urgent questions. Some were, "How do Negroes feel when the teacher discusses their problems right in their presence?" "Why don't the people want the Negroes to go to the same school? We're all of the same creed except for our color." "How would you answer the question that the United States is a country of equality?" "How many people of the South are actually opposed to segregation?" "Was [Arkansas Governor] Faubus' stand against integration for political reasons or sincere?" "How do Negroes, from sections where integration is no problem, react to the situation in the South?" "What do whites and Negroes of the North, and Negroes of the North and South feel about integration?" [19]

Later a young teacher described "the lack of suitable materials for instructing pupils in sophomore and senior English. The available books present middle-class morals which are completely meaningless to the youths." This raised a problem of communication, she said, quite separate from the problems of "low motivation, low measured IQs, or language difficulties . . ."

Some individual teachers take warmly to Mexicans and Negroes, like their "motivations," and show pleasure in working with them, perhaps because they appear exotic. Describing an elementary school whose pupils are 80 per cent Mexican, and which is traditionally segregated for Mexicans, an experienced young teacher wrote that he loved "the good old school."

It is a family, a vast network of connections who've been neighbors for more than three generations. . . . They turn events on school grounds, like the *cinco de mayo* [celebrating Mexican national independence and victory over the French at Puebla on May 5, 1862] into an all-Mexican fiesta, with *mariachis* [groups of singers playing musical instruments] and typical foods. These make Anglos and Negroes feel like outsiders—and it shouldn't be, since we're all Americans. At the last *cinco de mayo* celebration, Negroes stood around impatiently waiting for "the music" to start. I said the *mariachis* were music but they said no, that wasn't music, they wanted rock n' roll. Anglos felt the same.

[Unlike the stereotype of apathy, his Mexican pupils all want homework.]
They like school because things happen there! . . . Juanito is a delightful boy, he works and works. . . . My present class is a good one, and many do beautiful writing in their weekly themes. There's one 141 IQ in

class though I don't put much credence in ratings. Last year I had a class of clowns; their IQs were lower but they too loved school. . . .

Mexican parents do not attend PTA and hang all over one's neck like Anglo mothers at the other [middle-class] school, just to push their children ahead; but they know more about what happens at school than we do, through their children and the grapevine. . . . I don't find bilingualism a handicap, I myself talk Spanish occasionally when it puts a point across.[20] I can see no difference between achievements of these [unofficially segregated] children and the Anglos at the other school, where I taught four years.

The Mexican kids love the fruit-picking, and in their compositions they write regretting that they no longer go because their fathers have steady jobs now in industry. Prosperity is siphoning off our better families to superior neighborhoods. They're getting to be just like Anglos, can't wait to have a new car each year. . . . The children are honest; we leave supply rooms open and nothing is ever stolen. Some of our Mexican families are dirt poor but the children show up at school clean, even immaculate, and they do good work. . . . The school seems to attract creative teachers.

The two-year sequence with one city's elementary-school teachers, mentioned at the outset of this chapter, which related cultural factors to teaching, was introduced to improve accomplishments of Mexican and Negro pupils and parents. Ethnic enrollments at participating schools were roughly 51 per cent Mexican, 40 per cent Negro, and 9 per cent Anglo (white). At one school, Negro enrollment rose from 5 per cent to 15 per cent of the total during the first five months of the school year. Negro enrollment at another school rose from half of the predominant Mexican enrollment to equal it. Other communities said the Negro influx was "coming out of our ears." School boards were confronted with the dilemma of building schools to meet needs of soaring Negro numbers and thus appearing segregated, or of refusing to build and thus avoiding inadvertently segregated arrangements and the headaches of recruiting teachers for all-Negro classes. Some young teachers threatened to "crack up if I have to teach Mexican and Negro children, because I've never met them before."

Answers were sought to complaints such as these which the city's curriculum director recorded on tapes during exploratory interviews with teachers: "At R school, Mexicans don't come to PTA and attendance is mostly colored." "Children's irregular class attendance and truancy are due to parents' lack of interest rather than to true illness. It's possible that parents may have great worries and so do not notice children's failure to rise in the morning." "Parents' methods of control differ from our's, so they don't respect us." "We need education of parents to get their cooperation. Children don't read partly because parents don't. The lower levels of Anglo white families really want low standards of work." "Low-income parents say they have no clothes for the kids, so the kids stay home though they know perfectly well the school keeps a clothes closet. One Negro family kept its children out eight or nine weeks." "Our school has an 85 per cent Negro enrollment. These youngsters feel it's O.K. for them to fight. We use sociodrama to settle this. But results are only skin deep. At home they'll fight if somebody says 'chicken.' The parents say, fight back, trip them. We have real frustration there. The kids must be confused between school and home." "They're so limited in vocabulary. We've got to explain over and over. They're lazy in speech, just listen to their parents' way of talk. It's the perfect speech pattern for their subculture. They're slow in all movements, even in play." "Now, the high IQ kids are real quick."

To demonstrate that motivation and mutual understanding can be tapped and influenced, though hidden or supposed absent, the first year of the sequence was begun by considering the significant persons in teaching and learning—the teachers, pupils, and parents. Problems were reported at meetings by the school faculties and the Claremont observer led discussions so as to elicit cultural interpretations and solutions based on cultural knowledge. The teachers applied themselves to practical goals of discovering (1) how to induce Mexican parents, seemingly unreachable, to confer with teachers about their children, and (2) how to persuade Mexicans, who avoid school circles, to attend PTA meetings. Negroes, on the other hand, were relatively aggressive and accessible; at one school an able Negro woman newcomer was bidding strongly for a PTA office.

The curriculum director summarized the cultural recommendations as a guide for participating teachers, principals, and educators, charting these points:

1. People of Mexican background are accustomed to authoritarian procedures with the personal touch.
   a. Influence of leadership does not carry over. It must be continuous, even to the point of a nagging relationship. Two principals applied this and succeeded in getting equal Mexican and Negro representation on the PTA Board of Directors.
   b. Men of this background do not expect women to be in public positions of authority.
2. The American Negro subculture resembles the dominant American.
   a. Negroes are accustomed to women in all positions of authority.

    b. Middle-class Negro women may exhibit aggression and hostility.

    c. Negroes and Mexicans have nothing in common culturally, except the American experience of prejudice, and so cannot be appealed to similarly.

3. School personnel often show deficient empathy with Mexicans and Negroes, including children and parents, as revealed in voice tones, facial expressions, glances, body positions, and prejudicial language.

4. As schoolteacher and counselor are hosts to parents on school grounds, they are responsible for defining for parents the purpose of each conference in terms that will be understood and accepted. Parents can even be scolded if this is done in good faith, presenting school goals frankly, and showing respect for minority variations. Try to give parents agreeable reports on children, besides necessary criticism.

5. The teacher's use of language must adapt to the parent's background.

    a. It is possible to talk bluntly with Negroes when the school's good faith is evident.

    b. The Mexican parent responds well to clear direction initiated by authority, in our case, the school.

    c. Never allow prejudice to show on the job.

A month later, having applied these recommendations to the first goal, four schools reported success with parents' conferences. They said that for the first time, 80 per cent of the Mexican parents honored appointments; a third grade teacher reported 100 per cent attendance, and others approached 100 per cent. In the term before the sequence began, 423 parents of 776 pupils at R school had attended teachers' conferences; during the sequence period, pupil enrollment dropped to 758, but the number of parents attending conferences rose to 562. The R principal boasted that her teachers "went all out after parents," observing each recommendation, notably the first, fourth, and fifth.

Teachers scheduled appointments two weeks ahead, rescheduling when necessary. "As in big business," they said they followed up with personal notes a day before the conference. One teacher wrote and phoned dilatory parents. A Mexican-American teacher said she broke with custom and visited four homes where parents were confined, speaking Spanish to three mothers, which had never been done before. Several teachers led discussions in class about the importance of conferences with parents, and commanded each pupil to remind parents of the conference dates and escort them to school. A first grade and kindergarten teacher sent notes to some parents reading, "I *want* to see you today at 3 P.M.," and scored full success. The subject of parent visits constituted school projects for a class in composition and one in social studies. School V held class exercises of children's reports on their parents' views of the conferences; occasionally a grandmother substituted for a parent. The curriculum director felt elated that often a mother of several pupils grew interested or "cooperative" enough to confer one after another with her children's teachers.

At A school, pupil enrollment rose by 17 from 467 to 484, but the number of parents attending conferences rose by 63 from 345 to 408. One teacher roused her pupils to "cooperate" with her by pitting them against other pupils, challenging them by saying, "Don't we want our room to show 100 per cent attendance of parents?". She goaded them further by declaring that she would accept no refusals. In fact, all parents complied, except two who were sick, one who worked, and one who attended college. These she visited at home at suitable hours, attentions that had never been rendered before.

A man teaching at M school also made two unprecedented home visits, and was surprised to find "parents very receptive." One visit was to oblige a widow housebound with ten youngsters; another was to accommodate a woman with a hospitalized child and housebound with four youngsters, including an ailing infant. This teacher said he refused to "coax" certain parents but he was successful in "demanding" appointments with them. When torrential rains crippled transportation for those living in unpaved parts of town, several parents sent requests for later dates, a conscientious courtesy never before demonstrated.

These teachers felt a new regard for their pupils' families now and one of them made a blanket offer to visit homes when necessary. A teacher said that her visits actually "cured one boy of habitual truancy." All teachers reported improvements in children's behavior after conferences with parents.[21] It is also likely that the teachers' increased efforts led them to view their pupils more sympathetically.

Teachers agreed to encourage parents to express themselves at the conferences. This was quite a departure. Usually teachers monopolized the talk and the time, chiefly to issue reprimands. Some teachers reported how they guided parents to open the conversations, while limiting their own contributions to one or two remarks, or "points." Under the new dispensation, amiable feelings surged, and some parents confessed to the educators that, out of dread, they had never before set foot in school, even when agreeing to appointments. A teacher reported that a mother assured him, "I told David I wasn't coming if you told me bad things." Another mother was "dragged" to conference by her daughter. She so hated school that she would not allow its name spoken at home. Hence, she never knew her daughter headed the class. The teacher told her that immediately—"and did she ever relax and thank me!"

One teacher found that parents accepted criticism *after* they had heard favorable comments. Another teacher took the precaution of asking each pupil, "What would you like me to talk to your mother about?" Accordingly, she informed each mother, "Your child wants you to know this," and she would relate an accomplishment.

In this euphoric atmosphere it was necessary to caution teachers that the first successes would not continue merely on their own momentum, but would require continuing efforts, even to the extent of apparent nagging. Teachers would have to pursue every parental evasion personally, to convey sincerity, and to retrain parents' attitudes. This meant phone calls, home visits, personal notes. One teacher found it effective to write truant parents on their child's report card, "I missed you at conference." Such procedures are especially well-suited to Mexican inclinations. Months later, teachers reported again that their efforts brought mounting numbers of Mexican parents to conferences, open-house week, and PTA meetings.

Some Mexican fathers now attended conferences, "especially the better educated." The principal of R school counted over 300 Mexican parents attending PTA where heretofore the highest number had been 40, an increase of nearly 700 per cent. She helped a Mexican mother win a precedent-shattering election to the presidency of the school's PTA (with the cooperation of the Negro newcomer who generously agreed to withdraw her candidacy to insure this outcome). The installation meeting drew 314 mothers, fathers, and grandmothers, chiefly Mexican. The principal boasted that the ten new officers included "five Spanish-Americans (Mexicans) and five Negroes. Quite a few members now send in their 50 cents. The nagging works. Postcards and phone calls bring in the Spanish-American mothers. And they don't come alone." Another principal reported that his teachers' pertinacity maintained a 10 per cent increase in the number of parents visiting school.

To observe the strong influence of social background on children's classwork, responses of pupils in the city's southside minority-neighborhood schools were compared with responses of pupils in the city's northside "good" schools. Enrollments in elementary grades faithfully reflected residential patterns, so that the southside schools enrolled almost entirely lower-income Mexican and Negro children while northside schools almost exclusively served children of good-income Anglo-white homes. A teacher conducts classes differently in the separate neighborhoods because of the children's sociocultural inequities.

At the time of the Claremont observer's visit to the first grade in a northside school one spring Monday, it was Sharing Hour, when well-washed children rose individually to impart recent experiences. No smell of child pervaded the room, unlike the minority-neighborhood schools. The teacher was a pleasant-faced woman of early middle age, dressed in a charming, blue cotton frock set off by a coral necklace and coral-colored high-heeled shoes. She made her face expressive and affectionate for the children, spoke simply, and avoided words like "honey" and "darling." At her first request to "share," a boy jumped up to mention his "Chinese pheasant." A boy, sent off to Coventry in the rear, called out, "Turquoise, you mean." When a little girl rose and spoke with tense hesitation, the Coventry boy called out, "Don't lean on the chalkboard." Another boy stood to describe "this real scary movie on television, and this mummy crushed this man's head." Again the Coventry boy intervened, elaborating on "what the priest created" and on Chinese coins, and was not reprimanded. A little boy walked to the front of the room with a large clay cow in his arms, colored deep red and spotted black and white, to say, "I got this from our gardener who went to Paris."

All the children used fine language as a matter of course, eagerly reporting experiences unknown to southside children. All children were Anglo-American except the Coventry boy who was half Mexican, though this was indicated only in his surname. Here was fair evidence of the head start that a "middle-class" home affords young children, in language, poise, appearance, and interests.

In a sixth-grade class, the children awaited the Claremont observer and a school official impatiently to start a discussion in social studies. The girls were large for their average age of eleven years; the first speaker was as large as a woman. Holding up to the class an issue of a popular weekly magazine devoted to the President's family, she pointed to the several illustrations of dress and behavior. Boys followed, speaking easily of space stations; one described an industrial accident with "collapsing cranes" in New Mexico. An attractive blonde girl talked fluently about teaching machines in "schools of the future." A boy discussed educators' groupings of pupils by tests of ability, turning to the teacher for aid. The personalities seemed matured versions of the first-graders. The teacher listened carefully, rarely interrupting.

In a third-grade class visited, the Sharing Hour was on the theme, "What did you do over the weekend?" A girl said, "Saturday we went to a flood control area because there you can shoot without hurting anyone. Sunday we went to the desert." A boy said that Saturday they went to the movies and Sunday to their cabin in the mountains. Another said, "We are going to plant a cactus garden near the playhouse." The next boy spoke about planting yuccas. A boy said that on Saturday the family watched a movie showing how Abe Lincoln died. The teacher interjected for the first time, "What is the big word you use?" All hands shot up to answer "assassinate." A girl said the family went visiting on Saturday, and on Sunday "we went to the desert to study plants." Accounts tumbled out, describing weekends with Boy Scouts and Blue Birds, at weddings, Disneyland, the movies, Sunday school, bowling, ranching in Arizona, flower and stone hunts in the desert. The teacher observed quietly.

A southside school was visited to meet its Mexican and Negro pupils. In notable contrast to northside pupils' tales of parents and children going together to many different places, visiting other towns and the desert for weekends, these southside Mexicans talked about "cousins." In the school's grade-one class, the teacher asked the children to consider the subject of dogs. She struggled to elicit speech from the children, but they lacked vocabulary. A few pupils mentioned shepherd dogs, police dogs, and "just dogs." The largest amplification came from a husky colored girl who said that she and her father had nineteen dogs for hunting rabbits. The astounded teacher asked her to name the dogs, whereupon she produced five names. This teacher, and others in schools of underprivileged pupils, took the classes on walking trips to point out and name objects, hoping to enrich their stores of experiences and vocabularies. Exhausting the present topic of dogs, the teacher introduced the idea of birthdays. Mexican youngsters talked about baby brothers and cousins, and a Negro girl mentioned "My Ma's Birthday." The principal, who joined the Claremont observer and escorting school official, identified a little Mexican girl in the room as "the brightest one here because they talk no Mexican in her home."

Of a third-grade class numbering twenty-five children, the principal said that they fought frequently, concluding, "though the children are pleasant." All appeared well-groomed, nourished, relaxed, and gentle. They were divided into three reading groups, nine being in the fast group. When the teacher questioned, "What does the farmer do to make the ground soft?", none knew the desired word "plow." When the teacher read aloud to them, the children accompanied quietly, moving their lips and pointing their fingers.

In a grade-four class, the thirty attractive children were entirely Negro and Mexican. They were studying Spanish-mission architecture under the teacher's prodding questions. The southside teachers' massive efforts to elicit standard responses contrasted starkly with the easy pace of northside teachers. Patently, teachers and pupils in the northside school were of similar social stuff, that is, middle-class Anglo, with full understanding about classroom work. On the southside, the legal rulings about desegregation had no visible consequence. An eighteen-year-old Mexican-American boy of the southside, upon high-school graduation, was invited to spend a weekend at the home of an Anglo classmate. He accepted and on Monday declared, "Man, that's the first I've stayed with Anglos—and I survived!"

An extraordinary dividend on the initial year's work was the first complete turnout of Mexican and Negro parents having children at the three large southside K-6 (kindergarten through sixth grade) schools to vote for a school bond issue that would finance construction of additional high-school classrooms. Officials were certain that the teachers' newly extended friendliness had rallied this support of additional taxes. The curriculum director said this was unprecedented and attributed it to the special work with the selected elementary-school teachers.

Teachers in other schools of the city offered to join the monthly meetings, but the curriculum director limited participation to the original volunteers. Among these were a few who resented the unfamiliar labors required. Teachers were asked, for example, to report *if* the cultural approach led to improved handling of conferences with parents and *how* the improvements were manifested; they were asked to state new "goals" achieved, and to keep confidential files tabulating race, culture, and sex of parents and teachers who conferred, for subsequent analysis of processes. Teachers were reminded to visit homes and see how their pupils lived, so as to guide parents from mistrust to cooperation. The curriculum director urged principals to take over classes and so allow teachers to accompany the nurse or attendance officer into pupils' neighborhoods at least once a year. She commented earnestly, "I promise you a rude awakening when you discover, for instance, that even the best home and parents may own not a word of reading matter—nor a radio or TV. There's a big education job for us. We may discover that teaching elementary grades requires teaching minorities our culture, and ourselves theirs."

Without her strong leadership, few teachers would have ventured off campus, especially into Negro and Mexican neighborhoods, which frightened them. A young candidate for a teaching job on southside looked out of the school window and saw a Negro boy hit another, a Mexican. He turned to the man interviewing him and asked, "Is that the status of race relations here?" The other rejoined, astonished, "What do you mean?" "I mean, Negroes attacking Mexicans." The interviewer said, dead pan, "No, there simply wasn't anyone else around for him to hit. Didn't you ever hit, at the age of eight?"

The first experimental training period ended with the school year in June. It had tried to show that difficult behavior which frustrates educators may be illuminated by examining social and traditional backgrounds of the individuals concerned (including pupils, parents, and teachers), that the course of the behavior in known social situations is often predictable, and the dynamics of behavior often function below individuals' levels of consciousness. No opportunity existed for delving into some important matters, such as the relations between religion and culture which educators and social workers frequently ask about. It could merely be stated that the social scientist regards religion as a part of human life, with aspects that vary significantly in different cultures.

Among Mexicans, the Catholic view of existence pervades all activities and is vital to them, regardless of the effectiveness of particular priests. This bothers many Anglo teachers, though not Mexican ones, because Anglos interpret the Catholic outlook as anti-Protestant and antipublic education. Anglos themselves pit the church institution against the secular school in their assumptions. Most Mexican families, however, reason in terms of certain humanistic values, so that ideas and events become ordered as sacred or profane, as sacrificial or egotistic, as male or female responsibilities, and the like. Each pair and each member is elaborately developed, and all are interwoven within the Catholic life.

During this training period, the obligations of Mexican and Negro teachers to their respective groups were also considered, for a minority anxiously watches its successful representatives. Only members of a subculture or any other special interest world can clarify its nuances of language, emotion, and social relationships for effective use by the main culture in specific settings, such as schools. This accounts for the sound support northside parents gave educators, for each group approved of the other's ways and commitments. In effect, on the north side, education proceeded around the clock and year through parents' goals and acts. The parents supervised homework so closely that teachers often refused to accept pupils' typed reports, knowing they were actually done by parents. These parents prodded children with rewards and penalties, consulted teachers, and checked on school boards. Southside teachers harshly blamed their Mexican, Negro, and Okie parents for acting dissimilarly. Teachers called them indifferent and apathetic, in effect condemning them for being prejudicially excluded from northside's world and so being unable to learn northside's ways. This behavior was examined as the result of social processes that involve poverty, minority status, minority subcultures, and prevailing prejudices.

At the close of the first training period, the curriculum director requested her Claremont guide to propose some culturally apt arrangements for southside pupils during the summer months when these children were left at loose ends and were likely to forget how to read. Stymied by the failure of teachers to volunteer services and by the closing of the school library, the guide suggested delegating supervision of reading to an elder sister or brother among southside Mexicans, and to a mother, elder daughter, or aunt among southside Negroes, in keeping with each people's usual modes of meeting family responsibility. Teachers agreed to check out books to reading units of brothers and sisters, and of parents and children, which young neighbors and friends could join; and some contributed old magazines and catalogues. Pupils were directed to report on their reading in the fall to these teachers, not to their new teachers; and reading unit leaders were told to expect some official recognition from school.

The second training period was to commence with the new school year in fall. At the first fall meeting, a fourth-grade southside teacher announced that her old pupils who had checked out books were now presenting written reports and demanding recognition; the pupils wished to be called "Summer Associates." A first-grade teacher said fourteen of her old pupils had joined the reading enterprise following a form letter [22] she sent their parents, but only four could actually secure and read books. At 8 A.M. on the opening day of fall term, she had telephoned parents to ask their opinions of the reading experiment. All parents approved. A principal observed that more children would have read if the school library had remained open in summer; they could not visit the city library as the law forbade bus transportation out of school zones. All agreed that the evidence was convincing, even touching, that children could be readily encouraged to read despite poor circumstances. Thus, another heedless judgment of apathy was discarded.

The work on curriculum was linked to the prior work on behavior by exposing gaps that separated a minority child's experiences from the contents of school readers and social studies texts. Southside's minorities usually see fathers in work clothes, tired, unkempt, irritable at the end of the day, or snappish under prolonged deprivations; they see mothers harassed by baby care, cooking, washing, scrimping and scrounging to buy low-priced foods. The familiar Mexican tortillas, beans, and rice, and the southern Negroes' chitterlings or catfish do not figure in school texts. Drawings in these texts show fathers and mothers to be blond, relaxed, and well dressed, fathers often sporting felt hats (though this is generally abandoned in California) and playing cheerily with impeccable children on neat lawns before charming houses. Foods depicted in the texts include store-bought fruits, meats, breads. Characters in stories have ordinary English names like Dick and Jane, but minorities' names are often the Mexicans' sonorous Ignacio, Andrés, Guadalupe, Soledad, and the deep-South Negroes' Lincoln, Washington, Mahalia, Eartha. Mexicans, Negroes, and European minorities also use kinship terms (aunt, uncle, cousin, brother, sister) which appear in school texts as seldom as pictures of Mexican-Americans and American Negroes. Drawings of non-European or nonwhite types appear usually in books about foreign lands and colonial conquests.

The teachers knew all this, and criticized similar limitations in educational film strips. A principal said, "Fortunately many children's books are written about animals!" But the training program set teachers to consider the immense strain these gaps placed on minorities in their efforts to read. If emotional difficulties worsen stuttering, they also worsen poor reading. All agreed that the novice reader should be enabled to identify with the materials for which he is expected to cultivate motivation, either through the consistency of his life modes with these materials or through teaching devices.

Actually, the latter had been provided by Turkey in 1936 when her elementary schools used a primer [23] for adults and children whose illustrations were differentiated, in two editions, for the two social groups of peasants and city dwellers. The differences were in details of dress and activities in the illustrations accompanying the uniform text. Peasant boys were shown with typically shaven heads, wearing a cloth cap, a collarless, brightly striped shirt, baggy pants, knee socks, and rubber galoshes. City boys had a full head of well-trimmed hair, wore a school uniform including a cap, fine tailored shirt, tight Bermudas, casual store socks, and good leather shoes. Peasant girls wore long, braided pigtails contrasting with the city girls' smart haircut *a la garçonne* (boyish) with bangs; peasant girls, unlike city girls, wore earrings; they wore rubber galoshes unlike the city girls' one-strap leather shoe; they wore striped shirt, apron, pantaloons, black-ribbed cotton socks, kerchief, or long dress unlike the modish short city dresses, skirt, or school uniform and neat socks. Following the respective modes of life, the rural school was depicted with one story, the city school with two stories; the entrance to a city dwelling showed a push-button, the rural home a pull-button; rural children poured from a traditional clay waterpot and city children used a metal sprinkler.

From the identical texts (except those for workhorse and riding horse) accompanying the class-differentiated drawings, the whole population learned identical words in the then freshly introduced Latin print that replaced the original Turkish or Arabic. Bookcovers were identical except that the one with illustrated peasant details had a red border and the one with urban details had a blue border. Contrary to inferences of California teachers, Turks never thought to resent the pictured class differences but recognized themselves with a pride that their educators expected and deliberately invoked.

Again contrary to many educators' inferences, American minorities also have pride in themselves, along with the bitterness fostered by prejudice. Some schools appear to know or expect that minorities have such pride and accordingly use dolls of the several races and nationalities which mirror their pupils. A Southern California school in a good Negro neighborhood bought Negro dolls for its kindergartners. However, a white kindergarten teacher hung solely white-pictured people on the walls. Asked why she failed to include Negro ones, she said surprised, "Well, I *feel* this way. I don't see any difference between black and white." In the training group, a kindergarten teacher wondered why she never saw Negro dolls. Another said that they were available commercially but not of "durable" make, whereupon an order to buy some was sent the school purchasing agent. Another teacher wondered why she saw no Mexican dolls.

To compensate for the deficiencies in school texts and dolls, some teachers agreed to explain to pupils that middle-class types of parents and dwellings represented only one kind of worthy persons and homes. Teachers tried to adapt to their southside pupils the world's variety of dress, dwellings, games, foods, table-settings, languages, poetry, proverbs, and folklore. Class projects were planned to draw in minority parents, community leaders, and foreign consuls.

Teachers of fifth- and sixth-grade social studies asked worriedly, "What do we do about 'tolerance'?" As prejudice touches all lives, it was suggested that teachers discuss it in terms of legal defenses of equality,[19] legislative provisions for an additional official language in accordance with local language traditions [20] (New Mexico's official languages are English and Spanish, those of Louisiana and Quebec are English and French), the Supreme Court's various decisions on integration and segregation, contributions of minority geniuses to modern life (George Washington Carver, Albert Einstein, Louis Armstrong), and others. Children should dramatize characters of different ethnic sorts, in addition to enacting themselves. Members of class committees and research teams should be mixed ethnically, so that whites, Negroes, Mexicans, Indians, and others should work together, and chairmen should rotate; the same should be done in games, doll-play, seating. No one child should be obliged to bear the brunt of an unpopular ethnic representation but, like those of the dominant group, should have familiar partners. Volunteer reading teams could be organized among pupils with poor home resources, on a mixed social or ethnic basis. Even nonreading parents may be valuable exponents of their competences—say, in welding, cookery, music, sewing, carpentry. The need is to create an atmosphere of respect for all human beings without forcing undue favor for minorities or undue attacks upon the dominant group.

Such teachings below the level of senior high school will still take place in neighborhoods and schools that are to all intents segregated, that is, they will be predominantly middle-class white, or Negro, or Mexican-American, or European immigrant. However, no group learns the ways of another without doing them in the other's company, so that minorities will never incorporate standard American modes unless they can live them as fully as the dominant group. New York City's "Higher Horizons" program recognizes "that equality of educational opportunity means additional services for many pupils, in order to compensate for the disadvantages of the community and home . . . [and that] . . . college entrance is more a function of social class and economic status than of native intelligence and academic achievement." [24]

Each teacher was next asked to answer these four questions: In what curriculum areas do you believe you come closest to achieving your aims? What techniques seem most effective? In what curriculum areas do you believe your teaching is least effective? What techniques seem least effective?

In the session the following month, teachers thought their answers showed a "trend" to success in teaching the fundamentals of arithmetic and "language arts" (spelling, penmanship, music). Useful methods included field trips and other off-campus experiences, besides audio-visual aids in class and materials for work brought to class. Reports disagreed about achievements in reading and social studies. Arithmetic test scores of Mexicans, Negroes, and Okies were generally superior to the scores these pupils made in other subjects. It seemed plausible that the abstractness and impersonality of arithmetical symbols and processes escaped the touchy values permeating social subjects. Some teachers, however, interpreted the success of minority pupils in simple arithmetic to mean that "the lower classes are closer to life's realities. Children are sent to stores, understand counting, hear budget discussions at home." A teacher asked if particular social studies "units," like poultry care, bored pupils because they were unfamiliar subjects. Thereupon a Mexican-American teacher commented ironically that all poorer Mexican families kept chickens; it was rather the teacher who was boring.

The curriculum director strongly advised teachers to sense the direction of pupils' interests, and adapt to them the themes of the course. Once pupils got interested, i.e., motivated, the teacher could interweave such curricular themes as cooperation and competition, but, the director repeated, no unit was so "sacred" as to be preserved at a sacrifice of learning.

The program attempted a dramatic presentation of the idea that diverse social groups brought to class diverse life concepts with which the teacher had to reckon. On the wall of the meeting room hung a large, colored print entitled, "Covered Wagon Crossing the Frontier." The teachers were asked to name ideas that the picture aroused or to consider some prideful memories or other associations that the historic covered wagon stirred among families whose ancestors trekked West to homestead. Then it was pointed out that to Indians and Mexicans the wagon of homesteaders often meant terror, shame, and exploitation. This aspect of the West's history was hard to convey. An Anglo teacher protested, "But the children know about covered wagons from TV!" She supposed that there the pioneering purpose was presented convincingly. Another contradicted, "No, on TV it looks more like cops and robbers, fighting savage Indians."

A third teacher picked up the idea of pride and achievement as triggers to learning. Her face aglow, she told that one day, after weeks of plodding effort, a slow-reading child cried out, "Mrs. M! I can read!" Teacher and pupil were beside themselves with excitement, and the teacher's heartfelt praise kept the boy going. Teachers are aware of the magical possibilities of classroom success, which they call "achievement." Another teacher told of the strides made by a Negro boy who became filled with pride the morning he brought his father to class and listened to him tell about his skilled job at a Kaiser plant.

The problem remained of leading teachers to realize firmly that pupils' customary life concepts may be foreign to the school's "middle-class" atmosphere. Teachers were therefore asked to repeat with their classes a version of the covered wagon exercise, by showing some simple picture and instructing each child to tell his spontaneous interpretation to a tape recorder, out of the others' hearing. At the next meeting, teachers played back selected tapes.

The first tapes came from a southside school's fifth and sixth grades where the teacher had shown pupils a black-and-white line drawing of a young Anglo couple staring wide-eyed at a large volume labeled "City Directory." The first pupil's voice was full and resonant with the intonations of a southern Negro. He said, "They were looking in the paper for an advertisement about houses and were disappointed they couldn't find a house they liked." The next pupil, sounding much like the first, supposed that the couple was a husband and wife worried over high taxes, "and the wife was trying to cool him off so they were going to City Hall." The third pupil said, in similar accents, "They were looking in the paper and saw somebody they knew who was hurt." Pupil Four believed they were disappointed to see in the paper that Kennedy had been elected President. Pupil Five saw them disappointed over losing on horse races because now they could not buy a house or put their children through school. Pupil Six said they wanted to go on a trip but had lost their money. Pupil Seven explained, "They went to the hospital to see if it was their daughter who had been hurt. It was not, so they went home. Their daughter had gone to her grandmother. And they were nervous and frightened." Pupil Eight thought the couple was trying to figure out what the paper was saying about them. Pupil Nine stated, "Taxes are worrying the family and also they are trying to find somebody in this big town where they are visiting." Pupil Ten said, "They picked up the paper and saw that their daughter was in Juvenile Hall." Pupil Eleven lisped almost hysterically, with a heavy southern country accent, "The man and the woman are angry because the man didn't have a job. Or they saw in the newspaper that somebody got killed." Pupil Twelve said flatly that the man committed a crime. Pupil Thirteen was a California Negro girl with no regional accent, who said, "They look as though they are lost in the city." Pupils Fourteen and Fifteen said similarly, "They are disturbed to be in a new town and are looking up addresses in the directory. . . . They've got the wrong directions."

Of the fifteen pupils, ten perceived anxiety, disappointment, hurt, terror, violence, despair, and loss that were not recognized by the other five, or by the teachers. Someone said, "They didn't seem to read the words, 'City Directory'." However, these responses were more respectable than the tales of disembowelings and gunshots which Negro pupils reported to a teacher at another school as occurring in the home or street at any time. Yet, "the amazing thing," the teacher said, "is that the gory experiences do not seem to hurt their conduct at school."

When girls from the superior northside school were shown the line drawing of the couple and the City Directory, they saw only two people making plans for "a honeymoon" and "a vacation trip." Their contained, cheery voices contrasted startlingly with the ten emotional Negro voices that brought the southside world into the cloistered classroom. Some teachers found this knowledge depressing to "morale." Others, however, said they took the contrast for granted and "no one is surprised." The purpose of this training sequence was to identify the contrast for clues to fresh approaches in teaching those of unstandardized social traits.

At another southside school, the teacher had shown a highly colored picture of a tornado to a fourth-grade class. Again the taped voices were clearly southern Negro in accent and emotion. A boy spoke breathlessly, rushing to describe the violent scene. A girl declared, "It reminds me of a volcano that has busted out already. The whole world is running down. It will hit the wire." Another girl said helplessly, "It's a storm because it's windy."

Confronted with this capsuled evidence of socially heterogeneous speech, thought, behavior, moods, all forced to meet the school's Procrustean discipline, teachers asked, "What shall educators do?" They described their efforts to manage classroom consequences of social deficiencies. One said pupils mutilated those words in the reader that they never heard at home; her solution was to abandon the "syllable method" of teaching. Another explained that she could teach nothing to the moody, excitable kindergartners and first graders for a while after their daily arrival, so she established a "feeling time" for them to "blow off and let go" (fostering a roomful of "anarchy," according to her supervisor), after which they could proceed to lessons. When tension mounted again, as it usually did, she led group singing. Several teachers insisted that a paramount solution would have been the requirement for parents to help with homework, which parents presently failed to do.

The curriculum director stated that during home visits and school conferences, teachers could recruit parents to coach their children; and that the specific study units should be adapted to the children's irregular experiences. But some teachers were reluctant to switch from established curriculum guides and drills to the irregularities indicated. They raised obstacles such as this comment written by a fifth- and sixth-grade teacher: "Children do not apply what is learned in [the] Language [unit] to oral and written expression. I need to find a way to break habits. Most children are unable to work independently or in groups without my being right there. But they enjoy memorizing for spelling drill, if I check almost immediately." She did not criticize her compartmentalized notions of "language learning" and "memorizing" or her failure to develop broader skills in pupils.

A first-grade teacher objected, "In teaching these [Mexican] children Language Arts, the foreign [Spanish] language is a problem, as their English vocabulary is limited. Many of the English words have no meaning to them. Therefore, they cannot express themselves freely in English." A sixth-grade teacher complained, "Children don't enjoy reading from books they know are below grade level [i.e., for slow readers]. . . . My low sixth-grade group reads from . . . [a third-grade book] and dislikes it. But what are we to do with their poor English vocabulary?"

On the other hand, a kindergarten teacher at the same southside school personally organized study groups of parents and sent to the homes "bimonthly messages on subject areas and the manner in which parents might assist classwork." Still, she felt that the "social character" of the Negro group evaded her.

A second-grade teacher discarded the smoke screen of bilingualism to "encourage good work and listening habits in language stories and reading. I use a great deal of praise and try to develop a good feeling of working together. I try to make the period interesting for the children and give them varied reading and music experiences. I believe music should be fun for them and I try to help the 'out of tunes' enjoy music, too. I'm not very good in music but I enjoy it. I have had Negro and Mexican children. They are just like other children as they like and respond to praise. They do good work. I believe in taking children where they are and taking them as far as they can go, establishing good work and play habits."

A fourth- and fifth-grades teacher, according to her supervisor, "inspired confidence among [minority] pupils and parents, counseling them on family problems personally and at conferences, and inviting children to her home for barbecue suppers." A sixth-grade teacher at the school wrote of his awareness that, "in this [southside] district, I have learned that many children do not know how to study. . . . To teach the child better work habits . . . I am experimenting with an information sheet for my class on methods of study."

The empathy some Mexican-American teachers feel for Mexican and Mexican-American families, when left unguided by professional standards, blocked instruction. Thus, a young Mexican-American woman, once a pupil at a southside school, was "thrilled" to return to the school to teach kindergarten. All the pupils were of Mexican origins; to the teacher's surprise, several spoke only Spanish. One little Mexican girl was often insulted by the others because she was dirty and backward. The young teacher feared to tell the offensive facts to the mother. The principal learned of the situation only from others and took it upon herself to apprise the mother. Lack of empathy, however, seemed marked in the principal's impatience with Negro parents who failed to inform their children about race prejudice. At another school, on the other hand, a Mexican-American teacher fulfilled his traditional male part by undertaking to counsel Mexican families about school, even resorting to Spanish in class.

At this school, a fifth-grade teacher tried to uncover pupils' personalities and backgrounds through compositions and penmanship assigned as homework. Each child was to ask his family to help him select and cut out pictures from magazines and mount them on purple cardboard while the child wrote wishes bearing on each picture. Ornamental and interesting creations appeared.

A Mexican-American pupil named Priscilla wrote, "My wish is that even thow [sic] you don't have a pretty house like the picture, Remember you can be happy." A Negro pupil named Duane wrote, "I wish I had a big bag of cookies. I even wish I was out of school so could go to the beach an [sic] have fun. I wish my dog would come back home. I like fairy [sic] boats." Barbara, a Negro, wrote, "My first wish is I wish I had a car to go anywhere I wanting to go I would like to go to the beach or on a trap [sic] for about a week and take my family along with me . . . second, to go to the ocean to catch fish . . . or to look at the pretty waves go flowing by. My third wish is I wish I had a little cat to play with in the evening when I come from school and I like to feed them. And I would touch his furry fur and if it was a she I would have some kittens."

Joe, a Mexican, wrote, "My first wish—I wish I had a girl because

I just love girls. My second wish, I wish I had some gold so I could buy stuff for my girl friend. . . . My fourth wish—I wish I had a record player because my sister never lets me listen to her's." Porfy, another Mexican: "I wish I had that car [in the cut-out] because we don't have a car. We used to have a car but we never used it because it wouldn't go up hills. Because it was old. All the time we wanted to go to Colorado but it would never make it. So that is why I want the car. . . . My second wish is that I had a dog . . . because our's got lost and we couldn't find it. . . . I like those kind [in the cut-out] because I like their ears." Brenda, a Negro: "If I had my wish I would wish for that my parents an [sic] brothers and sisters could dine out. So we could have anything we wanted to eat. And that would be my wish." Her sister, Linda, wished first for a swimming pool, second for a [current] 1961 car, and "My third wish is I wish I had a big dinner the biggest dinner in the whole world. I'll have hot dogs and candy and anything I want." Cynthia, a Hawaiian, wrote, "(1) I wish to go to Hawaii, (2) I wish I could be a little fat." Crystal, a Negro, wished for a camera, a car, and finally "for all that food (in the cut-out). . . . on a picnic. Only Rita, a Mexican, desired a "lovely garden with many flowers in it;" and only she wished for a "long dog to give my teacher she wants one badly and if I had one I would give it to her so she won't feel bad." Betty's wishes were bound up entirely with her Mexican family: "If I had three wishes, I'd wish for a portable TV so that when I'd what [want] to see a moive [movie] I wouldn't have to see the moives [sic] my brother likes to see and I also could take it from room to room. And if I had a camer[a] I would take pictures of my family and not my big sister all the time and also so that I will have many, many remence [remembrances] of my family when they pass away. And my last wish is that [I] may get them."

Some educators feel that society's prejudice is inevitable but strive to advertise their personal goodwill by sentimental phrases. Characteristic is the turn of phrase of a southside principal, "The top pupil in a grade-four class is a Mexican girl with a real aristocratic bearing. There she is [he pointed to a slender dark child]. She stands out in this low-income area." A reactive, tough-minded view was expressed by a young man teaching a northside sixth-grade class. "The California social structure is so strongly anti-Mexican that our pupils can't hope for better jobs and therefore don't require academic courses."

Because of the south side's social inadequacies, the curriculum director accepted only provisionally IQ ratings of its minorities, and assumed further that the higher ratings had to be raised by some ten points, especially when English comprehension was rated below arithmetic scores. Many Mexicans were recent immigrants and others spoke Spanish because of established segregation. One rosy-cheeked Mexican girl, an immigrant in a southside kindergarten class of Negro children, was an ornament of starched frills and hair ribbons. Quietly she watched the others enact gay parts in fairy tales. After a time a Negro boy, youngest in a family of eight, approached her, coaxing her to join the choruses. But she knew no English. Curving towards her protectingly, he begged, "Say 'wagon,' say 'wagon'!" and he showed her how to hitch her little red wagon along with the rest.

At the city's four-year high school, the minorities' sullen and apathetic separateness influenced attendance records. The school's enrollment of 2,650 was 25 per cent Mexican, 15 per cent Negro and 60 per cent white. But 74 per cent of absentees were Mexican boys and girls, according to the Welfare and Attendance staff. A counselor said, "They attend school four days a week. You see them on downtown streets on Fridays, or they prefer to spend time with a visiting relative. In the worst cases, even if the child is under seventeen or slightly under sixteen, the school helps the parent take out a work permit for the child. Of our 156 worst offenders, only 10 are Negro but 76 are Mexican and 70 are Anglo [white]. It seems as though Mexican parents don't care. The Negro parents are very ambitious and *want* their children to finish school. They have the strong backing of their own organizations, like the NAACP. . . . Still, Mexican families are kind. Like Negroes, they always have room for one more at table."

High-school teachers were mystified that once cheery grade-school Mexicans became hostile adolescents, ignoring high-school sports, class bells, and the faculty's joking overtures. Yet teachers of a Southern California private military academy said their best students came from Latin America, including Mexico. The families of these children were well-to-do and educated members of their countries' ruling classes, usually active in foreign service and trade.

Educators, like their pupils, are often unable to cross social and cultural boundaries without help. But educators have the professional obligation to cross these if they are to teach in today's multicultural and desegregated schools. It is possible to train educators on the job to apply cultural information and theory to problems in the conduct and thinking of teachers, pupils, and parents. The considerable progress of the Claremont project in this training sequence rested on the curriculum director's strong leadership and on the care taken to design tasks to carry participants into fresh working relationships with parents, to provide insights into the different cultures, and to yield some control over the cultural processes. The tasks evolved as efforts to extract cultural meanings from particular problems in behavior and in curriculum, and as efforts to provide culturally appropriate solutions.

Notes

1. Allan Maxwell, unpublished Master's thesis in Education, Claremont Graduate School, 1962.
2. *Ibid.* In the first and second grades, two pupils had already attended five other schools, three had attended four others, four had attended three others, etc.
3. *The Los Angeles Times*, July 5, 1962, Part One, pp. 2, 17; and July 6, 1962, Part One, p. 6, in stories by Gene Sherman.
4. See, *Towards Greater Opportunity*, A Progress Report from the Superintendent of Schools, Dr. John J. Theobald, to the New York City Board of Education, on Implementation of Recommendations of the Commission on Integration (New York: June 1960, 196 pp.). This report states that three-fourths of elementary public school children in Manhattan Borough are Negro and Puerto Rican but two-fifths are in New York City as a whole.
5. *Ibid.*, pp. 114–115.
6. The Theobald Report defines an ethnically homogeneous school population as one 85 or 90 per cent so. Extreme "homogeneity" occurs in elementary and junior high schools, as these serve local neighborhoods; homogeneity is less extreme in senior high school, which draws from large areas of the city.

    Will Maslow, "De Facto Public School Segregation," *Villanova Law Review*, Vol. 6, No. 3 (Spring, 1961, pp. 353–376) writes that New York "school authorities in August 1960, adopted a new policy on transfers designed to obtain 'better ethnic distribution' in the schools. Under this 'open enrollment' program, all pupils from 21 designated junior or senior high schools with a 'heavy concentration of Negro and Puerto Rican students' were given the opportunity to transfer to 28 other schools, which were utilized at less than 90 per cent of capacity. Students in the boroughs of Brooklyn or Queens could choose any designated school in their borough and students in Manhattan or Bronx could transfer to any appropriate school in either borough. Parents however were required to provide their own transportation. The Negro and Puerto Rican enrollment in the 'sending' junior high schools was from 80 to 100 per cent and in the 'receiving' schools from .4 to 23.8 per cent. About 12,000 students were eligible to transfer.

    "The plan, winning wide public acceptance, was soon extended to about 50,000 children in the second, third and fourth grades of 93 predominantly Negro and Puerto Rican schools in four boroughs of the city. Free bus transportation is to be provided when the new school is more than a mile from the transferee's home . . . in the fall of 1961. . . . A first preference (in transfers) was given to pupils who would normally attend junior high schools

having a Negro and Puerto Rican enrollment of 85 per cent or more. A
second preference was given to pupils . . . scheduled to attend junior high
schools with Negro and Puerto Rican enrollments of 75 to 85 per cent . . .
the privilege to transfer is not given on a racial or ethnic basis; a white
student in a predominantly Negro or Puerto Rican school may also exercise
the option. . . . The open enrollment program is . . . almost a complete
break with the concept of the *mandatory* neighborhood school. . . ." (pp.
366–367)

In a report for the American Jewish Congress on "School Segregation,
Northern Style" submitted to the House Committee on Education and Labor,
March 29, 1962 (New York: Stephen Wise Congress House, 15 East 84th
Street, 15 pp., mimeographed), Will Maslow states, "The New York City
Board of Education reported recently that 4,965 elementary and junior high
school pupils were attending 127 schools outside their home neighborhood
under the open enrollment plan. . . . Any pupil of a designated 'sending
school' is allowed to transfer. . . . At present, the enrollment at Lincoln
School, as a result of the optional transfers of 267 children, now consists of
90 per cent Negroes . . .

"Perhaps the most effective method of reducing or even of eliminating
segregation is the so-called Princeton Plan, named for the city in New Jersey
in which it was accomplished. Under this plan, where there are two elementary schools, not too far apart, one . . . predominantly Negro and the other
predominantly white, one school is classified as a kindergarten to fourth grade
school and the other as a fifth to eighth grade school. This reshuffling of
classes makes for complete integration.

"A variant of this plan was recently developed in Morristown, N. J.
There a predominantly Negro school in the center of town was abandoned
and the children transferred to four other schools in the city with predominantly white enrollments. The Morristown plan is feasible, however, only
when these are 'white' schools with excess capacity not too far from the predominantly Negro school. . . .

"Desegregation is only one part of a school board's task. Indeed, were it
to stop at desegregation, it would not perform its constitutional duty of
equalizing educational opportunity for all its pupils. Negro and Puerto Rican
children, living in slums . . . will require more than attendance at a theo-
retically integrated school to overcome . . . handicaps. . . ." (pp. 7–9)

"The effort to raise the educational level of underprivileged Negro and
Puerto Rican children requires vast sums of money. In New York City, the
Board of Education spent about $300,000 in a three-year period in one school
alone (J.H.S. 43) in an educational experiment which demonstrated that
educational levels of slum children could be lifted spectacularly by saturating the school with remedial teachers, attendance and behavior counselors,
psychologists, social workers and auxiliary personnel. But as the New York
City Superintendent has pointed out . . . there are 200 schools in New
York enrolling about 200,000 Negro and Puerto Rican children that need
this intensive program. . . .

"Apparently recognizing that the program is too expensive even for
New York, the school officials of that city have now launched a modified
version of the J.H.S. 43 experiment, at a cost of only $50 per pupil per year.
This 'Higher Horizons Program' is now operating in 63 elementary and sec-

ondary schools in New York City involving about 40,000 children. Federal, state and municipal funds totaling about $1,500,000 are invested in the program. The Board of Regents which supervises public and private education in New York State has urged the extension of this program to every city in the state. . . ." (pp. 13–14). As of 1959–1960, "the Higher Horizons project is generally concentrated in Grade 3 in elementary schools and in Grade 7 in junior high schools. . . ." (Maslow, "De Facto Public School Segregation," pp. 375–376.)

The *New York Times,* November 21, 1960, reported that Negro and Puerto Rican "Pupils who have transferred as a result of the Board of Education's open enrollment program . . . have adjusted well to their new schools . . . in more integrated areas. . . . The metropolitan district of the State Congress of Parents and Teachers said a study showed 'the children are happy, behavior is better and there is more interest in school work.' " © 1960 by The New York Times Company. Reprinted by permission. Volunteer district groups, such as the prominent Riverside Neighborhood Association, steadily promote integration in schools, housing, recreation, health, human relations; and are commended in the Theobald Report for great services.

Some New Yorkers privately attack desegregation by transfer. A white retired schoolteacher, in a personal letter to the writer, vehemently condemned transferring the Negro children from their neighborhoods, on grounds of proper race pride and psychological dangers in uprooting old associations. Yet everywhere in our country, white rural children are transported distances to their schools.

Maslow, "De Facto Public School Segregation," p. 355, n. 18, mentions "ethnic homogeneity" of California schools: "In Berkeley, California (in 1959), although 28.7 per cent of the school population of 15,375 are Negroes, in six of the city's 14 elementary schools less than 1 per cent of the children are Negroes and in two schools the total non-Caucasian children constitute more than 94 per cent of the school population. . . . In Pasadena, California, three of the city's 26 elementary schools had in 1957 Negro, Latin-American and Asian enrollments of 97 per cent, 84.1 per cent and 86.2 per cent respectively. . . . In Compton, a city bordering on Los Angeles, six of the city's 19 elementary schools had Negro populations of 85 per cent or more. In Enterprise, California and Willowbrook, California, which are predominantly Negro areas, all three of the former's elementary schools and all six of the latter's have Negro enrollments of 85 per cent or more. . . . On the other hand, . . . Negroes are enrolled in 40 of (Bridgeport, Connecticut's) . . . 42 public schools although the 2,000 Negro children in that city (in 1960) constitute less than 8 per cent of the total school population."

Maslow notes that in Detroit and St. Louis, Negro elementary school children were bussed in 1960 from overcrowded schools in Negro areas to formerly all-white schools (*ibid.,* pp. 367–368 and 368 n. 73).

7. Louis Alexander, "Texas Helps Her Little Latins," *The Saturday Evening Post* (August 5, 1961).

8. Fred H. Werner, "Cultural Shock in Student Transition," research paper read at Southwestern Anthropological Association conference, University of California, Santa Barbara, Goleta, California, April 1, 1961. Werner adds, "Students will be heard to describe themselves and others as being 'apathetic.' . . . What is commonly called 'apathy . . . the sophomore slump . . . ennui

. . . meaningless diversions' seem to me to be manifestations of 'acculturation shock' in students whose core values . . . basic understandings of the world . . . have been challenged and are undergoing some . . . redefinition." See also Werner's "Acculturation and Milieu Therapy in Student Transition" in George D. Spindler (ed.), *Education and Culture, Anthropological Approaches* (New York: Holt, Rinehart and Winston, 1963), pp. 259–267.

9. The *New York Times Magazine*, May 15, 1960.

10. See Ruth Landes, "Biracialism in American Society: A Comparative View" *American Anthropologist*, Vol. 57, No. 6 (December 1955), pp. 1253–1263.

11. See Carey McWilliams, *North from Mexico, The Spanish-Speaking People of the United States* (Philadelphia and New York: J. B. Lippincott Company, 1949), pp. 280–283:

"Gonzalo Méndez, a citizen of the United States, had been a resident of . . . Westminster, in Orange County, California, for twenty-five years. . . . There are two schools in Westminster . . . (one) for the Anglo-Americans; and a Mexican school (with) . . . meager equipment. . . . Gonzalo Méndez . . . said that he didn't like the idea of his (three children) . . . growing up with hatred in their hearts for the children who went to the beautiful [Anglo-American] school. [In nearby El Modeno, the two segregated schools] . . . were side by side; but the Mexican youngsters were always served lunch at a different hour from the Anglo-American students. Concluding that this practice had gone on long enough, Méndez filed a suit in the federal courts on March 2, 1945, on behalf of some five thousand Mexican residents of the district, against the school officials of Orange County.

". . . The (California) School Code permits segregation (as of 1948) of 'Indian children or children of Chinese, Japanese, or Mongolian descent,' but says nothing about Mexicans or Negroes. Without formal sanction, the (school) practice of segregating Mexican children . . . came about in California largely through default of any determined resistance on the part of Mexican-Americans. . . . (The) superintendent (of a school) . . . involved in the Méndez suit wrote a thesis in 1939 in which he defended segregation on the ground of 'social differences' between the two groups; the higher percentage of 'undesirable behavior patterns' among Mexican students . . . and the 'lower moral standards' to be found in the Mexican group.

"In some cases, segregation was accomplished by a fancy gerrymandering of school districts; but the more common practice was to use the arbitrary linguistic device of assigning all children with Spanish names to a separate school. Occasionally the school authorities would examine the appearance of youngsters so as to prevent the offspring of a Mexican mother whose married name might be O'Shaughnessey, from slipping into the wrong school. . . . (The) general scheme was to segregate Mexicans from the first through the sixth, and in some cases through the twelfth, grade.

"In the trial of the Méndez case, the school authorities at first contended that Mexicans were a distinct and . . . 'inferior' race; but confronted by the testimony of some world-famous anthropologists, they soon abandoned this position. . . . (It) had been determined years ago—*In re Rodríguez*, 81 Fed. 337—that Mexicans of Spanish descent and of mixed Spanish-Indian descent were 'white persons' within the meaning of the naturalization laws. The superintendent of schools then testified that Mexican children were 'dirty'. . .

"In a memorable opinion handed down on March 21, 1945, Judge Paul J.

McCormick ruled that segregation of Mexican youngsters found no sanction under the California laws and . . . also violated the 'equal protection' clause of the Fourteenth Amendment. Segregation, Judge McCormick suggested, might have something to do with . . . Mexican youngsters (being) . . . retarded in English speech. It also had the effect, he said, of 'depriving them of a common cultural attitude . . . which is imperative for the perpetuation of American institutions and ideals' and of fostering antagonism. When the decision was appealed to the Ninth Circuit Court, *amicus curiae* briefs were filed on behalf of Méndez by the American Jewish Congress, the National Association for the Advancement of Colored People, the National Lawyers Guild, the American Civil Liberties Union, the Japanese-American Citizens League and by Robert W. Kenny, as attorney general of California. On April 14, 1947, the Ninth Circuit Court affirmed Judge McCormick's ruling.

"In a brilliant concurring opinion, Justice William Denman exposed (the school authorities') . . . shabby rationalizations. The segregation of Mexican students in the schools, he caustically noted . . . was part of a pattern of discrimination. . . . For, as he observed, the Rev. R. N. Núñez, a Catholic priest, Eugenio Nogueras, a college graduate, and Ignacio López, a newspaper publisher, had been forced to file a suit in the federal courts to enjoin the officials of nearby San Bernardino from barring 'Latins' from the public swimming plunges . . . *all* 'Latins' had been barred: clean or dirty, healthy or diseased, black or white; in fact, as Justice Denman pointed out, the prohibition was so broad as to have embraced the nationals of twenty-one South American nations, Mexico, Italy, Spain, and Portugal."

After "the filing of this precedent-shattering case . . . in a dozen or more (Mexican) communities similar suits were filed or movements launched to eliminate segregated schools; and in El Modeno the Mexicans followed up their victory in the courts by electing one of the group a member of the local school board." School segregation in Bell Town near Riverside, California, existed because "the school officials . . . frankly stated that the encroachment of Mexicans and Negroes would depreciate property values. . . . After a long fight, the (Mexican-American) residents of Bell Town won out. On September 16, 1946, the supervisor of schools told his staff, 'If there is as much as one segregated Mexican-American pupil, see to it that he gets unsegregated immediately.'"

12. Such as the volumes by Carey McWilliams, cited in n. 11 and in Chapter 4, n. 13; and Ruth D. Tuck, *Not with the Fist: Mexican-Americans in a Southwest City* (New York: Harcourt, Brace and Company, 1946).

13. A second Mexican-American teacher of Spanish handed the writer a note asking, "Are [certain] characteristics shown when a Mexican-American individual [is in sufficient] command of his [family] culture so that he can go on to master the Anglo-American culture?" Subsequent conversation revealed that he was thinking of aggression and competition. The writer answered that, "Initiative appears in pursuing higher education and better jobs. Then men leave the ghetto, though they keep in touch with the family remaining there. They want the children to speak correct Spanish, not the broken patois. They want the wife to have some education and be a companion, besides a housekeeper and mother. There is some ability to distinguish among individuals without reference to prejudice. There may be less display of *machismo*. The clergy exercise less influence. Girls also show initiative, perhaps more con-

sistently than men in keeping with their traditional domestic functions. There is more intermarriage with Anglos, because of freer movement in the general world."

14. *New York Times*, June 17, 1962.
15. According to Ignacio L. López, in 1963, editor of the now defunct *El Espectador*, for 28 years a Spanish-language weekly of Southern California. The paper served Mexicans of the Pomona valley, 1932–1960. Teachers discussing "the drop-out problem" did not stop to consider how the remaining Mexicans profited from their senior year.
16. Oliver La Farge, *A Pause in the Desert* (Boston: Houghton Mifflin, 1957), pp. 183–184, "The Happy Indian Laughter."
17. The *New York Times*, June 17, 1962, reports a federal government grant to help finance a Hunter College project training teachers for slum schools. A speaker is quoted as saying that teachers "often" experience "emotional trauma . . . (upon) teaching in a situation where the majority of students are from families of the lower socio-economic groups." Among the materials to be developed "are tapes that record the speech of children from deprived areas."
18. See Chapter 3, p. 56, and Chapter 3, n. 28.
19. Fred M. Hechinger in the *New York Times*, June 24, 1962, reports that "American legal and educational leaders . . . are seriously concerned about the lack of understanding of the meaning of civil liberties among young people.

"These experts assign much of the blame to inadequate teaching in high school. Last week, they outlined a course of action to bring about nation-wide reforms in teaching about the Bill of Rights and the idea of personal freedoms.

"The program is sponsored by the Civil Liberties Educational Foundation, Inc. . . . 200 Park Avenue South, New York 3. . . . The foundation has budgeted about $150,000 . . . for reform of the social studies curriculum within the next two years.

". . . Since teaching about civil liberties is largely concentrated in the eleventh-grade history course, many of the 30 per cent of students who drop out before graduation never get any instruction on civil liberties. . . . The essence of the proposals is that freedom must be understood in order to be preserved." © 1962 by The New York Times Company. Reprinted by permission.
20. Los Angeles City Board of Education requires Spanish to be taught in elementary curriculum. *Cf. Point of View: Educational Purposes, Policies, Practices* (Los Angeles City Schools: Publication No. 470, 1961 Revision), p. 30.
21. In other localities, ample cooperation was forthcoming to official overtures. A PTA meeting in an elementary school drew a 100 per cent attendance of young Mexican-American parents with their children. The program called on each child to rise and present his parents. Elsewhere the Los Angeles County Probation Department sponsored a picnic for clubs converted from youth gangs, attracting families from nine towns of three counties; the attendance was reported as 85 to 90 per cent Mexican. All refreshments were contributed by Mexican-American parents organized into Parents' Clubs; none were offered by parents of the few Negro and white children attending.
22. The form letter ran:

June 1960

Dear Parents:

We would like to encourage boys and girls to continue to strengthen their reading program during the summer. In order to do this, we are arranging to have older students help their younger brothers and sisters. Some suggestions are:

1. Older children read to younger.
2. Older children listen to younger read.
3. Older and younger brothers and sisters use library facilities regularly during the summer and share interesting books read.
4. Older and younger brothers and sisters keep records of books read:
   a. Book Title   b. Number of pages read   c. Brief statement about the story
5. Both older and younger brothers and sisters return record to respective schools in September.
6. STUDENTS WHO SERIOUSLY PARTICIPATE IN PROGRAM WILL RECEIVE SPECIAL RECOGNITION IN SEPTEMBER.

Please check and sign. . . .

( ) Yes, I will encourage my children to participate actively in the summer reading program as outlined above.

. . . .

Parent's Signature

(Attached was a card reading:)

MY RECORD OF SUMMER READING

NAME   SCHOOL

TITLE OF BOOK

TOTAL NUMBER OF PAGES

I ENJOYED THE STORY BECAUSE

( ) Yes, my son and/or daughter read the above book and shared some of the interesting parts of the book with me.

. . . .

Parent's Signature

23. Murat Özgün and İhsan Gökçe, ALFABE (Istanbul: Devlet Basimevi, 1936). The first author was then headmaster of Edirne Kurtuluş İlkokulu and the second was then headmaster of Edirne Gazi İlkokulu.

   This primer is now out of print. Copies were given to the writer, translated and explained by a young Turkish woman, Mrs. Nilgül Şanlı Matters, educated and married in the United States. Her assistance was timely and stimulating.

24. See letter to the editor of *The New York Times* (Sunday) *Magazine*, July 8, 1962, from Jacob Landers, Coordinator, Higher Horizons, New York.

6

Counseling
in Social Work

In its concern with public welfare, mental hygiene, and child care, social work,[1] since early in this century,[2] has been an arm of some systems of public schooling. This parallels its penetration as a "helping profession"[3] into industry, government, juvenile courts, hospitals, and psychiatric, guidance, and correction agencies. As schools serve "pupils" and medicine serves "patients," social work serves "clients"[1] through agencies and independent practitioners. Clients are individuals and groups that are identified as being trapped in hardships which also threaten community welfare. The hardships include notably: severe poverty, unemployment, delinquency, illegitimacy, attendant physical and mental disease, broken homes, senility, and catastrophes of nature (like flood, earthquake, fire) and of society (like war and economic crises), singly or in combinations. Social work's paramount goal is to help clients adjust to their world, or to help them rehabilitate themselves in it, through established institutions. Social work applies an eclectic set of concepts and methods drawn from medicine and psychiatry, political science and penology, religion and ethics, education, economics, behavioral sciences, dietetics, and legislation. Its characteristic techniques are case work, group work, and community organization.[4]

More pragmatic than educators, social workers evolve their standards on empirical bases in addition to theoretical ones. These are constantly tested, expanded, and reformulated, as in present concerns with minorities. From the daily encounters with clients, social workers expect variations of respectably established living modes, and

139

handle them in consultation with other agencies and the social sciences.[5] This orientation differentiates people who come to teaching from social work.[6] Unlike educators who are customarily confined in schools, teachers who were once social workers anticipate the unexpected in pupils' lives and are ready to attack problems by appealing to additional channels of the community; they focus on pupils', not on their own, pedagogic "frustrations." Though restrained by school customs, they often mention that they should visit homes, clinics, and service agencies for disturbed or distressed pupils and parents.

The former social workers who participated in the Claremont experiment were not appalled that pupils with subordinated traditions (like Latins, who cherish family needs above all) and unfortunate backgrounds (like otherwise typical Anglos who depart from standards, for example, in having practiced father-daughter incest for two and more generations) heeded private ties more closely than they obeyed the school. Earlier professional work with social ills, such as alcoholism or pregnancy of a minor, had shown them that erratic obedience to conventional standards, especially in districts that are isolated or of high mobility, was not to be punished but treated by "helping" clients through reeducation to meet the standards. School authorities, on the other hand, often condemn and chastise offenders. As transiency soars among all groups, including the middle class, social work treats a widening range of clients,[7] including schoolchildren of every social condition.

Unlike graduate training of school counselors, that of school social workers or visiting teachers [8] locates many causes and cures of people's problems in relationships with society. The approach is developed through class study and agency supervision [9] of workers' interviews with clients, the records and analyses of data, the plans for relief and therapy, and progress in awareness.[10] Some social workers help steer troubled youngsters through each one's entire development, which includes educational plans. Certain large city systems in California provide school social workers who may be experienced teachers but who must also be trained in post-graduate school social work; [11] because of severe difficulties in conduct or living circumstances, the client-pupils are referred to them by the teacher and school administrative officer. Specialized school counselors, in addition to vice-principals and deans, advise all students in elementary school, high school, and public college systems about schooling and jobs or careers only.[12] Principals and school psychologists provide supporting services.

The school counselor advises his numerous students in his office, reconstructing their out-of-school experiences in interviews, and planning academic or job prospects from psychological tests and other favored protocols. The attendance officer visits homes of truants; the nurse visits homes of the ill and those whose hygienic standards are substandard, often evidenced by impetigo, head-lice, or general scruffiness. The school social worker repeatedly visits pupils' homes and neighborhoods, bases plans for relief and therapy on the knowledge thus gained and on teachers' information, consults other appropriate authorities, and seeks to influence the pupil in his complex bonds with parents, friends, and clergy. This broad cultivation of a child's life sphere differentiates social work from other school guidance.

The following case illustrates manipulation of cultural factors by a school social worker to expedite the desired outcome.

A nine-year-old Korean-American boy with an IQ of 130 was reported for violence toward teachers and pupils, in acts that ranged from speaking offensively to throwing a chair at the teacher. The violence mounted for two years until the principal suspended the boy and threatened him with a long "medical exemption" from school. His brother, aged fourteen, was doing well at another school. For a long time the school social worker tried to reach the father and secure his permission to place the child in psychotherapy, hoping the treatment would save the boy from a "medical exclusion." The father evaded her. The father, proud of being the son of a distinguished musician, had been a violinist in his native Korea. The boy's mother was an American born of Korean parents, much younger than her husband. Though gainfully employed as a secretary, she told the worker that she could make no decision about the recommendation to take the suspended pupil to a child guidance clinic for psychiatric care; the decision had to be her husband's. As the husband continued to evade the social worker, even when she visited the house before breakfast, the worker asked the writer (who was then training social workers in cultural anthropology at the University of Southern California) how to deal with the obdurate Oriental. As an anthropologist knowing something of the culture of the Orient in general, though nothing of Korea, the writer surmised that some trouble lay in clashing notions of male and female responsibilities. Compromise here might open negotiations. Hence two social-work students of anthropology were asked to prepare studies on aspects of Korean culture. One, a young veteran of the Korean conflict, studied Korean education, and the other studied the family, aided by a Korean college student who visited her home. Relating their cultural findings to the present case, the writer and the two students saw that some Korean demands had indeed been violated and others ignored by school officials. In Korea, the father is the powerful family head, unmarried females are permanent minors, all females are subordinated to males, the elder son outranks the younger, individual and family prestige rests considerably on scholarship, and (male) teachers are revered.

However, school people, following American custom, had consulted only the mother about the boy. The social worker was an unmarried woman, easy for the father to rebuff. From what was learned of Korean preferences, it was agreed that the social worker cease consulting the mother and calling on the father. Instead, she was to write the father about the crisis and invite him to her office to discuss it. When he answered favorably, he was invited to school with his wife. Feeling it vital to exhibit the social worker's awareness of his male rank, the worker was to consult the father first, and alone. This procedure was calculated to restore traditional proprieties and permit the father to respond satisfactorily, by his lights and by American ones.

All followed smoothly. After the worker reported details carefully, the father expressed shock at his son's disrespectful acts and the paternal neglect this implied; he agreed sadly and earnestly to "give [his] son to the [psychiatric] clinic"; he commanded his wife to cooperate even if clinic hours conflicted with her job; and the principal satisfactorily reinstated the boy in school.[13]

The writer's teaching of social workers was facilitated by their special humanitarian interest in "adjusting" personalities through case work, group work, and community organization,[14] their acquaintance with highly diverse social circumstances [15] and behavior, and their disciplined self-examination linked with trained sensitivity to others. Social workers accepted the cultural view that it was improper to conceptualize "the normal person," but proper to conceptualize *standards* of normality and of deviation which are customary in every group and which vary among groups. In anthropological reasoning, individual personality emerges into strength and form as genetic potentials respond to pressures of the environment or culture. Pressures are exerted by personalities of cultural adepts—parents, teachers, police, and clergy—and by semiadepts—(juvenile) agemates—within relationships designated as family, school, government, church, friendship, etc. The child is a cultural novice who progresses toward adeptness and maturity as tradition decrees, acting through parents and other mentors. Only adepts or adults can be held responsible for maintaining concepts of "normality," so it is misleading to speak of the behavior of "normal and abnormal children." Children learn well or poorly, following standards of the environment, which function both externally to the person and internally as thoughts, emotions, and habits.

Much bad learning appears to result from poor exposure to norms. Learning, in a particular culture, is rated by highly specific criteria of success and failure. In our culture the criteria include IQ scores, earned income, scholastic advance, occupational titles, maintenance of status, physical and nervous diseases, sometimes creativity. The beachcomber and remittance man of an earlier day, the Skid Row habitués and subway sleepers of today are those who knowingly reject the criteria.[16] Descriptions of "wolf-children" found occasionally in forests of medieval and preindustrial Europe [17] and in contemporary India show the foundlings' nearly total inability to learn man's speech, gait, manners, interests, or even ways of survival in society. They suggest neurological injury and severely curtailed limits, functional or organic, to a child's ability to learn when tragic forces dominate the early years. Julian Huxley's concept of culture, or man-made environment, as expressing the functioning of human "minds-in-society" suggests how the wolf-child's long, early exile from society cripples his awareness of man's ways and concerns. This bears implications for the conduct of minorities, delinquents, and the mentally handicapped insofar as these groups are barred from participating in standard social life.

Correspondingly, behavioral science, including culture theory, hypothesizes that human potentials for learning are practically limitless when conditions allow suitable exposure to norms. Norms enter all social relationships, at any time of the clock or year. Besides inferences from the wolf-children, work with the mentally deficient [18] and mentally disordered suggests inappropriate learning by such children in abnormal situations. Psychotherapy may be described as normative retraining of culture bearers, who first learned inappropriately or undesirably in social relationships, manifesting the syndromes labeled Oedipus and other complexes or apathy under racial discrimination. Social work is committed to the psychotherapists' assumption that paths of abnormal or wrong learning can be retraced and righted. Medicine and behavioral science further infer, from geriatrics research, that under favorable conditions human aging of itself sets no firm limits on abilities to learn and create.

Anthropologists believe that members of a society develop as local traditions allow. Kroeber put the case vigorously, describing the limited variety of geniuses permitted by each historic culture though genetics offers no support of such limits.[19] He inferred that not more than 2 or 3 per cent of potential geniuses has found opportunity in culture, though without culture "the percentage would have been zero." [20] This is consistent with interpretations derived by Otto Klineberg and others [21] from studies of school performance of minority members and of others from poor social backgrounds. [22]

Today the total population of women rouses some interest as an untapped reservoir of potential talent for the space age. The historic preponderance of women in social work and elementary-school teaching, [23] though yielding to an influx of men since the Second World War, has accompanied the lesser prestige and rewards of these professions. In earlier generations, unmarried and widowed women took to these professions because they were respectable and unclaimed, and the women accepted pay significantly below the competitive standards for men. American working women have resembled a social minority because of masked conflicts between the American creed of equality and traditionally-ranked differentiations between the spheres of women and men. Women share the voting franchise and most schooling with men, but they are not equals in open job competition and consequently are not trained to develop incentives for jobs nor for exerting creative effort in science, mathematics, and fine arts. Differential training of the sexes has similarly differentiated results at any level of culture. Among hunters of an Ojibwa Indian tribe, [24] men anxiously pursued hallowed goals of hunting, war, magic, gambling, and romantic love; they gained expected rewards and suffered expected hardships of physical and mental diseases. Women were called on to meet these goals only in emergencies; usually they expected no rewards and usually they suffered no hardships of disease.

At this moment in our culture, the equality creed affects females of all groups, imposing on girls and women the motivation to succeed, regardless of ancestral tradition. The writer's social work students included young women of conservative families in their patriarchal homelands of Greece, China, Japan, Hawaii, India, the Philippines, Holland. They learned from observation that prestigious work in our country is measured by male endeavors; and that under "equality," women in the United States are spurred to men's work. Women reveal their anxious participation by adding to the male statistics of illness from duodenal ulcer, cerebral damage, and alcoholism. As yet, the glorious hazards of space exploration are reserved for men, though at least one woman astronaut has been described in the public press. Some critics complain that the prevailing winds of equality between the sexes turn men unambitious, content them with secure jobs and conjugal domesticity. The "normal man" has been similarly criticized. [25]

All service or helping professions are potential and profitable users of the cultural approach. In medicine, ministry, government, education, social work, immediate use can be made of known cultural facts about a people, including processes and trends clearly stated by or apparent in the culture and those inferred from comparisons of different cultures. Thus, the *New York Times,* May 20, 1962, reported from Abeokuta, Nigeria, the eight-year-long work of Dr. T. Abeoye Lambo, a Nigerian psychiatrist trained at Britain's Royal College of Surgeons. In 1954, Dr. Lambo opened a hospital for a "community system" of mental care of Africans. Treatment included traditional procedures, such as "animal sacrifices, rituals and dances for anxious Africans," besides modern psychiatric techniques. Patients were commonly tribeswomen suffering from anxious fears of sterility, and tribesmen anxiously fearful of sorcery and of being killed by sorcery. Dr. Lambo was quoted as saying that such ills needed to be treated by modes familiar to the patients and so the old rituals of sorcery were adapted to the ends of modern psychiatry.

In training social workers and educators, the writer presented the same assumptions about culture and personality and the same practical suggestions for counseling grounded on the assumptions. They included the following:

1. Since norms are first taught a child by his parents, who continue to teach him daily, social workers, teachers, and counselors must develop active associations with parents, both at school and in neighborhoods and homes. California and New York schools report that Spanish-speaking children, for example, can be taught more readily when their parents have been educated in public schools. California teachers could often recognize more tractable pupils as children of former pupils. When school officials reach personally beyond schoolgrounds, all parties learn, and gains soar. A famous teacher writes, "Good teaching depends for its effect on the personal relationship between teacher and pupil and must, in every case, be careful and special. For personal relationship there can be no substitute . . . it is the essence of inspiration." [26]

2. School and social work counselors and teachers should be familiar with the subcultures and languages of the groups they deal with. Even the English spoken by isolated groups—for instance, rural Negroes and Okies—voices an alienated tradition that grates upon that favored by school standards. Details, such as schooling, work, marital status, religion, and regional origins of each family, must be known, for these guide a pupil's responses.

3. Educators and counselors should be trained to study their respective individual cultural and family antecedents in order to more clearly comprehend their own behavior. Such comprehension helps to clarify exchanges with pupils and parents, including the disturbances that rest on cultural differences. By this approach, "apathy" can be understood as an adaptive mechanism in particular situations of prejudice, rather than as personal insolence or stupidity alone. The training requires a culture specialist, especially in regions of high transiency and many cultural traditions, like Southern California.

4. Recommendations for school action should follow careful observations of both child and parents. This includes silent watching. The words of an authority can frighten any group, and people tell a great deal without words. In the case of a Mexican-American high-school girl who did not transfer to a recommended enriched course, possible behavioral information was wasted because no educator understood her parents' fear of losing her through the transfer. Rather than weaken school standards, such approaches will support them by suggesting fresh tactics for achieving desired ends.

5. Educators and counselors should know the detailed forms and limits of responsibility defined by the pupil's family group. Asking, "Now, what shall we do?" often fails with a Mexican, Negro, Okie, or other boy accustomed to firm expressions of authority according to generation, sex, and status. In these groups, a child is seldom requested to make a decision bearing on adult duties or privilege; to do so may hint at a threat. When school authorities act in this fashion, they often rouse the confused responses conventionally labeled "hostile" or "apathetic."

6. School faculty should devise models of work and action for all parties. An effective junior high-school model in California was the Mexican-American cadet corps that taught Spanish. Careers of pupils and teachers were influenced by this; good will among the entire student body and respect from the general community toward the school were engendered. Printed materials on fields of humanities, arts, and sciences should be circulated and recommended.

7. In counseling those of unfamiliar backgrounds, the "normal curve of distribution" should be set aside. The curve serves only particular norms. The negative implications oppress vulnerable groups. Since 1959, New York City's Higher Horizons program among Puerto Rican pupils in elementary and junior high schools has supplied remedial and enriched teaching and guidance for the children and their parents. The pupils originally scored very low on standard tests and curves but responded with superior achievements to the new approach.

8. Educators and counselors should individualize their relationships with students. The learner's mind does not automatically process all environmental stimuli. Ideally, teaching should spark motivation, firing the student's desire to carry on. Our massive professionalization, however, seems to favor anonymity and social distance. In simpler societies and in our own society of the last century, even certain irregular personalities were allowed some social usefulness. American Plains Indians kept their berdache male transvestites and their male visionaries in the tribal community, endowing them with the responsibilities of their divergencies and making them indispensable. Berdaches, who were openly homosexual, cultivated arts and other visionaries cultivated war, the hunt, and medicine. Situations in works of Tolstoi, Dostoievski, Turgenev, and others illustrate how the Russians acted similarly with village idiots and eccentrics. To foster an individual's skills is the happiest show of respect.

9. Teachers and counselors should assume judicious initiative and responsibility toward pupils without expressing hostility. Students in high school and junior college are very aware of some educators' competitiveness and hostility toward them, though the educators themselves may be unaware of this. These attitudes, and also the failures of some educators to carry through responsibly, injure a learner's confidence in the right to the dependence that fosters learning, creativity, and ambition. Dependence on a responsive teacher, whatever the learner's age, serves the open limits of human genius, that mental plasticity which evolves culture.

In order to aid social workers to experience freshly and to analyze the traditional standards governing their behavior—personal, professional, routine, and spontaneous—from birth on, the writer directed each member of the anthropology seminars to record his own family culture, as was described for educators in Chapter Four. Each student spent weeks gathering data from kinfolk near and far; following intensive preparation, each one presented his study orally before the seminar and graduate faculty of social work. Members of the seminars brought to them the advantages of cultural and racial variety since they came from Europe and Asia, from Negro and white America, from the Mexican-American Southwest, and from Spanish-American New Mexico; their ages ranged from the early twenties to the late fifties.

Reports by each of the foreign women personally documented contrasts between women's positions in the home culture and women's positions in American life as well as conflicts and shifts of traditional standards under American influences.[27] The presentation of a Louisiana

Negro woman was paired with that of a Missouri white woman to bare conflicts and shifts of older Southern biracial norms in the freer California world. Presentations of a Mexican-American man and of an Italian-American man were paired to compare adjustments of immigrant groups, including recent changes of minority status among young veterans. The paired couples were of the same age. Differences of generation and status erupted when a senior faculty member occasionally objected that the family materials were public "confessions." The students thought otherwise and also willingly released their manuscripts for use in this book. In the discussion following each presentation, traditional social forces were identified by analyzing meanings of events according to the speaker's cultural background and interests. Then these forces were compared with those in situations of conflict and compromise during social work with clients.

An Anglo-American's examination of his family through several generations illuminated the cultural life of one American region and served as a first norm for comparing ways of other cultural groups. This student began the study expecting it to document his belief that he was of Protestant English origins, only to find that he was actually descended from Irish Catholics. Many of his remarks occur in a seemingly casual style of dry understatement, verging on humor, that is characteristically American, and he uses some idiomatic turns of phrase tellingly. He entitled his paper "The Cultural Role of the Male in American Society" and organized it in three sections, calling the first, "Ancestral History, or from Medicine Man to Millionaire," the second "Personal History and Small Town Cultural Characteristics," and the third "Characteristics of Family Structure."
The first section began:

My ancestral past has always been quite vague to me; this seems never to have been a topic of much interest in our family. I understand from the literature about American culture that this [indifference] probably means a long period of establishment, . . . always looking ahead toward the future and having no interest in one's past. . . . The information I give here was recently received from my mother and some relatives. It proves quite interesting.
First, I discovered that at least from my father's side, I am only third generation, my grandfather having been born in Ireland. Second, I discovered that I am practically full blooded Irish. . . .
My paternal great grandparents were farmers who came from Iniskillin county in southern Ireland, near Belfast. My grandfather was born in 1864, in this same county. My great grandparents came to this country about 1868 . . . probably around the time of the potato famine in Ireland. . . . They settled in Wisconsin and farmed there, moving in 1882 to Iowa for the remainder of their lives. My great great grandparents apparently also came

to this country about the same time, settling in and around Chicago and Iowa.

One great grandparent on my father's mother's side came from southern Ireland and settled in Iowa while my great great grandparents on this side came from Catholic Settlement in southern Ireland and settled in Pennsylvania as farmers. My great grandparents from this latter side supposedly became millionaires. Their millions were litigated in court for several years after their deaths.

My grandfather grew up and was educated in Illinois, Iowa, and Wisconsin, learning telegraphy and then railroad engineering. He married my grandmother in Iowa in 1892. In 1893, they moved to Superior, Wisconsin, where he was an engineer on the St. Paul-Omaha railroad. Here my father was born. In 1903, my grandfather and family moved to North Dakota where he practiced railroad telegraphy and later farmed.

Knowledge of the maternal family was relatively vague:

In all probability my great grandparents on my mother's father's side also came from southern Ireland. My mother is uncertain because, she said, her parents talked little about it. However they did come from Ireland and as they were strong Catholics, she supposed it was the southern part. . . . These people were also farmers and later retired around Chicago. . . . It is an interesting sidelight that these great grandparents came from about the same place and have the same name as my great grandparents on my father's mother's side, so possibly both sides are related.

My grandfather was born and raised in Springfield. He left home when about nineteen years of age, pioneered the midwest plains herding cattle . . . [and] finally homesteaded in Colorado.

The ancestry of my great grandfather on my mother's mother's side is unknown. Apparently he was some type of medicine man, dealing with medicinal properties of herbs, learned from his Indian friends; his clientèle included both Indians and white men. My mother states that he helped both white men and Indians dissolve a lot of their superstitions about medical practitioners. . . . Eventually he became a veterinarian and settled near a fort in Lupton, Colorado. As a small girl, my grandmother traveled the plains of Missouri, Arkansas, Kansas, and Colorado with him in a covered wagon.

My father was born and raised in North Dakota. [Discharged from the army after the First World War] . . . he traveled around the midwest. . . . Working on a farm in Colorado, he met my mother and married her. . . . She was about seventeen while he was twenty-three or twenty-four.

The second section related:

I was born into a coming family of four in a booming small town of approximately 500 population on the North Dakota prairies, when my father and mother were visiting his parents, shortly after their marriage in Colorado. . . . We went back to Colorado where I lived the first three or four years of my life. My father worked as a hired hand on some of the best farms there and also helped my mother's relatives with their farms. . . . I remember we lived in a rented house on one of the farms and that my mother's chief worry concerned my trying to ride my tricycle across the narrow boards straddling the wide irrigation ditches.

I do not know what persuaded my parents to return to North Dakota in 1928, though it probably had something to do with business propositions from my grandfather there. The trip of several hundred miles was made in a used sports car that we bought, an old Chandler. I remember fording streams with the car and my mother hollering in anxiety; the road would disappear into a river and following it, one could not know the river's depth. Apparently bridges were not too usual then. Getting stuck in the Black Hills of South Dakota was another event . . .

[My birthplace was] in the approximate center of North Dakota. The nearest large town was Bismarck, about 60 miles away. This little town of my birth was the thriving center of a prosperous farming community, the county seat and the largest little town for miles around. It boasted a fairly large drugstore, a kind of community hall where they later showed the first silent films, a general hardware store, a lumber yard, a couple of restaurants, a pool hall, a light plant, a bank, a couple of doctors, some fairly nice homes and last, but not least, plenty of churches and plenty of bars.

The light plant produced electricity from 8 in the morning until midnight or so. Only one man in town seemed capable of operating it, and if, as happened often, he had had a rough time the night before, the town might not get electricity until late the next day.

The business and professional men were of course the town élite, particularly . . . the owner of the bank and the drug store. Looking back through my childhood eyes, I remember that the owner of the drug store was so élite that he seemed unapproachable by the ordinary person, and was one before whom to be humble. He had the nicest home in town and set the social pace.

The two doctors in town were of course family doctors, general practitioners, about whom everybody always had something to say, good or bad . . . [such as that] one or the other was the best doctor in the state or a horsedoctor. The version . . . depended partly on whether patients found the doctors intoxicated or sober . . .

Next in terms of social status . . . were the farmers . . . [First were those] with the large, more prosperous farms; next were the small farmers or "almost" homesteaders. . . . The lowest class . . . was the foreigners or Russian thistle farmers, as they were called. . . . [They had come] to North Dakota from Russia sometime in the past. . . . To call someone a Russian or a "dumb Russian" was to show the contempt you had for him . . .

[My young father] . . . having no farm property of his own yet, worked for a time around town as a carpenter and then went into business with my grandfather operating what they called a "dray" business—a trucking line that my grandfather set up to haul produce from our town to Bismarck. One of my clearest childhood memories concerns my fifth or sixth birthday when my father promised to take me with him on his truck to the city. I stayed awake half the night to make sure I did not get left. This trucking business occasioned much dispute between my cousin and me. There were two trucks, his father driving one and mine the other, and we argued continually which father drove the more powerful truck. Here in embryonic development one can see a cultural factor of competition for recognition of power. After the trucking business, my father joined my grandfather managing the farm and eventually took over. By his death in 1930, we had built up a sizable farm. After his death, my mother sold the farm and we moved back to town.

Now my mother's cultural and personality characteristics came to the fore. She had two boys on her hands to take care of, one a baby and the other six or so years old.

The third section started:

Thinking about the structure of my family, I have tried to differentiate between characteristics of Irish culture and those more American. Traits of both seemed to appear together.

Characteristic of Irish culture, as well as of the American pioneer family . . . was a large family. My father's family included about ten offspring . . . [unlike my mother's]. . . . I know my mother did not believe in having too large a family. Most of my paternal uncles and aunts had large families, as do their offspring today.

Another characteristic of the old world culture is the authoritarian father. My grandfather was "It" in the family . . . [wielding power even over] married offspring. . . . My mother would get quite angry with my father for letting my grandfather influence him. . . . Primogeniture was a trait of our family organization and of Irish culture. My father was the eldest son and received most favors, as evidenced by his taking over my grandfather's farm. My grandmother had charge of the farmhouse and its events, besides the major burden of raising the children, while my father had charge of the rest of the farm. It was his duty to make a living for the family.

Another characteristic of the family . . . was its idea of kinship . . . probably another Irish trait. My paternal family was a close-knit organization, differentiating themselves as a group from the rest of the community. Some of this persists among the younger offspring. They visited with each other, helped each other when in trouble, and made gossip about relatives a chief topic of dinner conversation. When at times they got angry with each other, visiting stopped but not for long. The kinship idea included exchanging properties and renting houses to each other. Conflict among themselves was alright—but let an outsider say anything and they banded together against him, family conflicts forgotten.

A further family trait, which I think is from the old world, is respect for the older generation. My grandparents, particularly my grandfather, were respected and looked up to by offspring until they died. This seems also true on my mother's side . . .

My grandparents' family was an independent group, believing in doing everything for themselves; the less they depended on others, the better. Independence meant not being obligated to anyone, primarily financially. You owned your own farm, paid for everything in cash, had money in the bank, etc. This seems true of both sides of the family. My mother has often told how my grandfather was too independent even to ask people to pay bills owing him.

Another characteristic of the family on both sides, definitely Irish in culture and apparently also American, is covering up feeling about something. Particularly if the emotion is a tender one, you do not dare express it, more especially if a male . . . I remember being taught as a child that to express feeling was unmanly: if you did not want to grow up a sissy, you did not do this sort of thing. . . . A strong man was a silent one . . . with a stiff upper lip. . . . Some poignant memories of my grandfather concern this attitude. . . . If you hurt yourself, you did not weep but took it like a man, proudly. When I was nine years old, an event illustrated this. I was pushing my brother in a wagon on a wooden sidewalk, in my bare feet. Stopping the wagon all of a sudden, quite a large sliver pierced my heel. I limped inside to my mother but she was unable to pull it out. We went over to a neighbor and together they managed to get it out. That night when my father came home, he decided to walk about a mile and a half to my grandfather's farm; I begged to go with him and he let me. I remember that on the walk to the farm and back I was so proud that I had not cried during the whole process and still had enough courage or guts to walk the distance on a lame foot. I doubt if I'd have that courage now. . . . The fathers had a large hand in teaching the male children this.

Another way of demonstrating virility was through size and strength. The yardstick . . . was the physical prowess of the father and other family men. If you are not big for your age, chances are against your being much of a man, and as far as importance to kin is concerned, "you've had it." Further indications of boyish or manly behavior were rough talk, evidences of sexual knowledge, about women especially, wrestling, occasional tomfoolery like stealing watermelons from a patch . . .

Sex of course was a taboo family subject, something that just happened and was never talked about. The knowledge is expected to come naturally to boys. . . . The girls apparently stayed pretty ignorant . . . supposed to "endure" sex for love of their man. The sex I learned was from boys' discussions.

As I see it now, the great difference between my father's and my mother's families was that my mother's was more Americanized. She had more ideas belonging to the American success dream, more striving to get to the top of the ladder, the notion that urbanization and education made one better off. I infer this because my brother and I are the only two among the younger kinfolk who have followed such ideas and pursuits. The others seem to have followed rather the ways of their grandfathers.

My mother's ideas emerged dramatically after my father died. . . . Her primary aim . . . was for her boys to grow up cultured gentlemen. She had the idea, probably rightly, that if we associated too much with boys of our small town or with our own relatives, we would grow up too much like them. She disliked small-town ways . . . this seems to have been a general feeling then. Her method enforced a certain isolation of us and close supervision in neighborhood and classroom. She constantly brought our bad behavior before our eyes and pointed out that others' countryish behavior got them nowhere. When I returned from Minnesota for my grandfather's funeral, I saw how the small town regarded the larger world. I was fifteen at the time, and really looked up to by the other adolescents as a guy from the city, one who had been around. The Minnesota city I was living in had a population of 13,000.

In the interval between my father's death and my mother's remarriage, conflicts arose over male and female identifications for my brother and me. We boys strove to retain the male standards of earlier years against female encroachment. These conflicts were probably sharper than those created by the "Momism" of our general culture.

The difference or distance between generations in American life is noticeable in my family. Obeying my parents' wishes that I "get further ahead" than they, through education and material possessions, I find now quite a difference between them and me. My life view is unlike theirs, I value their advice less, I consider some of their ideas narrow. In short, I find somewhat of a gulf between us for much, if not most of what we share, derives from the past. According to our American culture, this is as it should be, the older generation always expecting to be left behind. This contributes to the older generation's feelings of being useless and unwanted.

In my immediate family, my wife works, and though I acknowledge the necessity, I still feel that she belongs in the home and that I should provide. This is a conflict in our present culture that must be worked out. . . . My wife and I chose ourselves to get married, not consulting our parents; and I never saw her's. There were a few passing comments on both sides but no outright objections to our "right" to act so. The marriage of my father and mother followed much the same pattern. I expect my children to receive higher education and, if not exceeding my accomplishments, at least keeping up with them. I want the best for them and would hope they could avoid some of the pitfalls I encountered although, as I have been taught, [surviving pitfalls] is the only real way to learn.

In doing social work, domestic or international, it is vital to understand varieties of social structures—such as the family, the school, the class system, the ethnic or minority-dominant system—and of their functions. Therefore the seminar students were set to apply methods and principles selected from psychology, sociology, and anthropology to the data of diverse societies. Besides gleaning data from published studies and from their own family research, students were urged to continue getting data from observing the behavior of groups living around them as clients, friends, neighbors, and others, among whom they could move freely. Their temperaments and professional interests led them to welcome this requirement to get out into the field of life for their studies. Each one then compared the cultures he had studied at first hand with those discussed in seminar, uncovering the uniqueness in each culture and also the similarities among those compared.

Using these approaches, a Nisei Protestant social worker examined and interpreted the social world of her people, and so depicted an American subculture very different from that described in the preceding Anglo-American account. She wrote:

I had intended to describe general characteristics of families of Japanese descent living in this country, and changes in family structure and customs during the past 50 years. I find this most difficult . . . as acculturative influences differ markedly according to the individual's family background, occupation, generational membership, education, residential locale —i.e., rural, urban, segregated, etc. [Hence] I shall individualize much of the content of this paper.

The three generational groups are the Issei, the first generation immigrant; the Nisei, the American-born Japanese or literally the second generation; and the Sansei, the children of Nisei, or the third generation. I will review main features of family structure in Japan at the turn of the century as the majority of Japanese immigrants came to this country between the late 1800's and 1924.

Filial piety, respect for the aged, male superiority and ancestor worship were dominant features. The family was patriarchal in form, the father a symbol and object of respect and authority, the mother a symbol and object of warmth and affection. . . . Marriage was usually arranged by a go-between, with little place for individual choice of a mate, as marriage served family purposes.

Family continuity went through the oldest son. Families without sons commonly practiced adoption; the adoptee might be the daughter's husband. Family continuity was so important that lineages of prospective in-laws were carefully scrutinized. Liabilities in family lines included tuberculosis, leprosy, prison records, and inferior social status.

The family was the chief agent of social control . . . extended to life in the local community and in the nation. From early childhood I recall my father as the head of the household. . . . Father [a Protestant minister] was very active in community affairs but mother's participation was generally limited to accompanying him on formal occasions. The patriarchal pattern was modified in our family, as we all discussed family matters informally at home. Though the final decision appeared to rest with Father, it also seemed to accord with the family's general desire, and its authority was benevolent.

Reviewing this point with father, he attributed the modification to his accepting the Christian faith and emphasis on individual worth. I imagine contributing factors included his extensive observations of American families during his student days in New Haven, Connecticut, before his marriage. [Possibly these observations led to] his choosing a mate personally, unusual at that time, and . . . his rapid acculturation to American community life through extensive participation in local events and through many close friendships outside the Japanese group. Our family doctor, of English descent, was like an uncle to us. He gave me my first dog, when I was five; he gave me a doll each year and my first highball. He taught my mother to plan American meals. Immediately after World War II he insisted that my parents stay in his home until they could resettle in their own. When well-meaning friends commented to him, "How nice of you to take them in," he would answer angrily, "This is part of my family." Another close friend was an Englishwoman, formerly headmistress of the school mother attended in Japan. She acted like a foster-mother to my mother and, for several years after my parents' marriage, resided in the upstairs apartment of our home. She assumed the role of our maternal grandmother. Mother's role as homemaker included managing the household within a well-defined budget.

The relationship between parents and children was informal and affectionate; the children showed parents great respect and the parents stressed happiness and well-being of the children. Family solidarity is strong. Mutual help is still considered normal in family life. Each child has played a part in helping a sibling further his education. Respect for the aged influenced the honor and love shown my paternal grandmother, who at 72 came to live with us. Mother had such a close relationship with grandmother that people often mistook the latter for the maternal grandmother.

Family continuity did not mean the same to us as to our relatives in Japan. My maternal uncle showed this. Head of his household in Japan, he asked to adopt the youngest of my three brothers to insure continuity of his family line; this is done through retention of name and property by one of the main family (i.e., not through concubines or lesser wives). The request was refused [and he] asked to adopt me. I recall how lightly my brothers and I considered the request, having no comprehension of its importance to the family in Japan.

I cannot remember that my parents ever questioned my brothers' independent choices of marriage mates. Lineage checks were foreign to our family's practice. But prior to World War II I had heard frequently of families making lineage checks on the family of a prospective child-in-law before approving the marriage. In recent years I have not heard of such checks, though derogatory mention may be made of a person's inferior class. Such mention is no longer well received, generally, as emphasis is laid on the worth of the *individual*.

At twelve years of age, I took a trip to Japan and became strongly aware of the highly structured class system. I still recall vividly my paternal uncle's dismay to find me conversing freely with servants of the house. He asked my parents' permission to keep me and raise me to become a lady befitting the family's standing. I was told tales, in childhood, of my grandfather's experiences as a samurai or feudal warrior before the Meiji era, and I saw the pride attached to this . . .

In my brothers' families, I note that wives play a more equal role at home and a more active one in the community. Last night I asked my fourteen-year old nephew who made the decisions in the family. His first reply was "mother." He added that his mother was home all day and responsible for disciplining the children, as his father was away from home all day. He explained further that it depended on the problem as to who made the decision . . . but usually a decision followed informal discussion. When the problem involved him, he said he joined the discussion and frequently had the last word.

As children, we spoke both English and Japanese at home, usually English with father but English and Japanese with mother. In all my brothers' homes, English is the only language spoken daily; the children also speak English to their grandparents. These Sansei children of our family have little if any knowledge of the Japanese language.

The American style of speaking is very direct. The Japanese consider it rude to make an emphatic contradictory statement in conversation. These differences in the manner of speaking took my attention upon returning home to Los Angeles after four years in a dormitory at Carleton College, Minnesota, for I had difficulty accustoming myself to the mode of speech of our first generation friends.

. . . Japanese meals are frequently served in all my brothers' homes, and their children seem to enjoy them as much as American meals. Chinese, Mexican, and Italian dishes are also frequently on their tables. Mother always cooked Japanese dishes for my grandmother, but she frequently cooked American dishes for the rest of the family. Our diet is regulated somewhat by our [Protestant Episcopal] faith, requiring, for example, no meat on Good Friday and usually no meals before attending a Holy Communion service. On all important national holidays, the entire family congregates at one home, where traditional American dishes are served, like ham on Easter and turkey on Thanksgiving Day; but on New Year's day the traditionally elaborate Japanese dishes are served . . . The younger generation celebrates New Year's eve in the traditional manner but on New Year's day, the Japanese customs are intermingled with such customs of the local community as watching the Rose Parade on television in the morning and the Rose Bowl game in the afternoon.

As a child I remember celebrating many traditional Japanese holidays. One was Girl's Day on March 3d when I displayed my collection of dolls, especially the traditional set of the Emperor, the Empress, the Ladies in Waiting and the Five Royal Musicians. On Boy's Day, May 5th, now known as Children's Day, large paper fish are flown from house tops, the number according to the number of sons in the family. I believe that only one of my nieces is familiar with the Girl's Day celebration.

Japanese customs have been retained by the second generation especially in relationships with the Issei. One custom is giving money to the family of a deceased. A familiar sight at funerals is individuals bringing a white envelope with written expressions of sympathy and money enclosed. There are still families who acknowledge these with a small gift, like tea packed in a lacquer container.

In Japan the people greatly respect education. In this country, too, the Issei willingly sacrifice for their children's education. Esteem for scholars and teachers is instilled in children. This no doubt accounts for the diligence of Nisei at school and for the large number that continue studies in universities.

Before World War II, there were very strong family and community controls over the individual but this has decreased noticeably. There is still strong group solidarity in caring for one's own. An example is the annual Christmas fund raising campaign, called Cheer, for needy Japanese families.

Independence is cherished. The first generation is known for industry and thrift. People taken to live in relocation centers close to Indian reservations have commented how grateful they were that the centers were closed immediately after the war because they feared that a dependency (supposedly like the Indians') could have been established.

Changes continue in assimilating to the dominant culture. A problematic one now coming to the group's attention is juvenile delinquency. This had not previously required group concern and action.

A Dutch woman, who came to California from The Netherlands to study social work, probed intently among her family materials for the distinct culture elements, processes, and changes in Holland that her family reflected through generations. She also hoped by this means to discover what *she* was in society's scheme and what she would become, and by empathic extension she hoped to learn what kind of social beings *others* were. This attitude was an elaboration of the graduate social worker's training in examining the psychological processes of those dealt with, usually colleagues and clients. Writing in English, this student entitled her study, "The Culture that Made Up Me":

Both my parents belonged to upper middle-class families of intellectuals in Holland. Both had long lines of forefathers who were ministers, schoolteachers, physicians.

The families belonged to a non-Calvinistic minority, though our culture is dominated by Calvinistic religious and political convictions. Throughout the ages since the Reformation, a group of liberal intellectual families has influenced certain aspects of life in my country of Holland. At the end of the 19th century they stimulated intellectual development and schooling for the "masses," thinking that so the world would become a better place to live in.

On my father's side, the family belonged to the liberal, religious humanistic group of Mennonites who questioned the divinity of Christ. My mother's father was a liberal minister in the Dutch Reformed Church; this was a religious political minority fighting against Calvinist domination *for* public schools and modern Sunday School teaching, and *against* the belief in predestination. These views greatly influenced my education, my attitudes towards people and my choice of vocation. . . . We were brought up to be tolerant, to live and let live. Yet we had to fight continuously for places in the dominant orthodox culture. This produced conflicts, at least in me. My mother's father was more involved as a minister than my [paternal] grandfather who was a surgeon and director of a hospital.

To describe my education, I must go back to my mother's mother, who was probably a frustrated woman. Daughter of a minister in the southern part of the country, she was intelligent, had a beautiful voice, and wanted a career; but a career was impossible then, even in liberally thinking circles. As she could not get along with her stepmother, she left for Utrecht to direct the household of her widowed grandfather, a theology professor and poet. She was then 18 or 20. She met many people at her grandfather's, had an unhappy love episode, then met my future grandfather, a student of her grandfather's, and married him when fairly old, at about 28. I often wonder about that marriage. My mother says it was the only way out because the times forebade women a career.

My grandmother had eight children, of whom three died. She gave the daughters and sons much intellectual stimulation. All her children went through universities except my mother, a weak child with a stomach ulcer. The two other daughters never married. One has a very successful medical career. The other, less fortunate, had to teach and did not like it.

My mother married my father at 22. She went through a girls' school while the others attended preparatory schools for university. She helped her mother after school, having no special training. She envied her sisters somewhat but went the other way, becoming engaged at 19.

I was named for my maternal grandmother. My mother always insisted that I finish preparatory school even when I was inclined to give up. Our high-school training is strenuous compared with the American. My sister, five years younger than I, failed the entrance examination and married at 19, having less education than I. In spite of being married, she admired education and sent her daughter to preparatory school. My brother did not complete training, attended a school for tropical agriculture, and is now in Indonesia.

I felt that both my parents put more pressure on me to be trained than on the other children. Perhaps I was to compensate for my mother's not having a career. My father resented the fact that he was the only one in his family without a university degree. . . . He stimulated me for he was proud of me . . .

My father was one of five sons of a very successful surgeon. My grandfather was a celebrated personality and generally liked. My father had been physically weak as a child, and his father did not think a university degree necessary for the kind of work my father had chosen. But as an adult, my father was seldom ill. As my grandfather thought outdoor life would improve my father, he had him thoroughly trained as a horticulturist and got him a farm. Then father married my mother, whom he met through her brother studying at the same university.

During the [financial] crisis, my parents lost all the money invested in the farm and nursery. They sold out and we moved. My father taught horticulture, my mother worked hard with paying guests in the house. I helped while still very young. We never learned to like the never-ending house chores. Of course the family helped us; my aunt gave us money for vacations. I went through high school, traveling to the nearest big city. Perhaps here I compared the lives of my mother and aunt; I am sure my mother did so often when saying that she resented the lack of special training.

I soon realized that study gave me a lot of satisfaction. My brother was slower in his thinking and had a hard time. We often heard approvingly from both parents, especially my mother, that I should have been the boy and he the girl. Moreover I resembled my paternal grandfather strongly; this made my father proud of me and stimulated me the more. I wanted to become a doctor. But after high school there was no money. My aunt did not offer any to me and I did not ask. This was partly because of a dramatic event in my father's family. A young girl cousin of his, trained as a veterinarian, married a colleague. The training had been paid for by her sister, a physician who had given up all personal interests when her father died. He had left her his medical practice and the job of supporting her mother, three younger sisters and a brother. When the younger sister achieved her degree and also married, it caused a sensation. I thought, this I will never do. Now my cousin has five children and a successful practice with her husband—but this is exceptional in my country.

Years later my aunt told me that she resented never having married and, thinking a career would prevent me too from achieving marriage, she never offered me money.

There I was at 18, with a scholarship to study home economics in the nearby city. I got my teaching credential and was ready for professional life at 22. But I had become interested in psychology and what we called pedagogy.

Now that I was ready for a job, an old friend asked me to marry him. He had a house and farm and wanted me to be his wife. Though I liked him very much, I said I wanted first to try being independent by means of my training; that perhaps after a few years I might be more interested. He did not care to wait, however. Thus began my working life. I did not want only to be in a home, a leading lady of the small town, with the life my mother had. I wanted to use my education and see the world.

I chose rural social work. I traveled around by train, bus, and bicycle, organizing courses for women in backward areas, giving information and help to large families. After a few years I supervised workers in the same area. I felt that our in-service training was insufficient. So a few years after the Second World War, when courses in psychology, pedagogy, and social sciences were opened again, I went to Amsterdam to study on Friday nights and Saturdays.

Religious and political convictions in rural areas were rigidly Calvinist or Catholic. Because of my liberal convictions, church authorities made my work difficult. . . . [After a time] I accepted a scholarship for America with the understanding that a year later I would return to Utrecht.

When I first started living away from home, I had to choose between a married life and a career. It is not very possible to combine the two. Sometimes a married woman can work part-time; I know some women physicians, lawyers, and pharmacists who work with their husbands. But in general a husband does not like it, wanting wife and family to be dependent on him. A man thinks, What would people say if the wife worked? Of course, the number of married women who work is increasing. Some men barely tolerate this, not many are proud of it, most do not like it.

My married women friends who gave up careers have attitudes that range from resentment to resignation about the careers, and some feel happy, because their dependency needs are met. Some plan to return to work after the children are grown.

When I first broke away from home, I symbolized the rejection by buying furniture completely unlike the old family pieces. Here in California, all of a sudden I realize that I am happy among Victorian furniture. . . . I would not have such furniture ordinarily but it belongs to the home culture which I have learned to reevaluate.

Briefly, these factors influenced my growing up:

1. My family background, which belongs to an upper middle-class minority group of liberal religious and political intellectuals. There is a certain pride in the ancestry.

2. The lives of women relatives who stress education and career and show ambivalence towards marriage. There is a wish for fulfillment and independence.

3. The financial crisis which blocked my real career preference and obliged me to make the best of it.

4. Interests in career and study that led me to gradually abandon the idea of marriage. The combination of work and marriage is not well possible.

A youthful, pretty grandmother in the seminar presented a study that returned us lovingly and calmly to memories of our frontier society, and linked these to Central European forebears. It was dramatic and instructive to see side by side, and in the same profession, representatives of a parent culture and of its American offspring, and to trace the clear social variations in the respective versions of life. The study read as follows:

My maternal and paternal ancestors came to this country long ago; no family member seems to have knowledge of the time. We do know that my father's people came from Germany. They may have had a shadow over them or may have wanted to become completely American for they dropped the "Von" from the family name when they reached here. Three brothers came, one traveled on West, one went up into Canada, the other, my father's branch, settled in the South.

My mother's people came from Holland and also settled in the South. I recall my mother's tales of a great grandmother who was breast-fed by a Negro mammy because her mother wanted to preserve her beautiful breasts.

My mother was the oldest of a large group of children. She was left a good deal of her father's estate when he died; she was then sixteen. Her father had owned a large farm, was the state surveyor in Arkansas, had a blacksmith shop, and taught singing school.

When my mother and father were married, they traveled to what was then Indian territory in the future state of Oklahoma. They homesteaded there and experienced good and bad times. Much of my mother's money was used up in those years. They had nine children in all, four girls born a few years apart, then four boys, then I came when my parents were in their forties. By the time I was born, my sisters were married and had children so that these nieces and nephews were older than I. At ten years, I was a great-aunt. Even for Oklahoma, this was a bit unusual. One of my sisters breast-fed me along with her own baby because my mother was unable to nurse me.

This sister moved into town at the same time my parents did. I don't know who decided on the move first. I was then six years old. Before their move into this town of approximately 30,000 population, my folks had always lived in a rural area; and the family had been pretty much patriarchal. After the move, things gradually changed.

My parents opened a grocery store, sold it, and then operated a hotel with a restaurant. The place was kept open seven days a week from early morning until midnight. We had one of those old player-pianos with the tinkling sound attachment; customers kept it going. Only two children, my brother and I, were now at home and we lived at the place of business.

Probably because of the long work hours, we had little social life but there was always much excitement.

There was always hired help and the family worked too. I remember my father then as a rather silent man and, looking back, as a lonely man. I remember I was surprised to hear from my sisters how much fun he had been when they lived in the country. It was a country custom, they said, for families to gather from miles around at a church or schoolhouse, with enough food to last a day or so, and plenty of bedding; they threw themselves, grownups and children, into dancing, singing, music, and games. It seems my father had been one who enjoyed himself immensely as he danced with my mother and others.

After the move to town, old family friends would visit us and stay for weeks. This presented real hardships, as it would not have in the country. In town our hotel rooms needed to be let for pay instead of being used by noncontributing guests; and all food in town was purchased from the store, no longer raised in the garden or on the farm. But it would have been unthinkable to my mother not to welcome the friends however long their stay, a continuation of behavior more appropriate to the country than the city. Not only old friends stayed weeks and months without paying: my mother never put anyone out, whether they paid or not. So we never were successful in business.

Alongside the hotel was a large, empty lot called the wagon-yard, where farmers left their wagons, horses and buggies when they came to town. It was usually humming with activity. I loved to stand around and watch the men sit there whittling on a piece of stick as they exchanged news, or I'd watch them gambling, or playing "stick-knife," a game where they threw knives. There was a lot of Indians, mostly Cherokee, considered the élite among Indians. I remember people looking down on Creek Indians, saying they were mixed bloods.

My mother took much interest in church, lectures, and politics. She always worked in political campaigns. I was taken to so many night meetings and lectures as a child that I am still able to drop off to sleep with no trouble at all by tuning in a speaker on radio or TV. My mother's interest in meetings was not always shared by my father. To my knowledge, he never attended a church service and I don't recall him indicating by word or sign that he believed or disbelieved in God. Sometimes he did go with us to political rallies. I remember the ones at night, with trucks carrying torchlights and huge banners.

My mother would sit at home with my brother and me around the lamp table on which stood a lamp with a heavily beaded and fringed shade. She read from a book called *Bible Readings Around the Home Circle*. At the end of each chapter were questions and answers, and it was a game with us to see who could answer most questions about what our mother read us. We memorized whole chapters of bible scripture.

Much of my childhood was spent reading. We always had stacks of books, and for years we lived a block away from the town library. I loved to spend hours looking at the old stereoscopic pictures in the library. This was when my mother worked for the local Welfare office. In those days, aid in food and clothing was dispensed over the counter to those who came for it. While our mother worked, we spent the time after school in the library if the weather was bad or in the park surrounding it if the weather was good. We never had a baby sitter and we never got into trouble. When I was around eight and my brother around ten, we loved to roll from the top of the park's grassy mound to the bottom, smelling the fragrant grass as we rolled. We were full of the joy of living.

Some of our folks had rather colorful nicknames. One brother, named William for my father, was never called anything but "Head," shortened from "Cottonhead," because of his white hair. Another brother named James was called "Jim Cliff." A sister named Dorothy was called "Cal-Bean"—I have no idea why. My mother whose name was DeMittre Ann was called "Mittie." I [named Patricia] was called "Billie-boy" until I started to school.

My family was not intolerant but in some ways they were ignorant about the Catholic religion. I have known of no relative in our very large clan to have the Catholic faith or to marry a Catholic. I grew up afraid of Catholics. I remember running hysterically up the nearest stairway one day when my brother and I were walking down the street and saw two Catholic nuns approaching. I thought sure they were going to take me away, shave off my hair, and never let me see my parents anymore. When Al Smith ran for president, my parents feared that the Pope would rule America if Smith were elected. The Pope in my mother's eyes was the true "Anti-Christ" spoken of in the Bible. We were taught to respect Jews because they were "the chosen people of God" and because Jesus was born to the Jewish woman, Mary.

I never saw a Negro until I was about twelve years old, when we moved to another town. No Negroes lived in our first town. A Negro woman came to the house to wash; my mother treated her with respect, as she did all people, so that I had no feelings about Negroes. Yet I could not help but notice that they were not treated like white people. I felt this was unfair, but the ones I saw were so dirty, thin and miserable looking that I did not want to associate with them, though I felt sorry for them.

In my 'teens, my mother died. I was impressed with my father's sorrow over her death. I had not realized he loved her. . . . He had always been quiet and reserved so that I was always a little in awe of him. My father lived for about fifteen years longer . . . and never remarried. Now I realize that my father could live more fully and richly on the farm than was possible for him in town. My mother, on the other hand, liked the city, always wanting us to have a good education and other advantages she thought the city offered. I could not say which was the better choice.

This student observed in class that "We social workers do not know enough about how individuals are affected by culture. For example, I think it necessary for caseworkers to know that when a father of European background is extremely strict with a daughter, this might be a natural, culturally formed indication of love and concern; while comparable strictness in a man of another background might indicate this man's punitiveness." A classmate fleshed out the idea in her own paper minutely examining the behavior of a family she knew in her childhood:

The Von H family moved into our neighborhood one windy day late in March. Their arrival was dramatic, almost tragic, for in crossing the frozen lake they had encountered shell-ice and been trapped for hours while they watched the horses drown and waited for a rescue party from the village. I was six, going on seven. I remember my father walking out in the dusk pulling a hand-sled and returning at dawn to announce that the family was safe. By noon the three older children of this extraordinary family were scouting the neighborhood for new acquaintances and reciting the gruesome details of their journey. All the next summer we played "drowning horses" . . .

Though we ran in and out of one another's homes, we seemed to live in different worlds. Mr. Von H had come from Prussia as a young man, bringing his father, mother, and a maiden sister. They had settled homesteads along the lake shore and river because at that time boats were the only means of transportation. They engaged in commercial logging and Mr. Von H moved to our village as manager of a Canadian-American company. For many years he ruled as benevolent despot over the ill and unfortunate of the community.

Mrs. Von H was of German-American descent; she never questioned her husband's decisions. The four eldest children were stalky blue-eyed blonds. Mark, named for his father, was nine; Lily, the same age as I; Rosie, a year younger; and the baby, a boy the same age as my sister, played with my sister and shared mischief for years. Mr. Von H referred to the two girls as his rose and his lily. With these two I "lived and had my being," sharing joys and sorrows, conniving for privileges and gratuities.

I soon learned that Mrs. Von H never had money in her purse. If Lily or Rosie needed a pencil or tablet she sent them across town to their father's office. They voiced their need often in the presence of strangers, when the telling was more difficult; but Mr. Von H's long black purse usually held an extra nickel in demonstration of his generosity. Mrs. Von H charged her groceries. All other items were brought home for approval by "Papa." Mrs. Von H knew when to show Papa the loot but there was always a day of reckoning when Papa paid the bills, and then everyone tiptoed to avoid his wrath. Monthly statements were unknown in those days; a merchant presented his account in person and the creditor paid up to maintain status in the community. Mr. Von H sometimes owed a merchant several hundred dollars but it was the consensus that what the Von Hs owed was as good as money in the bank.

Mr. Von H also exercised power by granting and withholding privileges. There was the matter of the movies on Saturday afternoons. We children worked out a technique for gaining his consent and the needed money. I would approach him, my spending money in hand and ask, please couldn't Lily and Rose accompany me to the movies. Mr. Von H would consider, pull a huge bandanna handkerchief from his back pocket and blow his nose tremendously. Sometimes he took a pinch of snuff and blew. No one breathed until he folded the bandanna and returned it to his pocket. "Movies?" he would ask meditatively, sending shivers of suspense down our spines. He would look at us and ask, "It's a picture mother would approve of my girls seeing?" We would nod emphatically. Slowly the long black purse was drawn from his pocket and he counted out the change. Yes, Mr. Von H had a technique too.

His father lived across the lake with his elder daughter Hennie, whom he ruled with an iron hand. His rages were magnificent and his infrequent visits to town were momentous. He spoke only German. Neighbors often heard him berating one or another of the family for neglecting his comfort. Even Mr. Von H caught the fury of his scowl and of his scathing tongue. It chagrined Mr. Von H that we saw him cowed by the old man, yet he never protested. In one of the bedrooms hung in an ornate frame a portrait of a grim-faced woman. The children were in the habit of gazing at the picture with a pious look and murmuring, "Grossmutter was an angel." This implied that she had been too saintly to go on living. I too paused to pay tribute to a woman I had never known; one day I repeated to my mother the remark about Grossmutter's angelic quality. She eyed me quizzically and said, "Yes, I guess she would have had to be." Now I observed the ritual with some reservations.

At the close of day, Mr. Von H's arrival demanded a set behavior. If we children were playing Big Casino at the dining room table we hurriedly dropped the cards, swept them into a pile, replaced the cloth, and helped the hired girl spread a fresh white linen cloth. Mr. Von H invariably entered via the kitchen door, to find Mrs. Von H busy in the kitchen. He pecked at her cheek, hrrumphed at the hired girl, and, arriving in the living room, scanned us closely. Out came the bandanna. If he blew loud, hard, and only once, we sensed that he was in good humor. Our toys and games had disappeared into a bedroom and we presented ourselves as dutiful children awaiting a father's blessing. He eased himself into the big leather chair and closed his eyes. He called, "Rosie!" "Yes, Papa." "My slippers, please!" Rosie ran for the leather slippers which were supposed to be by his bedside but were often lost back in the cavernous dark under the bed. It was my prerogative to slip out and help her find them if she delayed overlong. Mr. Von H then slid out of his Congress boots and shoved his feet into the slippers that Rosie placed on the floor just so. Next was Lily's turn. When he called to her, she knew exactly in which corner of the dresser drawer she must look for the fresh handkerchief. Mr. Von H then made his way into the kitchen where he reached into the cabinet above the sink, mixed himself a double dose of bromo powder, threw back his head, and downed the dose at one gulp. Then he belched. Then he settled himself in the chair again and read the paper until supper. When Mark was able to read well, Mr. Von H rewarded him with a "very good," emphasizing the "very" in direct proportion to his pleasure. This made Mark beam for the rest of the evening; we soon learned that at such times he was a soft touch to help us with our homework.

In that cold climate, food was important to our lives. Grossfader had a garden, planted and tended by the hapless Hennie. Each fall they sent the Von Hs casks of sauerkraut, pickles, sausages, and potatoes. This fare, alternated with huge roasts, heavy puddings, and white bread, comprised their diet. The Von Hs sat at a long table, Mr. Von H at the head, the plates piled before him, the serving dishes clustered about him. The children were seated according to age, with Mrs. Von H next to the youngest child so as to help him. The hired girl hovered anxiouly, refilling a bowl, slicing more bread; later she ate in the kitchen. Seldom if ever did the Von Hs sit down to eat without a stray neighbor kid or a guest from across the lake who had dropped into town. Mr. Von H cleared his throat after grace was said, flourished the serving forks and remarked, "Well now! Mark? meat? vegetable? potato?" and down the line it went to the last item with the last child. Once served, each individual was obliged to eat every morsel on his plate and no seconds were requested until Mr. Von H had satisfied his hunger. Between the main course and dessert, Mr. Von H brought up such matters as a poor report card or failure to complete chores or homework; the exposed culprit often had to blink back tears of mortification. At those times, Mrs. Von H never raised her voice to protest or blame. I never heard her utter a more drastic threat than, "What would Papa say?"

Grandma Tee, a practical nurse, exerted almost as much influence as Mr. Von H. Each of the small children, on a string around his neck, wore a small bag of camphor crystals to ward off germs; in the spring they were dosed with "tonic." When Lily reached puberty, Grandma Tee told her that she must never eat pickles or anything with vinegar during her menses because the vinegar would thin her blood. She left Lily to struggle with the import of such a catastrophe. I was present when Papa was filling Lily's plate and she said in a whisper, "No pickle, please, Papa." Papa Von H scowled and asked her to repeat. "Please, Papa. No pickle." Then looking around the table, he remarked fiercely, "My Lily's a woman now," challenging anyone who would dare to touch his Lily. Poor Lily cried afterwards and said that she had never been so embarrassed in her life, for one of Mark's teen-age friends was present and Lily liked him.

Almost every evening after supper Mr. Von H telephoned his friend, the local banker. The telephone hung on the wall. You took down the receiver, rang one long for Central, with a little crank on the side, and asked for 31-J or some such number. We enjoyed listening to Mr. Von H's side of the long conversations during which he addressed the banker as "Dearie" and we were given to understand that the banker called Mr. Von H "Sweetheart." We though this particularly funny. There was a great deal of laughter and Mr. Von H was always in good humor when he hung up the receiver. Sometimes he offered to read to us but more often demanded that we do our homework.

Simply because she worked from dawn until long past dark and seldom left the house, Mrs. Von H would not have recognized herself as a drudge. She bore several children after the family moved into the neighborhood. During the last months of these pregnancies, she seemed to derive strength from my mother and spent most of the daylight hours with her. Her sole conversation was detailed descriptions of all the deliveries at which Grandma Tee had presided. Mr. Von H always managed to be across the lake on an inspection tour of the camps at the times of her deliveries and Grandma Tee declared that the next time he wouldn't get away from her and she would show him what it was like to have a baby.

Confidence in Mr. Von H tottered when he refused to let Mark join his classmates enlisting in the army. Mr. Von H's reason was that Mark could not fight against cousins in the German army. Many heads were shaken in bewilderment. After the war, the logging company folded and Mr. Von H organized a company of his own. Prices were low and he did not do well. He began to have rages equalling those of Grossfader. He was crushed when the banker he called Dearie absconded and the bank fell into receivership. He died of a stroke following one of his tirades. None of the children has followed the old way of life.

A practically unknown American subculture was presented by a Negro member of the seminar. She had been born and reared in a quiet Southern town where her family was long established, respected, and possessed considerable farming land. She had been sent to a private school in New Orleans, trained in old-fashioned formal courtesies and notions of womanly conduct, and she married a man of similar background. The couple moved to Chicago and saw Negro slums and severe segregation for the first time. She became a welfare worker during the Depression of the 1930's and among her clients were Negro Moslems. For the seminar she described these people in a paper entitled, "The El and Bey Families":

Far off Chicago's Gold Coast, along Michigan Lake's Shore Drive, huge old industrial buildings have been converted into one and two-room kitchenette flats that house thousands of diverse persons. The people appear well content to inhabit the area; large numbers eke out their livings at menial tasks in households near the Gold Coast, in famous restaurants, and in hot night-spots.

Located in this converted section is a huge number of public assistance applicants and clients. I came to know them as a social case worker in a public assistance district office. . . . I met two groups of American Negroes who had migrated to Chicago from South Carolina and Georgia. In the South they had been migrant farmers and sharecroppers such as my father used to employ. Once in Chicago, these people claimed non-Negro status. The information I now give about them is from memory, as I can find no written material.

They substantiated their claim to be "Moslem" by using odd surnames and spectacular costumes. Regardless of the surname, the family gave it a hyphenated ending which was hyphen Bey or hyphen El. . . . The family Louis Sanders would be Louis Sanders-Bey, the family Christopher Anderson would be Christopher Anderson-El, and so on. These two forms were tacked on to any good old American name; otherwise there were no foreign family names in the two groups. The public assistance clients showed disappointment and hostility when government regulations forbade the hyphenated name-ending on their public assistance checks. However, the case records and all public assistance correspondence to clients and school authorities fully recognized these acquired names. In casual talk with the "Moslems," it was impossible to clarify the origin of the names except that people vaguely indicated that names were handed down by "Moslem" ancestors. Most of these people had very limited schooling.

Despite the large number of families in these two name-groups, there was something very cohesive in their pattern of living. Most resided in one area, a few families spilling over into other parts of the city. All their festive and religious activities took place where the greatest number resided.

Another distinguishing item was the bizarre costumes worn by women of the group, both young and elderly. They appeared publicly in colorful floor-length gowns of silk and cotton, made by combining horizontally wide strips of vivid reds, purples, yellows, fuchsia, heliotrope, shades of blue, green and others. Some gowns had many shades while others had fewer color combinations; perhaps these expressed the wearer's individuality. The gowns were usually held in at the waist with belts or sashes or wound around the body intriguingly. Tall turbans of matching colors were fashioned seemingly out of yards and yards of narrow strips wound around the head, sometimes completely covering the hair. Ear lobes were decorated with fancy inexpensive jewelry. Long strings of colorful bead necklaces completed the attire. Children wore ordinary dress, except for festive occasions in the neighborhood. Male members usually wore business suits but sported turbans and sometimes beards.

Their meetings were held in a large old dilapidated frame building within easy reach of most members. Several times yearly they held large conventions with visiting men dignitaries who distinguished themselves from group members by elegant flowing robes. Watching these activities made my field work delightful. No one seemed to know where these dignitaries hailed from, nor even if they were American or foreign born. The group usually assembled around their meeting hall, arranging themselves in squares, circles, and straight lines, singing and strutting to loudly played musical instruments. Men appeared to dominate all, leading lines of march, playing the instruments, moving about, calling for order. After the crowds disappeared into the building, male members guarded the entrance against the general public. All rituals there were strictly private and only the Els and Beys were admitted.

During many contacts with these "Moslem" families, I constantly observed their patriarchal structure in families and in other groupings. Men dominated their households. Male family members were considered family heads when handling public assistance matters, at the district agency office or at home. Male influence showed when protesting agency policy, when complaining over budgets, when requesting further aid. I understood that men decided the ritual acts of importance.

I found it strange then that in this patriarchal group it was mostly women who found gainful employment. The women worked as domestics and baby sitters and at other humble tasks in nearby Gold Coast houses. Perhaps this was because the males were too unskilled for the industrial work of the city.

Once I established a good relationship with these "Moslems," I secured, piece by piece, details of the religious activities. [By verbal accounts received, since outsiders were excluded,] their ritual was infused with mysticism. Their leader, a suave-looking young male, always appeared on the streets wearing chic full-length colored garb and the inevitable turban. The group referred to him as [its] prophet and appeared to consider him sacred. Not believing in earthly things, he demanded no fixed salary for his services. I learned that he was paid small tithes at births, marriages, anniversaries, and at certain stages of the moon, besides other goods and services. I would speculate that he received enough ego satisfaction from the hero worship.

Males of the groups constituted the religious hierarchy. At the head was the prophet; next the saints, the elect of the prophet; then a number of overseers; and last, the deputies. This line of leaders . . . governed meetings and other group and neighborhood acts. When disorder arose, the message was sent through this line of men to the prophet, who was always free, being unemployed, to set things right by counseling.

A group member told me that [its] ritual included the noise of the musical instruments mingled with song, dance, and heavy breathing. Some members got so absorbed performing that they forgot to pray. Some "passed out," speaking unknown tongues. The affairs could last all night. For the unemployed members, an affair might continue into the next day.

Diet patterns included much fuss about ritual cleanliness. They seemed obsessed with a fear that their foods might come in contact with something unclean. The orthodox washed all foodstuffs many times; they even washed vegetable seeds before planting them. Pork meats and scaleless fish were taboo, as were all intoxicants. However I understood that many males and females frequented taverns, mingling and drinking freely with the crowd once they were out of sight of their religious officers.

Another concern to the orthodox was sexual promiscuity. They considered this evil and vile. Officially they were monogamous.

Truth also got special attention. Lies could be told under extraordinary circumstances, for example, to save a person from great injustice and to keep peace between a man and wife. Truth told was an honor even if it held something unpleasant. A lie was considered humiliating even if it protected something dear. I was told once that a person known to be an occasional liar is suspect even when telling the truth.

In this subculture, dreams held great significance, many believing them messages from the unseen world. If one had no dream while sleeping, it meant that the mind was in free communication with God. Any dream of spiritual quality was believed to come directly from the Divine. When its meaning was not clear, the prophet was asked to interpret. A nightmare was supposedly caused by a great sin and the "devil" was its agent.

These people held that feelings about music were sacred, that music could produce ritual states of ecstasy facilitating communication with God. Members would sink into unconsciousness on hearing a song that harmonized with their mood of the moment. They concluded that, though valuable to worship, music held dangers that had to be contained within stated limits of musical use. They believed that danger might lie in the performer, the instrument, the song, the listener, or in combinations of these. Therefore instruments could not accompany drinking, nor could songs be immoral or irreligious, nor could hearers be too young and wanting in love of God. The "Moslems" believed that each person was born with specific traits and that little could be done to change him.

Their belief in the next world held some unresolved problems, especially about the abode of the soul after death. Many believed that there were individuals who died a second death, when their souls flew on birds to Paradise. The souls of prophets and saints had the choice of remaining in this world, for the purpose of appearing to good men in dreams, or they could ascend into one of the heavens.[28]

One doctoral student of Italian descent assembled a careful account of his parents' native culture. Like the Anglo-American in the first of these accounts, he said he had known little about his heritage at the outset and was obliged to learn by interviewing and writing to family members. In this way he discovered how considerably ancestral loyalties are retained in America through infiltration into assimilated American ways. In his account he traced the Italian and American veins of culture in his family's life in the following manner:

In a northern Alpine village called Rallo, both my parents were born. Rallo is one of four villages [forming] a commune. The chief occupation . . . is agriculture, fruit orchards and vineyards predominating. In my parents' time, the village had a populaiton of 500, all Catholic. The village church was a chapel since the priest, salaried by the government, lived in a neighboring village. The richest man in Rallo was the Count of Almiro, related to the Hapsburgs. One doctor and a midwife served the commune . . .

At the time of my parents' birth, their part of the Tyrol belonged to Austria. This caused trouble during World War I as some families considered themselves Italian while others considered themselves Austrian. The nearest city was Trento, about half a day's ride away. . . . The high court was at Innsbruck, Austria, several days' ride away.

North Italians often regard themselves as superior, perhaps because they have developed industrial and intellectual life more than have south Italians. . . . North Italians consider Southerners ignorant, poor, superstitious . . . and with some reason. . . . The Mafia or "Black Hand" comes from Sicily and the vendetta belongs to South Italy. South Italians devised a Catholic refinement in the "Major Vendetta," which brings death to the enemy after first placing him in a situation so sinful that his soul presumably would go to hell . . .

My parents' families felt a natural allegiance to Austria. Following World War I however, the Italian Tyrol was tied to Italy. . . . My father was born in 1885 and my mother in 1895. Hence, my grandparents lived in the period shortly after our Civil War and prior to World War I.

My paternal grandfather was married at 26 years to the 23-year-old daughter of a poor farmer with eight other daughters. His family did not approve heartily of the marriage because of the low status of her family. His family possessed a large orchard and a so-called villa. My great grandfather had been Mayor of the commune and held high status. . . . During his term of office, he built a viaduct which was said to have much reduced infant mortality.

My maternal grandfather was married at 28 to a woman one year younger. Both were uneducated. His family had been in business exporting wines, raising mules for the trucking cooperative, and raising horses for the Austrian army. Early in the marriage, he took his wife to Venezuela, where he worked as paymaster for a Swiss engineering firm constructing

Venezuela's first railroad. Here was born their first child, a daughter. He returned to Italy and the family business.

My maternal grandfather had four brothers and a sister. One brother was a baker, two were millers. One left for America because his mother disapproved of the girl he wished to marry. He settled in Colorado as a sheep farmer and owner of a general store, soon becoming wealthy. His morals were considered loose and he kept a mistress. The sister remained in Italy, marrying a farmer.

My maternal grandmother had two brothers and four sisters. The two brothers fled Austria to escape military service. One became superintendent for a beer distributing company in Colorado; the other started a general store in a Colorado coal mining town. The sisters married men of Rallo.

My family's migration to America began in 1888 when my paternal grandfather arrived with his ten-year-old son, for in Italy he did not wish farming or military service. In 1900 he was followed by his son of fourteen, my future father; in 1905 he sent for his wife and daughter. They settled in a small mining town near Florence, Colorado, about 25 miles from Pueblo, populated mostly by Slovaks and Tyrolean Austro-Italians. My grandfather worked briefly in the mines, then opened a saloon. There he learned some English; my grandmother failed to learn English during more than 40 years in the United States.

As the mining town consisted largely of Italians, my father and his brothers all married Italians. My father's first wife was a sister of my mother's who, with another sister, had run away from home to escape their father's drinking; an aunt in Colorado financed them. The aunt made a home for them until their marriages, about a year after arrival. No children were born to my father and his first wife. When his wife died, my future mother exchanged letters with her (then) brother-in-law; they had known each other as children. Her other sister in Colorado persuaded her to come, and my father also was interested in her, so in 1919 my mother arrived in Colorado and about four or five months later she married my father.

My mother was the third born, having two older sisters and four younger brothers, besides an infant sister who died shortly after birth. My grandmother had died in the childbirth. The oldest brother had died of tuberculosis in the Austrian army during World War I. In 1931, the second oldest son was murdered by a former employee; the youngest son married this brother's widow to support the children.

My mother states that family property was shared equally among males of the family. A single daughter was given an equal share upon the parents' death.

Here the student schematized "some cultural patterns of the Tyrolean villages" observed by his elders and transmitted partially to the American-born children:

The family is a close unit. In some households, though not in my maternal grandparents', four or five generations lived under one roof, including a great grandparent, grandparents, widowed daughters, unmarried children, and perhaps grandchildren. Silkworm culture was sometimes a household industry.

A Tyrolean village had no formal dating, but, my mother states, boys and girls had many casual opportunities for meeting. There were two or three carnivals each year, such as the Lenten Mardi Gras. Occasional dances were held in the town hall; older boys and girls were permitted to go to the local beer garden evenings and Sunday afternoons. The beer garden was approved because it was family-operated and the family was Catholic with children of their own. Sundays the boys played soccer and the girls a version of tennis. Winters, boys and girls joined in the usual snow sports. A young man interested in a girl made his intention known to the girl's father. There were no arranged marriages but parental disapproval sufficed to restrain young people. . . .

When father and mother approved of a suitor, a girl planned her marriage. Italy required a civil ceremony [owing] to separation of Church and State. Under Austrian rule this had not been necessary since the priest functioned like a civil servant, paid by the government. After a ceremony in church, the couple returned to the girl's home for a wedding breakfast. To this only close kin were invited. In the afternoon, there might be a dance for the couple but the celebrations did not last two or three days as it could with South Italians. Venice was the ideal honeymoon spot, and all tried to spend at least a day there.

Not all the numerous relatives are invited nor expect to be, but they do expect to participate in this custom: One of the family bakes many sweet breads, decorated with coarse sugar and shaped to resemble a wedding band. A day before the wedding a relative distributes these to second and third cousins and others.

The bride's dowry was usually a gift in kind, traditionally bedroom furniture handmade of cherry wood or walnut grown by the family. Sometimes the construction was let out to a local carpenter. The young groom, if a farmer, received a share of land; otherwise he was brought into the family business, if not otherwise engaged. Farming was done outside the village and such a couple purchased or rented a house in town.

At a birth there was little celebration though men of the family might drink. Most babies were born at home; many died of cholera. By custom, the family of the child first baptised after Easter brought a new lamb to church.

Rallo then had an elementary school. My mother, and others interested, attended high school in a village about a mile away. One of my mother's brothers got some college training. The families identified with Austria, like my mother's, sent their sons to live in Austria and learn German; in turn, they accepted sons from Austrian families. Sons who were to learn a white-collar occupation were sent to larger cities, before World War I, and preferably in the North.

On a death, the family usually moved out of the home. But the body remained, guarded all night by two male friends of the family. Family friends visited in the evening to say the rosary and the *de Profundis* (prayer for the dead). On the day of the death, church bells rang the *de Profundis*. A funeral was of more consequence than a wedding, attended by crowds that sometimes numbered 150 to 200 people, all carrying lit candles. The casket was transported by four men over the mile to the cemetery serving the commune of four villages. No flowers were sent, as in Austria, but the family of the deceased distributed gifts of salt or oil to those paying their respects. This symbolized the expectation that those salting their food would recall the deceased and pray for his soul. On the death of her eldest brother, my mother's family distributed over 500 pounds of salt. Businessmen immediately related to the deceased were to suspend business for a week. The men wore black mourning bands, and still do, and women still dress in black for two or three years. A mourner faced disgrace if he or she attended any recreation before at least a year.

On All Souls' Day, November 2, all bells in the villages rang the *de Profundis*. Families visited each other expressly to recall their dead. At three in the morning, everyone visited family graves in the cemetery, where they sang the *Miserere*, and proceeded to mass in the local church. Everyone was expected to sacrifice for a month or so in memory of the dead and funds were given to the church and to missions . . .

Upon a kinsman's death, one person took it upon himself to notify the relatives in neighboring villages and towns, up to tenth and eleventh degrees of cousinship. Oldtimers were consulted and they strained to recall the distant relatives who should be notified.

My mother said she knew of no unwed mothers except for a couple in the neighboring village during the war. In her town she knew of no prostitute or mistress although she heard there were such in Trento, the nearest large city. She knew of one girl who fell in love with a Protestant but did not marry him because of family opposition, which was heightened by the priest in the family.

This way of life is still followed in the Tyrol, though some customs change, as illustrated by a female cousin who married an Italian from Ravenna. Her family had disapproved because the man was a sort of foreigner, of whose family and Catholic belief they were unsure. Besides, they were a family of produce haulers and so did not like his occupation of agriculture inspector. But the young lady, who was 19 years old, traveled to Ravenna with an aunt and forced her family's approval.

Then the student appraised himself as a cultural amalgam of his family's heritage and the practices of American life:

In 1921 I was born, an Italian-American, in the Colorado coal-mining town to which my parents had migrated. Until the age of four I spoke Italian and a little English. During my fifth year, my parents moved us to California, persuaded by a friend and former business partner. My mother was disappointed in the United States and particularly with my father's family for spending their days in the coal-mining town. She feared that her children too might end their days in the mines and fail to get a good education. My father saved money for the move and for starting a small grocery store in a residential community near Los Angeles. When we arrived there, we knew no Italians locally but we had Italian friends in the greater Los Angeles area.

One of my first recollections of the new neighborhood is that we were regarded as different. Perhaps I sensed this when my mother forbade us to leave our yard or bother the neighbors. Later I learned that a neighbor to the rear immediately built a high fence against us "kids." We were four in number. He could as effectively have drawn a white line for we knew our mother's worry and the possible consequences of violation.

Growing older, we began to move around the neighborhood. My first boyhood chum was of German-American extraction; we both attended the local parochial school. I recall four or five Italian-Americans in school. Occasionally I was teased at school about being a "dago" or "wop." Coming home from school once, I got into a fight over being called a "dirty so and so wop" and Catholic. This was the extent of aggression against me as a child though I understood at a very young age that it didn't really pay to be a "foreigner" and a Catholic.

There were no Italian professional men then in the community, but there were two or three thrifty Italian merchants who in time accumulated much property. The story went that Italian merchants made their money bootlegging. This might have been true of one or two but the others were plain, hardworking, thrifty people. I recall one Italian shoemaker who worked extremely long hours and by the sweat of his brow accumulated enough money to buy property in the community; at death he left his widow and children well provided for. Untrue stories made the rounds about this man's supposed bootlegging.

In adolescence I personally encountered no overt hostility though I knew that townspeople regarded Italians as potential gangsters. My family would have liked to blame this on South Italians or Sicilians, but they had too many friends among them. The concept of the Mafia or "Black Hand" did not strike close to home though I heard the term, was given to understand the society existed, and that it was one reason Italians were disliked.

During my childhood our family's social life was with Italians in other parts of Los Angeles. Occasionally my father took me with him to North Broadway where Italians lived as a colony. There he drank his wine, played *bocce* and *morra*. We especially enjoyed visiting an Italian family who lived on a farm in the San Fernando valley raising grapes, onions and potatoes. . . . Many evenings were spent listening to our elders talk of the old country.

We knew the children of our parents' friends only slightly and found few things in common. During the week we children played in the neighborhood with friends who were mostly non-Italian; Sundays we joined in our parents' Italian sociabilities. Children of these Italian friends spoke Italian, as they lived in Italian neighborhoods. I remember feeling badly at my parents' friends' surprise that we spoke no Italian. However, my mother was most anxious to learn American ways and to speak English; she spent considerable time with a neighboring retired school teacher. At this stage my mother practiced her English at home on us and so we heard little Italian. My father spoke English proficiently, having come to America young and gone immediately into business.

As a teen-ager I resented accompanying my parents to their Italian friends and soon they allowed me to remain with my own friends from the neighborhood and school. However the five younger children continued to go with my parents. Often staying for lunch or dinner at a friend's home, I was soon introduced to new eating habits. But I recall as a teen-ager begging my mother to make meatballs and spaghetti for Thanksgiving dinner, after learning that my sister had persuaded her to cook a turkey.

I had become aware that my friends enjoyed my mother's Italian cooking. In fact, she learned much of her Italian cookery after reaching this country, since macaroni and spaghetti were somewhat foreign to Tyroleans, who prefer German dishes or their own provincial plates like "polenta'" (a yellow cornmeal cake served with meat gravy).

In 1935 [I had] my first cultural conflict with my mother over her attempt to have us follow an Italian custom. She had lost a brother and her father within three or four months of each other. She began wearing black immediately and in her grief asked us not to play the radio. We complied briefly and then balked. I convinced her finally that it was unfair to impose European customs on us. She agreed but herself continued to wear black. In later years, she too changed. For example, a few years ago, another of her brothers died but she did not mourn in the traditional way, though she prefers to wear dark clothes.

As a young adult I found no problem in being Italian. My friends enjoyed my home and I was accepted in theirs. Graduating from seminary high school, I went to work in an aircraft firm. Finances forbade my attending college. Beginning to date girls, I found no objections to non-Italians from my parents. I learned that one girl in the church's young people's club was dissuaded by her mother from dating me because I was Italian. Entering military service, I found no problems about my heritage since I was thoroughly Americanized. Returning from the service, I again dated girls of my own and neighboring parishes. Among these was a young war widow to whom my mother objected because she had not mourned her husband a sufficient time. I suspect there was also the idea that she was a "used" woman.

One of our South Italian friends let my parents know that he and his wife would be happy for one of their children to marry into our family. Nothing came of this except that it was mentioned. My parents did not attempt to arrange a marriage though we knew our mother would disapprove of marrying a non-Catholic. All of us children have married non-Italians. . . I approached my wife's father [Irish-American] for her hand in marriage.

Four of my brothers and sisters married non-Catholics; three of these were married in the church, one outside. Two of the non-Catholics are now Catholic. Each has two or more children. One sister is married to an engineer, the other to an aircraft worker studying electronics by correspondence. Two brothers are contractors. The remaining brother has a civil service job as a fire marshal.

The food eaten in my brothers' and sisters' homes is American. Now it is a treat when my mother cooks Italian dishes for us. Most of the wives have learned to cook at least one Italian dish.

The marriages in our family were in American style though my family attempted to provide the treat of an Italian wedding feast as they had heard of it. There was plenty of food and drink, music and dancing.

Death is also handled the American way. On my father's death, the family came together. Italian friends brought food they had prepared. Aside from Catholic rites, an observer would not have recognized differences from another American funeral. The children did not wear black though my mother did. On the anniversary of father's death and on All Souls' Day there is a religious remembrance for family members together or in their own churches.

My brothers and I are typical American husbands, sharing with wives the responsibility for decisions. Child rearing is somewhat in the [permissive] American vein though I feel my siblings aspire towards the [more authoritarian] ideals of our parents. They have not forced the issue, to avoid conflict with spouses. Though we brothers were never expected to do household chores, since marriage to Americans we all help with dishes, changing babies, and other light housework.

Now I reside in the community where I was reared. Among us are at least two Italian-American doctors, several Italian-American schoolteachers, and at least one Italian-American attorney. The attorney is married to a non-Italian; one doctor is married to an Italian-American and maintains close ties with other Italians in the community. Several prominent Italian businessmen are active in community affairs.

There is an active Sons of Italy Lodge. I am not a member, probably because I have never identified myself with other Italian-Americans and also because the majority of members are South Italians. Being late arrivals to this country, they tend to be clannish; I notice that they have close family groups. . . . The number of Italians in the community is not noticeable perhaps because there is no ghetto; but the existence of a lodge indicates the considerable number. In my work with parish young-adult clubs, I find many officers carry Italian names. . . . Outside the local community, many of my Italian friends have entered professions as doctors, attorneys, teachers, social workers; several are already respected businessmen. Their children will increase the number of professional and businessmen carrying Italian names.

These vivid glimpses into family life mirror the vigorous diversity of America's cultural soil. The dissimilar Japanese and Italian death customs; dissimilar social expectations of men and women among Japanese, Dutch, German, American Negro Moslems, and Italians; the special views of kinship among Irish, Japanese, and Italians; the varying styles of marriage among Irish, Italians, and Japanese; the intimations throughout of some convergence toward standard American modes among those entering the middle class, while the narrators still recall older traditions; all indicate that standard official approaches must fall short of the many-faced realities. Discussion of these in seminar—and reference to each student's sudden awareness of the cultural nature of his life as he confronted cultural differences among historic groups, seeing them as variations on universal human themes, while noting each group's passionate devotion to its own variations and supposed uniqueness—roused lively sympathies among students and efforts to understand one another. These attitudes were deliberately extended to clients, who also belonged to the historic groups examined.

Other seminar projects for exposing cultural influences were devised to illuminate students' immediate professional tasks. Students' age-spread and diverse origins (Dutch, Greek, Italian-American, Mexican-American, New Mexican, Hindu of India, Negro and white Americans, Hawaiian of aboriginal and English descent, Chinese, English Canadian, Filipino, Nisei, Issei, Catholic, Protestant, Jewish, Greek Orthodox) were capitalized on in choices of projects. Some individuals worked in teams, others singly, examining problems among adults and among juveniles. These social workers used a broader range of approaches and evidenced wider interests than the later Claremont teachers, who pursued projects singly and oftener with pupils.

One team of four men and a girl, placed for training at a Public Assistance agency, organized "A Research Study of Skid Row" since some clients lived there. The men included a young Catholic priest who wore his formal garb until he saw that it hurt research for it cued the responses of his subjects narrowly. The team charted and tabulated findings, thus describing each informant by sex, age, race, language, religion, nationality, education, occupation, marital status, and residence. The team tabulated each informant's drug and alcoholic addictions, his "incidence of incarcerations," his kinds of "relationships to police authority," to "fringe people," and to "transients." The team itemized the dates, duration, and number of interviews, and charted the ties among persons studied according to residence in the Row's neighborhoods, patronage of the Row's facilities, and drinking habits. The team recorded the special phrasings used by informants and itemized peculiarities of conduct, appearance, and clothing. Each team member consulted published literature and his own running diary of notes to prod his insights into situations, and he recorded these at several stages.

When visiting the Row, members of the team proceeded to "walk among these men and women, listen to stories of their lives, join in their conversations, eat and drink with them. . . . Our discussions were open ended though we directed the very informal interviews by a common pattern of questions. Our findings represent about 90 hours among people of Skid Row, a short time to spend among those who pass their lives there."

Students were asked to explore situations imaginatively and venture inferences. Accordingly, the Skid Row team concluded its report:

The social relationships of these men are stifling. Relatives and true friends have no parts in their lives. Even among themselves, with one exception, there is no companionship, for most of the men prefer anonymity.

. . . The remark of one fellow is typical, "I don't know anyone and don't want to know anyone, don't want anyone to know me. The secret is to keep moving."

Of course they know the police and the police know them. Sometimes they win the game, sometimes they lose. . . . There is an unwritten and generally silent league against authority which occasionally breaks out in bitterness, hostility, and vengeance. They can't trust anyone. I was driving one fellow across town, after some acquaintance with him. Reaching his destination at a mission, he got out of the car, pulled old leather gloves from his pocket and carefully wiped window, door-knob and window-opener to remove finger-prints as he said, smiling, "I don't trust anyone, Mac, not my own mother."

Skid Row is a bowl of maladjusted personalities, which can be found in any other social milieu, only here they are concentrated in the bottom of the city. The same types of deviant walk the more respectable Beverly Hills and Pasadena, only these have avoided the economic blight and social stigma that dog the heels of Skid Row.

The young priest learned further that the garb of his office, charged with merit for him, did not always stir respect and trust but often warned the frightened to dodge the help he hoped to give. He found strength in looking past his trappings and focusing on the human messages exchanged with others, across the diversities of class and culture.

A school social worker mentally organized her life-long familiarity with her fellow-Hawaiians and wrote about their great diversity. As a *Kamaaina* (born of the land) observing the *malihini* (newcomer), she saw that:

Contrasting with the Japanese family, the Filipino cherishes girls above boys. To dress his wife and daughters finely is a Filipino father's major delight. Sons shuffle for themselves early, many enlisting in the armed forces on finishing high school. Girls with any ability go to college, to judge from the number studying at the University of Hawaii . . .

Puerto Ricans resemble Mexicans, the young people being indifferent to higher education and marrying young. . . . Samoans are simple, happy Polynesians, as Hawaiians once were. Most are Mormons, do not drink but love to eat, sing, and dance. Expert machinists and welders from Pearl Harbor still do the knife dance evenings for tourists at swank Waikiki hotels. These modern Samoans cling to old clan relationships and refer all negotiations to their traditional Talking Chief, who might also be a sailor in the navy.

The large influx of States-side *haoles* [foreigner, stranger, American white] into Hawaii, since World War II, began with skilled war workers and discharged servicemen. They are transients, like thousands of servicemen based on the Islands. Unlike local *haoles*, who are settled, the transient ones show mainland prejudices. These caused the only racial flare-ups the Islands have ever known; even this slight friction gives concern to old residents.

A mainland school social worker focused on middle-class America and conceptualized the "value system" of W, a prosperous midwest suburb:

My views of W are influenced by my different background. W is almost entirely residential, having only single-unit homes. A few blocks are devoted to grocery stores, one or two small clothing shops, garages, small filling stations, banks, and other modest businesses. Everyone in this town knows who everyone else is.

As there are no apartment houses, few single persons are resident. The homes are occupied by young families enough established to have children and to have moved here on their upward climb. Most of the men work in professions or highly-paid industry in Chicago and other nearby cities. But most of those working in W live elsewhere, many commuting from Chicago. Besides those in local businesses, people working in W are domestics, teachers, staffs of protective services, and others needed to serve a community.

The small family characterizes this suburb. As neither grandparents nor other relatives live in W, children are reared solely according to their parents' values; these can be vague. However, everyone is devoted to money and possessions, as is manifest in roles of family members. The man is primarily the earner, and wife and children evidence his adequacy . . .

Authority is supposed to be equal among husband, wife, and children. This actually means that each one is respected as an individual and that children's wants and needs are considered equally with those of parents. In fact, this falls short of realization because parental ambitions for children conflict with parental intentions to allow children free choices. Besides, the daytime absence of fathers leaves women to direct life at home and in the town.

. . . Home is for family comfort but, besides, symbolizes the family's financial success and therefore serves also as a showplace for entertaining. Almost every family has domestic help. This is usually a maid, plus additional help for washing and ironing plus sometimes a chauffeur and yardman. Freed of most household duties, husband and wife interest themselves in community work, social affairs, sports, and club work. Children are also freed of home chores but the prevailing individualism leads them into separate activities.

Nearly every family has children and through each one, the future-oriented parents reach for the success, largely financial, that they may not achieve themselves. Parents take responsibility for the children's upbringing but often leave actual care to the maid or another employee, though not to a special nursemaid. Parents give affection and make careful decisions about their children, yet often turn to specialists for help. Hence, there is great parental interest in schools, and mothers are as active in school as children.

W's school system is one of the most progressive. Besides classroom teachers, the elementary school where I worked had teaching specialists in music, rhythms, art, physical education; it had a full-time librarian, an audio-visual aids expert, a special teacher for children with academic problems, a consultant in science and a consulting school psychologist. School authorities constantly evaluated and experimented to achieve the best education. The luxury of so many specialists seemed part of the community's ambitious style of life.

Schools had a weekly coffee hour for parents during the school day. Teachers were free to attend during the periods that specialists had their classes. Parents were encouraged to visit classes. The PTA built a teacher's room and kitchen, furnishing them with two expensive dining-room tables and matching chairs, wall-to-wall carpeting, a couch, coffee table, occasional chairs, and assorted objects. Certainly the parents wanted teachers to have a comfortable place for relaxing. At Christmas, teachers received expensive gifts from pupils. These efforts to provide teachers with over-adequate surroundings helped instill W's values.

At school the children expressed parental values. Three children were disliked by other children for bragging about family possessions and for "showing off" with extravagant buying. Their parents employed a maid and chauffeur, owned two Cadillacs, and built a house on such a scale that they could afford to furnish it only piecemeal. These parents were disliked by other parents. The worst behavior problem in my school was a boy of relatively poor family, perhaps because W's children and parents stressed money income so greatly.

The focus on children was shown extremely the night *Peter Pan* was on TV. The whole town then settled down with their offspring to watch. The next day at school, any child who hadn't seen the program was outcast during the heated discussions. On Peter Pan night, fund raisers visited to collect money, knowing every parent would be home.

A young woman studied deviants from middle-class norms in "The Al-Anon Member," reconstructing lives of four members by lengthy interviews. She tried to explore backgrounds of individuals married to alcoholics to see how Al-Anon, a group therapy program, helped them, the spouses, understand the alcoholic and themselves. Interviewees had belonged to Al-Anon for several years. She met them at meetings and elsewhere. Interviews were informal, taking place, with one exception, in various homes. Her conclusions provided insights for professional care of the alcoholic and the family.

The considerable duration of the marriages to alcoholics indicates a definite need for [sober] spouses to be married to personalities with the defects that result in excessive drinking. The marked abuse tolerated by spouses indicates a sadomasochistic relationship . . . satisfying to the partners. The alcoholic is likely to be "charming," with extremes of mood and behavior; the spouse is likely to be a motherly "suffering martyr" type.

Both partners are unable to conduct self-fulfilling lives. The alcoholic blames his wife for his drinking; she tries to help but in questionable ways, like hiding the bottle. Both parties evidence guilt feelings and active projections. The alcoholic tends to marry a much younger person. Mary's [alcoholic] husband appears 10 to 15 years her senior; Ethyl's first husband, while not alcoholic, was 30 years her senior. This seems a search for a father-figure.

The Al-Anon program is modeled after Alcoholics Anonmous, stressing belief in God and prayer. . . . The program appears intended for the middle-class American with sufficient ego-strength to change when aided by others in similar situations. Al-Anon members learn to concentrate on their own problems rather than on the alcoholic, and so become more self-reliant . . .

A number of students focused on cultural factors in delinquency. In a research class of twenty-five, two students joined to examine predelinquency; [29] a team of eight reported opinions of delinquency held by interviewees within different social groups; [30] three formed a team to study views of delinquency held by interviewees among different social groups of adolescents.[31] All these students were preparing themselves for child counseling in schools, clinics, or welfare agencies. Seven students individually examined views of intermarriage among interviewees in their communities.[32] One student also described his own experience of such a union:

Mine is a marriage with a Japanese woman; I am a Caucasian. Over the fourteen years of our happy union, many slurs have been cast on us which did not become clear until I spent much thought on the present paper. Those in our situation gloss over the affronts of colleagues, acquaintances, and even immediate family as pointless except to lead us to friends with similar marriages. [After marrying during the Second World War in Hawaii] my wife was told never to come to her home Island again; and my family wrote scathing letters about "blackening the family name."

[After comparing the hostile behavior of his American and Japanese relatives, noting his eventual closeness to the Japanese and his only bare civilities with the American, the student concluded that we]

had little trouble adapting to one another's culture. Of course, I often forget to remove my shoes before entering the house and still can't get used to cooking fish with their heads on, but she found it difficult to be married to a person ambitious for higher education, wanting potatoes at every meal, and not wanting to work in the garden. We compromised all our differences and have reached accord almost completely. She eats her Japanese food with rice when she wants it; I eat steak and rice whenever she wants it that way; she works in the garden and yard, I do cooking and dishes. Here in a rental apartment we do not worry about wearing shoes in the house, and she is coming so to like it in California that I am much more anxious to return to Hawaii than she is.

An interracial marriage like mine has many difficulties but none that cannot be surmounted with understanding and acceptance of the other's background. . . . Social problems present themselves but will seem small against the satisfactions of mutual respect and understanding.

Other projects directed students to analyze novels, autobiographies, and short stories that revealed personalities of different cultures under stress, such as Oliver LaFarge's works on American Indians, Willa Cather's on Central European immigrants in the Far West, Richard Wright's on Negroes. Another project directed students to study gait, mannerisms, and dress of unknown passersby and so alert them to social stimuli and responses outside the medium of speech and usually outside of conscious awareness. For example, their attention was drawn to the fact that a farmer treads more heavily and slowly than a city man; that a Russian, in all Soviet films, walks as if in one chunk, while an American college boy (and many Negroes, Britons say) moves from the hips, swinging his arms; an English person of upper class avoids the direct gaze, as even news photos reveal, but an American demands it; Americans stylize deep voices for men, light ones for women, but the opposite is often true of upper class English and lower class Latins.

Still another project was to analyze uses and effects of words in newspaper columns and on radio and television as models for analyzing conversations with clients of different origins. One other project required students to select a vital issue, such as divorce or careers for married women, to interview persons of different backgrounds about it, and then to relate responses to the speaker's background, examining details in the light of culture and personality. A young Jewish matron and a newly arrived Filipino girl, both students, conducted an unrehearsed interview before the class to demonstrate the procedure.

Counselors, social workers, and educators ask how to differentiate between disturbances of personality and peculiarities of culture. It is an anthropological generalization that to know the regular practices and expectations of a culture is to recognize when an individual "carrier" or personality steps abnormally out of line. It is not possible to appraise order and disorder of conduct in a local group except by reference to norms of the native culture. The "normal" person, then, is one who learns well the standards and modes of normality and of deviation in the culture, whereas the "abnormal" is one who practices deviation from the standards and modes.[33] In certain societies, even homicidal mania, cannibalism, genocide, infanticide (of females, especially), and epilepsy have a proper place. In the modern Western world, far more physical violence is allowed individuals, and even demanded of them, among groups outside the middle class than in that class itself. For example, slum dwellers tolerate or invite physical beatings, dangerous weapons, and aggressive drunkenness among family members and youth gangs, regardless of race, religion, and national origin.

Strict, even harsh, authority has characterized European and Asiatic societies that, unlike twentieth-century America, have been governed by elders, especially by males, who delegate varying authority to women and younger men. In the United States this authority may survive longest among segregated and subcultural families. It appears as a grave deviation to the middle-class eye but not to the parent subculture, which persists in the shadow of our system of discrimination. Californians observe, on the other hand, that Mexican-Americans who enter the middle class show corresponding modifications, as when men discard their ancestral mode of showing bravery or self-assertion by great swings of temper and responsibility. The project in family culture documented this as did workshop studies of social work clients. The cultural approach to the signs and dynamics of disorders—whether mere idiosyncrasy, mild neurosis, or personal or social pathologies—visibly relieved students' tensions, freeing them from much self-recrimination as it revealed the grandness of the traditions.

Notes

1. Harold L. Wilensky and Charles N. LeBeaux, *Industrial Society and Social Welfare* (New York: Russell Sage Foundation, 1958), p. 144, quote "An international study by the United Nations . . . that social work seeks to assist '. . . individuals, families and groups in relation to the many social and economic forces by which they are affected. . . . The social worker . . . cannot exclude from his consideration any aspect of the life of the person who seeks help in solving problems of social adjustment . . . [or any] of the community's social institutions that might be of use to the individual.'"
   See also Philip Klein, "Social Work, General Discussion, Social Case Work" in (eds.) Edwin R. A. Seligman and Alvin Johnson, *Encyclopedia of the Social Sciences* (New York: Macmillan Co., 1934, 1954), Vol. 14, pp. 165–183.
2. See Nathan Edward Cohen, *Social Work in the American Tradition* (New York: The Dryden Press, 1958), pp. 116, 142–143: "The first program of school social workers was introduced in 1906–1907 in Boston, Hartford and New York under private agencies. The first public school sponsorship of the program was in Rochester in 1914. . . . By 1916, 8 states were utilizing a total of 41 visiting teachers in their program." "With the financing of demonstration programs of visiting teacher work in some thirty centers throughout the country by the Commonwealth Fund in 1921, the number of visiting teachers grew from 41 in 1916 to 275 in 1931. In 1919 they organized the American Association of Visiting Teachers (now the School Social Workers Section of the National Association of Social Workers)." Wilensky and Lebeaux, *op. cit.*, p. 296, speak of "School social work, more commonly known as Visiting Teaching . . . In some jurisdictions social work training is re-

quired for employment, in others the stress is on training in the field of education combined with some lesser preparation in casework . . . (The) high educational requirements of the NASW . . . (since) October 1955, will henceforth prevent all but those who complete graduate social work training from joining the professional association." Reproducing U. S. Department of Labor figures, the authors list 1,210 school social workers in 1950 (*op. cit.*, p. 292). In a letter to the writer, August 1962, Jerry L. Kelley, Assistant Dean, University of Washington, School of Social Work, said that these 1,210 included untrained social workers, that presently "about 1,100 members of NASW (National Association of Social Workers) designate themselves as (professionally trained) school social workers . . . (These are) more numerous in elementary schools but serve high schools too." For a general discussion, see Arlien Johnson, *School Social Work: Its Contribution to Professional Education* (New York: National Association of Social Workers, 1962).

Claremont College Education Professor, Donald McNassor, told the writer that he finds Visiting Teachers in many urban elementary schools, teaching the home bound and secondarily doing social work. He finds counselors, guiding education and careers, universally in high schools since the 1930s; and he finds school social workers in occasional urban public schools.

3. This phrase and variants are used generally. See Cohen, *op. cit.*, p. vii; and Wilensky and Lebeaux, *op. cit.*, pp. 300–301.

4. See Wilensky and Lebeaux, *op. cit.*, pp. 289–291.

5. See Wilensky and Lebeaux, *op. cit.*, p. 331.

6. Wilensky and Lebeaux, *op. cit.*, p. 147, say some social workers believe "that public education might be classed among the social services, as it is in England . . . In the United States there is apparently a tendency to exclude from the welfare category any service, no matter how identified with welfare . . . in origin, which becomes highly developed, widespread . . . and professionally staffed by persons other than social workers . . ."

7. Albert I. Gordon, *Jews in Suburbia* (Boston: Beacon Press, 1959), pp. 242–243, 9, 245, examines high transiency among young successful middle-class Jewish families in suburbs: ". . . the very mobility which has produced these suburbs has created many challenging and often frustrating situations. For before these new families have really settled in the suburb, they seem ready to move on again, searching for a new suburb that will represent greater wealth, hence a higher social status. Because homes can be sold easily, new homes in even the newer and more exclusive suburbs are being purchased and occupied for comparatively short periods of time. Suburban Jewish community leaders report that this transiency is a major problem affecting the organized Jewish life of the community." Leaders of Boston suburbs "are concerned because the number of families who really fix roots in the community appears to be declining." California's San Gabriel Valley suburbs "have a considerable degree of transiency . . . One in 7 families . . . in the Los Angeles area reported in 1958 that they intended to move . . .", according to Jewish community leaders. "Transiency makes it difficult if not impossible for religious leaders within a suburban community to help the family integrate properly." "New Yorkers have been in mass flight from Manhattan to the suburbs." This transiency stirs fear of losing traditional Jewish identity.

8. A description of training for the professional social work degree appears in Wilensky and Lebeaux, *op. cit.,* pp. 311–314.

9. See description in Wilensky and Lebeaux, *op. cit.,* p. 306 and p. 308n.

10. See Wilensky and Lebeaux, pp. 237, 308.

11. See California State Department of Education (Division of State Colleges and Teacher Education, Sacramento, California, December 1954: California State Printing Office), Article 34, General Pupil Personnel Services Credential. See also the pamphlet, Council of Chief State School Officers (1201 – 16th St., N.W., Washington, D. C.), *Pupil Personnel Services.*

12. See "Guidance Roles of School Personnel," Evaluation and Research Section, Los Angeles City Schools (California), 1961, especially p. 27.

See also Lawrence H. Stewart, "The Counselor and the School Guidance Program: Some Considerations for a Framework," mimeographed report of a conference, University of California, Berkeley, 1961, pp. 1–4, 7–10, 16, 19. Professor Stewart writes:

> There appears to be a considerable amount of confusion about the role of the school counselor. School officials do not agree on the duties which he should be assigned; teachers and students are not sure which services to seek from him; . . . the counselor himself does not appear to be confident about the image he wishes to promulgate . . . [National] concern is reflected in the enactment of the National Defense Education Act of 1958, which provides federal support for guidance in the secondary schools through scholarships for counselor training and grants to state departments of education for improved guidance services, and also in the recent heated debates over the degree of excellence of American public schools . . .
>
> . . . The school counselor is depicted as [having] . . . a major role in the discovery and motivation of talented students to meet . . . manpower needs. But while the school counselors are performing roles of increasing importance in our educational institutions, there is also an increase in attention to [their] . . . adequacy . . .

Illustrative of the school counselor's "confusion" are

attempts to answer questions of fundamental responsibility such as: Should [the] . . . school counselor acquiesce to the demands that he work to further the immediate needs of society or should he be primarily concerned with the specific needs of each individual?

. . . [The] lack of role definition stems from many sources. Perhaps the most important . . . is the tradition . . . [of] the profession . . . Formalized guidance work began at the turn of the century as a response to needs . . . of the industrial revolution. During the 30's the movement became involved with problems associated with the Depression; during the 40's it was World War II, and now, it is the shortage of scientific and technical manpower. . . . [The] profession has been primarily oriented toward the solution of pressing social problems and little attention has been given to . . . helping . . . prevent personal and social problems before they arise. . . .

A second factor related to the confusion about the roles of the school counselor may be the practice of recruiting counselors only from the teaching ranks . . . [Then] . . . a counselor . . . may carry over his perceptions . . . learned as a teacher . . . Also, a school administrator, who was first a classroom teacher and then used a counseling assignment as a stepping-stone . . . may tend to make assignments to his counselors which he deems appropriate because these were the functions he performed as a counselor . . . [Is] teaching the *only* way or even necessarily the best way to become familiar with an educational institution? . . .

A third factor related to the confusion about the school counselor's role is the concern with the uncertainties of the decades ahead particularly [regarding] . . . the occupational structure. . . . The rapidly accelerating rate of change of the labor force suggests that occupations . . . important in 1961 may not even be in existence in 1975. . . . Lack of clarity about the counselor role in helping students plan careers is compounded by the fact that these students must be making decisions now about fields of endeavor which they will not be entering until 1970 or 1975.

[School] . . . guidance should be a continuous process from kindergarten through grade 12 and if . . . possible through college. The present practice of segmenting guidance services for elementary, junior high school and senior high school makes meaningful articulation among various parts of the program exceedingly difficult. . . . [Much] of the counselor's time at present is devoted to the atypical child. If the focus is to be the maturation processes of *all* students, the current practice must be changed . . . [We] must learn how to work with these (problem) students without such work being at the expense of the rest of the student population . . .

. . . [Counselors] have long held the belief—in word if not always in deed—that the student has the right to make his own decisions about the way he wishes to use his talents and about the kind of life he wishes to live. However, on the matter of the student's obligations to his society which go along with his right to free choice, we are not at all sure . . .

. . . [The] obligation of the counselor to insure that the counselee has access to adequate information on which to base meaningful choices is less often recognized . . . is often vague and a source of conflict to the counselor. To what range of information should the counselee be exposed? How much of the counselor's effort should be expended in making sure that the counselee is interpreting the available information properly, particularly in view of inadequacies in the data on which such information is based?

Unless the counselor recognizes and accepts his obligation to equip the student to make decisions, it is difficult to see how the counseling process can be effective . . . [It is an] . . . obligation of the counselor . . . to help the student implement his decisions—even though the counselor may not feel that the decision is necessarily a wise one! . . .

. . . Perhaps the present emphasis on individual counseling is not the most efficient or effective way to work with the developmental problems of youth. It is conceivable that the counselor could realize more . . . [by] helping teachers understand their students . . . The counselor's time spent with the teacher gains in significance when one considers that it is the teacher who spends the most time with the student and that many of the problems . . . [to] reach the counselor's office have their origin in conflicts between students and teachers . . .

. . . [Until] his various roles have been clarified . . . [it] is unlikely that the counselor will be seen . . . in any meaningful way.

13. These are excerpts from the school social worker's report of the meeting with the parents:

The father cleared his voice two or three times, . . . [showing] humiliation and anger, said he was embarrassed and apologized for his son's behavior "at the school." At the word "school," his tone dropped, was almost reverent . . . [After hearing the social worker's presentation, he] said, "Miss—, I am here to listen to your recommendation." His tone was both arrogant and courteous. After he had made remarks to the effect of "I'm here at your mercy and waiting," I wondered if we might not now have his wife come in. He thought it might be well . . . When she was seated, I said I had already spoken to her husband, that the boy's behavior shows definite need of help, for himself and to prevent a school exclusion. She looked at me and at her husband, shaking her head in agreement and said yes. The father said soberly, "Miss—, we are here for your recommendation." I said that my recommendation was for them to go with the boy to the PTA Child Guidance Clinic at the earliest possible moment. [To the father's remaining objections, the worker repeated that the child's temper tantrums and vile language] mean only that the child needs a doctor, whom he would have at the Clinic. The father looked at me searchingly and said, "I'm so sorry he talked this way at the school." . . . Most of the time the mother was glancing back and forth from me to her husband . . . The father questioned in a hopeless tone if he should give his son to the Clinic and let them take over. I immediately said that this was not the case, that it simply meant that he and his wife would join hands with the people at the Clinic so that all could help . . . In a loving thoughtful tone, he repeated "join hands," and I did likewise saying, "Yes, you join hands with those at the Clinic." The father said, "Then this we had better do."

The mother asked about the time it would take. The father turned to her saying, "However long it takes, we must go." I inquired about the mother's . . . [taking] time from her job. She was asking about Saturday appointments, which are impossible, and was interrupted by the father who said, looking sternly at her, "This is the most important thing and we must do what is recommended." . . . I asked if he could take time from work for the Clinic appointments. He said it would be hard but the Clinic was important and he would make arrangements . . . He turned to his wife and said, "He will not always have me and he will leave, he will go out on his own and I want him to be ready even if it takes many years." . . . [Later, discussing the boy's earlier years] . . . the father said he had found the youngster "out of hand" and had to "straighten the matter out." Looking intently at me, he asked falteringly if he had been "too strict?" I said that in any case I felt certain that he did what he as the father thought best. He nooded agreement and said, "The boy will not mind anyone else and never has." He asked what the boy's reaction might be if he, the father, was advised to become less strict? I thought he should talk this over with the Clinic social worker.

I told the parents I would recommend to the principal that the boy be reinstated, on the basis of their willingness to get him psychiatric help . . . I asked if they both could go immediately for a conference with the principal. The mother mentioned her work but the father intervened to say that getting the boy back in school was most important and so they had better see the principal now. . . . I said I would like their son in for a few minutes so that all of us together would understand about the Clinic. [The parents] left for the principal after much handshaking.

14. This is described in Wilensky and Lebeaux, *op cit.*, 289–291.

15. Wilensky and Lebeaux, *op. cit.*, 137–228 discuss social problems and welfare services.

16. According to Ruth Benedict's concept of personality and culture patterns, their temperaments (or personalities) were not congenial with their culture's bents.

17. Ruth Benedict, *Patterns of Culture* (Boston and New York: Houghton Mifflin Company, 1934), p. 279, refers to *The Wild Boy of Aveyron*, by Jean-Marc-Gaspard Itard, translated by George and Muriel Humphrey (New York, 1932). She comments, "It is probable that some of these children were subnormal and abandoned because of that fact. But it is hardly possible that all of them were, yet they all impressed observers as half-witted." Discussing such abandoned children, pp. 12–13, she says,

    . . . they were all so much alike that Linnaeus classified them as a distinct species, *Homo ferus*, and supposed that they were a kind of gnome that man seldom ran across. He could not conceive that these half-witted brutes were born human, these creatures with no interest in what went on about them, rocking themselves rhythmically back and forth like some wild animal in a zoo, with organs of speech and hearing that could hardly be trained to do service, who withstood freezing weather in rags and plucked potatoes out of boiling water without discomfort . . . [What] they had all of them lacked was association with their kind, through which alone man's faculties are sharpened and given form.

18. See Nancy Rambusch, *Learning How to Learn: An American Approach to Montessori* (New York: Helicon Press, Inc., 1962). *Time* magazine, May 12, 1961, p. 12, summarizes Dr. Maria Montessori's successful training of feeble-minded and slum children in Rome in 1907. In the United States the Whitby School, Greenwich, Connecticut, adapts the Montessori method to American children of low-rated mentality with brilliant results. The *New York Times*, May 20, 1962, states,

    There are now thirteen schools from Washington, D. C. to Los Angeles employing the Montessori method and thirteen more are scheduled to introduce classes in September. "There would have been twenty-five more if there were qualified Montessorians to man them," Mrs. Rambusch said. [She is] President of the American Montessori Society and headmistress of the Whitby School . . . Instruction begins with children aged 3 in an ungraded setting with children of different ages and levels of achievement working independently in the same classroom. © 1962 by The New York Times Company. Reprinted by permission.

19. Alfred L. Kroeber, *Configurations of Culture Growth* (Berkeley: University of California Press, 1944).

20. Alfred L. Kroeber, *Style and Civilizations* (Ithaca: Cornell University Press, 1957), p. 61. Copyrighted 1957 by Cornell University. Used with permission of Cornell University Press. He says further,

I computed that even in the greater civilizations of history . . . when their more and their less productive periods are taken together, there must be at least three-fourths, perhaps nine-tenths of their potential geniuses that never come to flowering for posterity to recognize. And if we take the whole human population through its whole history, including conditions alike of great and of lesser civilization, of semicivilization, of barbarism and primitivism all together, then the percentage of realization of genius is of course even less, possibly only two or three per cent.

21. See W. Lloyd Warner, Robert J. Havighurst, and Martin B. Loeb, *Who Shall Be Educated? The Challenge of Unequal Opportunities.* (New York: Harper and Brothers, 1944.) Also Allison Davis and Robert J. Havighurst, *Father of the Man.* (Boston: Houghton Mifflin Co., 1947.) Also Kenneth W. Eells, Allison Davis, and others, *Intelligence and Cultural Differences: A Study of Cultural Learning and Problem-Solving* (Chicago: University of Chicago Press, 1951).

22. See Robert P. Crossley, "The Secret of Getting Into Harvard," *McCall's* Magazine, July 1961, pp. 45, 134–136. This describes Harvard's successful experiment with 19 boys from poor backgrounds and with low College Board scores, 75 to 100 points below classmates' scores, but with high ambition. Quoting Harvard's dean, "It is painfully clear that we do not know much about measuring human ability." Crossley concludes that, "In Harvard's view, the project proves . . . that a poor cultural background will make a boy look worse on a test than he really is. It proves that high school grades are a better barometer of ability than test scores. And it proves that no qualities are more important than ambition and perseverance."

23. See Wilensky and Lebeaux, *op. cit.,* 322–323.

24. See Ruth Landes, *The Ojibwa Woman* (New York: Columbia University Press, 1938).

25. During May 1961 the *New York Times* and other news media, including radio, discussed results of the American Psychiatric Association's completed twelve-year study of fifty male subjects. The composite portrait presented the "well-adjusted normal American male," deplored as dull and uncreative.

26. Agnes de Mille, *To a Young Dancer. A Handbook for Dance Students, Parents and Teachers.* (Boston: Little, Brown and Co., An Atlantic Monthly Press Book, 1962). Foreword.

27. See the foregoing discussions. One seminar program was a Symposium on the Changing Position of Women by the four participants from India, China, Greece, and Holland. The presentations and discussions were tape-recorded. All students' reports to follow were condensed by Ruth Landes. Students prepared the work for this use.

28. A lively account of a famous American Negro cult is Sara Harris' *Father Divine: Holy Husband* (Garden City, New York: Permabooks, Doubleday and Co., 1954). An account of celebrated Brazilian Negro cults with African traditions is Ruth Landes' *City of Women* (New York: Macmillan Co., 1947). An account of similar cults in Haiti is Maya Deren's *Divine Horsemen: The Living Gods of Haiti* (London and New York: Thames and Hudson, 1953).

In 1962, American newspapers and periodicals published stories of American Negro Muslim militancy, e.g., The *New York Times,* August 26,

p. 64; *Newsweek*, August 27, pp. 26 *ff*.; *The Saturday Evening Post*, September 8, p. 19. Moslem and Muslim are variants of each other.

29. They set out to answer, "What traits distinguish the potentially delinquent child from others, what appear as primary social causes of juvenile delinquency, what preventive measures seem effective?" Besides studying publications, they interviewed six professional people (a woman high-school counselor, a woman juvenile delinquency officer of sergeant rank, a male probation officer, a male high-school vice principal, a male director of a neighborhood center, a minister directing youth work for his church) and "5 females aged 16 through 42 years," all white. Interviews were reported in narrative detail and then in tables.

30. The team product was entitled, "Study of Parental Attitudes toward Juvenile Delinquency." Chapter headings were: "1. Middle-Class Caucasian American Working Mothers. 2. Lower-Class White American Mothers. 3. American Career Military Parents. 4. Catholic Parents. 5. Filipino Parents. 6. Japanese Parents. 7. Negro Parents of Professional Class. 8. Professional Social Workers. 9. Summary and Conclusions."

31. The team product was entitled, "Juvenile Delinquency Viewed by Three Groups of Adolescents." One group interviewed had eight boys, 13 to 17 years old, from "upper-lower to upper middle-class families" of Mexican-American and Anglo-American Catholics, of Anglo-American Lutherans and of a Mormon family. Another group interviewed had six girls, 13 to 14 years old, from affluent Jewish families. The third group interviewed had twenty "teenage boys and girls living in a Jewish children's institution."

32. The concept included every construction respondents chose to attribute; these were chiefly racial, cultural and religious intermixtures, occasionally touching on national and class aspects. A caseworker concluded her report on "The Question of Intermarriage" thus, "To me the most interesting aspect of the interviews is the use that 3 individuals made of the question posed. One expressed guilt and hostility about her own marriage; one, who was ⅓₂ Negro, tried to justify her desire for a group identity; and one tried to feel out where the interviewer's approval lay . . . An individual's answers to a question of intermarriage reveal much about his own feelings of social identity and security."

33. See Ruth Benedict, *Patterns of Culture*, *op. cit.*, Chapter 8 on "The Individual and the Pattern of Culture." Also Ruth Landes, *The Ojibwa Woman*, *op. cit.*, Part 4 on "Abnormalities." Also Ruth Landes, "The Abnormal Among the Ojibwa Indians," *Journal of Abnormal and Social Psychology* (Vol. 33, No. 1), January 1938, pp. 14–33.

7

Teacher Research
in Culture and Education

In all training lectures and field projects about culture, education, and social work, the Claremont undertaking kept to the front the concept that a culture limits and stylizes the raw, pulsating materials of mankind like a mold or pattern. The nature of culture is to organize human life everywhere and also to vary the great and small details. Herein lies the mystery of culture, but the training focused rather on *applying* culture concepts and knowledge to school and welfare needs. Hence, if educators and social workers are not to lose their way among the different traditional cultures, especially of the minorities, they must learn to understand them. This approach releases information and provides insights for practical use.

The imaginations and curiosities of teachers were stirred by the field projects [1] as the research carried them to the world beyond the usual limits of school building, grounds, and curriculum. Teachers gave more time to each successive project and to "the public," as they described parents and others outside school walls. Projects grew more complex and touched sensitive areas as teachers grew more familiar with the research methods and ideas and with their own emotional responses, now disturbed, now exhilarated. Through their work in the field, more than through any in libraries, individuals became alive to varied cultural forces acting in them and through them on others. They saw these forces also acting in pupils—such as the Anglo's expectation that it is normal to see authority shared unequally by men and women working together, unlike the Latin's expectation of seeing the sexes in sharply differentiated spheres of activity. They found

190

that research on unfamiliar peoples trapped in significant situations—
such as conflicts between Mexican standards of adolescent behavior
and Anglo standards enforced by schools—served inevitably to illuminate also, though obliquely, a researcher's own personal problems.
This oblique gain, embedded in research insights, apparently cush-
ioned shocks in personal discoveries. Thus, the minorities in school
areas provided living texts of culture and also clues to self-discoveries.

The teachers also read published studies about remote peoples,
borrowed ideas from them for their projects, and wrote their findings
and reflections with care and imagination. They ceased to use "culture" as a faddish label but employed it as a meaningful attribute of
behavior, describing customary practices or conventions. Thus, they
recognized that Anglo "culture" justified the school's approach to
Anglo mothers for decisions but not to Oriental ones. They saw that
unfamiliar conventions clashing with school conventions or standards
—as when Mexican pupils evade rules to undress in open showers—
had to be recognized as such and deciphered for hidden meanings to
facilitate appropriate negotiation by authorities. Conventions were
seen as staging or defining situations, relationships, trends, and ideas
—such conventions as the biracial practices of the old South, sub-
ordinating Negroes and Indians to whites; as the etiquette which
Spanish-speaking peoples elaborately differentiate for the sexes; as
limitations on actions of minors, which vary among groups and
which define the subordination of minors to elders, as in European
demands that children never intrude on adults and American demands that pubescent boys refrain from sex relations. Many cultures,
including minority subcultures, were examined and compared in
order to single out conventions that variously meet universal human
needs for order, comfort, power, pleasure, and perpetuation.

Each project was designed to embody one or more cultural concepts pertinent to education and welfare [2] and to demonstrate basic,
simple research procedures.[3] Each project was intended to amplify
the educator's usual focus on individuals with realizations about society and culture, especially in view of the vast continental migrations,
which brought into Los Angeles county, for example, 464 persons
daily from different regions.[4] Besides the social instability accompanying the migrations, new antidiscriminatory legislation opened opportunities for minorities, altering locations of power, releasing unfamiliar
encounters among traditionally separated, ranked groups, and bringing home through talk and feelings such unrest in the greater world
as nation-building by Africa's former colonies and hostilities against
the United States in Latin America.

To emphasize sociocultural forces, American public education was defined as the sanctioned practice of the dominant group which transferred official knowledge through selected agents, called teachers, to all children under the age of sixteen, called pupils, and to elders meeting formal qualifications. But the public authority, which in the past decade established the standard of universal desegregated schooling, did not provide for the consequence that uncontrolled cultural elements—like foreign speech and Mexican youngsters' docility—would enter classrooms. The oversight, and the accompanying failure to train teachers in cultural factors, reflect prevailing blindness to the desegregated subcultures and to the ways in which culture influences learning. Both reflect persisting stereotypes about the inferiority of minorities. The lack of cultural controls, however, exacerbates the "frustration" that teachers profess at all levels and the undesirable behavior that delinquents and predelinquents cultivate. Through their projects teachers learned that cultural controls were feasible and advantageous in professional applications, as illustrated later in this chapter.

Research procedures utilized direct observations of individuals and groups, when people were silent, talking, or behaving otherwise. They stressed interviews of the "open-ended" sort which allowed informants to express their own interests in response to fairly general questioning. Research records included questionnaires, diary accounts of observations, interviews and other flows of data, snapshots of events in the field, drawings, tables, and simple statistics. Research problems were phrased in the light of a selected literature but keyed to professional application.

Teachers were led to concentrate on how individuals and groups conduct social business—as, for example, how decisions about discipline are made and enforced, how marriages and divorces are accomplished, how family name, status, and real property are transferred. The "how" was an omnibus concept stressing functions that also carried questions about who, when, where, what, and why. An informant's housing and employment experiences were recorded for their revelations of values, goals, and techniques favored or not by informants, on one hand, and by society, on the other. It was vital for these students to discover which language a multilingual person or family spoke on a given occasion, and possibly why. Students examined parental authority in several unlike groups. They compared the cultural data secured from all groups to learn which traits and trait complexes might be unique, which shared, and why.

With their own work, therefore, they provided evidence of cultural designs, dynamics, values, services, liabilities, and relativity.

Students' reports of their work document the range of problems and interests examined, the research procedures followed, and the insights gained. The reports also convey a sense of the personalities at work. To illustrate all this, portions of some of the reports are given.

About Teachers

Several reports, though prepared by different persons in different years, constitute a series focusing on teachers, pupils, families, and their troubles with education. One study, by a young woman teaching high-school English, presented "The Shifting Image of the Teacher in America." The subject concerns all educators, many of whom voice distress over their profession's low prestige and over the place of individuals who teach. In her report, the student identified the atmosphere around educators as one of "anxiety" and accepted the anxiety, nurtured in generations of teachers' families, including her own, as an index of educators' "subculture." She told her seminar mates, twelve men and a woman, "I'm ashamed to admit that when a school administrator asked me if I were a dean of girls, I answered, 'I'm just a teacher.'" Except for one Mexican-American man, her listeners nodded in concurrence.[5] Hunched in avowed "embarrassment," the young woman read aloud her report of interviews with six female and two male "successful high-school teachers and administrators" about the status of teachers in urban communities; she had anticipated self-depreciatory responses. Sections of the report follow.[6]

[To her first question] "Do you ever hesitate to state your occupation?" a woman answered: "I was pleased that on a world tour, the others didn't suspect I was a teacher. . . . They expect you to be staid, stiff, and proper. But in a way we're proud to be teachers."

Another woman said, "I'll always remember this incident. In my first year we were to attend a teachers' convention, but instead we all decided to go to Chicago. On the train we met an army colonel, considerably older, and we told him we were actresses! I can hear him yet. He said, 'My dears, there are worse occupations than schoolteaching.' But if I'm asked, I never deny being a teacher."

A young man said, "My first thought would be whether the group I'm with would feel awkward, inferior, like groups in the army. If so, I keep my occupation in the background. . . . Sometimes I hesitate, sensing that people will expect too much of me concerning standards, morals, etc. I want to be accepted as a human being."

A man school administrator who had transferred from teaching, responded, "I don't hesitate as much now as when I was a teacher. It depends on the group. I have a young friend who's a self-made millionaire. Once on his yacht he introduced me with the old remark, 'You better watch yourselves! He's a teacher!' There comes this reaction in others you have to break down."

A woman said, "At times I haven't admitted I was a teacher to an individual with prejudices. But I've never lied about it. Nor have I ever apologized that 'I'm just a teacher.' "

Another woman said, "I don't advertise it, but if asked, I answer truthfully."

[To the second question] "What is your reaction when someone guesses you are a teacher before you tell him?" [respondents' answers fell somewhat in the same sequence but are not all reproduced here]. A woman said, "I resent it! Three teachers and I were starting down the Grand Canyon on a scheduled donkey trip when the guide said, 'Now, don't you teachers give me any trouble.' I turned to the others and said, 'He doesn't even recognize a good secretary when he sees one.' Another time a car-park attendant asked me and my girl friend, 'Is that teachers' meeting at the hotel over already?' I said, 'We're not teachers.' My friend teased me all the way home. She's not a teacher."

Another woman declared: "I feel a flash of annoyance, like a reflex."

A third woman: "I'm horrified! It always shocks me. Recently I gussied myself up for a dinner with my husband and his business associates. Opposite me at table a woman gushed to her husband, 'Doesn't she look like an ideal teacher!' My reactions were mixed."

A young man: "I have spent a lifetime trying to rid myself of that mental image. Now people tell me, 'You don't look like a teacher.' "

A woman: "I want to know why they think I'm a teacher and not something else. Most teachers aren't proud to be that. A teacher bristles at the question because the profession has been so maligned."

Another: "I feel embarrassed . . . [as if I] must justify something."

[To the third question] "What undesirable characteristics does teaching bring out in individual teachers?" [the same respondents answered].

A woman: "Teachers sometimes steal an idea for their own, often to ingratiate themselves with the principal. It's a form of cheating. One type of teacher cheats to make her pupils look well on tests."

Another: "The voice becomes strident, as teachers talk too loudly. We're trying to be correct most of the time. Sometimes we give absolute answers though we know differently. We talk to others as if they were pupils in a classroom situation."

Another: "We fuss about details, get overly critical of pupils, talk too much. The work is so demanding that often a teacher cannot see beyond the job—it's with her 24 hours a day. There's an emotional exhaustion because we're forever on stage. Then we lose sight of our purpose, which is teaching . . ."

Another: "I say to the kids, 'Will you stop making a fishwife of me?' "

[To the fourth question] "What does a man teacher look like?" an unmarried woman said, "He is generally effeminate unless a coach."

A married woman said, "He is effeminate, not too manly, introverted, with limited interests, rarely concerned with the world outside his subject, socially ill-at-ease."

A young man said, "He's a middle-aged man, wears a navy-blue or other conservative suit, has a quality of tiredness in the way he walks and stands. There is always an unkemptness, chalk on the suit, necktie not straight . . ."

A divorced woman: "We don't have any men in our system! When I started teaching, there were a few men, typically effeminate. . . . The GI bill changed the picture, bringing in manly men. It also brought in some who are only after a fast buck."

A woman: "He isn't a man among men. He's insecure, resentful, lazy, threadbare-looking. Takes on more and more jobs to earn money and doesn't always do them justice."

[To the fifth question] "What is a typical woman teacher?" [a woman responded] "I resent being categorized with other women teachers!"

Another: "She wears longer than normal skirts, ground-gripper shoes, hair drawn to a bun, glasses, dark drab clothes, looks stern, pale."

A young man: "I think of my math teacher, hair parted and severe over the ears, severe drab clothes, efficient, warm, strict, formal . . ."

Another woman: "She is opinionated, insecure, prim, hypersensitive, self-pitying, has a strident voice and closed mind, is covetous of materials and ideas for teaching, has a neat appearance and is lonely."

[To the sixth question] "What can teachers do to improve their status?" [one woman said] "Be as natural as possible. Drop the dogmatic teacher role outside the classroom."

A man: "Be human."

A woman: "To gain respect, we need more control over punishment."

Another woman: "Do a better job of teaching! And mix in community affairs . . ."

Another: "Make contributions outside the classroom . . ."

And another: "Do a better job of public relations, as a group and as individuals . . ."

[To the seventh question] "When you attend a large gathering of teachers, do you feel a sense of belonging?" a woman said, "No. I come out blue as a Negro. No one can be more dowdy than teachers. I feel almost trapped at teachers' meetings."

A young man: "I always feel like an outsider who just wandered in, even among our own faculty. . . . Because older teachers make innocent remarks like, 'You're too young to know . . . You're capable but immature.'"

A woman: "I always feel insecure, as if we're all criticizing each other. Often we have nothing in common but our occupation."

[To the eighth question] "If you were starting again, would you still choose teaching?" two middle-aged women answered that they would not choose teaching because of better opportunities. But a woman of thirty-five said, "I don't really think I'd be happy outside of teaching though sometimes after a bad day, or facing a weekend with papers, I would almost rather scrub floors."

Another woman said: "I enjoy the work but if I had known how exhausting it is, I wouldn't have gone into it."

A young man asserted: "I'm very happy and can't see myself in any other role."

An older man said: "I never have regretted teaching because I'm happy in it. I do regret the poor money return."

A woman said she would again choose teaching where "I like my little theatre in which, by turns, I play many parts."

[To the ninth question] "What is the typical attitude of students towards teachers?" several women answered in versions of "It's between tolerance and liking." One woman elaborated, "I think they like us more than they did because today's informality lets them see us as individuals."

A young man thought that "Pupils are taught to dislike teachers by their parents. But they have an underlying desire to like us."

"A woman suggested that "if we were called something else, they might accept us more readily."

Another woman said, "Pupils come for grades and we're supposed to help. A few resent us and a few admire us deeply."

The student also asked thirty adults residing in a middle-class neighborhood, parents of children in all grades from kindergarten through junior college, to answer her questionnaire of fifty items about "stereotypes of teachers in the thinking of adults." All these persons responded approvingly, with "heavy emphasis on the positive traits of teachers," surprising the researcher and showing that the profession's anxieties were perhaps twenty years outdated in this neighborhood.

Another high-school teacher, married and a grandmother, expressed teachers' dread of superannuation and reported her study (mentioned before) of "Changing our Attitude towards the Aged." She began, "Youth and vigor are a traditional American ideal. How will this be reconciled with a life span of 120 years unless our society becomes culturally adjusted to old age?" For answers she combed geriatrics literature, interviewed elderly active people, and visited lively communities of the retired.

A Mexican-American high-school teacher devised a questionnaire to gather opinions from Mexican-American pupils about Mexican and Anglo teachers. He gave the questionnaire to 28 Mexican-American high-school seniors and found that "Mexican-American teachers are well-accepted. Since most of these teachers are so 'Americanized,' probably most students do not identify them with Mexicans in the community. . . . Mexican-American pupils do not seek out Mexican-American teachers for help except occasionally but usually they ask no one for help. The question arises, How can Mexican-American teachers provide greater help to Mexican-American pupils?" This man held that his professional rank laid on him a special and honorable duty to aid children of his own minority group.

A young woman on home leave in California from teaching at a mission school in Ethiopia described obligations and trials of American teachers and Ethiopian elders in the African kingdom:

There is satisfaction in knowing that you, an American, are accepted as a true friend by those of another culture though you keep your place in your own culture. You alter your thinking about people but you do not become one with the other culture. The relationship is somewhat like that of teacher and student. Friendship and understanding are gained by knowing another culture without imposing one's own culture's interpretations. . . . Our school's American and European teachers are a foreign minority group who conscientiously adjust their ways to Ethiopian ones, and this prevents confusion because of different cultural origins. For example, we learned to cope in accordance with the Ethiopian hierarchy of age.

It works this way: added years bring added respect, so older pupils in a class with younger ones automatically receive the respect of age or seniority. A pupil would not address his elder classmate by the given name without prefixing a title. Age-respect means that a mature eighth-grader has more opportunities for leadership at school than has a younger eleventh-grader. The choice of leaders is made by pupils or teachers.

In an Ethiopian back-country community, tribal elders are the governing body. Seated under the nearest tree, they hear cases. . . . Our student council is called the board of school elders. Pupils choose an elder from each tribal area to be responsible for those of his own group at school, including girls. To combat tribal rivalry, several elders are chosen at large. An elder jealously watches his tribal name. If unable to solve a pupil's difficulties, he calls upon other school elders. Usually the pupil listens to the group of elders; if not, our teachers, foreign or Ethiopian, talk with him. Good school elders set a fine tone in the school generally and in counseling.

We learned also that the Ethiopian way of settling quarrels requires the parties to call their witnesses before a group of elders and recite their grievances at length. After each one has testified and has answered the elders' questions, the elders voice a decision. Though this process is time-consuming, we follow it at school. If a problem occurs in the elementary grades, an Ethiopian, who is usually our blind pastor, and I sit in on all discussions. If it is a high-school problem, a discipline committee of the two school principals and two or three Ethiopians takes over. Formal peace between offending parties must be made with handshakes and kisses, whereupon the matter is forgotten. Little regard is shown for differences of rank between the parties. Peace must be made. Ethiopians may exchange harsh words in a private dispute. After a few hours or a few days, the guilty party realizes his obligation and makes peace by asking pardon unofficially, as between father and son. An affair is never considered closed until the peace is made in the traditionally proper way. When the trouble is serious, a third party makes the peace. If a foreign teacher offends an Ethiopian pupil, even unwittingly, he must make peace in the traditional manner or there is trouble. Since our foreign men give the dressing down, often severely, but do not follow the custom of the peace settlement, . . . their actions build resentments in the students, which crop out later. When an Ethiopian teacher wrongs an Ethiopian pupil, he must make amends. If the wrong was done publicly, he must apologize before the school assembly or even drop out of teaching briefly. Only then is the matter forgotten.

We learned, too, that the Ethiopian likes to use a spokesman or middleman. Last year a mature eighth-grader, who is a good friend of mine, asked another teacher to approach me about changing his school program. I felt rather flattered because this showed that the student knew I understood the Ethiopian tradition of showing respect by communicating through a spokesman. Frequently I ask teachers or mature students to pass my advice on to other students and often this is more effective than direct advice.

We learned the traditional peculiarities surrounding an Ethiopian patient. The teacher's greatest difficulty arises when a pupil has a prolonged illness. Back-country people show a completely fatalistic attitude toward illness. In each family, several children die before maturity. The people do not know that the month-old baby's dysentery comes from the whole milk and butter dripped from the mother's unwashed hand or fed out of the seldom-washed ox-horn bottle. They do not know that infection comes from the leaf-wrapped dung poultice they commonly place on sores. . . . Illness is expected as part of life. Pain is to be borne as long as possible without remedies because, if you are to die, you will . . .

The customary help during illness is sitting by the sufferer's bedside with a long face and reciting stories of others who have been ill . . . During a typhoid epidemic I had charge of ten critically ill people. Other pupils, though knowing that the disease was contagious, did not stay out of the sickroom. Relatives and tribal friends joined them. They had all learned about germs but could not apply the knowledge against their customs. One of our Ethiopian teachers repeatedly told a patient that he would probably die. I could not rely on Ethiopians to keep other Ethiopians out of sickrooms.

We had to learn that the Ethiopian scorns work, an attitude which opposes our denominational philosophy of education. In all our schools around the world, we expect each student to work some hours each day, regardless of fees. Our purpose is to show the dignity of ordinary work and to give the worker pride in his labor. In Ethiopia, the fatalistic attitude prevails. If a man does not plant enough corn, it is God's will that he go hungry. If the corn does not mature, it is because a man did not make proper sacrifice to the rain-god. In the past, government schools did not require students to work. Servants cleaned rooms and did personal laundry. Students were paid to go to school, that is, schooling was free and pocket money was provided. This is changing and our students now work more willingly.

To induce a favorable attitude to work, our students are divided into small work groups with a foreign or Ethiopian teacher who supervises and works along. Assignments are rotated. Good workers get responsible jobs, such as driving tractors and helping in the office. Very few Ethiopians are willing to give or take directions from their own people, and so leave most administration to foreigners. This, too, is beginning to change. Now I have an Ethiopian assistant in charge of the elementary school . . .

Comparable clashes arose between East Indian and American students at a California college. A young administrator of the institution studied the explosive incidents, personal griefs, and resounding fears that flourished while authorities remained ignorant of the alien ways; and he investigated efforts to manage them. He wrote:

During 1959–1960, three students from India were enrolled at our college. Relations between them and American students appeared quite friendly; the Indians were invited to American students' homes and were liked. The cordiality was reported in Indians' letters to friends and relatives at home and helped attract twenty-one more students from India the following year.

The Indians wanted to live in the residence halls with American roommates. But after a few weeks, the Americans were requesting transfers to rooms with Americans only or were making their Indian roommates so unwelcome as to cause them to move. Calumnious tales spread of the Indians' unacceptable hygiene, dirty clothing, black magic performed at night, odd eating habits, worm-infested digestive tracts. Relations between Indian and American students sagged badly . . .

To cope with this, a Foreign Student Advisory Committee was appointed by the college administration, including faculty and students of both cultures. . . . Free discussion of the complaints generated sympathetic understanding. It was learned that twenty-three of the Indian students belonged to the same Hindu caste, one was Moslem, all but one came of wealthy, urban homes, the one came from a village. . . . All desired to fulfill their families' hopes of success. . . . The Moslem sensed that the second group of Hindus disliked him and he joined the Americans in expressing resentment.

The Advisory Committee opened discussions cautiously with the Indians by remarking that dermatologists criticize Americans' frequent bathing as it removes vital skin oils. The Indians readily explained that both Hindu and Moslem honor bodily cleanliness and that the orthodox usually bathe twice daily in India because of heat and humidity but rarely use soap. Thus, religion was eliminated from the Indians' failure to bathe regularly. Then the Indians added that they could not endure the college's community showers, for even in their poorest villages Indians demand privacy in bathing. Hence when the shy Indian students did shower, it was late at night while others slept, and not for sorcery. . . . A few failed to bathe at all, causing offensive body odors.

Further, in their wealthy families the Indians were not required or prepared to perform menial housework, like cleaning rooms, laundering linens, and making beds. Their families would lose caste if they did such work, much of which is performed in India only by Untouchables despite recent legislation. . . . In the villages, many common tasks are executed only by people of specific castes and subcastes. Hence, the committee agreed, regardless of the Indian student's urban or rural origin, on arrival he is not equipped to live in our state college residence hall . . .

The Indian must be taught what to do, and how. The American has been trained to take soiled wash to a commercial laundry, a laundromat, or home to parents. The Indian requires some time to learn where, how, and why he can provide himself with clean clothing. Until that time comes, students often wear soiled garments a week or more, which spreads the notion that Indians are "dirty." Even when Indians saw American roommates tidy up it took time before they could bring themselves to do the same . . .

Americans have few religious taboos on foods but Moslems and Hindus have many such taboos. Hence, they experience profound difficulties among us. The Moslem may not eat pork, the orthodox Hindu may not eat any meats or meat products including eggs and is expected to live on vegetables. Students in residence halls eat at the college cafeteria and are generally unable to pay additionally for outside meals. The vegetarian Hindus could not subsist well on the vegetable side-dishes provided with cafeteria meals. Noticing their weights drop markedly, some moved off campus into a communally rented house. But most remained in the residence halls and eventually ate meat with the private excuse that health was at stake, and they needed health for study. One Hindu said that for over half a year he could not persuade himself to eat flesh; then he started to eat meat regularly, vowing that "I shall never eat meat again once I leave this country." All but one Hindu stated that they did not dare inform their parents of the meat violations.

Thus, the Foreign Student Advisory Committee opened the way to solutions and bettered relations between Americans and Indians.

About the Community

At this period of American history, the relationships among dominant and minority ethnic forces in the community hold the attention of educators and welfare workers. Stereotypes and statistics flourish but not intimate knowledge. Hence, an Anglo-American teacher studied "reactions of successful Anglo-Americans toward minority groups in their city." By a questionnaire and interviews he examined six married men, a bachelor, four married women, and two single ones of varied ages and occupations. Interested in their "hidden motivations" toward Mexican-Americans and Negroes, he found "the majority of respondents unopposed to integration in public schools but considerably reserved about integrating social relations. They would actually prefer having minorities teach their own. . . . In dealing with minorities, there was more consideration of the individual's worth than of the group's status. . . . Racial intermarriage is considered disastrous chiefly because the children would be half-caste. . . . It was conceded with reservations that all are created equal. . . . While admitting the complex problems of minorities, only 23 per cent of these respondents would give time to them. . . . Perhaps successful integration of races and cultures is not yet possible. Or perhaps demands of the space age will erase prejudices."

Despite the conservatism of his findings, this teacher felt much stimulated by them because the feelings generated in his discussions were high, though controlled, and he felt he had touched something more real than newspaper articles or educators' abstractions. His own views were exactly those summarizing the report.

During the two years of the Anthropology and Education project, only one student chose to study the American Negro. He was a mature teacher, a white man originally from Oklahoma, who had taught for years on the faculty of a white denominational college in the deep South.[7] Because of his church interests and interests in civil rights, this man wrote an essay on "The Negro's Unique Resources in Developing Effective Nonviolence."

Beginning with allusions to the history and philosophy of nonviolence in the Judaeo-Christian world, he proceeded to Ghandi's nonviolence in India, and related to these the contemporary nonviolent programs of American Negroes in the old South. He concluded:

> Inspired by a Jewish carpenter two thousand years ago and by a Hindu of our twentieth century, the American Negro may lead humanity to a new nonviolent love. . . . As the Hebrew people, during four centuries of slavery and forty years in the wilderness, acquired resources fitting them to lead humanity to a high ethical monotheism, so three centuries of slavery and a century of humiliation have bequeathed the Negro resources for leading humanity to a highly ethical effective nonviolence.

This view of the Negro role in the world community is, of course, a special one. Further, it does not provide understanding of individual Negroes in the white-dominated world. A white woman teacher came closer to portraying a worthy Negro member of the general American community when she fulfilled a class assignment to interview a person of unfamiliar background by conversing with a Negro teacher:

> Our talks now clarify certain acts and the tensions under which this teacher, Mary, works. Though I have known many Negroes, adults and children, I have never discussed personal feelings and problems as with Mary. Our talks were at school, at home, when driving in her car or mine and at other odd times.

She learned about Mary's impoverished segregated childhood and schooling in Oklahoma, about her family's slave ancestry and its mixtures with American Indian, European, and African races.

> After one year in a segregated school, Mary's mother insisted that she attend a "mixed" school, to be better prepared for the world. Mary preferred to go where she could "have friends rather than just smiling acquaintances . . . where I could meet someone to marry." So she went to a teachers' college in Kansas that had been integrated shortly before and had enrolled about fifty other Negroes. Here she met her future husband, Dick, a football hero and son of a well-to-do doctor. . . . They came to California during Dick's army service, now are buying a $16,000

home and new furnishings; they drive a Mercury station wagon and a foreign sports car. Mary is working toward another teaching credential, Dick teaches and holds another job with the city recreation department. She appreciates greatly the opportunities in California and cannot understand the children in our [chiefly Negro and Mexican] school who do not take advantage of the chance to learn and advance.

In our last talk, Mary spoke more freely than ever about color. She said most Negroes disapprove of intermarriage. Negroes are prejudiced against the darker ones of the race. She lost her babysitter because the three-year old persistently asked if she was "black" or "brown." This was after the neighbor's children, themselves black, had told the three-year old that she was black. Actually she is light, like her parents. Dick was nearly expelled from the Kansas college when the dean heard a rumor that he was dating a white girl. The girl was Mary; and Mary and Dick had to see the dean to correct the rumor. Mary feels that their light skins give her and Dick a hard time in the Negro community. She says they are accepted only about as well as a mixed couple. Her light-skinned family has always had this trouble.

Since the end of the Second World War, American Indians are coming into some recognition as a minority group in many local communities. This is partly a response to tribesmen's activities in war industries, in military services, and in civil rights' programs on their own behalf. It also reflects efforts of the federal government to "relocate" or remove many from reservations to large cities, like Los Angeles, offering industrial jobs. California public schools usually find Indian pupils "frustrating" to cope with, especially since the federal relocation program and the Supreme Court's 1954 decision ordering desegregation. Various churches intervene to promote friendship between Indians and others in the community, and one such undertaking was observed in the summer of 1961 by a young elementary-school teacher.

A church group brought some Indian children from reservations outside California to visit families in the teacher's California town. The young woman spent considerable time with a few tribal visitors in their hosts' home, read works about the tribes, and reported her views in a discussion called, "Ten Traits of Navajos in New Surroundings." [8] She wrote that:

The Indian children, nine to fifteen years old, included seventeen Paiutes and Shoshones from Bishop and Death Valley, and eighteen Navajos from an area between Farmington and Cuba, New Mexico. It was said that many had never been off their reservations. Now they were to spend two weeks with Anglo-American families in our town.

The visit was to show life off the reservation so attractively that the children would want to leave their reservations and would copy our American culture and manners when they did make homes off the reservation.

Also, the visit was to create understanding between the Indians and the hosts' children.

Hosts of the Paiutes and Shoshones commented on the ease with which these Indians adjusted, saying frequently "He does everything my boys do!" I felt the same when I interviewed a teen-age Shoshone girl and a teen-age Paiute girl attending public schools and found them acting much like my teen-age cousin. But hosts of the Navajos found differently and worried that "they don't talk, you know. We just have to guess as we can. What does she like? What will she eat? and do? We don't know."

I assumed that the Navajos were following traditional behavior. But what were they expressing? I observed carefully two Navajo girls and their brother, their mother who stayed in another home, and the children's hosts, Mr. and Mrs. A.

Mrs. A was a retired high-school teacher and principal, proud of getting along with children. Her husband was a retired postmaster who cultivated his garden and honeybees. They were financially comfortable, their two children were grown and had academic degrees.

The Navajo children were named Maria, Marilyn, and Doug. Doug told me they were fifteen, twelve, and fourteen years old respectively, though the mother and girls said the ages were actually fourteen, nine, and thirteen. Doug said the father had been dead some twelve years. Their mother, Mrs. P, worked for clothes and board at a mission school; the church had built her a one-room house without running water. The family owned thirty-five sheep, ten goats, four horses, two cats, and two dogs. Depending on who was talking, ownership of the animals was attributed or delegated to various family members. Mrs. P sold wool and carded some for weaving her rugs. Doug attended sixth grade and Maria the ninth in a government boarding school eighty-five miles from their home. Marilyn was in the fourth grade of the mission school near home. Maria was usually the spokesman for her brother and sister and also amplified her mother's remarks. An eighteen-year-old sister was entering college in fall; she and another Navajo girl had gone to Mexico for a month's stay at a work camp.

Books about the Navajo mention characteristic traits and attitudes that I recognized when observing the children or hearing others talk of them. These traits seemed most noticeable in our Navajos' behavior:

1. Navajos present an *expressionless face to strangers*. Except for Maria, who occasionally smiled, the Indians showed no expression during my first visit. Seeing them more often, they lost this aspect and all of them frequently smiled. The day after the children's arrival, I asked Mrs. A, "How are you getting on?" She answered, "Oh, blah! They don't do anything. They don't say anything. When asked a question, they don't even nod their heads. Their expression is just blah!" Oliver LaFarge wrote that the children are taught to act so from an early age, that under stress the face carries a mask of emptiness and absence.

2. Navajos believe *strangers are enemies* to be fought or *intruders to be shunned* and ignored, according to works of Ruth Underhill and Alberta Hannum. One afternoon, I went with another teacher to the A's. When we entered the living room, the P's almost ignored us, glancing quickly, then bending down their heads to read. They gave me a queer feeling of

intruding. We got responses only by dint of repetition. Finally the Indians looked only at their magazines so that we felt that they, not we, had concluded the interview and withdrawn. . . . In Alberta Hannum's *Spin a Silver Dollar,* an old Navajo says, "My son . . . you have learned to ignore by your manner the people who annoy you. You should learn to ignore them with your mind. Then nothing they say or do can hurt you, because for you they do not exist!"

3. Navajos have an excellent *sense of humor,* according to A. H. and D. C. Leighton in *The Navajo Door.* Lunching with the children, I noticed their humor among themselves. When I peered and failed to distinguish a tree among distant bushes that Mr. A was pointing out, Marilyn commented in Navajo and the others laughed heartily. Mrs. A asked Doug a question which he seemed not to hear but he glanced at Maria and she giggled. Later when the family visited us, my father showed them his pet white rat, and the P's all played with it, laughing.

4. To a direct question, a Navajo answers *what he thinks you want.* Alberta Hannum says in *Paint the Wind:* "Ask the thorough-going Navajo a leading question and he . . . tell[s] you what he thinks you want to hear."

Often the P children varied their answers to a repeated question. By our standards this resembled lying. Once at lunch, Mrs. A asked Doug how they got to school, "Do you walk?" Doug said no. She asked, "Do you ride a horse?" He and Maria said no. Mrs. A asked, "Do you go by truck?" Doug looked at Maria, both laughed, and Maria answered, "Our mother takes us in the car. The school is too far to go any other way." Later Mrs. A asked Mrs. P about her car. Slowly she answered, "No. We don't have car." Once Doug answered Mrs. A that his dog was named Lassie and another time he answered that the dog was named Shepherd. When Mrs. A offered to help Maria sew a skirt, the girl said she did not know how to sew. Later Mrs. P said, "Sure, Maria sew." After Mrs. P spoke in Navajo to her daughter, the girl was asked the question again and she replied, beaming, "Yes, I sew."

5. Navajos *do not like their real Indian names known,* according to many published sources. The P's denied having Indian names.

6. Navajo etiquette *forbids staring in another's eye,* according to La Farge. Marilyn and Doug would avoid looking at me when talking, though Maria came closer to it. They stared at me when I did not appear to be noticing. When Marilyn sat beside me at table, she turned to glance at me, then quickly looked down.

7. Navajos *rarely thank* one. In *Laughing Boy,* LaFarge says, "Navajos almost never say thank you, save in return for very great favors; ordinary gifts and kindnesses are offered and accepted in silence. They regard our customs as obsequious."

Mrs. A complained: "Those Indians never say thank you or please! I haven't heard them say those words yet!" So when the children came to my house for a barbecued dinner, I was totally unprepared for Maria's smile and words as they were leaving, "Thank you for having us to your house tonight. It sure was good." I learned that Mrs. A had lectured the children beforehand that, "Here when a person does something for us, gives us something or has us to the house for dinner, we say thank you!" But ordinarily the children behaved according to their own cultural training.

8. Navajos will *take everything offered,* if they like them. Hannum says in *Paint the Wind,* "Offer a Navajo his choice . . . and he takes the lot." Mrs. A said she felt disgusted because, when "good clothes" were brought to the church for distribution among the Indian children, Mrs. P arrived first, went through everything, chose the best for her children, and left little. Mrs. A exclaimed, "They came with just a few clothes but, boy, they have lots in their rooms now."

9. Navajos *cannot be hurried,* as shown in Hannum. The trait exasperated Mrs. A. On the last Sunday of the Indians' visit, the children were given time to prepare for church but spent it just combing their hair. Mrs. A went to church without them though this was one activity they had seemed to like. She said, "I got fed up with the whole mess. They take their own sweet time about everything."

10. Navajo *parents and children have mixed emotions about school attendance.* R. M. Underhill, in *The Navajos,* quotes a mother who said she hated to send her son to school for she knew he would return a stranger. LaFarge's stories describe culture clashes at boarding school and on the return to the reservation. The P's gave conflicting and evasive answers to questions about school and it seemed that the questions touched sensitive spots.

Observing merely these ten traits, it seems clear that actions exasperating to us are nonetheless proper cultural traits of The People.

It seems likely, from the writer's experience in discussing cultural factors with educators, social workers, public health nurses and physicians, and psychiatrists that such provisional chartings of conduct for encounters with individuals of unfamiliar backgrounds give useful clues to meanings and pertinent directives for action. After the behavior traits of a strange group have been charted from authoritative sources checked against observations of actual people, it is possible to venture into the significant nuances and qualifications of behavior that infiltrate situations. These present variations on the traditional ground plan of behavior which indicate the range of normal and deviant conduct within the group's tradition.

About the Family

It is generally assumed that the standards of the middle-class family set norms for education and social work. A young teacher tried to see what this meant in some familiar, modest activity, so he recorded his systematic observations of middle-class fathers coaching their eight- to twelve-year old sons in proper competitiveness during Junior Little League Baseball. He found that by word and deed, fathers indoctrinated sons in the sportsman's notions of winning, losing, cooperating, and competing. He watched children practise, from ages eight through the teens, until their fathers' standards of success were met. He even distinguished a crisis of behavior change in twelve-year olds, when they abandoned habitual prompt obedience, hesitating and casting a surly look at the commanding adult before complying as though on their own initiative. The student concluded that fathers' acts determine the sons'. He noted:

When parents took active interest and encouraged their boys' parts in the game, the boys were less critical of others, more confident, steadier and more relaxed than the boys whose parents showed no interest. However, parents' overanxiety was reflected in children's conduct as shyness, fear of making errors, and lack of self-confidence. Sometimes undue participation by a parent, a father who stepped out of line to complain to the umpire, caused extreme emotional outbreaks among the children in forms of sulkiness, attacks on teammates, and heated self-defense against umpires. A parent's overindulgence caused a son to fumble or to become immobilized. The presence of many parents in the stands heightened tension in the boys enough to sharpen alertness and efficiency with the ball. . . . When a child hits the ball for the first time, contributes to defensive play and other teamwork, his success induces the crucial change from passiveness to activity. Now the boy wins praise, acceptance, and identity with his fellows. Hence I urge parents and school coaches to encourage boys to assume aggressive roles.

This analysis of the close attention middle-class fathers pay their sons throws some light on the superior achievements that a young vice-principal recorded when he compared eighth-grade test ratings and report cards of Air Force children and civilian children at his school. He found marked differences between the two groups, favoring the former, and attributed them to differential socioeconomic factors. Air Force children, about half of the school's pupils, were chiefly "sons and daughters of career enlisted personnel, a few the children of officers, many having traveled extensively in the United States and overseas . . . [The achievements of these pupils show] the rough equality of Air Force enlisted men's life. Among the rest of the children, there is more socioeconomic variation, as parents chiefly work in construction, factories, service trades, and on farms; there are occasional small ranch owners and business and professional men; there are one or two moderately wealthy landowners. Housing is mostly in lower-income areas." Air Force fathers had more schooling than the rest, to a statistically significant degree; the mothers did not. The vice-principal concluded that "the high mobility of the Air Force group apparently has no ill effect on children's achievements . . . [contradicting a common view] that frequent change of schools handicaps adjustment and achievement. . . . "Transiency" is expected in an Air Force career . . ." but not in the civilian world; the Air Force family prepares for it deliberately and often meets old friends at the new bases.

One of the research projects sought out the forms and goals of authority in families of different social and cultural origins, as described in Chapter 4, children's awareness of these, and their accounts of adults' uses of authority, according to sex. Consequently, one teacher, a young white mother, questioned her eighth-grade class of white, middle-class pupils about their adult aspirations, their expected conduct on becoming parents, and the standards of conduct they would uphold if they were of the opposite sex. From their responses, written as a class assignment, the teacher concluded that "not the young are confused about where authority should lie in the family but the adults, who are either afraid or unwilling to accept the responsibility." Like the others engaged on the project, this teacher found her pupils proposing that "parents should impose restrictions and duties on all children, as such discipline shows parents care." One pupil wrote, "The real opinion I would *not* like my children to have is that I don't care about them. Children can get this idea very easily if a parent puts no restrictions." Another pupil wrote, "I think kids like some discipline because it shows their parents care."

Boys and girls emphasized different aspects. Girls tended to be quite specific about duties they would assign their future children and stressed the hope to be regarded respectfully, as a friend, by their children. Boys were concerned that their future children (*a*) show adults respect and (*b*) save money for college. Boys gave more evidence than girls of planning for the future, wanting to finish school and get a job to support the family. Several girls planned for careers but most voiced desires for marriage and a home. Girls said that if they were boys they would want to be tall, good-looking, and dance well. Several boys said that if they were girls they would not want to be smarter than their husbands. Boys often mentioned that if they were girls they would want a sense of humor, would wish to be a lady, understand children, and spend time with husband and family.

Another teacher asked her tenth grade low- and average-achieving classes, "If you were mother or father of a family, how would you discipline your children?" The children wrote their answers as essays, which formed the basis of the teacher's report:

Five among the *low* achieving group described the happy family as eating together, attending church, picnics, shows, and trips together. This was never definitely stated in the *average* group, though implied by a few. Low achievers stressed teaching good manners, including respect for elders. Though never explicitly stated in the average group, perhaps good manners are generally expected, along with the respect for elders this group mentioned frequently. Mentioned equally in both groups was love shown children, but the average group stressed discussions with children about problems. Only the average group mentioned making decisions in the family, phrasing this as "showing good judgment."

Cited equally in both groups were house rules about dates and their locations, curfew, telephone, chores, church. Only one average pupil mentioned parents as an example (or "model," in current academic idiom), but this was mentioned frequently by low achievers. The low group's frequent mention of cleanliness contrasted with the average group's silence on the matter. Both groups felt it important to get an education, but the average group specifically mentioned homework and good grades.

Both groups advocated punishment by reasoning and withholding privileges. The average group stressed techniques of scolding and isolation; the low group stressed whipping and spanking. The average group saw rewards in going to specific places; the low group saw rewards in dress, allowances, use of the car, later hours.

The average group saw mother as the disciplinarian because she was home more than father. They saw father as in grumpy control, but not the enforcer of discipline upon returning home lest he be viewed as the "mean one."

The differences expressed by this teacher's two groups raise questions about the presence of authoritarian elements among the "low achievers" that appear milder or are entirely absent among the "average achievers." Are the possible authoritarian elements in the cultural backgrounds of the pupils, or in the personalities of their immediate families, or in their own personalities? Is the low achievement in class related to the suspect authoritarianism in some personalities? Some teachers tried to pursue such further questions raised by their studies.

A related study was made by a young father. He approached his 160 junior high-school pupils, in their six classes, about "notions, ideas, values with which children in this school are growing up." He assigned pupils to read an article on "Proper Parenthood" by Art Buchwald and presided over the discussions in the six classes. He wrote in his report:

There was dynamite in the students' reactions. Though their feelings were sincere and spontaneous, I was shocked. I have never had groups open up like these. They were hungry for understanding, wanted to prolong discussions and returned after class to talk. They reflected disturbances of their parents. I felt that the parents have spun a web which the children want desperately to escape but know they cannot. Yet they try to escape. I got a lot more than I bargained for here. To my mind, these youths were clearly saying, whether Anglo, Mexican, or Negro:

1. We want firm discipline and known boundaries. We know where home base is, but how far out is left field? We need places to go and things to do. There isn't much we can do without getting into trouble.

2. We want authority and responsibility. We can show you that we can handle them.

3. We want honesty and have not been given it.

4. Our parents are in pretty sad shape, too worried about money and things. They have forgotten how to have a good time and are forgetting about us as a family. We want to do things together.

5. We want Dad to be head of the family, both parents to carry authority and to back each other up, like a team.

6. When we are punished, we want to be told why and what the penalty is and we want to be allowed to pay our debt. We resent hearing the same things over and over when we are being punished. Most parents are too easy on us so we lose respect for them.

7. We hate comparisons with others, and nagging.

8. Our parents live their lives through us.

9. We want parents to give us encouragement and praise for a job well done. Their praise means more than any other.

10. Nevertheless, we love and need our parents very much. We want them to understand and love us and do things with us. One girl said, "My worst punishment is to see my mother cry."

An experienced high-school teacher, also a father, asked his 80 senior students and their parents to tell what each expected of the other. He wrote:

The class was heterogeneous in mental ratings and in socioeconomic backgrounds. The students were 62 Anglos and the balance of 18 was Mexican-American, Negro, and Oriental. I asked them to list five or six statements explaining "What a Teen-ager Expects of Parents." I urged them to ask their parents to list five or six statements explaining "What Parents Expect of a Teen-ager." All students complied, but only 60 parents did.

Students responded with generally selfish demands for independence, recognition, and responsibility. Parents' responses showed a tendency to cling to the teen-ager, to hold him within the family where he would refrain from disruptive acts. Only three parents expected teen-agers to follow the religion in which they were reared, which was Catholic. Parents implied reluctance to acknowledge the teen-age struggle for recognition. *Not one parent or student mentioned education.*

When I asked students about desirable child-rearing, 65 per cent of the 38 boys stated that there should be a clear understanding of father as head of the family; 85 per cent of the 42 girls made this assertion. When I asked how they would answer if they were a parent of opposite sex, only 42 per cent of the boys, acting as mother, responded the same; but all except two of the girls, acting as father, responded the same. The father as family head seems in no great jeopardy during the next generation; this includes the duty of religious instruction.

A white mother in the seminar working as a juvenile probation officer compared "Notions of Identity and Authority" held by 26 pupils in a Juvenile Hall class with those held by 36 pupils in an average public-school class. She was aided by two men teaching social studies in the respective institutions. The team wanted to see if youngsters caught breaking the law differed from others. The Juvenile Hall class included grade levels eight to eleven, with 10 girls and 16 boys aged thirteen to seventeen years. The public-school class was eighth grade, with 18 girls and 18 boys aged thirteen to fifteen years. All children were of varied European ancestries except for one American Indian and four Mexican-Americans in Juvenile Hall, and two American Indians and one Mexican-American in the public school.

The pupils were asked to write essays telling (1) How, when they became adults, they would rear their children to understand authority, obedience, and responsibility; and (2) What their conduct would be if they belonged to the opposite sex. Each pupil wrote his first name, age, grade, national origin, parents' occupations, number of brothers and sisters, and his ordinal place among them.

In the probation officer's report the team found "no significant differences" between the Juvenile Hall and public-school essays about standards of parental care. The report grouped pupils' stated standards into categories named Parental Dominance, Parental Laxity, and Intermediate. The first category represented statements like, "I will make my child do as I say. He must be home at 9 o'clock and tell me where he is at all times. He must obey me, police, school, and church. I will take full responsibility for my child." The report noted that "seven of the eight boys in Juvenile for the most serious offenses stated that they would expect complete obedience from their children. Parental Dominance was most strongly supported by oldest siblings' statements at Juvenile."

The second category represented such statements as, "Allow children almost complete freedom. I would make my child take full responsibility for himself." The report noted that "Laxity was most common among middle and youngest siblings at Juvenile but least common among youngest siblings at public school. . . . In almost every instance, Mexican pupils stressed Parental Dominance while the Indians inclined toward Laxity."

The third category represented statements seeming "to show good balance in handling authority, responsibility, punitive acts, and obedience. . . . Taking the two groups as a whole, a majority indicated the Intermediate attitude toward parental authority . . . and very few cared for Parental Laxity. . . . Intermediate standards were most common in Juvenile youngest siblings but least common among the same in public school."

The report sought to relate essay statements to further aspects of the children's lives:

Two pupils from two-parent homes, one at Juvenile Hall and one at public school, did not commit themselves about parental authority. One said nothing. The other said, "I wouldn't know as I'm not going to have children." An outstanding expression of Parental Laxity came from an intelligent but seriously disturbed girl at Juvenile Hall: "Probably I will let my children come and go as they wish. I wouldn't care what clubs, activities, sports, or anything else they joined. A boy could join the Scouts, I wouldn't care." She was the only pupil to state a clear change of attitude as a father, saying that father should be dominant in the family. . . . Does this small survey suggest that the law violators will be more responsible when parents?

Among children of unskilled workers, a large proportion at Juvenile Hall expressed greater fear of legal authority than of parents' authority. Those at public school did not mention public law but stressed respect for parents' authority. Fifty per cent of these children in both groups expressed the Intermediate view of parental authority; as did 75 per cent of the children of skilled workers at Juvenile Hall and 58 per cent of the comparable children at public school . . .

Responses to the second question, about conduct as a member of the opposite sex, brought only eight Juvenile responses out of the 26 but 31 from public school out of the 36. The answers ranged around similar points. A public-school boy aged fourteen wrote that, as a girl, "I'd be completely different, would have more responsibility, and would have to control myself better." A fourteen-year old girl at Juvenile Hall wrote that, as a boy, "I would try to get a girl that has a good personality. If she had a bad reputation, I would try to get her to straighten up. I would call her everyday and do anything I could. I wouldn't let her spend any money on me." An American Indian and a white boy in public school, with fathers doing unskilled work, wrote that if they were girls they would "take more responsibility and have higher moral standards." The daughter of a professional man wrote similarly for herself as a boy, "I would have more manners . . . would start thinking of a job so when I got married I could support my family." Four girls, white, Indian, and Mexican, with fathers in skilled work, all stressed fine manners and morals for boys. The Mexican wrote, "If I were of the opposite sex, I would respect all girls and try never to get dirty thoughts in my mind. Sure, I would also like to know the facts of life." The Indian girl wrote, "I have always wished I could be the opposite sex for a day or so. I would try to act like a good guy, have a good job when I got older, do good work and be respectable. I would try to raise my family in the best way and in the best neighborhood." The daughter of a European, doing unskilled work, wrote "I would try to be a well-rounded person and respected by all. I would be a square!" Public-school girls with fathers doing unskilled work and girls of minority origins voiced higher standards for the opposite sex.

This report showed, like the others, that teen-agers can speculate and write clearly about their emerging ideas. The reporter's expressed surprise showed, as did the surprise of the others, that adults are far distant from youngsters' yearnings and potentialities. Reports showed that even young children respond sensitively to social influences. A young unmarried woman teaching a fifth-grade class of well-to-do children, of whom "80 per cent intend to go to college," reported her astonishment that, in a class discussion of Identity and Authority, pupils said they "want parents to be strict but fair. I had not introduced the word 'strict' but they did so repeatedly. . . . It interested me that the poorer [-rated] pupils expect their children to do well in school. Many approve of spanking as a last resort but talking [reasoning] is important to them. It amazed me that parents use money for punishment and reward."

A mother teaching homemaking in a junior high school asked her middle-income girl pupils, aged fourteen to sixteen, to help her study "Rewards and Punishments." She asked one class to design a questionnaire and another to answer it. She coded the girls by characteristics in the light of which she planned to interpret their responses. The characteristics included family background (as two were Mexican-American, one was Korean, and the others were Anglo-American of several European ancestries), parents' marital status, number of siblings, ages, school achievement, and personality traits. The teacher explained in her report that she divided up the work of the pupils on the questionnaire "to insure that my explanations to the class designing the questionnaire would not direct responses. This class worded and reworded the questions and pretested them on each other. Then we gave eleven of the questions to another class of 24 girls of about the same age. [Most of] the questions were: What would you do if your daughter wanted to run with a fellow four years older than she? If you thought your daughter was running with the wrong crowd? If you, a parent, came home to find that your daughter had cleaned the house and had dinner ready for you? If she brought home A's on her report card? If your daughter were one and one-half hours late coming home from school? Or, that late coming home from a date? What and how would you punish your child for average misbehavior at home, such as fighting with brothers and sisters or not doing a chore? How would you have fun with your children? How would you act as a boy at your present age?"

Responses appeared as censorious, ironical, indulgent, and mature (rendered by one respondent as "machure"). A fourteen-year-old wrote the following answer to the last question: "I would act like a boy. Yes! Because I hate to curl my hair everynite. And I get tired of babysitting. And boys can stay out later than girls because people say girls can't protect thereselfs and boy's can take off anytime they want and don't have to worry about cleaning the house, cooking, bathing the kids and everything else girls have to do."

Excerpts from some other responses were:

1. "Yes I would act like a boy because they get away with almost everything, ask girls to go steady, don't worry about getting new clothes for a dance, go cruising in a car, go places without being policed with questions and answers."

2. "As a boy, I'd be scared to death of girls. I know, being one, how sneaky women are. I guess I'd wonder about the same things girls worry about. I'd take an active interest in sports, in driving, in hobbies, have a collection of girls and be popular. A girl has to walk a line down the middle between what gives her a shady reputation and what makes her be called a goody-goody, where a boy has more leeway."

3. "As a boy, I would be polite, modest, respect girls and not be a show-off. I would like to be a boy because building model cars and running electric trains, which I love to do, are more acceptable."

4. "I've wanted to be a boy so I could be like my father and my name could be Jimmy. I don't like Sharon."

A mentally retarded girl wrote, "I want to be a boy because some of them get by with murder. But I wouldn't act like a monkey." Eight preferred to remain girls "in the long run."

Even kindergartners aged five and six expressed clear ideas. An experienced kindergarten teacher reported:

We had a group discussion among our 25 children about the policeman and fireman and their relationships to parents. A week later I started interviewing each child separately about the matters discussed, calling our talks a Pretend game. We pretended we were grown up, married, and had children. Twelve of the children were born in California, one in Germany, and the rest in the eastern United States. I asked, "What do you expect of your children? How would you punish them and reward them and who should be boss?"

Larry answered that he expected his children to mind mother, be punished by spanking and not watching TV for a week, be rewarded by letting them take out the garbage and polish the car and watch TV, know that Dad is boss "because he buys the most things and does work for Mama. Mama should be boss only when Dad is gone." His twin, however, considered Mommy the boss "and sometimes the daddy when Mommy is gone . . . well, both of them."

Ernesto expected his children to "eat all their food and pray nice, keep their money and be nice with it, be nice to father, mother, cousins, and grandmother." As punishment, he would "give a spanking and send them to their room until they say, I'm sorry." He would reward them with money and "give them something good to eat." Father and mother are boss, "the father because he eats all his food and grows bigger. When mother eats all her food, she will grow bigger and be the same size and then she can be boss too."

Robert stated definitely that "Mother should have most authority because she is the one who went to the hospital and got the baby" while Tommy held "My daddy is the bigger boss than Mommy because he makes the money and is bigger."

Scott's precocious answers were, to show reward, "I would love them. Probably make them proud of me. Is friendship the next best to love? I love both parents but like Daddy best because of our friendship." He affirmed that Daddy was top boss but "the grandfather would be the judge. The grandmother will give the papers to the judge to tell me how to boss my children and I will show these papers to my wife so she can boss the children the same way I do."

Jaime saw authority in "Father and Mother because they are the ones who teach us how to protect ourselves." Douglass saw authority in "Father, because the mother [wasn't] smart enough." Dorothy held "Father should be the boss because he is oldest." Six little girls agreed severally that Daddy should be boss because he spanked harder and that Mother should punish in his absence.

The kindergarten teacher summarized:

Though we had talked about authority, I was surprised that the children understood so well. Only in a few cases did I need to use the term "boss." The children said "boss." Two mothers work outside the home and some mothers tend to let daddy administer all the punishment. When I asked them to pretend to be of the opposite sex and say how they would look and be and do, they laughed! I noticed that almost every boy, pretending to be a girl for me, wanted to have wavy or curly hair and play with dolls. Are these little fellows telling us that playing with dolls does not mean being a "sissy" but that they have the same desire to cuddle dolls as a little girl? Not one of these boys had a doll. Some had toy animals or a teddy-bear but they still wanted a doll. I was surprised that no little girl, pretending to be a boy, wanted a gun to play Cops and Robbers or Cowboys and Indians but thought chasing girls would be a lot of fun.

The day after each interview, the teacher permitted the child to be father or mother in the playhouse "and noticed that the actions were consistent with the remarks to me. Thus, whipping was a favorite discipline, by word and deed, in the playhouse and the interviews."

Another teacher questioned her first-grade pupils about discipline through reward and punishment. She learned that one family of Mexican extraction found Anglo middle-class stress on not fighting in conflict with the Mexican family's idea of manliness. "The child quotes his father, 'What is the principal trying to do? Make a sissy out of you?' The child shows effects of the opposed demands in spells of crying, restlessness, and talking. The father told me he may be over-emphasizing the matter with the child, remembering that a timid friend of his schooldays committed suicide after allowing boys in junior high to beat up on him. The father swore to himself at the time that if he ever had a son, he would not let him grow up to be a coward." The teacher decided that the father's personality explained his strict interpretation of the traditional *machismo*.

Eighteen junior college students responded like the lower division schoolchildren, their psychology teacher reported. The students ranged in age from eighteen to the early twenties and belonged "basically to the lower class." Anticipating themselves as parents, they would demand "obedience and respect" from children, who "should not talk back [and must] do what they are told. They did not want their children to regard them as pals or buddies, but rather as 'a friend, some-one they can talk to, who is understanding.'" They said frequently that they would enforce family standards strictly. One of them said he felt leniency was a form of rejection or neglect. Nearly all stated that they would set up duties for the children and supervise them with care, fairness, and love. These students seemed to expect responsible adults to assume authority. When exercise of authority fell below expectations, much doubt and insecurity were generated. They were not concerned with permissiveness, perhaps because they would view it as "weakness or dereliction of duty."

A Mexican-American father in the seminar, employed as a finance officer at a California correctional institution, reported on group discussions about Identity and Authority which he held with fifteen male "wards," aged sixteen to twenty-one. The discussions fitted into a group work program of therapy and instruction. Five of the youths were Negro, five Mexican-American, and five Anglo, all from Southern California, only two from comfortable economic circumstances. The group was unique in emphasizing education for the prospective children. The Mexican-Americans were less emphatic than the others, largely "because of uncertainty about their limitations and opportunities. They preferred sons to earn their way through college by part-time jobs though they were willing to help sons attain college and professional goals. Generally, they felt it more important to educate sons than daughters. They would not care to change themselves much nor would they shelter their sons. Rather, they would teach their sons to avoid gangs and certain types of trouble, such as smoking marijuana, crashing other people's activities, contributing to the delinquency of a minor, or showing race prejudice. At the end of the program these wards thanked their caseworkers, parole counselors, and teachers for guiding them so that they now knew how to protect their sons."

It greatly surprised teachers and welfare workers that many youngsters, from kindergarten to college, and even in correctional programs, could express themselves aptly, and that the statements composed a body of coherent information and criticism which none had expected. It was also striking that the reports, gathered independently, showed the same trends of ideas and criticisms from young people and their families. Furthermore, all the information was applicable to needs of educators and welfare workers. Evidently teachers and others have much to learn about youngsters of school age and about their own relationships to them. They can achieve this to a considerable extent through their own first-hand research.

About the Children

Children of families tagged with minority status—because of race, religion, nationality, or marked poverty—are often regarded by those in more comfortable or authoritative positions as strange, even suspect and alarming unknowns. At the same time there are friendly stereotypes, though these may be as remote from actualities as the Indian "noble savage" in the romantic philosophy of earlier centuries. The friendly stereotypes rest heavily on descriptions of Negroes, Mexicans, and others as "musical, rhythmic, happy, naïve," given to dancing, singing, romantic or passionate love, displaying flashing teeth and eyes, and sensuous bodies. Some minorities, like Jews and Orientals, do not lend themselves to such amiabilities but are covered by prestigious though ambivalent attributes of cleverness and ambitiousness.

Through their field projects, teachers learned to put such stereotypes and fears in better balance with realities of human nature, or the behavior permitted by specific social and cultural surroundings. Many teachers discovered increased confidence in themselves as they reflected systematically about the child behavior they described. They were obliged to be explicit about vague, goblinesque notions. They discussed their troubles with others who had similar ones and learned of solutions they could adopt and develop further. As soon as they understood the high regard held for fresh understandings and techniques based on controlled field observations, teachers produced useful materials of considerable variety and challenge.

A young man, teaching driver-education and English in a high school with an enrollment of two thousand, felt challenged by some fourteen- to sixteen-year-old Mexican-American boys. He wrote:

They do not feel they need be on time to class, behave courteously, or wear the same haircuts and clothes as others. They razz Mexican-Americans who "go with gringos" or "study all the time" or "try to get in good with the probation officer or teacher." [He asked a handsome sixteen-year old for explanations.]

[The boy told him] "We dress in khaki pants, dark grey shirts, french-toed shoes with a beautiful shine because we have done this for very long, since our fathers had block gangs in East Los Angeles. . . . We won't change. It's in our blood to fight. If a guy from Puente runs around East Los Angeles, he might get killed. We get in trouble, go to [police] Camp Five, go to Juvy [Juvenile Hall] and we might even return to this school with a good probation officer!" [Later the boy was expelled from school.]

[The report continued with the teacher's account of another "extremely handsome" sixteen-year-old. For five months the boy had resisted the teacher's questions. Then during a driving lesson on a busy street, the boy said] "That car over there is the dope man for the police. I know all the cops. My three brothers are up at [the police forestry] Camp Five. They say they get good food. We all like to ditch school, get up in the canyon, climb the cliff and go swimming. I'm scared of the snapping turtles, though. The cops stop us all the time. The other night they stopped us three times. We had our girls and we was just riding around, drinking beer, and, you know . . . well, the cops stopped us, asked for our licenses and gave us the once-over. We weren't doing anything wrong but they all know me, they've seen me in the police station so many times." The boy, a nonreader, spoke also of San Quentin prison as a good place for food.

I think the problems with such boys should be attacked in several ways. One is to hire more Mexican-American teachers. This might eliminate the resentment the boys express when they tell me, "You treat the gringos differently." I don't know, maybe we do. At our high school, there are only two Mexican-American teachers. Another way to attack their problems is to reactivate a friendship club we had for Mexicans and whites, called Los Amigos [The Friends]. A third way is to train new teachers in better techniques than our present punitive ones which we express as "You've got to handle those Mexicans [usually in remedial and slow classes] with an iron hand. Show them who's boss. Don't let them get the upper hand." This doesn't work anyway.

I found success by carefully planning lessons to suit my students' abilities. Speaking a few words in español and a big grin did more than any iron-whip method with boys who were slow learners and happened to be Mexican-American. Above all, the two hundred Mexican-Americans in our school must be made to feel that they are treated as fairly as the whites. This means compromises, a daily problem for many teachers.

A woman teacher sought to discover social conditions accompanying low achievement in her school, where pupils were 74 per cent Mexican-American, 13½ per cent Negro, and 12½ per cent Anglo-American. She wrote in her report:

My third-grade class of eight- to eleven-year-olds has twenty-five Mexican-Americans, five Negroes, and four Anglo-Americans. Only the lowest economic level of Anglo lives in this poor neighborhood; the transient pupil here is almost always Anglo, from Texas and Oklahoma. Many Mexican-American families have resided years in the same homes, sometimes two generations. Most of the Negroes have come only in the past ten years. Compared with pupils of schools in more prosperous parts of the district, our children rate low academically. Last year nine pupils out of thirty-one could read at third-grade level; this year there are nine out of thirty-four. Even in music and art, where reading ability is no factor, these pupils fall below standards of schools in better parts of town.

All twenty-five of my Mexican-American pupils speak Spanish and several parents speak no English, yet what of the other nine children who know only English? Last year and this, the top reading group in our class has been entirely Mexican-American. This seems to disprove the idea that bilingualism is the main handicap to achievement.

The school assembles a cumulative family background record on each pupil. According to the records, one in my class is an only child but over half of the others are of families with six, seven, ten, and eleven children. This means inadequate funds for food, sanitation, medical care, and education. According to my present incomplete information, the highest school grade reached by any father was the ninth, by any mother the eighth, while four parents had not attended any school. . . . Fathers' occupations are mostly in the category of unskilled laborer, a few are semiskilled and two are skilled. Ten families live by state aid. . . . In the crowded quarters at home, the children get no proper rest. All but three of my pupils stay up with the family watching TV until 10:30 or 11 at night.[9] We see many tired, bemused faces in the classroom, and some children cannot forget the horror show of last night.

The low incomes, large families, crowded housing, and poor education of parents constitute a meagre backgrounod for our pupils. Only nine of my thirty-four ever visited a zoo. Our spring visit to the county museum was the first any pupil had made to a museum. . . . At home all pupils receive physical punishment for misdeeds and all but four state that it takes painful forms. Negroes especially use a belt for punishment.

There is no conflict among our three ethnic groups; personalities are deciding. A sociogram shows the most popular boy to be Anglo, the most popular girl to be Mexican, the least liked child a belligerent Negro boy.

But older third-graders are beginning to recognize "race" conflict. An eleven-year-old Mexican girl dreads junior high because "the Americans" sometimes beat you up after school. Several Mexican boys described a fight between "Mexicans and Americans." When I said they were Americans also, they ignored this as something they didn't believe or understand.

As the teacher seeks ways to help these warm, affectionate Mexican children to master reading and to speak English, she often wonders if other teaching materials are not needed. It seems ridiculous to present books illustrated by immaculate middle-class homes where father comes home in a business suit, carrying a new briefcase, and mother is almost glamorous, with never a hair out of place. I hardly blame the ten- and eleven-year olds in the lowest reading group when they yawn over antics of Spot and Puff and Baby Sally. However they enjoy learning about other cultures. We studied Hopi Indians, and several Mexican children pointed out similarities in customs, such as carrying a pottery water jug on the head, both by the Mexican grandmother over the border and by the Hopi woman in New Mexico.

A young Anglo-American man, teaching in an elementary school consisting predominantly of Mexican-American children, found the children's lives and the once segregated school interesting and delightful. He wrote:

G school is small and old, having ten teachers and about three hundred children. About eighty per cent of the children are Mexican-American and the rest evenly divided between Anglo and Negro. The building seems like a rather large house with a large yard and a rather large number of children. All the children walk to school and their recreational play is an extension of home play . . .

. . . Almost daily, local newspapers report neighborhood crimes of physical violence, drunkenness, narcotics, and vandalism.

School records show truancy, gross health problems, TB histories, common-law households, abandonment by father or mother, complaints about apathy toward school of parents and children, poor PTA attendance, hunger, poverty, neglect, and abuse of children. Perhaps a third of the children receive . . . public assistance. Absence slips returned by truants usually say "no shoes . . . headache . . . baby-sitting. . . ." [Yet] most of the children appear happy, eager, and active. . . . It seems inconceivable that outstanding children sometimes emerge from frightful backgrounds. Perhaps conditions that horrify school personnel are not actually so damaging. The total weight of trouble is rarely concentrated on one family and misfortune is more easily borne when not borne alone. A hungry child may have an otherwise acceptable life and be able intellectually. Outsiders who live and work in comfort view these conditions in the light of losing their own comforts . . .

Teachers working outside the school make a point of expressing sympathy for those brave enough to work there. They offer us mild patronage, mild apology, amusement, or ridicule. New teachers in the district often show embarrassment, when meeting us of G, and blurt out questionable remarks. Yet I, for one, chose this school, leaving the supposedly superior "white" school in town when the vacancy arose.

For at G, life is not a daily round of weapons confiscation, abuse, or drama. Discipline is not a major concern even with children becoming delinquent or actually so. Many children are shy or aloof, but at school their behavior is friendly, curious, cheerful, and delightfully frank. One teacher, who had not announced her pregnancy, but wore a smock, was approached by a fourth-grade girl who asked if she were "in style or in trouble." Children pester one half to death, offering themselves for errands, office duty, or clean-up chores.

G school is too small for the time-consuming activities that occupy larger teaching staffs, such as grade-level meetings, committees, public relations programs, and the countless hours of nervous busywork generated by assembled teachers. G teachers are singularly free to devote themselves to teaching . . .

Their effectiveness is illustrated by the following results of our testing program in March 1960. All scores are averages; most median scores were slightly higher.

California Reading Test, *Upper Grades*

Grade	Norm	Vocabulary	Comprehension	Total
4	4.6	4.6	4.2	4.4
5	5.6	5.2	5.2	5.2
6	6.6	6.2	6.3	6.3

California Reading Test, *Primary Grades*

Grade	Norm	Vocabulary	Comprehension	Total
3	3.2	3.7	3.5	3.6
2	2.6	3.1	2.8	2.9

California Achievement Test, *Sixth Grade*

Arithmetic	Norm	Reasoning	Fundamental	Total
	6.6	5.9	6.4	6.1
Language	Norm	Grammar	Spelling	Total
	6.6	6.2	6.5	6.3

If these figures are valid, showing above-grade achievements for everything tested except "arithmetic reasoning," they indicate surprisingly high accomplishments in a very handicapped group of minorities. Does the prevailing culture pattern explain this?

The commonest cultural behavior includes high ideals of personal conduct, generosity, acceptance of hard work and adversity, intense desire to better conditions for the children, rich family life, loyalty to the group, and a keen sense of guilt when commendable standards are violated, as they often are.

The poor PTA attendance of parents does not necessarily reflect poor support of education, as a 100 per cent attendance does not guarantee it, however fine this appears to the public. Here are questions of form and substance: in the last two years, despite feeble parental cooperation, G's PTA has earned a large amount of money and spent most of it on welfare. Though few parents worked, pupils and ex-pupils did, and most of the neighborhood attended our carnivals, held on May 5, a Mexican holiday.

People spent freely, so G made the largest contribution to a fund for emergency dental care. Dentists in the program found trouble getting support from the service clubs, however, because they did not want their contributions lumped anonymously with those of other groups.

Poor PTA attendance does not mean neighborhood ignorance of school matters, when large numbers of families have been residing many years in the school district, sending numbers of children to the school continuously. The people know a great deal and overlook or forgive much of what they disapprove.

There are strong lines of communication between home and school. Messages are conveyed by telephone, relayed by an older child and by the parents who visit school in greater numbers. Children enroll and transfer themselves, take milk and lunch money to younger brothers and sisters. School secretaries learn the intricate family and neighbor relationships so as to contact families without telephones. So the school functions, though exasperation is felt by those who demand formal accurate records.

The children's actions express good acculturation to school needs. The children serve more valuably than do the safety patrols and the pupils' kangaroo courts established by teachers. At present, ex-pupils of G, who live in the neighborhood, compose a group that has won the city council's support in improving a neglected little park, and the PTA is donating playground equipment.

Some of my pupils wrote these pieces after playing volleyball at a new school:

"I like G because it's small and we have lots of fun. The yards are green and large."

"I don't think I would like a new school because they look like deserts. New schools don't have grass or trees and hardly any books. I like G because it's prettier than other schools . . . and green in the front. . . . But a new school looks like a desert."

"I think that good old G is a pretty good school because of the books we have, the activities, and all the good friends and teachers I have. I also like it because of the shade in the front yard. I think I would never like to move out of this town or this neighborhood."

Such open affection for low-status pupils and schools is uncommon. These pupils responded with good achievements and motivation.

Another teacher, freshly confronted with enforcement of desegregation, reported on "How Fourth Grade Children Adjust to an Integrated School":

For the first five months of the school year, we were assigned to an all-white school but the class knew we were moving to an integrated school in January. The children, all lower middle-class, were apprehensive about a school with colored children. One child remarked, "My father says the colored kids fight all the time." Another added, "They carry knives to fight with. I heard about it on TV." Another commented, "My mother says we'll move if there is trouble."

On a day of general uproar, each child tried to give examples of interracial horror. When order was restored, a blond girl stood up to say, "My father *wants* me to go to that school and learn to get along with everyone. He said he went to a school with all kinds of people."

Several mothers moved away and others talked to me about "the problem" of the new school. But most decided to wait and see. In January after the move to the school, the children were delighted with the new room and furniture but were tense and uncertain outside, clinging to me and to each other. On the second day, a colored boy threatened several of our boys and hit some. These boys actually feared to go on the playground and walk home. For weeks, every contact with a colored child was reported to me in detail. Then the fear died down.

[Two Mexican-American and two Negro children joined the class. Because of her physical aggressiveness, one of the Negroes was resented.] She entered the room saying, "I'm scared!" and drew back, hanging her head. For no apparent reason, she frequently hits the children with her fist. When the boys get angry with one another, they call out insultingly, "You love . . . [the Negro girl]." No one wants to sit by her and the boys refuse her as a partner in square dancing.

From further observations and a questionnaire asking the children to write about their likes in friends and house guests, the teacher concluded that one of the white children was "more actively disliked than the colored girl . . . Apparently in our area there is little prejudice against the Mexican race but a colored child has to prove himself. These children judge other children largely as personalities, influenced, however, by their cultural background."

A California school attendance officer reported on her study which asked whether race prejudice played a part in assigning youngsters to an adjustment school. This institution is described in the the manual of the particular city's public-school system as "an outlet for those students who have not adjusted satisfactorily to a regular school program." Its pupils were described by the attendance officer as those "referred repeatedly by a variety of teachers for disciplinary action [and] whom nobody wants." She wrote:

Many of the adjustment-school candidates come from our minorities. This year, 35 per cent of adjustment-school pupils were Anglo-Americans. Frequently they are referred to as "Okies" or "white trash," and their neighborhoods often carry appellations like "little Oklahoma." Thus, their classification as Anglo-Americans does not truly remove them from the minority-group category.

Granted that youngsters in adjustment school show severe behavior problems, that they are defiant and their parents uncooperative, it still appears that the overwhelming numbers of nonminority schoolchildren must show more of the undesirable behavior requisite for adjustment school than are referred. Remarks of teachers throw some light on adjustment-school referrals.

S taught boys at Juvenile Hall and now teaches in a school of minority pupils. He told me his mother was an Okie and his father a European immigrant, and that neighborhood playmates of his childhood were Japanese, American Indian, and European. He assumed that prejudice had no part in his life. However at his present school, he says, he is becoming prejudiced: 'It's the Negroes. They [cause] prejudice by the way they act. The Mexican kids are all right. But these Southern Negroes! I can't stomach them." These families are recent arrivals from Mississippi and Alabama, with chips placed so precariously on their shoulders that just once keeping a child after school brought the whole family pounding on the school doors.

J is in his first year as attendance counselor at the roughest school in the district after adjustment school. His initial enthusiasm has diminished visibly. He shakes his head hopelessly, saying, "These people! Look, I'm Italian. My folks were born in the old country and still don't talk good English but *we* didn't act like this." On numerous occasions he has said to me, "I'm almost in favor of a police state for these people. Somebody should have the authority to *make* them conform. Force is the only thing they understand and the way things are now their behavior contaminates the good kids."

Another teacher in this school teaches the MRs [mentally retarded] who, of course, are largely minority-group children. He said, "There are eighteen in my class and each gets one-eighteenth of my time, no more. If they can't understand what I'm saying, that's their problem. We didn't ask them to come here."

The counselor at another school, after one semester of attendance work, asked to be returned to the classroom. The supervising counselor was taken aback, for quitting seemed uncharacteristic of this man, reputed to have a persevering interest in pupils. The counselor said he was shocked to see "these people" living in apparent satisfaction with filth and slovenliness, refusing to better themselves despite his greatest efforts. When he didn't know "what they were really like," he said he felt no prejudice; but observing them in their homes brought the adjective "dirty" into his thoughts about their national and racial identities. The dean of the school says, "We have no prejudice in our school, we are very careful not to. We have a Negro teacher, you know, and we have made that work. We had to."

If the youngsters feel prejudice acting against them, they have learned to keep their mouths shut. I have never directly questioned them or their families about this. But I have noted evidence that they do feel prejudice. For example, Rosa, now at adjustment school, says, "They just don't like Spanish-speaking kids anyway." She barely remembers her father, who is in a state prison for killing her grandfather when drunk. Rosa's temper propels her into screaming arguments with her mother and into pitched battles at school. She baits the teachers by speaking Spanish, in a major violation of school policy. She explains, "I couldn't say that in front of a man! It's personal. But I *had* to have a nickel and I had to explain why to Maria."

Carlos is an attendance problem. When I call at his home to determine reasons for his absences, he and his mother ask, "Why don't you make Bill Green go to school? He stays out all the time." They mean that Carlos is being pursued not for absence but for being Mexican. There may be some truth in this.

Cherry is a Negro at adjustment school. When she was transferred there, her mother protested that it was only because she was Negro. Usually when disciplinary action was taken against Cherry, she pointed out that an Anglo [i.e., white] girl had been doing the same thing without reprisal. On occasions known to me, Cherry had a legitimate gripe. She often muttered, "Us colored kids always get the blame."

I could fill pages with similar cases. Instead I will give some rough statistics. From a tally made toward the end of the school year, the groups at adjustment school were 43 Mexican-Americans (45 per cent), 34 Anglo-Americans (35 per cent), 19 Negroes (20 per cent), aged twelve to fifteen years, in grades 7, 8, 9. Of the ten junior high schools in the district, three made 73 per cent of the referrals, who were 60 per cent Mexican-Americans and 27 per cent Negroes. It is notable that 52 per cent of the Mexican-Americans and 88 per cent of the Negroes at junior high schools in the district are found in the attendance areas of these three schools. Among the 101 teachers on combined staffs of the three schools, there are two Negroes and no Mexicans . . .

These statistics seem to present disproportionate numbers of Mexican-American and Negro referrals to the adjustment school, based on total enrollments of the groups in junior high school, compared with Anglo-American numbers in the same schools. At one of the three schools, the pupils number 5 per cent Anglos, 53 per cent Mexicans, 42 per cent Negroes; at another school, pupils number 57 per cent Anglos, 22⅔ per cent Mexicans, 2⅔ per cent Orientals, and the rest Negroes; at the third, pupils number 20 per cent Anglos, 50 per cent Mexicans, 30 per cent Negroes. Referrals to adjustment school from the first school were 66⅔ per cent Mexican, 33⅓ per cent Negro, no Anglos, in the total of 18 per cent [of the school's population], sent the past year. Referrals from the second school were 77 per cent Mexican, 20 per cent Negro, 3 per cent Anglo in their total of 15 per cent. Referrals from the third school were 50 per cent Mexican, 30 per cent Negro, 20 per cent Anglo in their total of 40 per cent . . .

This report was based on information the attendance officer gathered from enrollment and attendance summaries at the school district's central office, from interviews with administrators and teachers of the junior high schools, from the schools' yearbooks and enrollment lists, from personal contacts with pupils and parents, and from professional experiences during five years in the field.

A California junior high school dean wrote about her work with segregated and ignored pupils:

While the community denies practicing segregation, nevertheless segregation has been the deep-seated rule. So we find many Mexican and poor white families living south of town, close to the washes or in the lowlands. When the attendance counselor names certain streets, these mean a shifting population and pupils in and out of school several times a year. People of these areas practice mores strange and difficult for teachers to understand. We school administrators are guilty of ignoring problems affecting these minorities.

For example, five of our students live on the Indian reservation, over three miles from our school; one student lives a quarter-mile south of the reservation. City schools furnish no transportation for these Indian children. Why, you ask? So do I ask. The county school district transports the Indian children attending grades kindergarten through six in county schools. But our junior high is in the city system. One can understand why Indian children at our junior high become attendance problems when the weather is inclement. The father of one family drives some of the children to school in his car when there is money for gas.

When I came to this junior high six years ago, I saw that the Indian and Mexican girls and white girls of financially poor families, though of average or better intelligence, had no part in social activities. They didn't seem to belong and were often truant and fighting. I felt that I must make up for the rejection by the problem girls' peers. I asked the Social Living teachers to help me single out some problem girls with whom to start clubs.

Within a week, teachers gave me thirty-four names. I called these girls to a meeting, described my plan and asked them to participate. My plan was to permit each girl to drop an elective class or a science class in order to work that one period daily in the office or library or for the nurse. I said that a fight would mean removal from the job for a semester, as would truancies, smoking, or foul language. I encouraged the librarian to form a club of library helpers, including boys. The nurse organized her group into a club called The White Caps. The girls working for me in the main office became a club called The Note Toters.

Each club elects its officers and levies dues of about ten cents a month. Local and city newspapers and the school annual have carried stories and pictures about the clubs all year. The clubs are responsible for each year's Mother and Daughter banquet, attended by over three hundred. We encourage the clubs to join community projects. Last year, out of their dues, the Note Toters purchased necessaries for dependent children in Juvenile Hall, like combs, hair brushes, bows, toothbrushes and toothpaste, crayons and coloring books. A committee of five girls did the actual shopping when I took them out on school time. Another committee wrapped the items and tied them with colored ribbon. I escorted a third committee to deliver the items. The girls said they never knew it could be such fun to shop for others. At the close of the school year, the three clubs attend a swim party with the other school service clubs.

The girls in the office are trained in office and telephone manners, filing, delivering call slips and announcements, picking up and alphabetizing attendance cards, and picking up tardy slips. I believe the most difficult office practice to teach teen-agers is not to repeat things they overhear. The White Caps, who are nurse's aides, are trained to take temperatures, read a thermometer, file, alphabetize, administer first aid, apply simple bandages, and tidy rooms and cots.

You can guess that the three clubs now have quite a waiting list. Students often want us to promise them office practice for the following year. I always work through recommendations of the Social Living teachers and I aim for a fair proportion of the status groups on campus. This year I have three Mexican-Indian girls, one Spanish [i.e., Mexican], and one Italian girl, and the rest are of various economic-status groups.

The dean of boys and I explained to our PTA that we needed a Morale Fund on which to draw for hair permanents, haircuts, corsages, an occasional pair of shoes, or that something enabling a needy boy or girl to attend a social function or raise his social standing on campus. Our PTA gave us $138. With this I have bought several pairs of shoes, three permanents, one corsage and seven tickets for girls to attend the Mother and Daughter banquet. Three of these girls were Mexican ninth-graders and had never attended a banquet. I took seven motherless girls of low economic status to the banquet. One girl was too proud to accept my invitation but said she would work, so I put her on the banquet serving committee.

Our agricultural community is undergoing tremendous cultural change. Orange groves shrink as subdivisions replace them. Many parents commute to work. The schools have a tremendous responsibility to teach children of families newly arriving from many states and from other countries to live appreciatively with every other group; and to teach members of the old families to accept and appreciate newcomers.

Desiring integration of his multiethnic pupils, a junior high-school principal devised programs for accomplishing this, through broadened activities of his faculty and by strengthening self-confidence and initiative among Mexican-Americans and Negroes. He reported:

Pupils become young adults at junior high-school age. While having to solve the special problems of adolescence, the youngsters must simultaneously learn to live with those of other backgrounds. At this school level, minority groups are often required for the first time to integrate with Anglos. The junior high-school teacher and administrator require every ingenuity to create an integrated school community.

. . . A man teacher might well spend a spring vacation picking oranges or grapefruit to get the feel of how many Mexican-Americans earn a living. Teachers should attend Mexican fiestas to see how traditions still influence Mexican-American life. The school administrator can volunteer to work in community settlements and meet the minorities in their own environments. He can help raise scholarship funds for minority pupils. During the noon hour, he should visit with minority pupils on school grounds, talking over their interests and problems. It may be necessary to organize groups for shy Mexican youngsters, then eventually pool them with Anglo groups. Such gradual integration is often done with Scout groups, Y Teens, HiYs, and others. At senior high school, segregated groups often disappear by merging.

Minority students should have responsible positions on the Student Council and other governing bodies. It may be necessary to run two students of one minority for the same position on the Council to insure the minority's representation. Perhaps a minority should be represented on the Council in the same proportion as it occurs in the student body. Such activity provides valuable leadership training.

A small but strong organization of minority students can be formed by the administrator to help influence actions of other students of their race. This has been effective in our school with Negro boys. I have called meetings of five to ten Negro boys about problems concerning their race; and they have pledged themselves to counsel other Negro boys about poor conduct. Building race-pride and self-respect in minority youngsters guarantees their good efforts.

It may seem advisable first to establish the minority as a worthy group. We did this in my junior high school by the following method.[10] Once weekly, three teachers of Spanish especially trained two Mexican-American pupils in every one of the 42 homerooms to teach conversational Spanish to all other pupils at the school. These eighty-four Mexican-American "cadet teachers" reviewed grammatical construction, pronunciation, and teaching methods. Within the first year, they won respect and recognition from the others; at the same time, intergroup hostilities on campus disappeared.

Teachers in schools and colleges blame students for being "dull" but are far less critical of their own teaching. It would seem as if they expected "motivation," a favorite word in the educator's vocabulary, to spring from every pupil's forehead, a veritable Athena out of Zeus, without themselves exerting special effort. The so-called unmotivated pupils are also often the ones designated as "bilingual . . . underachieving . . . delinquent . . . drop-out." Such was the eleventh-grade remedial reading class of Mexicans, Negroes, and whites, or Anglos, led by a teacher to compose poetry, as noted earlier (see Chapter 4, footnotes 6 and 7).[11] The Mexicans, constituting most of the class, were children of uneducated Spanish-speaking workers; like their classmates, they scored a zero rating on the Cooperative English test [evaluating language use, vocabulary, spelling, grammar], except for one who was rated in the first percentile and another in the second percentile. That is, they were rated as lacking any competence in English. Yet within a few weeks, the inexperienced Mexican-American teacher had all the pupils writing original English verse.

When the teacher later joined a seminar in anthropology and education, she was directed to reconstruct and explain the practices by which she had achieved her results. She found this difficult, for, like many creative talents, at the time she did not "know" what she had done. On first consideration, she thought it important that "I showed them that I am a lover of poetry, especially the English and Spanish, and that I myself write." Finally, after much discussion, she wrote this reconstruction of twenty sequential procedures in her work:

It was my first teaching assignment. I had no special training in remediation but they give these classes to new teachers [as first choices go to senior teachers]. Heightening my tension and frustration were colleagues' remarks like, "The remedials are stupid, no matter how you try with them. They just can't learn! Don't try to make them write, just give a lot of seat-work to keep them quiet. If you can do that, you're accomplishing a lot. I've had them before and, boy, do I feel sorry for you. They're nothing but a bunch of monsters."

1. Instead of buying a suit of armor, I made an appointment with the counselor of my prospective monsters. The class list had names of seventeen boys and three girls, whose ages ranged from sixteen to eighteen. The counselor explained that these pupils, on a group intelligence test, scored from

69 to 98. Iowa scores [testing school achievement and past learning] were very low but not all were available. Several pupils had long been classified as "nonreaders," others were three to five years below their grade level in reading. There was much truancy and many attended school only sporadically; some had been in Juvenile Hall, a few were on probation; only three belonged to school clubs. A number resembled adults more than teen-agers. The counselor was very helpful in explaining each adolescent's cumulative record of test scores, class grades, health checks, and family details.

2. I also consulted the attendance officer, whose discussion of the delinquencies and of family aberrations, such as incest, proved invaluable later on.

My classroom was typical with its three bare walls, one row of windows and endless rows of hard desks set rigidly before the teacher's desk. On the first day, as I waited and the bell rang, in marched one, then another of the twenty pupils; they filled the seats. Were these the "monsters" who would attack at slightest provocation?

3. Hardly, I told myself. They're too beautiful. I know them already and they wouldn't look so sullen and suspicious if they realized I knew their secrets.

4. The first class period was spent gathering information. I passed out cards that confidentially requested each one's name, parents' names, parents' places of employment and of residence (some were in jail), the number of brothers and sisters, hobbies, club affiliations, plans for the future, etc. This occupied most of the period as many pupils needed help with spelling.

5. The next day when I called roll, they were surprised that I pronounced difficult Spanish names correctly. Some were pleased. They said things like, "You're the first teacher who's said my name right . . . How did you know how to pronounce my name?" The cold walls began to thaw.

6. My formal instruction started with a lecture, the only one I gave that class, on social conditions and minority groups. Intense interest lit their faces as I explained that all races have similar potentials for intellectual learning, that no race is superior to others, and that every individual has something to offer society. I stressed the importance of each individual. Pupils then discussed discrimination, segregation, and the great contributions of some minorities.

7. All the pupils had made D's and F's the previous semester. I said I would disregard this, that they could make better grades if they wished, that I would ignore the policy of not grading above D in remedial classes, that they would be rewarded if they performed well or only tried to. I said, "I don't care if your hair is blond, black, or green, or if your eyes are blue or brown. I want you all to do your best." Noticing that some wore poor clothing, I added, "I'm not interested in Mary's pink sweater or in John's flashy shirt, only in your success here."

8. I allowed pupils to choose their own seats and, like adolescents, each chose to sit by his best friend. I couldn't expect them to be quiet all the time but I had to set limits to the talking. Not to seem arbitrary, I said, "You may talk with your friends whenever you like. Talking doesn't bother me if it isn't loud and rowdy. But when someone is reciting or I am explaining to the class, there must be absolutely no talking. You may

work with others when you find it necessary but during tests you do your own work."

These limits were observed well by the whole class and never did I need to quiet them during recitations. I do not want to give the impression that they were always quiet but they did respect the rules. Pupils who were reciting seemed to feel important with everyone listening to their words. At times they were a little noisy but so happy about their work that I stressed their achievements and not the keeping quiet. One of the delinquent boys enjoyed the lessons so much that he attended faithfully even when absenting himself from all other classes!

9. We had a "workshop" period when the room was a little noisier than usual, because everyone was working. Pupils brought their portable typewriters, scissors and paper, hobbies, rocks for our study of geology, and other projects. Who would expect the room to be quiet then!

10. From the work they were turning in, I saw that these "remedials" were not dull. Their writing was good, the oral expression of most was good, their vocabulary was *not* exceedingly low but fairly average. At first, some lacked motivation but I took care of this quickly in different ways.

11. For instance, instead of punishing or ignoring one boy who constantly drew pictures and passed them around when he should have been doing other work, I admired his efforts and asked him to monitor the bulletin board. He drew pictures and artistic letters for our bulletin board and was consulted about contributions for the board. He said he wanted to become a commercial artist. For our class he did research on Italian Renaissance artists and wrote some essays on them.

Then these questions arose in my mind: Why were these children, especially the many Mexican-Americans, put in remedial classes year after year? Do they really lack intelligence and learning tools? Are they always rowdy and lazy? Can they become creative? Have they actually been misplaced in these "low" classes? I graded one boy "B" on his fine work but he refused the grade so he could remain in the class; he asked me to lower the "B."

12. A unit of work that proved satisfying was writing poetry. Children of this age commonly dislike the love and other sentimental themes of poetry. I asked myself whether the pupils could not be made interested in poetry if I were careful to choose unsentimental examples. I answered myself affirmatively and proceeded. I told them to look for poems at home or in the library and to copy one or two. I thought that writing would make them feel the rhythm. I said the writing had to be done neatly, in ink. Some complained that they had no pens; I said buy them, and if you haven't money, go to work. They bought pens! Some complained it was a chore, but not for long.

13. After all poems were handed in next day, I proceeded to read to them from my personal selection of modern poetry, Benét, Poe, Vachel Lindsay; I read the light verse of Edgar Guest, Shakespeare's sonnets, and works of Spanish and Mexican poets. The girls especially enjoyed works of Gabriela Mistral, Chilean poetess and Nobel prize winner, probably because of the deep maternal feeling she showed. I read aloud poems of Robert Frost, Carl Sandburg, T. S. Eliot, Lope de Vega, Garcia Lorca (the *Blood Wedding*), and others. From the astonishment on some faces, I pre-

sumed they had never heard so much poetry all at once. Next day I pinned on the bulletin board the neatest copies of poetry turned in.

14. After saturating them in literature, past and present, I described highlights of some great writers and musicians, especially Tchaikovsky. I said that some personalities belonged to minority groups and some had been poorly educated, but with the creative gift that is in everyone and that should be explored.

15. I read my own poetry and commented on it only to say that the joy of creating a poem was indescribable, and that if they would attempt to write, they might also be pleasantly surprised by hidden talents.

16. I told them that no one was being forced to write. Poetry could not be forced in the absence of desire. Those not wishing to write could choose other work.

We then proceeded with the mechanics of writing rhythmical lines, of describing abstractions in words, of testing different meters. Pupils were attentive as I explained Spanish meter and music. On the blackboard I wrote lists of nouns and adjectives for objects and for sensations, which I told them to call out. For example, we listed different "smells" of baked bread, garbage, perfume, talcum powder, old books, shoes, fruit, foods.

17. All of their original writing was voluntary. This is important. At the start only two or three pupils were brave enough to write. As soon as the first poems appeared, I read them aloud to the class, not naming the writer, to forestall criticisms of the topic or expression. But I noticed that beforehand, the youngsters read one another's poems and commented on them. Nevertheless, I had the policy of not naming a writer.

18. My emphasis on the beauty and rhythms of the first poems they composed, which I read aloud, prompted others to follow. Perhaps the teacher's public reading of their work made them feel important, and this may have led others to follow suit.

19. After they had written many poems, the pupils brought their portable typewriters to school on our "workshop" day to type and mimeograph all of them. Now they felt proud and no longer wanted to be anonymous. For Back to School Night we pinned the poems on a display board. Happy parents, who had never before visited, came to see the display. Pupils brought friends to read and reread their work.

20. This was a new experience after years of ridicule about low school achievement. All pupils wore satisfied proud smiles over the lyrical beauty they had brought to life and the emotions they expressed in what to most was a second language.

Basic to their accomplishments were the trust, encouragement, and understanding I felt.

Here are some of the poems, [published with the permission of the teacher].

Down on the Farm

Down on the farm where I used to live
I slept in the barn, the roof leaked like a sieve.

The farmer treated me mean and cruel
He'd chase me down and whip me with a rule.

He raised Cain to a hickory stick
He'd beat and whip me, with his shoes he'd kick.

When I reached the age of twenty-one
I was much relieved to run no more.
I went to the city with buildings tall
I was so glad to get away from it all.

Home

High on a hill stood a young lad
He was naughty and would not listen to his dad
He stood so high and watched the trees sway
For lo! and behold, he'd run away.

He soon grew cold, tired and weary
He wanted to go home but was kind of leary.

Soon he saw his dad run up the hill
He didn't know whether to go or stand still.
He soon ran to his father's arms
And found he had some lover's charms.

This poor lad who had no mother
Found he and his dad were meant for each other.

So, if you ever plan to roam
You'll soon find out, there's no place like home.
                    (*D.S., Anglo-American boy*)

God Made People

God made the people
God made them at night
God was in a hurry
He forgot to make some right.
     (*J.B., Anglo-American boy*)

Her Eyes

Her eyes are like cat eyes gleaming in the night
Her eyes remind you of a star and all its sparkling light
Her eyes have the image of the moon and all its light
Her eyes are like a cavern with a crystal for its only light
Her eyes are like a song with lovely tone and its delight
Her eyes are the color of the sky with the clouds all in flight.

To Be or Not to Be

To be or not to be
That's what my mommy told me.
To be is to be a bumble bee
Making love to a honey bee.
To be a bee you must know the birds and bees.
To be a honey bee
You·just have to love me.

The Ocean Sound

It's very hard to identify
Those whispering sounds of the ocean cry.
It makes you think that we shall die
And be beyond those clouds up high.

The Beatnik

Here is a beatnik, a beatnik is he
He dances a round to the bongo beat
He jumps and hollers as crazy as can be
He wears a beard as long as can be.

He tries to make poems like you and me
He wears a funny looking hat to be cool
But don't let this poem get you
Cause you see, I'm a beatnik too.
                    (*R.M., Mexican-American boy*)

The Sky

Looking at the sky
Where clouds run together
Doves and other birds fly
With only one feather

The Ocean

Every time I hear the sound of the ocean
Everything looks bright and gay
The sea gulls, the sky and the sun's rays

But best of all is the smell of the ocean.
That you can never forget
Though you live hundreds of miles away.
                    (*D.T., Mexican-American girl*)

A Poem

When you try to think of a poem each day
    You might as well put it in the lay-away.

A poem is something hard to find
    If you even look into the mind.

You will never find the answer there
    So don't even give it another care.

You could write about a Dancer and never find the answer.
    You could write about a Lancer and still not find an answer.

But if you write about the Lancer and the Dancer
    There will be the answer.

Snow

The black and white clouds up in the sky
Huddle the mountain tops very high.

It's a very beautiful sight to see
With a layer of snow on every tree.

Soon the sun peeps from out of the sky
And children all around begin to cry.

You'd think they're crying without a reason
But they'll see no snow until next season.
(R.T., Anglo-American boy)

The Autumn Leaves

The night was dark
And the moon was mellow
The leaves withered down
Upon the soften(ed) ground
Soaking up the smell of the earth
That smelled of fallen oranges
Made into a soft pillow.

The leaves no longer crunchy
From mixing into the ground
Help to form spring colors
Of apple blossom, cherry pink
Topped with chocolate cream
Hiding the rotten scum
That we see through the day.

The Cool Ones

The gang hopped in the cattle wagon
To make the fine rounds
Where there were fine units
They made a cool sound.

The high saddies longed to see
Where the creeps linger
With untied and fine threads.
They had no reed to spend.
To the creeps known to them
The high sadditries were jitter bugs to them
They seem so cool with their bucks (buck shoes)
They were sent to their pads on a rail
After they were wiped out in a fine whale.

The Jitter Bug was cool
The Bongo beat was hot
He cooled it all night long
To make the sound waves strong

So he could be the coolest one
To beat the Bongo beat
That his fine threads may be knit
So may the cool ones have a beat.

(H.W., Negro boy)

Wind

There is a wind I'd hate to hear
A wind of mystery and of fear
They say when it is near
Its voice will call
"Come here, come here."

There is a wind I'd hate to hear
A wind of death, a wind of fear.
It's coming! Its voice is near.
Listen, listen, can't you hear?

Slow Down

On the freeway there's a smell
A smell of danger, a smell of fear
As you drive along the way
You hear your tires say,
Slow down, for death is near.

The Whisper in the Sky

There's a place where birds fly by
High as the endless sky
This is a place where clouds float by
Way up in the endless sky.

There's a whisper in the sky
A whisper that will never die
A whisper without a cry
A whisper from the endless sky.

The Bird of Families

There's a bird I'd like to be
The prettiest one in the trees
He's the one with long white wings
That glides along the sky with ease.

They say that those white wings
Bring people here with ease
They say that bird is called
The stork, the bird of families.

(W.W., Anglo-American boy)

The varied themes and styles—dramatic, lyric, narrative, balladic—
tumbled out readily, after brief guidance, upsetting the pretentious

tests of intelligence and achievement. Nor were these manifestations a mere fluke. Everyone in the class wrote repeatedly, revealing distinct personalities and talent. An experienced Anglo teacher tried the method the following year in another city with ninth-grade classes of "slow" learners (IQs of 70 to 90) and "average" learners, and produced similar remarkable results. This second teacher had learned of the method from her husband, also a teacher, who was in the Anthropology and Education seminar with the Mexican-American woman originating the method. One of the poems, evoked by the second teacher from an "average" pupil, was chosen for publication in the school's literary magazine, having been singled out by the magazine's poetry advisor, a member of a university faculty. The husband reported, "My wife's best results last year involved reading to the class some of Shakespeare's works. She found the pupils not only receptive but eager to hear more, even to the slow learners, who suffer as well from family pathologies and delinquency." 12

Another teacher remarked on pupils' equally keen awareness of common *adverse* classroom techniques. A young Negro told him that after reading Little Black Sambo to her first-grade class, the teacher asked the pupils, "And who is *our* little black Sambo?" A Negro teenager added, "The reading divisions in school are always the 'white paddies,' the 'beans' [Mexicans], and us niggers. That's how reading ability is scored." Hence "reading readiness" and the English language were inseparably mixed with hostile feelings about race prejudice. It does seem impossible for a young American, having all of his mental faculties, to rate a true zero in English usage. The poetry method evolved in teaching remedial readers exposed the true competence.

About Communication

Because of the great recourse to verbal modes of communication in our highly transient, socially unstable communities, and the paramountcy of these modes in teaching relationships, it was vital to have teachers discover and test repeatedly the unreliability of the spoken word. In the project described in Chapter 4, teachers interviewed people of different social backgrounds about the meanings of seven much-used words, and they wrote useful interpretations. Since academic ability is rated chiefly against verbal familiarities and glibness, and educators proceed as though these are standard qualities of all social groups, the teachers were astounded at their irregular findings. A woman, principal of an elementary school, wrote:

Not only are there very great quantitative differences in individuals' vocabularies, but also great qualitative differences reflecting varied experiences and backgrounds. Words carry feelings special to each individual.

The minister I interviewed works closely with people and their feelings, and defined words accordingly. The engineer I interviewed treated vocabulary like cold hard material. He quickly assigned a one-word definition to four of the seven words. The mother I interviewed explained words according to experiences with her family, particularly her ailing small daughter. The fruit packer gave no exact meanings but each word was referred to things and experiences of hers. The Negro steelworker showed high awareness of society's standards. The words had social significance for all my interviewees except the design engineer. This was especially noticeable with the word *interaction*.

He hesitated over it and finally said, "Actually it has no damned meaning for me at all." His concerns were for fact and figure and how an analogue computer performs mathematical operations.

It struck me that the word *role* or *roll*, having fifty-eight meanings attached to it in the dictionary, received the least comment. I spoke but did not spell the word, to see the aspect chosen. The minister and the engineer chose to define r-o-l-e. The others defined r-o-l-l. The housewife asked why the word was in the list, imagining she saw connections among all the words but r-o-l-l.

The word approached with perhaps the greatest care was *delinquent*. All interviewees raised questions of right and wrong. All except the engineer said they wanted it dissociated from youth, yet they all mentioned youth when defining the word. The minister wanted it understood as an individual volition rather than as an inherent quality. The steelworker said he heard the word daily and thought of it with reference to meeting or failing a set of imposed standards.

Now I see that full communication is not easy to achieve. Albert Schweitzer said, "We wander through life in a semidarkness where none of us can distinguish exactly the features of his neighbors; only from time to time through some experience we have with our companion or through some remark he passes, he stands for a moment close to us as though illuminated by a flash of lightning." [13]

Writing of his six interviews, a high-school teacher isolated a contrast between the well-educated and the less-educated respondents. "College graduates picked the form *role* while noncollege respondents chose *roll*. However, a civil engineer chose *roll*. On the other hand, a product designer, aged forty-two, who had been educated only at high school and night art school, gave the most definitions for each word, talking at length about possible ramifications.

"Only one interviewee responded to *deviation* with *sexual deviation*. This was my brother-in-law, who perhaps felt more at ease and had been for years a newspaper reporter. He took time and care to complete the answers he gave. Throughout other interviews, I wondered how many actually had that concept of *deviation* in the back of their minds but were reluctant to bring it out."

A young social science teacher in junior college examined interviewees' responses for clues to their life-styles. Observing a young man of twenty-three in the college coffee shop, he found that "much about him escaped neat classification. Dressed in the clothes of any sloppy waiter or bus boy, his haircut and leather sandals, of a type I have seen Germans wear, were contradictory."

His replies to the first three stimulus-words (delinquent, crisis, diagnosis), indicated that "he was college-educated and bright. When he defined *role* as 'the part taken by an actor,' I asked him if he were a literature major. He was. When he finished the definitions, I asked him if he were bilingual in German and English. He was. His speech, including expressions known to me from my similar background, cued me. He gave a few definitions of latinized words, like *interaction*, as close translations of the Latin components. I asked him and, yes, he had a Latin background, besides knowledge of French and Russian. His occupational (bus-boy) words were misleading as when he said 'white coffee' for 'coffee with cream.'

"Another male subject, aged twenty-five, married and a father, gave definitions acidly, explaining that was the 'only way' he could feel about 'sociology jargon.' He responded to *prevention* with unusual definitions, like 'birth control, precaution against the acts of fate.' He defined *role* as 'surrender of self to the role.' I know that . . . personal identity is very important to the subject. For the first time in his life, he is deliberately attempting creative work."

Teachers found that asking about isolated spoken words, free of an imposed context like a sentence or a particular spelling of a sound-complex having more than one written form—such as, role and roll—was a quick way of unearthing notions in the informant's mind. These notions are of the sort psychologists term "free associations." The associations yielded by this project included some evident cultural and bilingual errors and confusions. This was clear in the response of the Mexican-American janitor who explained the spoken word *race*, which the investigator had in mind, as though it were *raise*. In his Spanish-accented English both words were pronounced identically; in the absence of a context, he mentioned what was uppermost in his mind—bringing up children and increasing his earnings. Suddenly it dawned on teachers that here was a tool with which they could test "retarded reading ability," "poor motivation," "bilingualism," and other classroom inadequacies of children coming from foreign, subcultural, and substandard homes. Teachers and social workers were pleased with the handiness of this instrument, and were startled by its unsettling revelations.

About Intermarriage

Since American racism taboos intermarriage, as do religious and national prejudices, and class pride in stratified societies elsewhere, though these may be less fierce, policies of desegregation and integration instantly provoke questions about permitting such marriage in states without restrictive legislation. Schools outside the old South, from kindergarten to the topmost academic reaches, must provide for desegregated and integrated programs; these throw the sexes together. Mixed couples are seen around the campuses of many institutions. Welfare agencies care for mixed families. Consequently educators and social workers requested a project illuminating intermarriage, which they conducted as described in Chapter 4.

Their field studies around this theme roused powerful disturbances in all parties, like those reported by a young counselor at a junior college serving a highly varied population. During coffee breaks he interviewed colleagues in faculty rooms as they happened to enter. A married counselor, aged forty-three, the father of single daughters, replied thus to an initial question asking his feelings about intermarriage:

"I'm opposed to racial intermarriage." [Question: Why?] "Because I've been where I saw that the children have no status, living in a kind of never-never land." [He had been stationed with the Air Force in several parts of the South.] I asked how he would react if his oldest daughter were to date a Negro. He said, "I'd point out disadvantages and if this didn't work, I'd forbid her to see him." [Question: If this didn't work?] He answered forcefully, "It would!" [Question: What would you do if it didn't?] He said he'd move away if necessary. [But if they eloped before?] Hesitatingly, he said he wouldn't reject them. [How would you feel toward grandchildren by such a marriage?] He said, "Don't know. [pause] I couldn't accept them." He refused to pursue this.

[What would you do if you discovered now that before your marriage your wife had dated a Negro?] Immediately he replied, "She wouldn't have." Then after reflection, he said, "It wouldn't make any difference because you build up a marriage to mean so much that what happened before wouldn't affect it. . . . That's a stupid question."

[How would you feel about integration if it led to greater intermarriage?] He said, "It won't." [But sociologists believe it will.] "It won't."

[Why do more white girls marry Negroes than the converse?] Registering shock, he said, "It may be that they feel sorry for them." [How do you feel about a caste system that allows white men to exploit Negro women but permits no reciprocity?] He said, "I know it exists but I don't feel it's right."

Another married counselor, aged thirty-seven and a father, also said, "I'm against marriage between Negroes and whites." [Why?] He said, "If racial barriers didn't exist, it would be all right. There's too much stigma, especially in the middle-class." He would not like his daughter to date a Negro, but did not know what he would do if they married and had children. [Had his wife dated a Negro before meeting him?] "I wouldn't have gone with her." [If you first learned about it now?] "I'd stay with her. Wouldn't like it, though."

He favored the Supreme Court decision (of 1954, ordering desegregation in public schools) though he felt that integration would further intermarriage. He had attended a mixed school in Ohio where all worked out well because social pressure kept each group apart. He had noticed white girls with Negro boys but didn't mind. "As long as racial problems remain academic, I give good answers. When they affect me personally, I feel otherwise."

Next I interviewed a sociology teacher, married, forty-eight, and a grandmother. She said she opposed racial intermarriage. Like the others, she interpreted "intermarriage" to mean this. [Why?] She said, "It's not a matter of superiority or inferiority," adding that both groups might reject the children. She felt there were enough problems in marriage without adding to them. [How would you feel if your single sons were to date Negro girls?] She answered as before, adding "they might fall in love." [Suppose there were intermarriage and grandchildren?] She said, "I would accept the baby. Babies have universal appeal. I would feel sorry for the child but love it." [Are racial intermarriages becoming more popular?] She said, "We're not ready for that. I suppose it would come about by doing it. But I don't want my sons to lead the way. . . . Integration will result in more intermarriage."

Unlike the others, this subject was poised and confident. I felt that she was aware of her prejudice and accepted it without guilt.

A high-school counselor questioned three Methodist clergymen in California about intermarriage. One was a naturalized Mexican, the others were native-born Anglo-Americans, originally from Pennsylvania and Florida. These men were concerned only over interfaith marriages, mentioning Protestant, Catholic, and Jewish faiths; they thought there were no real problems in marriages mixing "whites and Negroes." The Mexican, aged sixty-two, "pointed out that in Latin America, the word *negro* [also] connotes 'darling' and is used between spouses. Favoring especially Anglo-Latin intermarriage, he foresaw great increases in all intermarriages, the trend being marked since the end of the Second World War. He thought the older generation more than the younger objected to intermarriage and that it was no problem to individuals having no religious interests.

"The Pennsylvanian, aged about thirty-eight, thought intermarriage with Catholics presented the most difficulties, especially with regard to children. He felt that under the impersonal conditions of large cities, intermarriage offered fewer possible problems. His denomination's clergy do not refuse to marry people of different faiths and races but strive to counsel them.

"The Floridian, aged about thirty-three, held similar views. Success of a racially mixed marriage depended on the local group, he added, as he knew from some years in tolerant Hawaii. He found the average young American less biased than his parents, and so the American GI contributes to the rising rate of intermarriage. He found no biological objections to intermarriage."

One young housewife and mother, a former teacher, interviewed a white Catholic neighbor and European Jewish friends. The neighbor said, "You mean Negro and white intermarriage? I was brought up not to be bigoted. But the strongest prejudice is against the colored. My husband and I talk about it; if anyone colored moved in the neighborhood, we wouldn't go out of our way to make trouble. But my husband says, as long as it's not my daughter marrying one of them. It's bad for the [mixed] children. But if my daughter brought one home and said, this is it [I'm marrying a Negro], well, if that's what she wants, it's O.K. with me. Only their children will ask, how come? So, I suggest no children. . . . The white race is in the minority over the world. It's not a subject I would get steamed up about. The way I was brought up: I believe what *I* want, you believe what *you* want, just don't try to palm off your beliefs on me."

Though this woman seems to speak against bigotry, the interviewer reported "hear[ing] her shriek invectives at her children that included 'nigger.' When the family dog becomes a nuisance to her, she addresses it as 'nigger.'"

The neighbor sent her high-school daughter to be interviewed, saying that it would be "real interesting to find out what a teen-ager thought." At the question, "What do you think of intermarriage?" the girl became flustered, "opening her mouth several times, smiling broadly, looking away, leaning on my desk, finally asking, 'You aren't going to put my name on this, are you?' I said no. After a silence, she said, 'It's all right for someone else but not for me.' Following more silence, I asked, 'What are you thinking of as intermarriage?' Startled, the girl asked if I meant racial intermarriage because 'their children would have more problems than they.'"

Later, the subject of intermarriage was introduced with dinner guests. "The couple seemed taken aback. Aged about forty, they were born in Czechoslovakia where they lived until after the Second World

War and married after the liberation. As Jews, their families were sent to concentration camps during the Nazi era. After the War they were harassed because the husband's surname sounded German, so they changed it to the Czech equivalent of Brown or Smith. For the same reason they named their first child Jan. From a DP camp in Germany they were taken to Israel and lived there nine years until they came to California about three years ago.

"To my question, the wife asked, 'Do you mean marriage of Gentile and Jew?' The husband laughed, 'Between dog and man? Or between human beings?' The wife continued, 'I first heard the word here, referring to Caucasian and Negro. In Europe the expression is "mixed marriage" and is thought of as mixing religions.' The husband said, 'In Israel, "intermarriage" is a very strong word. They prefer to say, he is married to an Arab. But in Israel you can't marry unless both are Jews, by birth or conversion. Or you go to Cyprus to be married.'

"When the wife and I were alone, she asked me, 'What does intermarriage mean to you?' I said that in our country, though I too am Jewish, most of us think of 'race,' that I respond emotionally to the idea: He is Negro, she is white. The wife said, 'What did we Europeans know of race? The only Negro I ever saw was in a circus. In wartime England, there were the mulatto babies. And this Negro dentist, married to a white woman. When I asked him if they would have children, he said no, they were very happy and would never have children. Maybe he underwent sterilization. . . . To me, the worst possible thing would be my son's marriage to a gentile.'

"She explained that she felt she belonged only in Israel. It was her husband who wanted to leave. 'Israel took us when we were in need. They didn't need us then but they do now. There my son did not have to ask, What is it to be a Jew? Here he does ask. What do you answer? There he knew only Jew and Arab. Anyone who wasn't Jew was Arab. Here we find anti-Semitism. I saw my son walk home from school with a Catholic girl and he finds nothing wrong in this. My punishment for leaving Israel may be that he will marry a Gentile.' "

Various factors influence the meanings a person assigns to a concept, this interviewer commented. The relation of interviewer and informant is important. "The teen-ager may have failed to express ideas she feared would be carried back to her mother. The Czech woman, lonely for Jews, may have told much simply because I was Jewish. Authoritarian elements influence responses, as in my neighbor's awareness of the Supreme Court decision and of TV comments on civil rights legislation. If there is a kinship between the idea of inter-marriage and the individual's self-concept, the idea becomes laden with emotion, as in the Czech woman's selection of religious inter-marriage as the threat."

A blond, young kindergarten teacher questioned the Mexican-American mother of a pupil when she called at the school, putting the issue of intermarriage in a specific social setting. She said, "If you needed partners for a bridge game at your home, would you invite mixed couples, like Mexican and Anglo or Negro and Anglo?" The woman answered that it made no difference. The teacher asked how she felt about mixing religions. The Mexican answered that it de-pended on the individuals: "If I like them and we have a good time together, it wouldn't matter. We have Negro neighbors next door and we get along fine. We have Mexican neighbors on the other side and don't like them as well. We have Negro and white friends who are [inter] married and proud of it."

The teacher asked if there were cases of intermarriage in the Mexican woman's family. The woman replied that her brother was married to an Italian whom her family liked and who liked them. Both were Catholic. Asked what would happen if their religions were different, she said she thought her family would accept another religion after a while "if the person was nice and not acting better than [i.e., superior to] us. It might take a while to get to know the person and like him or her. In high school, I had a Protestant friend and we never talked about it [religion] because it didn't matter. She married a Catholic who became a Protestant. We never talk religion with them. I think that there won't be many differences in five years anyway. . . . Maybe I'm open about mixed marriage because it comes down to people, and all people have feelings. It's the rich who are prejudiced, not people like me."

The teacher repeated her question about intermarriage and mixed couples to a young Jewish woman, a teacher, married to a Protestant. The woman replied, "Race makes no difference. Close friends of ours are a Negro man and white wife and also a Chinese couple. Maybe I'm the wrong person to ask this because I am Jewish and my own marriage is mixed. . . . Originally my mother objected to my marriage, fearing our relatives' remarks, but now she loves my husband. . . . The crucial point is reached when confronting the person, not the idea. . . . To some I would recommend intermarriage but not to others. Great maturity is needed to face the added prob-lems brought to a marriage linking two religions or two races. The outcome depends on the individuals. My husband, God bless him, has been open to the Jews and my eyes have been opened to other faiths."

The interviewer observed in her report that each of this couple was "much wrapped up in a new religion. Both spend hours trying to convince others of this glorious new truth. Are they trying to cover up some insecure feelings? At present they are childless but parenthood may reveal other facets to their marriage."

Finally this teacher interviewed a Mexican-American man of forty, a shoemaker, whose children she taught. She put to him the same question, of social relations with mixed couples. He answered, "I wouldn't care. I feel every man has a right to his own religion. Some of our friends have different religions. Basically, they're all the same anyway. I was born and raised a Catholic and will remain so and I suppose my children will be the same. [What about racially mixed couples?] Well, we mix with them but not often. A good friend of our's married a girl from Guam and we like her because she fits into our way of life. It would be different if she were Negro. I can't accept [racial] intermarriage. I was brought up this way. My father used to talk to us boys about marriage. He never said not to marry out of our race but we knew he wouldn't like it so it never entered our minds. [What about your boys?] I think I could learn to accept it if the boys married an Oriental, Italian, or French woman but I would find it very hard if they married a Negro. The Negroes are becoming so aggressive. . . . I doubt if the next generation will accept intermarriage but maybe the one after will."

The interviewer added to this report, "Furrows in his brow revealed anxiety at the idea of his sons marrying Oriental, Italian, or French but at mentioning possible marriage to a Negro, there came a solid look of opposition."

A middle-aged Negro woman probation officer told the white colleague interviewing her about intermarriage, "Opinions vary with geography. In Negro parts of San Francisco, you see all kinds of mixed couples, and at church no one even turns around to look. In the [Southern California] city where I grew up, I know five or six happy couples where the man is white, the wife Negro. This combination seems more successful than when the man is Negro, the wife white, perhaps because a Caucasian man can get our best girls but a Negro man nearly always chooses white trash. Caucasian in-laws, especially professional people, are quite accepting. I know a Caucasian woman who introduces her son's Negro wife proudly as 'my little brown daughter.' I suppose the better class of Caucasian feels more secure than the lower class. Negroes accept intermarriage with Orientals better than do Caucasians. In a Negro classroom or at a Negro party a Negro-Korean child is considered Negro without reservation. But Caucasians notice instantly [censure] a white-Korean child's slanted eyes. However, in a white classroom, a white-Korean child is accepted better than a Negro-Korean."

Although this woman foresaw ultimate broad reception of racial intermarriage, she opposed religious intermarriage. "I don't believe at all in marriage between Catholic and Protestant," she said. "It would be disastrous also to marry into a religion like Jehovah's Witnesses where chastity is required after a period of time."

Her behavior matched her views. She married a Negro minister of her faith and adopted a Negro-white child. Being employed, she engaged a maid to care for the child, "a Mexican without race prejudice." She told bitterly that the child was not accepted by a private kindergarten only "because of her race."

In a junior high-school faculty room, a teacher interviewed colleagues on intermarriage. He wrote:

The discussion was not heated but showed rank differences of opinion. John was much bothered over issues. Aged thirty-two, with a master's in education, he has a young wife and a small child. He declared, "I hate to see a white man married to a colored woman, it looks awful. It makes me sick to see colored and whites living together." Going on like this, he was interrupted by Frank, aged over sixty, with a master's in education, formerly a school principal and superintendent in the South; he has a very young wife and three children. Frank said, "Farmers have developed fine hybrid cattle by mixing breeds. Maybe we can do the same with the human race." He paused and John said, "Sociologists would like to see intermarriage happen right away but it won't for generations." Frank observed, "There are enough nonconformists in our society to make this happen rapidly. It might not be as far away as you think."

Dick entered, a man of forty-five, a counselor and math teacher, thoughtful, and loving an argument. He said that he strongly favored intermarriage, that intermarriage was absolutely necessary if our country is to endure as a democracy. However, the partners must share interests. But the typical colored man loves a big black Cadillac while the typical white woman loves a great big house.

John said, "This sounds good in theory but it is fundamentally wrong. Intermarriage with Japanese and German war-brides is well accepted and common and successful. But the Negro is not in this category and will never be. Mixed marriage (Negro and white) is bad for the children."

Frank said, "I see two problems here. One is racial, and we are solving it. The other is religious, and it grows more divisive."

The group's real concern with the Negro held no hate. All felt that the problem was most difficult but would be solved.

A middle-aged white man, teaching at a high school and at a junior college in a rich California city, interviewed a middle-aged

Negro man who was counseling vice-principal of a junior high school and an ordained minister. The former asked, "In this explosive period, how do you regard intermarriage?" The latter answered, "In our community, [Negro-white] intermarriage probably has considerable acceptance. But it will be many years before it is accepted widely. Religious intermarriage faces lesser problems since the church no longer can enforce disapproval. Marriages of whites with Orientals and Mexicans may favor marriages of whites with Negroes. But the race pride of the Negro mother will delay this. She objects especially to her daughters marrying white. The mother is the bulwark of the Negro family, and the ordinary father shirks responsibilities. Have you ever heard Negro boys call each other 'son of a bitch'? I doubt that you have. The worst insult among Negro boys is verbal obscenity against the mother. To help a Negro boy in trouble, do not appeal to family pride or the father but work through the mother and through the boy's attachment to her.

"The Negro does not want general social intermingling. He wants equal treatment in jobs, housing, education, recreation. People fear that integration must incite mass intermarriage. That is not so. . . . Now, I want to be considered one with my colleagues, not just as the person handling Negro problem kids. Going home at night, I do not expect to visit *your* private social world, or any one else's. I enjoy my own group and do not expect to share with any one not of my choosing.

"Negroes are not agreed on all issues. Take race pride. Many of us opposed NAACP efforts in World War II to integrate combat units, because the Negroes chosen were the most promising and educated of us. Integrating them in combat meant risking their deaths. Many of us were content to keep the all-Negro units or we would have preferred integrating service units such as Quartermaster, Ordnance, Food Services."

The interviewer wrote reflectively that he "had stumbled on reactions considerably different from those (he had) expected. I had not imagined so much race pride, and that this pride would deter intermarriage. I had not realized the prestige of the Negro mother, having imagined her only as a jovial fatalist.

"Now I see," he conceded, "that I may have erred with Negro students. I had approached indifferent ones by arguing that though the father was unsuccessful, there now was opportunity for the ambitious. Perhaps I could have better motivated these students if I had concentrated on the mother. I must investigate the patterns of the Negro-American family to follow the confusing ramifications in our society."

Next he reported his interview with a white lawyer seated for years on the municipal bench. He asked the judge if he thought school desegregation favored intermarriage. The judge answered, "Most great social changes are well under way before the law catches up. If the Supreme Court had not ordered desegregation in 1954, there might have been widespread revolt. . . . Intermarriage has long been a reality, especially among different religions. Accepted racial intermarriage may take longer. Even upper-class Southerners tell me they know they must confront the likelihood of biracial marriage. I don't think intermarriage is the basic issue in today's changes. It is only one feature in the great social revolution of our time."

Next the interviewer reported the views of a white woman directing municipal welfare services. The welfare agency's Negro clients were unskilled workers newly arrived from the South and openly resented by local Negro residents. The city's Negro population had come to outstrip numerically the older Oriental and Mexican populations. The welfare director said that "racial intermarriage presents no problem here. Only when a mixed marriage breaks up, usually after five to six years, does the agency become involved, often to aid the children. We notice that the white wife abandons the children. The Negro husband refuses responsibility for the children, as it hinders his next marriage. Yes, mixed marriage is increasing, especially between whites and Mexicans. We receive mounting requests from distraught white mothers to stop budding romances between their children and Negroes. White girls might be the aggressors. Seldom do we find a Negro boy wanting to marry the white girl.

"Recently I had a case of a white girl wanting to marry a Negro," she continued. "Her family had turned her out though she'd had no physical relationship with the boy. His mother took her in and sympathetically tried to dissuade her from marrying. But the girl insisted. Another mother asked the school principal and dean to help end her daughter's romance with a Negro but they said the matter lay outside their authority and furthermore such relationships should be expected and provided for. The mother was frantic."

Asked how she felt about intermarriage, the director responded, "At present I see only disadvantages though there will be increases in all sorts of mixed marriages. The offspring are the sufferers, unfortunately. First we must solve the general problem of integration. Why aggravate it with intermarriage?"

About Illness and Pain

As minorities are deterred from sharing marriage, schooling, jobs, recreation, and housing with the ruling middle class, and often, therefore, do not share the respectable, standardized language, so this ruling class does not expect minorities to share the generally admitted states of suffering. Thus, there lingers a belief that American Negroes are always happy and strong, and never commit suicide though they may commit murder and rape. Authoritative statistics from medicine and social science have long shown, however, that Negroes suffer much grave illness and maintain a high suicide rate, facts which certainly are consistent with Negroes' centuries-long state of deprivation and with such cultural productions as Blues songs and spirituals.

One curious expression of middle-class prejudice is to suspect minorities, or those of low social rank, of feigning troubles to exploit the rich, or of indulging them willfully, and of practicing cures that the middle class considers morally dubious or rankly superstitious (such as many remedies that include herbal folk cures, incantations, amulets, medals, and even prayers), as it does the folk curers. The middle class often talks and acts as if only it were entitled to states of real suffering.

Giving illusory substance to middle-class skepticism is the fact that those of minority or subcultural position often show sickness or hurt by symptoms that appear to differ from those of the Anglo or white middle class. Usually this means that the low-status symptoms appear in unfamiliar settings or in a person of the wrong sex and are treated by unfamiliar modes. Generally, most differences of any category are suspect at schools, welfare agencies, and other public institutions receiving the poor and socially handicapped. Judging from reactions of many school nurses and other officials, even familiar ailments—colds, headaches, digestive disorders, fatigue, skin eruptions—appear questionable in minority children.

The minorities are seldom invited to explain their ailments on a serious or respectful basis. The minorities' views of their disorders, their etiologies, meanings, and cures, and of responses shown by their betters are known only to occasional scholars and novelists.

Recent behavioral research suggests that all stressful aspects of life appear in forms of illness and pain which are somehow patterned by the local social environment. These aspects include the local cultural roles of men and women, the traditional social controls, traditional objects and modes of love and hate, of religion, science, and superstition, the preferred and tabooed food and drink, and the local forms and consequences of poverty, wealth, war, and migration. Suffering—of body, mind, and emotion—is considered by many authorities to contain information about stress; some anthropologists see this information as couched in bodily idioms that are special to the patient's traditional background.

Teachers and others in the seminars became acquainted with the general behavioral viewpoint through the project examining cultural factors in illness and pain. Their studies uncovered unlooked-for facts which included vigorous practices and beliefs retained from prescientific times, along with adaptations to modern knowledge, folk sayings about classic diagnoses and philosophies of suffering, and changes rung on these in different groups.

Teachers studying Anglo-American children in middle-class neighborhoods found that the children cried more readily over *emotional* hurts than physical ones. Weeping by males was viewed dubiously. A teacher reported a sixth-grade boy's statement, "I wouldn't have sympathy for a crying father because it would show he had no guts." Most pupils were reported as finding it acceptable and moving for a *mother* to cry. Boys agreed that they cried less and less as they matured. A teacher wrote that at her elementary school, "more antiseptic and dressings are used than elsewhere in the school district and children are quick to report feelings of illness. Most of our pupils have been in the same school system since kindergarten and have learned how clinic and teachers handle indispositions." The nurse at a neighboring junior high school concurred, stating that "proportionately fewer illnesses are reported by our Mexican-American students than by our Anglo ones. Mexican parents are very cooperative when contacted and extremely concerned about their children." Where Mexicans tolerated anyone's tears, a German-American family restrained their children with the proverb, "Tears are self-pity."

A tenth-grade English teacher wrote, "It is generally accepted that Negro pain tolerance is lower than the Caucasian. The school nurse verified that the largest number of chronic visitors to her office are Negro low-achievers with poor attendance records." This teacher sought no further confirmation of her statement. But another teacher reported reading that whites possessed "superior sensitiveness to pain." A school nurse reported that Mexican-American "children exaggerate their illnesses. [This is] to avoid some issue though their parents never seem excited or unduly concerned." The usual opinion among Mexicans and Anglos, reported by educators, was "that illness in the Mexican-American family is accepted calmly, almost fatalistically."

A woman probation officer reported that "young adult Mexican-Americans do not retain many beliefs in their forebears' unscientific treatments of disease. They do retain the traditional attitude that illness must be accepted calmly as inevitable." She adduced the Mexican proverb, "Life is like that" (*así es la vida*). A teacher quoted to her the proverb with which a Mexican-American cattle rancher opposed immunization of his cattle and children: "Some live, some die." This meant that he accepted fate or would not resist it. Another fatalistic Spanish proverb was: "A tree that grows up crooked will never straighten its branches." The probation officer learned that even Mexicans of the tradition-bound lower class "seek modern medical aid for severe illness and pain. At other times they rely on home remedies, the 'witch doctor' and priest." Other Mexican proverbs that she heard were: "A [curing] remedy in time is more valuable than repentance. Fear kills much more than sickness." The last partially explained customary supplication of the Blessed Virgin, by Catholics and Protestants alike, to cure anything from a mother's cancer to a baby's indisposition. Usually such supplicants did not resort to physicians and hospital clinics.

Some families feel that the medical doctor's treatment would be "too strong" for an ailing child and might cause death, so they call the herbal doctor. This may reflect tales of patients who did not receive medical attention until too late.

The mother cares for her ill children and explains disease to them. The illness is often blamed on the child's state of being *empachado*, or of suffering from indigestion; then purgatives are administered. The father may make recommendations but usually leaves things to his wife.

The *bruja*, or woman witch doctor, is highly regarded by older Mexicans. Three *brujas* practice now in the Mexican *barrio* (quarter) of my town. They use their own brews of herbs, weeds, animal organs, blood, and human secretions, besides using spider webs, massage, and visions. One *bruja* told a young Mexican-American man, who told me, about her brews and her mistrust of medical doctors. Besides being a midwife, she also treats sore muscles, colds, headaches, bruises, mental illness, TB, and other ailments. She believes that some medical "quacks" have learned much from her traditional lore of herbs. She competes keenly with the other two *brujas*, rating herself the best because she is most successful with patients.

My Mexican gardener says that as a Protestant he rejects the *bruja's* magic, that only superstitious Catholics use it. Shuddering, he told how "witch doctors" place cats' glowing eyes in ashes, stare at them until entranced, then diagnose "supernatural" cures. He mentioned miracles accredited to a statue of the Lady of Guadalupe in Central Mexico, which effected immediate cures so that the lame danced upon nearing the statue at a given number of paces. When he treats his own colds with boiled water, lemon, and whisky, he is careful to cut the lemon in a cross.

Laboratory technicians at the county hospital tell me that Mexican-American families *fear* the hospital's elaborate modern equipment and the blunt approaches of doctors, nurses, and technicians. Yet they behave quietly, showing no hysteria. One said, "They abandon themselves to fate, though not in a completely passive way. They want to get well." Small children may cry but they obey authority, as they are trained to do at home. Unlike Anglo patients, these children do not tease or plead with a parent for their own way; nor do adult patients speak profanely or demandingly with doctors, nurses, and technicians. Mexican-Americans *accept* the situation.

A nurse at Juvenile Hall said that when the Mexican children there fell ill, parents showed little concern, as if the child were no longer part of the family. The parents surrender responsibility to those in charge of the child though to nurses it looks like "out of sight, out of mind."

According to a young Mexican-American probation officer, psychosomatic illness among his people allows the sufferer's withdrawal. The excuses offered may seem irrelevant to Anglos, but Mexicans do not challenge them openly. Proverbs from Mexico expressing the situation are "Chicken fever and disease of the kennel are reasons for not going to school," and "Headache of a lazy person is reason for not going to work."

A teacher learned that Mexican-Americans "do not need rest homes for their aged. They never feel that the presence of old folks harms children. They rely on oldsters to pass on the culture. Grandmothers on both sides doctor the sick with inherited remedies. A simple cure for earache consists of stuffing a clove of garlic wrapped in cotton into the ear. Supposedly, the garlic generates a soothing heat. If the patient lives, his sickness is an enriching experience for he is then surrounded by numerous kinsmen, hovered over, aided in work, never left alone, made to feel wanted in the world. To the Mexican, putting his relatives in the *gringo* hospital is to neglect them. Such people are not necessarily poor or illiterate. Nor is the herbalist grandmother only a simple peasant. I have known such in families of college graduates. In one prosperous Mexican-American family, the herb-doctor grandmother had been well educated in Mexico City and later created recipes and marketing procedures for the family's flourishing cheese factory."

Another teacher reported changes in traditional practices:

When I first taught in an all-Mexican-American junior high school, most youngsters were poor and most families were on welfare at least part of the year. Children feared the hospital, saying, "Anyone who goes to the hospital dies." Probably some had died because of delayed medical and hospital care. One day a girl came to school with a small blue cross on her forehead. I asked if this were required by the Catholic religion. My error. The cross had nothing to do with religion. Her mother had put it there to ward off disease. I had in fact read that, in Mexico, dye of the indigo bush is used for this purpose.

Another time a boy said that he could not attend his mother's funeral or go near her body because he had a cut on his hand. In Mexico people believed that fatal disease, like his mother's, would enter the cut.

Often I have heard girls say that their mothers warned them against eating lemons and avocados during menses. But lately I heard a little seventh-grader declare, "Lemons are good for you. They have vitamin C. My last-year's teacher told us." Our Mexican-American girls seem to crave lemons, eating them like oranges in spite of mothers' warnings.

Lately I notice that most of our Mexican-American children visit the school nurse, the doctor, and the hospital. However, when a relative is in the hospital, the family visits *en masse*, including cousins, aunts, uncles, and grandparents. Everybody is important. The present trust in hospital and medical care results from schooling the children and from the influence of increasing numbers of educated Mexican-Americans, Negroes, and some whites in tract-home sections.

A Mexican-American man observed health problems, especially headaches and colds, in a correctional school for young men, aged fifteen through seventeen, and discussed them with these wards. "The Mexican-Americans among the wards had a deep-rooted belief that they were stronger and resisted more illness than Anglo-Saxons. Hence, they seldom remained as convalescents. They broke any prescribed diet, eager to resume favorite dishes. Youngsters who obviously should be in bed or resting were seen playing outdoors or at school. Many Mexican-American boys were ashamed to admit illness and undergo vaccination. To them heart and mental disorders characterized gringos more than *la raza* [our race], because greedy Anglo-Saxons overworked while Mexicans adjusted themselves to life as it came.

"The Anglo-Saxons, on the other hand, gave little thought to heart and mental diseases, though they agreed with the Mexicans about competing with the Joneses. The Anglos guessed Mexicans were easygoing, unconcerned about tomorrow or with bettering themselves. Men who lacked ambition, these youths believed, would never have heart disease. Male prisoners, aged forty to sixty, expressed the same views."

It seemed clear to this observer that "beliefs about traditional differences supported convictions that one race was healthier, richer, or poorer than another. The poor say as long as we have good health, we are richer than the rich with heart troubles, ulcers, and mental breakdowns."

An unmarried young woman doing social work reported on health problems in the Well Baby clinic of an old Mexican-American quarter:

The nurse said that though these Mexicans have ready access to stores selling milk, fruit, and vegetables, and the money to buy these, families still eat the traditional beans, tortillas, and mole. Meat is served chiefly to men, as the "working" members of the family. This diet often produces severe anemia in pregnant women and their offspring. The clinic tries to correct deficiencies in the children by giving iron and vitamins, but it does little to develop a diet that is both nutritious and satisfactory to Mexican taste. Principles of diet are observed less by younger Mexican mothers than are principles of sanitation.

The visiting nurse described the doctor's problem with Mexican mothers. It seems that a Mexican mother always lays the baby down to drink his bottle, not caring if he drifts off to sleep while eating, wakes up to take more, and sleeps again. The doctor calls this a feeding problem, believing that activities of sleeping, eating, and playing should be *separate* in the child's mind, that the child should not be allowed to *drift* from one activity to another. I asked the nurse if a specific health danger lay in the baby's "drift." She did not seem to know of any. The doctor just did not think it a good idea. Mexican mothers cannot see much reason for his thinking and, frankly, neither can I. The doctor's worry seems to illustrate how the Anglo culture's time and place categories conflict with the Mexican custom of not making a production out of small children's normal functions and behavior.

An elementary schoolteacher reported on "The Stigma of Disease":

The following incident occurred in 1946 when I was teaching fifth grade in a California Mexican [segregated] school. Rosa, a beautiful Mexican girl, did not come to school one day. The other children said that Rosa's father had died in the county hospital but would not tell me the cause of death. For several days they whispered a great deal among themselves. When I approached the little whispering groups, they disbanded or resumed work.

After two weeks, Rosa was still absent. The nurse visited the home and reported that Rosa would be in class next day. But we saw no Rosa. However, the principal appeared, saying that one of my little girls was in the hall, refusing to enter the room. I walked out and there was Rosa on the floor, sitting crying. I got down to comfort her but the more I talked, the harder she cried. I waited until she stopped. Then I took her by the hand, saying, "Come, Rosa, let's go into our room. Your friends are waiting for you." The child said she could not because the other children made fun of her and avoided her. I asked why. She said it was because her father had died of TB, and that was bad, real bad.

I took Rosa to the principal's office and went back to talk to my children. Then I learned much, for the children were eager to explain that their previous whisperings had been about the badness of TB. The children had known Rosa was crying out in the hall. They were superstitiously afraid of TB, as though a TB victim was being supernaturally punished. They had been told this by relatives.

Ten years before, I'd had a comparable experience in Western Pennsylvania when teaching in a two-room village school. I taught primary grades and a Mr. C taught intermediate grades.

Mr. C's large family were old residents with a lot to say in running the community. However, one sister was very poor and lived out in the mountains. Her son, Richard, attended third grade in our school.

One afternoon Richard had a *grand mal* epileptic seizure. I sent for Mr. C, the uncle. When he finally arrived, I had the child on the floor with a coat under his head. Mr. C seemed to know what to do and did it; the child fell asleep.

After school, Mr. C asked me to accompany him to take the child home. Arriving at Richard's house, Mr. C lifted the boy from my arms and carried him indoors. Though it was bitter cold, I was not invited in. On the way back, Mr. C asked me to telephone the doctor but not to describe symptoms over the party line, saying only that the child had a high fever. I did so and am sure the doctor thought I was nuts.

Next day, Mr. C told me that the doctor said Richard had a convulsion, not an epileptic attack. I was no doctor but as a child had often witnessed a neighbor in *grand mal* seizures. I was beginning to suspect Richard's relatives.

Some weeks later, Mr. C admitted that Richard was epileptic. However, the family considered this disgraceful and tried to hide it so as not to be ostracized in the village.

Recently, while teaching in a California kindergarten, I had a child with *petit mal* epilepsy. But the mother said the girl had temper tantrums, causing rigidity of the stomach muscles. At school, the child had several of the so-called tantrums, when she always ran to me and asked me to hold her. I would do so until her body relaxed. For several days after each attack, the child stayed out of school. The mother would explain that her daughter had a cold and would ask why I didn't paddle her when she had the tantrum. Only after a bad attack months later did the mother allow the necessary encephalogram. This confirmed a diagnosis of *petit mal* epilepsy. Under daily medication since then, the child has suffered no attacks.

A young mother, temporarily retired from elementary-school teaching, organized a little field investigation of "Illness in Mexican-American Children." She wrote the head nurse of an adjacent school district about her wish to observe cultural aspects of illness, submitted sample questions, and requested the privilege of visiting a school for two or three days. She reported how later, on the telephone, the head nurse "implied that a morning of observation plus a conference should yield all the data. The nurse said, 'I don't think you will find any difference between Mexican-American children and the others. Mexicans are not the roaming group they used to be.' Any differences, she thought, were individual."

Several days later, the two met in the nurse's office at S school, where a doctor was scheduled to examine a mixed group of children. The nurse was in her late thirties, the mother reported, "with ladylike graces and style."

The nurse said that the city health department had better information than she. As to the percentage of Mexican-Americans at school, she said, "They are less than 50 per cent at this school and we try to keep it so in the classrooms. This was a problem when they lived in concentrated areas. Anglo mothers would telephone us and complain. But now the Mexicans move all over town."

I asked about the change she had mentioned on the telephone. She replied, "Since I was at school in this city, there has been a real change. We used to be separated, the Mexicans on one side of the building, Anglos on the other side. The town was mostly migrant Mexicans. The laws weren't as strictly enforced, in or out of school. Mexicans didn't attend school much. They still stay out more than others on rainy days. For some, it's a clothing problem. But most of them feel that if they get wet, they'll get sick. They won't bathe or wash their hair if they feel any indisposition or are menstruating. In the fifth grade, we show girls films on menstruation. Mexicans feel the food they eat affects menses, especially sour foods, pickles and lemons. They used to wear something on a string for general protection against illness. They used fig leaves for something about their teeth. I know, because my mother had a fig tree in her back yard and they used to take leaves from the tree."

A Mexican-American girl of about eleven entered the office through the hall door. The nurse rose to meet her. Trying to be unobtrusive, the interviewer turned her back to them and so saw nothing while overhearing their conversation. The child explained her absence of the day before: "I had a bad stomach ache yesterday. I still have it," she said.

"The nurse inquired, 'What are we going to do then?' Her tone conveyed, 'You have failed and I don't like you. You could redeem yourself but we both know you are incapable.' The girl did not reply. After a silence, the nurse went on, 'Do you think you could go home this morning and be clean by this afternoon? Do you think you could have a bath this morning too?' The girl answered 'Yeh.'

"The nurse continued, 'You should be able to come back at noon, don't you think so?' The nurse's words charged the child with responsibility and threatened her with dislike. Coming from an authoritarian but affectionate type of family, with the philosophy of adjusting to the world as one finds it, the Mexican child must have found the nurse's remarks hard to understand. Besides, the reference to 'clean' probably differed between nurse and child. Perhaps the child was hoping that a laxative would ease her stomach ache by noon. She spoke hesitatingly, 'Well, I'll try' and left the room.

"The nurse told (her visitor), 'That girl's family just came from

Monrovia. They receive county aid because the father has deserted. They are one of the few families with head lice. The child is filthy. Did you notice what a strong odor she had? It filled the room.'" The visitor had noticed nothing but in her report of her visit commented that her sense of smell was poor.

The nurse added, "She's absent most of the time. She has a pretty low IQ and just can't compete. Is learning the real problem, and then other difficulties get attached?" She seemed puzzled and concerned. "In the larger families, they don't feel it wrong at all to keep older girls home for babysitting, washing, cleaning. Boys and girls take care of younger children. Some large families keep children home because they have nothing to send for lunch. I ask the mothers, Why not send beans and tortillas? They're cheap and you have them. But they're embarrassed to do so and instead keep the children home."

Asked if Mexican-American families, or parents, followed her recommendations when children showed loss of hearing or of sight, the nurse said, "The parents do as a rule but not as completely as Anglos. The state has an aid program for the severely handicapped, which follows through."

Asked about folk medicine among Mexicans, she said, "Sometimes when you ask a child to have his mother take him to the doctor, he says, 'My mother will take me to a *bruja* or *curandera* (curer, or untrained practitioner).' About ten years ago, when I worked in a local doctor's office, I learned of two or three women on whom Mexican women depended for curing sickness. They were mostly first-generation Mexicans. Often the women would bring their curers to the doctor as interpreters. One Mexican woman performed abortions.

"At school, we struggle to keep Mexican cliques from forming. Do you know what they say when we break them up? That they are being picked on." She smiled scornfully, "We encourage mixed groups. Many class officers have been Mexicans; two Mexican boys have been student body president. They support each other in politics." She smiled again.

Asked how Mexican-American children behaved when they fell and hurt themselves, the nurse answered by referring to patients in the local doctor's office. "The real tiny children are stoic. You know, they have a lot of Indian blood . . . Since the War, they've upgraded themselves terrifically, in economic advantages and housing. They used to be in one little area; now they're all over town. Did you know the *pachucos* (youth gangs) started here?" Smiling uncomfortably, she digressed more. "Mexicans have a different attitude toward marital infidelity. Anglos try to conceal infidelity; they don't expose it to everybody. But in the Mexican group, they talk about it freely. They don't try to protect each other about that kind of thing."

The inquiring mother asked if Mexican mothers showed emotion when picking up sick children at school. "Not as much emotion as some Anglos," the nurse replied. "They don't have cars so we take most of their sick children home. In the past few years, two Mexican doctors have come to town. One is an osteopath and they go to him. We have a fine new Cuban M.D. who speaks Spanish. He just walked into town and got a thriving practice. They used to visit a doctor only when near the bitter end but I think that now they're trying real hard to be just like us. More and more often, they can't speak Spanish, only English. Some who have really elevated themselves don't want to associate with the others; it's a class distinction."

The nurse now took her to P school to observe physical examinations conducted by the school doctor in the nurse's office. "Boys and girls were told to remove their top garments but were never in the room at the same time. The doctor and the P school nurse insisted that differences among pupils were not cultural but individual or linked to social class. The P school nurse said, 'Take Mary. She brought a note from the doctor that she had neuresthenia, she was in and out of school for quite a while, then finally she had a ruptured appendix. Another girl was a nervous wreck [the nurse mimicked this girl's large body jerks] but she was Anglo. I notice no difference at all between children. Some are chronic complainers to get attention. They are more apt to be Anglo than Mexican-American. Mexicans get lots of love and attention. A Mexican child was having a GI series because of intestinal trouble, and do you know what I found out, purely by accident? She'd eaten a can of tamales for breakfast.'

"The P school nurse smiled wryly and shook her head, like a mother who cannot understand her many children but loves them all the same. She proceeded, 'Considering the lack of milk in their diet, Mexicans' teeth are as good as Americans'. . . . Our principal's biggest problem is that Mexican children stay out to take care of the house and their younger brothers and sisters.'

"She remarked to the doctor, who was examining children, 'Well, we finally got Mary back in school. She said there was something wrong with her blood.' The doctor and nurse smiled and the doctor asked, 'Tired blood?' The nurse answered, 'Yes, she's had something wrong for three years now: a low IQ. Just doesn't like school.'"

When there were no more children to be examined, doctor, nurses, and visiting mother met for coffee with some teachers. The doctor said, "Mexicans are great believers in the occult, especially for chronic conditions. To relieve terminal cancer, they seek a witch. Still, about three months ago I read an article in *Time* magazine about someone in England practicing such therapy."

Over coffee the teachers and nurses talked about Mexican-Americans' poor hygiene: "Once a month the county nurse comes to delouse them at school. Then they go home and sleep with the dogs and their brothers. But they don't delouse the house. Now, an Anglo mother had her house fumigated—'for termites,' she said." Everybody laughed. "But really she was upset because her daughter's pretty long blond hair was full of nits . . . Lots of Mexican-Americans are afraid to bathe their children in winter and are afraid to send them to school when it rains because of colds."

The doctor amplified, "TB is prevalent among Mexicans and they consider it a disgrace. . . . Maybe there's something to folk medicine. I used to wear a garlic bundle around my neck to ward off disease. It probably helped too. Who would want to come near you with that around your neck?" The school nurse added, "Lots of people believe that milk makes you cough when you have a cold."

Back at the nurse's office, they found two Mexican-American girls waiting. "The doctor asked pleasantly for one child's name. She answered rapidly, grinning, 'Brenda López de Puente.' (The girl may have grinned because the name as given was in the Spanish form proper for a married woman.) The head nurse and school nurse leaned toward her, asking her to repeat. The doctor frowned, for there was no Puente in the office file. The school nurse asked for the mother's name. The girl answered, 'Mrs. López de Puente.' She asked the father's name and the child answered, 'Jess López.' [This is incorrect, if the mother's name is given correctly, suggesting that the child was confused. In the child's own name, the Spanish form has her patronymic precede the mother's patronymic, so that her name should have been given as Brenda Puente López.] The head nurse exclaimed angrily, 'I don't know where that extra name came from.'

"The doctor turned to the other child and smilingly asked her name. 'Sally,' she said. He asked, 'What's your last name?' She said, 'I forget.' The nurse provided it, mispronouncing the Spanish. The doctor told the child, smiling to reassure her, 'Well, that's a hard name to remember.' "

The former teacher wondered "if Mexican girls are taught more physical modesty than Anglo girls. There seemed a subtle difference in the way the bodice of the dress was held up during the examination. Mexican-American girls did it with greater ease, holding elbows or upper arms against their sides so that the bodices did not drop.

The Anglo girls kept losing their tops and pulling them up. . . . The little girls were continually warned by the nurse to keep chests covered and to stay out of the room when a boy was there."

A highly trained teacher described a "flight into illness" among a group of thirty Austrian Jewish boys brought to England from Nazi-occupied Austria just before the Second World War:

Nearly all these children, aged five to thirteen, had undergone recent traumatic experiences. Several were orphaned by the Nazi purge of Jews. Some parents were in concentration camps. Stormtroopers had shot other parents before the children's eyes. England was strange to all the children and so was the language. I, their housemother, came from the children's Austrian homeland.

During the first five weeks of the children's stay in London, six of the younger boys came down with appendicitis, one after another, and all underwent surgery; the appendices of two boys had ruptured. One can hardly assume that six cases of appendicitis in a period of five weeks might have been coincidental. Appendicitis is not communicable. No one had complained of abdominal pains previously but only of slightly sore throats. Each got violently sick during the night, vomiting severely so that I called an ambulance and accompanied each child to the hospital and operating room.

The attending physician and surgeon were greatly puzzled. They wondered about the drastic change of diet. Several undernourished children had eaten ferociously upon arrival. Many had gained several pounds during the first month in England. But it remained doubtful that overeating or a strange diet would cause appendicitis in six simultaneous cases.

All were children under stress. Hence, we may speculate on what illness could have meant to them. As all came from the middle class, it can be assumed that formerly the mother had shown a sick child greatly loving care. In England there was no mother. I, the housemother, spoke their language and had had experiences similar to theirs. To each I was father, mother, sister, brother. Nights I was always available to a patient, in an open bedroom adjoining the sickroom. On falling sick, each child was assured of more of my individual attention. Appendicitis brought pain and also compensations.

But why appendicitis? Published studies in psychosomatic medicine report cases of chronic and acute appendicitis as gastro-intestinal responses to severe stress. Dr. Flanders Dunbar found that stomach and eliminative upsets are directly linked to conflicts over dependence.

Our six boys had not been allowed to grow independent gradually but had been forced from total dependence, typical of European children, into sudden unwanted independence by the removal to the unknown country. The boys may have regarded dead parents as "abandoning" them and themselves as "abandoning" the parents taken to concentration camps. Overwhelming guilt feelings might have developed readily in the boys for not staying with parents to the bitter end.

Anna Freud and Sophie Dann, studying greatly deprived children of similar background, described children's feelings about the peer group.

Each child perceived himself and the group as one. When one child would not walk, none would. If one would not eat, none was hungry. If one did not feel well, all were listless. There were striking similarities to such conduct in the illnesses of my refugee boys.

About Culture in Families

The project of reconstructing a family culture through the three latest generations exposed enormous social variety in the origins of teachers despite the teachers' usual middle-class appearances and professional oneness. The ranging differences—of religion, national and regional descents, race, parents' economic class—behind the standard appearance contain unsuspected cultural factors, which are hidden points of behavioral reference heightening an individual educator's troubles with those of other ancestries because they are as unknown as the behavioral standards of minorities at school.

If every individual teacher were securely set by descent from generations of the same American tradition, a strange people or minority might seem less disturbing or threatening. But the teacher who rests heavily on his certificate to symbolize the community's standards, and who must instruct accordingly, is revealed in many of the family analyses as only a first- or second-generation comer. Recent converts take few risks with the authoritative creed, and, at the same time, strive to invalidate a divergent one. On the other hand, old heirs know their latitude: thus, among socially strong and impeccable white Southerners are found some of the regional racism's most stubborn foes. Judging from the family studies, educators of subcultural origins feel anxious about conforming to middle-class referents because of the clash with certain ancestral standards, habits, and comforts over which the individual has little conscious control. The clashes and anxieties gave meaning to the educators' reiterated term, "frustration." Then suddenly, work on the family cultures appeared to give students the right, as it were, to feel proud of their origins! This was an unexpected consequence of the project. Studying cultural dynamics, individual teachers rediscovered enthusiastically their deep roots in the family's ancestral traditions. It seems that the middle-class demand for adherence to its single standards, or "equality," attacked divergent ancestral loyalties and the personal identities of many teachers trying to earn professional recognition and social comfort from the middle class.

The writer expected that roused family pride and stirred-up sympathies would alert and attune teachers to their minority pupils' similar attachments and needs. They did. Teachers came to recognize the strains placed on a subgroup, on its culture, and its member personalities when defeated by another people and forced into other ways by poverty, prejudice, immigration, and ignorance of the ruling or host society.

Each one who engaged in the research stated in one way or another his new knowledge that culture was a generic function and life-condition of all men, a mysterious creation of such power that some culture theorists call it "superorganic." Each one glimpsed the crucial reality that man's culture has taken diverse forms in time and space, and that the historic diversities were cornerstones of existence for the heirs. In the United States, the crucial reality has proven tragic as well for certain groups, notably those of the minority peoples; but the teachers now had firm hold of the idea that, regardless of minority labels, the diverse cultural or subcultural groups were treasuries of human resource for the heirs, and for other groups —like educators—who understood them.

This family project was planned as instruction and not as therapy; but, as with some experiences, the project cast a healing light on knotty situations in submerged areas of students' careers. Each time students resorted for information to relatives, to relics in family trunks, to libraries, and museums, they explained some version of, "This is what life is about! This is how we know we're human!"

Most of the family studies were written with the great feeling we call love. This did not exclude some hostile feelings. Students said, "I left things out because I didn't want to hurt my people," or "I hesitate to read this to the seminar because of what it reveals." One woman, on the contrary, read and wept over her devoted recollections. As director of the Claremont Anthropology and Education program, the writer's view of the supposed omissions was that "What you left out deliberately is immaterial. The purpose is for your report to give a coherent picture of your parental tradition."

The points about which a student declared himself to be privately sensitive, as he felt shame, hate, and pride surge, invariably eluded the listeners when he read his paper aloud. Listeners showed the reader a purblindness similar to that which authorities showed regarding sensitivities of minority persons. After this startling experience, and with heightened insight, students now readily guessed how handicapped and oppressed groups suffered humiliation, anger, and bewilderment—states normally inconceivable to an outsider lacking empathy. One high-school administrator concluded discussion of his family culture thus:

This was an extremely difficult assignment for me. By describing my (European Jewish) parents, the lives they spent, the anti-Semitic prejudice to which they, their parents, and grandparents were subjected, I have alluded to factors leaving deep imprints on my own life.

This is the first time that I have ever discussed my background outside the immediate family circle. I guess there are many things one wishes to repress, consciously or unconsciously. While much is unsaid, I believe the major objective of the assignment was attained: namely, that by experiencing a strong resistance to writing about myself, I have sharpened my sensitivity to the deeper feelings, the inner conflicts of other persons with whom I come in daily contact. Yet I had already experienced anti-Semitic prejudice as a child, in school and on the playground; as a student in college; as a member of the Armed Forces during World War II; as an employee on various jobs; and sadly, as a member of the education profession.

A teacher, born and reared in Vienna, described changes in her life brought about by migration to the United States after the Nazi conquest of Austria:

It was difficult and painful to be uprooted from the culture and country of which one felt a part. It was as hard to grow roots again in a strange soil and learn to become part of the new land. Yet I felt able to retain much of the culture in which I grew up, and still have space left for absorbing the new.

Living most of my life in an authoritarian society only to begin life anew in a democracy is an experience hard to describe. It is almost like learning to walk again after a long illness when one does not quite know what to do with the new freedom of locomotion. Only slowly one learns to adjust and love freedom. Compared to the rigid social patterns of Europe, the United States is almost classless, for it is really possible to move from one social rank to another. This realization takes time and requires good understanding of how American institutions function.

Meeting and living with people of different racial groups impressed and depressed me in equal measure. I never met a Negro until I was eighteen and never saw an Oriental until I was twenty years old. I was deeply impressed that, according to the Constitution, we were equals in sharing the democratic way. But I was depressed to find segregation of races not very different from the segregation I knew in anti-Semitic Europe. Is it possible that freedom, given to those who never knew it but longed for it, seems of greater value to them than to those having it as a birthright?

Changing cultures may provoke a sense of impossible contrasts. Listening to American-born teachers describe their family cultures, the Austrian-reared teacher exclaimed tartly, "I'm amazed at these long American genealogies! I'm not that interested in my family. I never even met my grandparents, who died early." This view may reflect special aspects of Jewish history, where the people wander under persecution, strongly rooted in an ancient tradition but not for centuries in a geographical terrain until the establishment of the state of Israel in 1948.

This was one of the American genealogies that amazed the former Austrian:

I regard myself as a typical product of the American melting pot. My grandparents and greatgrandparents came from five different countries of Western Europe and the British Isles: England, Ireland, Scotland, Holland, and France. It is even possible that the French greatgrandmother was part original American.

My paternal grandfather came to this country from Bolwiggie, Scotland, where the family had been weavers. Tradition says he came by steerage when he was fourteen. His name was Alec and in the Civil War he became a drummer boy under Lew Wallace, who wrote Ben Hur. After the war he worked as a carpenter, building depots for the railroad running west. He stopped in Kansas at the then Grasshopper Falls, later renamed Valley Falls, and bought a store. Here he met and married a Dunkard, Alice Ann; but she was known to dance! Alec sold his store, moved to a farm, did custom harvesting with a new steam-engine harvester, and later turned building contractor and cabinet maker in Topeka, the state capital.

Alice Ann was of English and Dutch ancestry. Her mother's parents had left Holland for the United States, homesteading and clearing land in Illinois. This was later sold and the family, including six sons and a daughter who became Alice Ann's mother, homesteaded and bought some thousand acres of farm land near Springfield, Missouri. As Dunkards they opposed war; when Missouri pressed men into the Confederate Army they traded their land for cattle and mules, at far below value, and left for Kansas. Heading for a Dunkard settlement north of Kansas, they were asked to settle in the Dunkard community near Valley Falls and Topeka. Later the six boys served in the Union army, one as a doctor . . .

My father, Clarence, married a girl of English, Irish, French, and possibly Indian ancestry. He learned telegraphy because weak eyes prevented his studying medicine. He was a relief telegrapher for several years in western Kansas and eastern Colorado. My mother, whose family lived in Central Missouri, visited, for her health, some relatives' ranch near Colorado Springs. Here my future parents met and married. My father then went into banking with a friend at Jennings, Kansas. There I was born and lived during the first part of World War I.

Our little community had a rather large Bohemian settlement, which gave a cosmopolitan air. Each year the community held a dinner where families of different racial origins served foods of their countries. I watched the burning of the Kaiser's effigy at night in the public square . . .

We moved to Topeka, where I first met colored children, at school and play. My home training was that all men are brothers. Two mulatto girls, whose Caucasian father and full-blooded Negro mother were legally married, taught me race prejudice. We used to roller skate down a long hill by the State Fair grounds. At the foot we met two very dark Negro girls, who asked us to skate on to their house. The mulattoes would not let me go and said my parents would disapprove.

After college I married a man of English and German origins. His mother's family had been knighted under Cromwell and with the king's return they left for America. His father's family had left Germany for England, where they remained over two hundred years before any members migrated to America. This family valued time; wasting it was a sin. This is quite a shift from the Celtic love of life I had absorbed from my Scotch-Irish ancestors. . . . We became acquainted with educated Indians. Some of our best friends were proud of their one-eighth, one-sixteenth, or one-thirtysecond fraction of Indian blood. Moving to California, we bought a small ranch among Mexican-American neighbors. . . .

Another teacher, born in Hungary and brought to America at the age of four years, described her recollections of culture shifts, vivid after more than thirty years:

My maternal grandfather's family was gentry, being large landowners in Hungary. They traced their land title back over four hundred years, near a little village called Komarom-Szemere. Although untitled, the family was law in town government and society. The estate grew wheat and had large herds of livestock. Until World War II, life there was still somewhat feudal; the same families worked on the estate for generations, and my grandfather's cousin's son operated it. My grandfather was a good landowner, prosperous and beloved; he was the village arbitrator and political figure. He gave his own funds to the village school and other institutions.

My maternal grandmother was a doctor's daughter; she married at sixteen. She ran the household, including my grandfather, unbeknownst to him. Their large manor house was an overnight stop for important travelers in Hungary's agricultural area. In my mother's memory, the travelers even included the Emperor Franz Joseph and his entourage . . .

The children were educated by governesses until, when my mother was eleven years old, they moved to Budapest for better schooling. My grandfather gave the management of his estate to his cousin and started a wholesale meat business in Budapest, marketing his own cattle. Despite changing to a merchant class, the family lived in style on the estate's wealth. The family's attitude during this period is symbolized in an anecdote about my maternal uncle. His classmates were discussing their fathers' professions of law and medicine. They asked him what his father did. Puzzled, he finally answered, "My father? Why—he's a gentleman."

In contrast, I know little about my paternal antecedents. My parents met by a wartime fluke. Normally they could not have met because of differences in social standing. My father was graduated from Budapest University as a veterinarian. During the First World War he was veterinarian to a Hungarian cavalry regiment, with the rank of major. My mother met him and married him against her family's strong disapproval . . .

My father dreamed of coming to America, feeling he could never succeed in Hungary. Their final decision to emigrate roused great consternation in my mother's close-knit family in which there had been no mobility because of the estate. My maternal grandmother finally solved the bitter arguments. Quoting the biblical story of Ruth, she stressed the sanctity of marriage vows against her private inclinations.

Thus, we arrived at Pearl River, New York. I remember odd things such as learning that you need not curtsy when you enter a room of adults, that you need not kiss the hand of very old people, that the way to tell girls from boys is *not* that girls wore rings in pierced ears, and that Americans were stupid, understanding neither Hungarian nor German. I remember being puzzled and intrigued at seeing my first colored person . . .

My father had to be treated with the respect of one whose word was law. He rated with God in my early childhood. Only when I was about ten, and we both collected stamps, did I realize he too was human. I learned that behind his tall frame, military bearing, and deep voice, he was gentle and kind, though still awe-inspiring. He appeared the stern European *pater familias*. Now elderly and ill, he gives himself to his grandsons as he did not to me in my childhood. He feels that somehow he has failed me, from the standpoint of today's American father. But I know that mother and I were the center of his world . . .

In the rural Long Island of my childhood we were the only foreign family. At home, my parents and I generally spoke Hungarian. They both speak English fluently but in my early teens, I was ashamed of their accent. To overcome this inferiority, I felt I must be spectacular, so I worked to become the best scholar, the best swimmer, and the best basketball player at school. . . . Now I realize that my early self-consciousness was unfounded. My father was respected in his profession and received honors. Yet I know that he too had some inferiority feelings about his foreign background . . .

My mother had an easier time making friends because of her superior or more worldly family background, and she turned her accent to good advantage. She brought American friends to our home, unlike my father who always found it difficult to unbend in small talk and social niceties . . .

After college I worked as a chemist and married an engineer. I made a free choice, with my parents' consent, unlike my mother's free choice with family opposition. To my surprise I received a dowry and much household linen. My mother had collected the linen for years, unsuspected by me . . .

In my own family we speak English at home, though there are a few words and phrases from German, Hungarian, and Russian because they are untranslatable. However, these languages will be lost to our sons.

I believe we are quite assimilated in our habits and thinking. Our friends are entirely American. I am sympathetic to Hungarian customs, from a highly interested American viewpoint. My husband, born in Moscow, educated in Prague and New York, with an erudite Russian background, is, of course, violently anti-Communist and is perhaps more removed from Russia than I from Hungary.

The most obvious foreign influence is perhaps in my cooking. Much of it is Hungarian, much is American, some is Russian. . . . Assimilation to another culture is a very difficult and long process but it can be accomplished . . .

A youthful mother, of Anglo-Russian parentage, married to a Swedish-American teacher and herself teaching high school, interviewed French-Canadian parents who had migrated five months earlier with their children from Trois-Rivières, Quebec, to California. She reported that this Catholic bilingual family felt "a loss of status as a result of the move which one could sense though they did not express it. Parents and their five children all worked hard to be successful in the new situation. They found California different: 'So many autos, so much to do!' The numerous women drivers confounded them. Few women in Trois Rivières worked outside the home. The husband said he would never approve of his wife's working."

In Quebec the children had attended Catholic school, as did 95 per cent of the local school-aged group. In California they attended public school.

The interviewer found that "the family is close knit, having few outside activities. The father is undisputed head and the parents supervise their children more closely than do Americans. There is a cheerful camaraderie but no impertinence or belligerence from the children. May this family not become too Americanized!"

This sympathetic attitude contrasted with that of a colleague, a young man who wrote that his father "took a job teaching dumbbell English to underprivileged Mexican children." Neither party was satisfied. In offhanded words the father was scorned for his work, the Mexicans for their status.

A mature man, a high-school teacher, told of cultural shocks and conflicts, generated by his Mormon upbringing, in his personal life:

One of my earliest recollections is of my [Mormon] parents' emphasis on education. Both parents continually impressed this on us six boys, though my mother only finished eighth grade and my father left school even earlier. Yet both were well read and possessed abundant practical knowledge.

This attitude, it seems to me now, characterized most Mormon families. My grandparents on one side of the family, my greatgrandparents on the other, were Mormon pioneers who crossed the plains with followers of Brigham Young.

These pioneers were taught by the Church that "the glory of God is intelligence," and that "as man is, God once was; and as God is, man may become." So it was the purpose of each life to develop the intellect. It was proclaimed often from the pulpit that the only thing one took on leaving this life was the intellect one developed.

Not all the Mormon attitudes were as positive. Few of the darker races came to Utah in early days, but there developed an intolerance of them despite the Church preachment that "all men are brothers in the sight of God." Church *practice* makes it impossible for a Negro to hold authority or "priesthood" in the Mormon Church because the Negro was cursed by God with a dark skin and is an inferior: "the time was not yet ripe when God would forgive him and accept him into His church."

With this background it is particularly difficult for me to accept Negroes as equals. Personal analysis has helped me to realize how ridiculous the attitude is; yet I fear mine is an intellectual rather than an emotional tolerance.

I do not recall ever doubting that mine was the one and only true church until I was well out of high school. For I was born into a Mormon home, in a Mormon town, in a Mormon state, and attended a Mormon university. Certainty of the truth of my beliefs rested on my lack of exposure to other beliefs. There was no other church in our small community; and non-Mormon families could be counted on the fingers of one hand. At the university, I first had opportunity to analyze religion objectively and to examine my own beliefs more scientifically. This is now beneficial to me as a teacher . . .

It seems to me that, though the Mormon people are part of the greater American culture, they developed patterns peculiar to themselves during their long isolation from the rest of the country.

Another teacher described her parental culture complacently, as though it lifted her above stress: Her middle-class family, she said, "had little opportunity to see how 'others' live . . . My maternal grandmother traces her line back to Miles Standish, though I would never have known without asking because she believes that the only important things are a person's acts.

"There has been no real contact with other races and only limited contact with the Catholic and Jewish religions," she related. "I like to think I am very broadminded about others' problems. I realize, however, that this is only a rational philosophy about cultural differences. My sole travel has been to West Canada and to Mexico City, though my parents sacrificed lovingly to give me a good education, wide interests, and understanding."

A colleague of similar age and ethnic roots was, on the other hand, strongly alive to the continual stress and change in American life, as exemplified in her family. Her account said:

Paternal grandparents both migrated from England before 1900 and settled in a little town near Vancouver, Canada. After the births of six children, my grandfather died, my grandmother moved to Tacoma, Washington, and later remarried. The second husband also died early, the family was extremely poor . . . and the children began working very young. My father could not even complete elementary school . . . but he and others helped the youngest boy finish college and become a pharmacist.

The family was close and valued homemaking. Traditional recipes were handed from mother to daughter and traditional menus were served on occasions such as Christmas, marriage, showers, births, deaths. Whether from destitution or custom, all members of the family seemed very frugal . . .

My maternal grandparents migrated from Germany, settling eventually in Seattle, Washington. They produced six children and, when my mother was about ten years old, her mother left home and divorced my grandfather. A housekeeper was brought in. My grandfather, a shoemaker, later married her and four more children resulted. Great friction between stepmother and stepchildren followed, so that most children of the first marriage left home in early adolescence. My mother left at 12 years to do housework with a family; this way she put herself through high school and studied piano and voice.

My mother felt little affection and happiness in her father's home. The family was run on dictatorial lines, was poor, and was lucky to have the barest necessities.

While a housekeeper my mother took a boat trip to California and met my father, a carpenter, in Los Angeles. He courted her in Los Angeles, they married and built a home there, and remained until after my birth. Then my father moved us back to Washington, hoping to better his prospects. He always felt hampered by lack of education, despite his good mental ability. He was always dissatisfied with manual labor, developed psychosomatic ailments, and still suffers untold misery. He has managed to eke out a living through real estate, occasional jobs, and my mother's occasional employment.

My father long held rather autocratic control over his wife and me, his only child. He did not approve of a wife working outside the home, or having outside interests. Only he could handle money and dole it out. Housework was solely for women.

But through the years his ways changed. My mother came to earn money and control much of the spending. When mother worked, father helped with such house chores as dishwashing. Mother developed outside interests and new friends after they began spending part of each year in Southern California. They had moved far from old family habits until about a year ago when my father's worsening health returned them to his home town of Tacoma. I believe he has an overwhelming desire to live out his days there and be buried in the family plot which the relatives decorate attentively.

As a child I feared my father's anger and tried carefully not to displease him. Though we had poor times during the depression, we were always well dressed and fed. Most of our social life was with my father's family—dining, visiting, and driving together. At times I longed to get away from this close relationship. But now I believe I had considerable freedom—swimming, boating, roaming the woods, playing without someone to organize games or "protect" us . . .

I was expected to and did graduate from high school, but had no plans for college until my senior year of high school when I got a college scholarship. Besides, we traveled summers with a small carnival, operating concessions, and we decided that all money earned in my concession would be saved for college.

After one and one-half years of college and the outbreak of World War II, I married and quit school. We moved to Portland, my husband as a sheetmetal worker for the Oregon Shipbuilding Corporation and I on a job in the transportation office. We both took college extension courses.

A year later my husband was drafted into military service and volunteered for paratroopers; later he was commissioned in the Air Force. George and I lived a very democratic marriage, partly through war and our life with the service, partly through personal ideas. We both believed in equal sharing. An Air Force wife necessarily assumes much responsibility for family affairs, often travels alone, finds a house and job, and develops independence. Both our children were born when my husband was away on assignment, the first time as far away as the Philippine Islands. In those years we had maids . . .

When our son was a year old and our daughter nearly four, my husband was killed in a plane crash. It seemed best to bring the children to my parents in California. We soon learned that three generations seldom live happily together. I bought a house for the children and began studying to be a teacher. Teaching seemed the best employment for a mother with two small children.

I taught a year when plans were underfoot for remarriage. Almost three years ago I remarried. We had been acquainted for several years, during which time his wife had passed away. He is much older than I but we seem to have much in common. His one grown daughter, unmarried, opposed our marriage until lately.

Having been single so long, completely independent, and responsible for my children, it was quite an adjustment to marry one a generation older. My husband believes quite autocratically that all family authority is vested in the husband. I believe, more democratically, that husband and wife should plan together and give children some voice, especially about things concerning them. Doubtless we are both modifying our views. However, the children *are* being reared differently from before.

Family ties are now loose compared to the close ones of my childhood. We do not visit our relatives. My children will not have any feeling of family closeness except for our frequent correspondence with grandparents, now in Washington. Nor are the children free to have parties at home, though they may bring friends in casually. Unlike their father and me, they are well provided for financially through their [deceased] father's estate and can afford good medical and dental care, lessons in music and horseback riding, and, eventually, college. I hope that material things are not coming too easily to my children.

A young missionary teacher described explicitly and approvingly the American family values she carried to remote Ethiopia:

In my life philosophy, I recognize beliefs grandma or an uncle taught us children through stories, axioms, and little talks, and which mother taught us when she punished us.

I think our family's first tenet is that *anyone* with ordinary powers can succeed in almost any work if he is willing to struggle. Mother often said, "You can do anything if you want to badly enough." We expected to study, help ourselves financially, and not feel particularly sorry for ourselves. We chose denominational schools, though we could have gone to public schools more cheaply. We all earned board, room, and tuition from the time we were in high school. Even though one sister and her husband are financially able to provide well for their children, they insist that the children work and contribute to their educational costs.

Another family tenet is that each person has his worth, to be valued above material possessions. Often I have heard family stories illustrating the proverb that a good name is to be preferred above riches. My uncles who farm and train horses are as esteemed by the family as my uncles who are college professors and ministers.

We also believe that we should make the world better for having been here, that a life of service brings more satisfaction than abundant material wealth. Our family has three ministers, two nurses, three foreign missionaries, several teachers, a cousin doing cancer research, and an aunt working for retarded children.

Consequently there is little race prejudice in our family. When I asked my mother how this was, she said that her father forbade the children to talk disparagingly of anyone.

When her young brother ridiculed the humpbacked cloth peddler, a Southern European, my grandfather took this uncle out to the barn for a long talk reinforced with the razor strap. My grandmother and several younger aunts worked in San Francisco's Methodist church; so, in the early 1920s, one aunt wanted to marry a Japanese. She was dissuaded with difficulty, and only by arguments about the hardships for future children. Lack of prejudice allowed the opportunity for a serious friendship. Another aunt married a foreign-born Armenian, and my stepfather is from Holland.

Although several denominations appear in our family, religion always means a personal dynamic relationship with God, a relationship that shows in daily life. I went abroad to teach in our denominational school, feeling I should, and I am content doing the best I can.

One teacher, of Anglo-American Protestant origins, in boyhood acquired a Franco-American Catholic stepfather and a large Franco-American stepfamily settled three generations on California farms. Through charts showing the lineage and social status of his kinfolk, and a lengthy exposition, this young man schematized the culture into which he was introduced by his mother's second marriage and to which he became attached sentimentally though he felt apart otherwise. He thought his sense of cultural separateness was consistent with his mother's choice of a "Frenchman" who was openly rebellious against his own family's French background

The student's report postulated cultural homogeneity in the immigrant generation.

All were born in Southern France, received some eight years of formal education there, and came to the United States before the age of twenty-one. All males were farmers, all females housewives, all were proficient in their French language, all settled in the same part of Southern California.

The men came as hands on large ranches, the girls came as domestics in ranch homes. Social life centered on the ranch, limiting the pool of potential mates. Those in France often saw to it that an unmarried daughter went to the same ranch as the family friend's unmarried son. This simplified acquaintanceship and courting, and led to semiarranged marriages for all in that generation except E. He was much younger and when he reached marriageable age, conditions had begun to change. Attending high school, he broadened his social circle. His two marriages followed Americanized styles of dating and courting. But he limited his choices to the "French community," subject to traditional chaperonage.

Even in the 1920's and 1930's chaperonage was still required by parents of most French girls. All men of the second generation, that is, the first generation of American-born, rebelled against chaperones, except R. They enjoyed much greater freedom than their fathers. High school was the general rule, and college was for some in this generation. They learned that dating was more fun without the "old people" around to chaperone. Generally, they "wanted to be like the other kids in school." Their parents did not care for this but could do little about it.

The girls found it more difficult to rebel. Hence the men's rebellion greatly reduced the girls' chances of marriage. Two of the girls in this generation therefore married late and one of these marriages had to be arranged. The attractiveness of the French-American girls was not an issue.

All men in the immigrant generation are farmers. By 1915 all owned farms, acquired in one of two ways. Either the men saved enough to purchase land, which was then rather cheap, or the ranch owners gave land to the immigrant workers. In the second generation, only two are farmers, while none are in the third generation. Reasons for the change are more education, rising land values encouraging sale, higher earnings in other occupations, and the young people's attitude that they are "sick and tired" of farming.

Among the immigrant generation, only two had more than eight years of schooling in France. In the United States they had no time for study, often expressing strong regret about this and even becoming fanatics for schooling. All agreed that children and grandchildren were to be better educated, even if this caused the "French community" to disintegrate and the young people to give up the land.

Among the second generation, most felt the same. But this pressure inevitably met second-generation resistance, to the regret now of all. One first-generation father "always wanted a doctor for a son" so he pushed and pulled his Jean in the medical direction without once considering Jean's feelings. Jean is not doing well at medical school and is unhappy, less because he doesn't want to be a doctor than because of the terrific pressure on him to succeed.

The immigrant generation learned English to varying degrees. Justin and Appolonia learned mostly from their sons. Also, when Justin was fifteen, he attended the second grade of school one year to learn English. The poor English proficiency in immigrant parents of two other families accounts for their children's relative proficiency in French, without injuring the children's competence in English. LeRoy's poor French is a consequence of living with his English-speaking mother. Jean understands much French as his mother has spoken this to him during most of his life, but now he hates the sound of it, refuses to answer in French, and wishes his mother "wouldn't do that."

[Family pressures were dramatized by sketching the personalities.] Justin was a tyrant, Appolonia and the boys little more than slaves. Appolonia's role was to bear children and keep house, then work in the fields when she wasn't busy with the first two obligations. For the boys there was nothing but work and study. Justin provided well for the family's material needs, but completely neglected their emotional needs. There were never picnics, trips, other family entertainment, or even after-supper conversations among the family. The home was not happy. The boys were very fond of their mother but towards their father, feelings often reached the point of hate.

[The account ended with a summary.] There are four main areas of change among these families. The areas are marriage, ocupation, education, and language proficiency. Changes are discernible in each family and generation. Succeeding generations become less traditionally French in marriage and language. They acquire more schooling, their occupations leave the soil and become diversified; these widen their social contacts, they speak English more and neglect French.

In these areas of change, different degrees of change are also discernible. These seem to be linked to a family "personality" or ethos, by which I mean the family atmosphere of relative happiness and closeness. Justin's family shows the greatest degree of change, or Americanization. To his hard-driven boys, "the French way" became synonymous with "the old Man's way" and so was to be avoided.

A widowed elementary-school principal wrote exuberantly of her Scandinavian-American family in Wisconsin, producing a paean to domestic love, stability, and prosperity. "In both the maternal and paternal families," she said, "authority lodged in the father but the goals and means were different. The paternal grandfather exerted quiet, firm pressure; his wife was the mouthpiece. From earliest years, his children conformed. My father felt this strongly and practiced similar ways. There were no harshly spoken directives, but a quiet implying and sensing of direction. Grandfather was a man more of deeds than words; his most effective tool was silence. My father also attained control through directed silence. Silence did not mean consent. My realizations of when to act, and when not to, reflected my father's behavior and his silence or voiced encouragement. He never said no. He never had to. We all knew."

Her maternal grandfather, she said, exerted authority by voice and act, and his wife, fully trained in voiced directives by her father, without kind overtones, understood and accepted her husband's authority. The grandfather did not hesitate to raise his voice. His conduct was above reproach but it included an amount of "do as I say rather than as I do." Children of this line could divert from authority because of their trust in words; that is, they could discuss matters. The paternal line, in contrast, lacked such recourse. Relying on nearly absolute silence the children had no mode of response permitting choice or disagreement.

The principal felt the influence of both family lines. "I could talk to my mother," she said, "but if she felt that my father might uphold her against me, she would say, 'Ask your father.' That was the end of the line; I knew what to expect, though my father was less rigid than *his* father in that he permitted some discussion. I cannot locate the boundary between strict authority and some freedom in my parents' home. I was never terribly afraid. I was confident of the chance for some discussion leading to a calm decision.

"Each family line defined its own goals. The paternal goal was 'a good life,' that is, wealth sufficient for needs but not necessarily more. Most members wanted approval and acceptance. Social status had no great value but unpopularity implied social failure. A 'good life' required conformity to patterned behavior of the class and region, including the standard religious beliefs.

"The maternal family valued land highly, and monetary worth, and cultivation of talents. This meant emphasis on education. The maternal grandmother often said, 'It is nice if you never have to do these things, but it's wonderful to know how if you need to.' So the children were given every opportunity to be prepared for life's demands."

Relatives neighbored one another over a great extent of land, the principal related. Each family had to succeed on its own and contribute to the community by its talents and by returning the body of each deceased member for embalming and burial in the family cemetery. Each bride received a dowry; each deceased received a burial casket—of copper or wood and concrete for a woman, of steel and concrete for a man, materials supposed to defy extinction. At a death there was to be no weeping and also no remarriage. She had supposed these modes of burial and mourning to be general. She felt committed to support all her family traditions. At the time of writing about them she was feeling obligation to return as a teacher to the ancestral community.

She concluded her account: "Mother's family influenced my father greatly. His primary goals remained the same but he also followed his wife's people in acquiring more land, money, prestige in the local community, county, and state than did any of his own family. My mother strongly encouraged him in the goals he adopted from her family.

"I also am continually adding new goals to my life. It is an ever upward struggle and I always question my ability, in the spirit of my paternal line. However, if all one needs are determination and effort, I have not a doubt of succeeding, in the spirit of my maternal line."

A quiet, young teacher described his family culture with details more unusual, even exotic, than are ordinarily attributed to the middle-class public schoolman:

My maternal grandfather, Jacob, was born in Saratdorf, Germany, the youngest of a large family. He appeared to have been the black sheep, leaving home at an early age, traveling around Europe and ending up in Turkey. There he fell in with a band of raiders. When the raiders heard of caravans traveling the desert, they would intercept them, take the goods and sell them in the markets of some Turkish town. After about a year Jacob fell out with the Turks and fled for his life to Siberia. There he brawled and gambled until he met my grandmother.

My maternal grandmother was also born in Germany, in an unknown town. Her parents died when she was very young and she was sent to an aunt and uncle in Siberia. There her aunt made her do the hardest and most distasteful chores. She told me of the times she carried the wash down to the river for scrubbing; there she exchanged gossip and news of friends and relatives.

When girls reached the age of marriage it was then customary to have them seated at a window sewing or quilting until they were noticed as attractive by young men. An interested young man would follow up by approaching the parents to discuss marriage.

When my grandparents were married they moved around Siberia considerably, having inherited a small sum of money. They had four children in quick succession. In 1905 they sailed for the United States on the ship *Missler.* Jacob worked as a farm hand in Colorado, bought farm machinery and land, and they produced six more children. The Depression wiped Jacob out. Now bankrupt, he and the family worked in fruit fields and canneries until he had paid all his debts. Then grandfather again worked as a field hand and turned religious until death . . .

My paternal greatgrandfather was born in Aleksanderthal, Russia, a small village of German descendants. After marrying and having eight children, my greatgrandfather came to the United States in 1893. He worked as a railroad section hand in New Jersey, traveled as far west as Wilson, Kansas, then returned to Russia. There my grandfather grew up and married, sailing to the United States in 1901 with his wife and baby daughter.

Working as a section hand on the railroad, he moved his family to Colorado where all worked as farm hands until he staked dry claims to 640 acres of land and acquired other holdings. In 1921 a flood wiped them out. They left to work on California fruit farms and in canneries.

My father was a farm hand until 1941 when he worked at an air force base until after the War. Then he entered a factory. . . . I was the eldest son. I completed college and my two years of military service, I married and now have a year-old son . . .

The goals of my family, like those of all living from the land, contained the quality of hard work. My father would tell me, "Do the job well the first time so it will not have to be done again." He also said, "For an honest dollar, you must give an honest dollar's work." Actions of my grandparents spoke these points louder than any words.

I believe my father never gave less than the very best to his employers. He worked hard days, and nights he brought home study manuals so as to become even better at his job.

My grandparents and parents believed that hard work would raise us to the middle class. My own goals were to go to college and to become a schoolteacher. Now I have raised them to cover further study and my ambition is to be a *good* teacher. This means hard work in our constantly changing world, but I am extremely satisfied. I enjoy working with students and helping them in their problems.

[Having established the family creed of honest, hard work, he described Americanization in his family.] In Europe, the eldest male of the whole family was the leader. Others obeyed his orders even when the younger men had families. With time in the United States, my family lost some of these ways, and the head of each separate family took control. This lessened authority of parents over grown sons. But my father long continued absolute in his family and would swing from extreme severity to indulgence.

I am less absolute than my father was. I share responsibilities with my wife. Also I find that my parents now share in making their decisions, noticeably more than during my younger days. When our children are old enough to understand rules, I feel that my wife and I should be democratic about establishing rules. Until then, my wife and I will carry out the duties of punishment less severely than in my childhood, for I still resent authority that has not proven itself, such as my father exercised . . .

My family expected me to be polite and respectful to all my elders. My family taught me about race prejudice. Probably they did it in the reverse of the usual way. In their time, they had been discriminated against as Germans, as had their parents during the First World War. So they would tell me I was as good as anyone. I personally experienced no difficulty but their advice made me aware of racial problems. I came from a town with many Mexicans, where whites opposed Mexicans in snowball fights, soccer games, and otherwise. I remember telling myself, "They're as good as I am" but I went along with the crowd.

My father also stressed my responsibility to admit when I was wrong. Once I threw a rock and hit a friend, so my father ordered, "Go over and say you're sorry." I answered, "Why? Nobody ever does that to me." He insisted, "When a man is wrong, he should always admit it, no matter how it hurts." So I said I was sorry, and from then on tried to make sure I was never in that situation again.

[The elder generations' views of respect, authority, obedience, and integrity included] keeping the family together. My father's father gave each son a portion of land, from his own lands or adjoining ones, to keep the sons from scattering. But when he lost his lands in the 1921 flood, the children sought employment elsewhere and scattered far and wide.

The older generations also took care of their aged. But I would not want my children to support me and my wife. Children feel, as I did, that they must escape parental authority, move away to where they can be free. The same is true of religion. After a rather carefree youth, my maternal grandfather repented and joined the German Congregational Church. My parents were brought up in this church, hearing sermons in German. My grandparents expected everyone to follow their religion and repentance. This somewhat alienated my parents and now I hardly ever attend church without thinking of my grandparents' extreme conduct.

I am the only one in four generations of my family with a high-school education and more. But the story is not ended, for there is no ending while the family exists.

Showing major similarities in social forms and conduct to this German-Russian-American account is the brief description given by a young junior high-school counselor, of Pennsylvania Dutch or German-American antecedents. The social design outlined accompanies these families tenaciously even on far-flung travels, as was shown later by German-American Lutherans long settled in the French Catholic stronghold of New Orleans. The counselor wrote that arbitrarily starting with the birth of his greatgrandparents in Missouri, about 1840, "the husband was the final authority. In the parents' generation there was a shift towards more equal cooperation. My own generation shows equal status of husband and wife in family affairs. For the first time, wife and mother work out of the home and experience new satisfactions.

"Formal education reaches higher levels. Grandparents could not have gone beyond the eighth grade, nor did mother. Father finished college, and children continue into graduate study. Women are now expected to have completed high school and to aspire further.

"Religious emphasis is not on church attendance but on total behavior and thought, equated with democracy and with the family's interpretation of the American way. Religious education comes through the church organization rather than through family devotions.

"Family members are no longer close bound, owing to geographical distances. Grandparents and their brothers and sisters reared families within fifty miles of one another, exerting strong reciprocal influences. In the maternal line, parents followed children across the country, keeping the close ties. Ability or readiness of parents to move such distances marks change from the previous generation, to whom a move of one hundred miles seemed impossible. But many obligations persist as taught by older generations. For example, care of older family members is considered necessary; neglect of them is unthinkable. The needs of parents are heeded readily."

A young Greek-American teacher, who had heard no English before entering public school, described the midwestern settlement of Greek immigrants that included his parents:

Over the past half-century the small Greek minority tried to preserve traditions. Families have lived together in great intimacy and know each other only too well. The second generation finds it most difficult to marry within this compact unit. Most have married into other Greek communities of the region.

The immigrants of our community were welded together by the same social and economic forces, the same language, religion, and customs. Their peasant forefathers had lived very frugally, and the immigrants lived similarly. They did not speculate in their American businesses, but expanded slowly. Their personal lives were not spectacular, they did not try to keep up with the Joneses nor make the society columns. Comforts in the Anglo-American home were considered extravagances in the Greek home. Our Greeks' first goals were not a new car, new refrigerator, new furniture, or a new house; but rather money for security, the children's education, elevated status, and strengthened identity with the Greek heritage. These four were life's important goals.

Greek culture affected every phase of existence. Within the home, only Greek was spoken; some of the second generation heard English first at grade school. At table, the food was predominantly Greek. Records of Greek music and folk dances often preceded knowledge of American music and dance. *Atlantis*, the Greek-American newspaper, appeared in every home. New Year's Eve, Apokreas or Carnival, Easter, and name days were all festive occasions for the entire group.

Many of these people were vaguely aware of their great heritage. They had heard of Plato, Xenophon, Aristophanes, and Euripides, but had not read them or otherwise understood them. They had been told stories from the *Iliad* and *Odyssey* without distinguishing whether they were history or legend. Though sharply aware of their language, they were vague about Greek civilization's great ideas. They were cognizant of the world's admiration for Greece's past. Therefore why should they embrace all ideas and practices of the adopted land? They sat reluctantly, waiting and observing . . .

The dozen or so boys who went to war in World War II returned as men. For the first time they had been exposed to completely American surroundings. This second generation now took responsible parts in Greek community affairs. English replaced Greek at all formal meetings, including meetings of the church council, and in the recording of minutes. The younger generation moved into occupations and professions where the elders could not counsel or interfere.

Although today only a few of the immigrants remain, their opinions are heard and rarely opposed vocally. At all social gatherings these men are the first seated, served, and recognized. Sons still ask permission of their fathers to marry and seldom enter marriage without parents' approval. Families are formally introduced when their offspring wish to date. When possible, families contribute materially to establish the newlyweds. The whole community dances at weddings.

Most of the second generation marry in their late twenties. Many marry other Greek-Americans, but some do not, against great parental objection and family heartache. Such pressures often force these young people to leave for other parts. Today a number remain unmarried, victims of rigid tradition, searching for ideals combining their hearts' wishes and their parents' dictates. The marriage barrier crumbles slowly. A few of the elders accept American in-laws. The degree of acceptance seems to depend on the Americans' understanding and tolerance of traditional Greek society, customs, and authoritative elders.

The daily life of second-generation Greek-Americans blends the traditions. Greek is spoken in the presence of elders. American food is served as often as Greek. Gala parties and religious festivals are fewer and less gay. The priest is American born; sermons and Sunday school are in English. An annual formal ball, including Greek folk dances as intermissions, has been started by youth groups. The city's chamber of commerce sponsors "Greek Week," importing a professor of classical Greek to discuss the Greek theatre and also programming youth groups to demonstrate traditional dances, foods, and dress.

More of the youth devote time to play, doing it outside the Greek community, than did their older brothers who had to work in family businesses at comparable ages. However, grandchildren, no longer understanding or speaking Greek, are still named traditionally after grandparents; popular songs of Greece are collected on stereo; youth groups study classical Greek literature, and whole families make pilgrimages to Greece.

The era of the elders is ending, but the second generation will carry on the community. There is no ending. Time and the community move on, heedless that the first immigrants had planned to return home to Greece with enough American dollars to buy a farm and start a family there. Today, most of the city's Greek population is middle class and self-employed; there are a few millionaires. No members were ever on a relief roll, there has never been a juvenile delinquent, and there is almost no divorce.

The last illustration of work in family cultures presents our dominant group—the white Anglo-Saxon Protestants of good repute and colonial or American Revolutionary origins. These dominant families are our traditional measure of social accomplishment. The family record to be summarized was assembled during months of effort by a young man teaching high school. The genealogical zeal of successive generations produced oral and printed histories of member families, accounting for every person in lineal and collateral branches. Wherever these kinsmen wandered, they kept in touch. Men and women of the member families contributed actively to their times, founding a university, a major industry, a church, a political movement, having careers in learned professions, in industries, legislatures, judiciaries, commerce, governmental administration, and the military. If the kinsmen had not privately kept in touch, they would have known one another's circumstances through public news and monuments. The student records that none in the family was reputed wealthy, though "comfortably well off"; and none was a social snob, because "the spirit of public service persists through the generations." Some women of earlier times were called "bluestockings" because they taught in university and high school; they were also "such perfect ladies, very formal, sweet and proper."

In the grandparents' generation, a number of men and women failed to marry. Like the bluestockings, "many of the girls educated themselves out of the possibility of marriage; while the men were so committed to public service that they may have lacked the time to get married! Branches of the family tree disappear without male descendants. Thank goodness, my father eventually married to perpetuate the name. He was also the first of his name to leave the Middle West permanently," where ancestors had founded the university and kinsmen still study.

There were no evidences of black sheep. The student's father attributed this to "a solid church background in all generations and to being surrounded by many relatives living within a small geographical range. I am sure this extensive world of my forebears and living relatives, always present in my background, must have weighed on me tremendously as a great debt needing payment, or as a great reputation needing to be sustained, or as a heritage to be fulfilled. Nobody ever said this in so many words. It must have come to me when I was too young even to understand words. It must have been conveyed in attitudes, expressions, and family recollections of dozens of aunts and uncles, great-aunts and great-uncles, and other relatives."

Family records noted that the ancestors migrated "originally from Scotland. In defense of their Presbyterian religion, many fled to northern Ireland in the seventeenth century. Even here they suffered 'civil and religious oppression,' according to the family history, and hence, many moved to America." Aristocracy was not this family's boast, but in America the student's greatgreatgrandfather, a greatgrandson of a Virginia settler, became damned as "that — aristocrat" by those opposing his demands for public education.

The student observed that "the importance of being able to trace the family back to the first American settlers seems to have overwhelmed earlier generations of our family. Our [printed] history is loaded with references to various relatives accepted for membership in the DAR or the Colonial Dames. This seems to have little merit for the present generation." What mattered rather was that the young man, like his predecessors, should earn a living at something he enjoyed. "Accidentally I fell into teaching, after journalism, advertising, radio broadcasting, and management. In this I am happy. I just want to be a teacher! New cars, a big and flashy home, the finest of clothes have *not* been among my goals. The home, car, and clothes we have are fewer and older than those of anybody else I grew up with.

"What we have are four wonderful children. If I sound conservative, I cannot ignore the fact that through all my gentle radicalism goes a paternal strain of conservative Scot and a maternal strain of conservative New England. My radicalism has always been within close bounds."

In this student's long, detailed, and chart-enriched account, expressing an exuberant love of kin—people living and dead—and of the world they patterned, shared, and carefully transmitted, there is a high sense of the family's strong social position. There is not one mention of the great minorities struggling through American history. One would never guess that fateful national issues rested on special social uses of different races, creeds, classes, and nationalities. This omission, no less than the affirmed "spirit of public service," marks a dominant group who, in the words of an English aristocrat, "never meets anyone else." Yet the recorder of this family had been in the American Army during the Second World War. He served a little over three years, of which a year or so was spent in India. "There was nothing I liked about it except that I was smart enough—three cheers for my ancestors!—to qualify for the Army's college program and so spent six happy months at the university. And there I met the girl I later married."

The student concluded: "I am proud of my forebears, full of a sense of obligation not to let them down, filled by the duty to pass their heritage on to my son. Our family's insistence upon quality in all work, upon devotion to doing the best always, have been practiced and communicated down the generations. My father said that these traits characterized every relative he knew."

All accounts show that pride of family and its ways is not confined to special students, traditions, or families—it is universal. It seems to be an aspect of the psychic quality we call morale, which persuades human beings to go on with the hard business of living, perpetuating, and creating. The concept of the family-style of life—its hereditary patterns taught, enacted as life, and transmitted down generations, even centuries—seems to exalt every student's awareness of himself and even of others. Through the systematic communications with persons of his lineage and about them, at distances that lighten pressures and allow conceptualization, the student feels ennobled by an active sense that the family's tradition is his property, and that he holds it as a precious trust. This feeling surprised most students, as a discovery, though it usually did not surprise their kinsmen of older generations.

Perhaps the discovery is surprising only to this century in America, to our epoch of rising social equalities, elevating children of every humble origin, leveling every social diversity to produce a surface of anonymous Americanism. Our creed of Americanism today holds no grand reference to family life but incentives to self-reliant individualism on the one hand, and to joining the army of organization men on the other.

A consequence of the students' work was each one's sudden conviction, by empathy, that the minorities also, even under grinding poverty and humiliation, share similar commitments to their ancestors' traditional past and its future. Occasional Negroes, Mexicans, and others who agreed to serve as informants, made it clear that their families also boasted of great persons, achievements, and standards within their own cultural and social realms, even when the group was denigrated by the dominant middle class. Greatness does not rule out meanness in any group, but, on the other hand, its mean status does not erase the group's conviction of worth. And the students found their conviction justified in the minorities' family cultures, whose designs and details captured their imaginations. For these students, the stereotypes about minorities now proved insufficient, and minority persons of all ages and positions became interesting, comprehensible, and worthy fellow humans.

Through all projects a fresh style of thinking was encouraged: to expect tremendous cultural variety in American populations, to ask the meanings of behavior in terms of ancestral family and community traditions, to listen and observe, to question formalistic or stereotyped judgments (like "retarded" or "unmotivated" pupil), and to search for the creativity in each child which might be masked by the educator's own cultural and professional (called at times "subcultural") predilections and by the child's culturally conditioned or class-conditioned disorientation at school. Students were urged to keep abreast of our revolutionary social changes by reading widely outside of their professional publications, by searching the news media for signposts, and by reading creative writing for invaluable information about man's ways. Conscientious and highly disciplined as a professional group, and considerably overworked by extra tasks, educators had to be urged to trust themselves to look beyond their usual limits. And they did. Some went to extraordinary lengths, as when two women studied a ponderous work on cultural theory and presented a condensation of it as an educators' manual. All took intellectual and professional pleasure in understanding culture's operations affecting schools, including biases of each one's cultural nature, manifest in teacher, pupil, parent, and community.

Notes

1. See before, Chapter 4.
2. See before, Chapters 3, 4, 5.
3. See before, Chapter 4.
4. From the *Los Angeles Herald-Examiner*, August 8, 1962. The *New York Times*, July 22, 1962, states: "According to estimates of the Bureau of the Census, California's population is expected to burgeon from 16,000,000 at present to about 21,000,000 by 1970. This will be almost double the rate of expansion projected for the United States as a whole . . ." The part of natural increase in this forecast may be surmised from this statement, printed by *Newsweek*, August 13, 1962, as a letter written by Becky Holmes: ". . . in Cleveland, Ohio, the Maternal Health Association reports that our inner cities are reproducing faster than India or China."
5. This report is mentioned before, p. 19. The young Mexican-American protested earnestly, "I'm proud to be a high-school teacher. Maybe because it shows how far I've progressed beyond my illiterate parents." An Anglo colleague said that teachers face a brighter outlook in the disappearance of "spinsters," whose earlier preponderance in teaching explained the profession's historically low status. Teachers often express satisfaction with the growing numbers of young men entering education.
6. Each student wrote reports knowing that the work would be used in this book, as a source for understanding cultural factors in education. The students agreed to this use generously. All reports are edited and condensed by Ruth Landes. Usually local and personal identifications are changed or omitted.
7. This is mentioned p. 87, before.
8. This is mentioned p. 87, before.
9. In this connection it is useful to consider Stuart Chase, *American Credos* (New York: Harper and Brothers, 1962), pp. 196, 134–136:

> Three out of five adult Americans in a recent study admitted that they had not read any book—except possibly the Bible—during the previous year. Comparative surveys show Britons reading three times as many books per person as Americans; Germans and Australians twice as many; Canadians almost twice as many. Compared with the time the average American spends before his television set, the time he spends reading books is miniscule . . .
>
> . . . American teen-agers [are] not precisely bookworms . . . [A] study found that more than half U. S. citizens lived within a mile of a public library but only 20 per cent of these had entered its door during the previous year . . .
>
> Roper, in 1950, found 18 per cent of adults who claimed to be currently reading a book of any kind, even a cookbook. The figure is probably too high, since many Americans call a magazine a "book." Another 18 per cent said that they had *never* read a book that was not required for school or business. "Book reading has little status in the U. S. unless it is job-connected." . . .
>
> . . . 15 per cent of college students draw no books at all from the library in a given academic year.

Allan Nevins, *The State Universities and Democracy* (Urbana: University of Illinois Press, 1962), p. 6, quotes Charles W. Eliot of Harvard: "When I asked in the Medical Faculty in 1870 if it would be possible to substitute an hour's written examination for the five minutes' oral examination . . . the answer came promptly from the Head of the Faculty: 'Written examinations are impossible in the Medical School. A majority of the students cannot write well enough.' "

But Nevins cautions, pp. 130–131, ". . . no trustworthy means exists for determining which students are exceptional, which average, and which dull . . . (Besides retardation) by environment, or by inner repressions . . . talent depends on relationships, and a man dull in one context may be brilliant in another. . . . (Furthermore) from the home of the dullard may come the supremely gifted, as from Thomas Lincoln's cabin came Abraham Lincoln. It will make a difference if the Thomas Lincolns have been given their full chance . . . In this hazardous zone the trustees of the Carnegie Corporation, acting with (presidents of six universities) . . . have offered a set of cautionary rules. Their first injunction is that the diagnosis of a youngster's abilities should ideally be a process continued over long years. . . . The second rule is that appraisals should be founded on many kinds of tests . . . In addition, full weight must be given to what modern pedagogues call motivation and our grandfathers called earnestness . . ."

10. This program is discussed before, pp. 56, 227, and Chapter 3, n. 28, Chapter 5, n. 18.

11. Further discussion of this teacher's work and the implications for education are in Ruth Landes, chapter on "Culture and Education" in George F. Kneller (ed.), *Foundations of Education* (New York: John Wiley and Sons, 1963). This teacher's work is also described by Marianne Wolman, "Cultural Factors and Creativity," *Journal of Secondary Education*, December 1962, pp. 454–460.

12. The teacher is Mrs. Herman G. Stromberger, living in Pasadena, California. The success of these two teachers with Shakespeare and other classics contrasts with the complaint on p. 33, "Does the school culture oppose Shakespeare?" Here we may be encountering unfamiliar emotional elements in creativity and the effectiveness of pupils' self-expression over the more passive functions of reading and listening to others lecture and recite.

13. John C. Lilly, *Man and Dolphin* (New York: Doubleday and Co., 1961. Copyright © 1961 by John C. Lilly. Reprinted by permission of Doubleday and Co., Inc.) makes observations pertinent to culture and education. Thus, p. 108, ". . . to understand man, we must investigate what a particular individual has in his mind rather than presuming that he has a prescribed set of ideas." His discussion of his experimental communication with dolphins illuminates educators' problems with pupils of estranged social groups and other cultures. Thus, to give dolphins "the same chance that we would give a human child to learn our language and ways, we must modify our own behavior and meet them at least halfway in their own medium . . ." (122) ". . . [A] continuous verbal barrage is necessary if the young human is to learn the speech of his species." (123) "The essence of taming is changing an anxiety-provoking situation to a reward-producing situation: the same situation is changed in its motivational value to the animal by means of learning." (169) After an experimental dolphin "had heard only human voices for several

weeks, his vocalization began to be less 'dolphinese' and to break up into more humanoid, wordlike explosive bursts . . . [despite] a vocal apparatus quite different from ours." (178–179) For a child to learn to speak, he "must be exposed to effective language experiences in an environment presenting simultaneously several things: (a) language packets in the proper media, (b) personal rewards and personal punishments contingent on the proper use of these packets, (c) examples of other similar individuals exchanging rewards and punishments with proper accompanying packets. A child must be rewarded for making attempts to speak so that he will repeat the experiments of speaking. . . . [A] young human being or other young animal with the obvious prerequisites for intellect needs proper living conditions for well-being . . . [If] he is put in conditions on the very edge of survival he is so busy with survival necessities that there is relatively little chance of acquiring additional language . . . except on a very primitive level." (269–270) Taming, or learning life with humans, requires "chronic and continuous contact with human beings . . . Among humans, this procedure is known to produce extremely rapid learning in certain controlled directions. It is commonly used in education, in brainwashing, and in psychotherapy . . ." (170)

8

Summing Up

The purpose of the Claremont project for educators [1] and the program for social workers was to promote efficiency in achieving professional goals by applying cultural knowledge to problems arising in schooling and welfare. As the work of indoctrinating and applying anthropological concepts and methods developed, it stressed theory and modes of confronting students with evidences of human nature as shaped by culture. The evidences included the human nature in themselves and in any others, in the dominant middle class and in the submerged minorities—in all peoples anywhere. This approach stressed the view that all peoples live in a universe of *meanings* which are of the same generalized sociocultural order but cast in different tongues. The key to this universe is knowledge of the local cultures that embody the local meanings, including knowledge of the languages spoken.

California today is a laboratory of man's social and cultural varieties. They exploded upon the social horizon with the Second World War and the tremendous industrial and commercial complexes that developed. Riches came to California with war industries, including those devoted to electronic missiles and space equipment. Migrants came in waves from all quarters to partake of the Southwest's fine climate during the Great Depression of the 1930's; their numbers accelerated with the Second World War and its train of full employment. They brought firm and clashing ideas about living customs,[2] notably those about social rank, race discrimination, and civil liberties. California's peoples are also evolving a local ethos that fosters great freedom in the forms of opportunities and dignity for all. Old discriminations, presently condemned by judicial decisions at all levels of authority and by federal and other legislation, are also being

284

attacked by California's state and local legislation. Carried on such tides of progressive thought and action, educators and others studied at Claremont how to discharge their duties among the subcultural sectors in ways respectful of them and supportive of public education. Similar things are happening in New York, which California now paces in population, riches, and social complexity.

Training in the anthropological discipline seemed to assure teachers and others that, despite the highly fluid, changing fronts of California society, there are behavioral constants on which to rely. These are the traditional practices in each and every group that await the sharpened eye. The first problem for educators was to identify the practices, the next was to decipher them through obfuscations of ignorance and prejudicial stereotypes, the third was to employ them for the best gains of all parties. This required the investigator to shelve his professional ego in favor of the problem, usually concretized as pupil or client, but more properly to be regarded as the *relationship* between the investigator (in his professional capacity of teacher, social worker, physician, or police officer) and the pupil or client.

Teachers learned that the constants—such as modes of effecting parental authority or male superiority—usually appeared as dissimilar customs in the different groups, whether the groups are ancient ethnic ones, regional ones, or those of class such as are found in most societies outside the United States. Teachers learned how to interpret the dissimilar appearances both in their native context and in the context of middle-class America; and they learned how to adapt some of them for use in school programs, undertaking translations, as it were, from middle-class norms into subcultural ones, and back again. They reached the fundamental understanding that customs channel human energies, and that the direct way to tap a people's energies is through their group customs. They saw that a people's customs are interrelated systematically, so that action upon one custom, such as sending once-cloistered girls to school on an equal basis with boys, sends reverberations through other enmeshed customs of the system, as when coeducation seems to loosen male authority over daughters, wives, and sisters among Mexican-Americans.

An incidental consequence, which teachers and others remarked on, was the changes in these education and welfare students' own habitual ways. Many had started out with the widespread American inclination to condemn and resent the differences of others. Anthropological insights eased fears about the different, newly desegregated groups and undermined fixed ideas about minority traits such as race and language. Students learned the usefulness of focusing on cultural variety for itself alone when they charted customs and tested inferences. They realized that customs that are relatively different are to be examined with equal seriousness, since they are norms for people trained in them; the effect is consistent with our American tradition of civil liberties. The broadening of ideas accompanied increases in professional confidence.

Students were advised to distinguish between their job standards and their personal sentiments with respect to race prejudice, in view of the state's considerable legislation against discrimination. That is, racist preferences could be expressed only in private life, where presumably they were learned, but never on the job. Many people thought that the officially condemned racist ideas and language were "the truth" and had no idea, often, that they were offending. The distinction was offered partly to indicate that students could relax their new discipline at home if they felt they had to. Actually, however, the study and the new professional experiences influenced private conduct. So here again educators saw how it was that a pupil's career at school is involved with experiences outside.

The teachers had been trained to work in the school system's routine channels, always expecting supervision. Now they were advised that, in explorations of culture and its involvement with learning, no observation was wrong and no method poor if it was instructive. This experimental approach applied to the main end of adapting cultural knowledge to schoolteaching. Accordingly, the most unpromising or aberrant pupil, or the most backward minority could be a source of useful knowledge. Thus, concepts and methods were used to test and amplify one another in studying society, culture, personality, and learning.

When the applied knowledge, or even hunches about culture, made difficult pupils manageable, it was important. If particular changes in behavior of pupils and parents was indeed referable to particular culture signals, the teachers felt they had an answer to "frustrations" over the stupidities of pupils and their own professional inadequacies. Teachers also came to see that the panic in their frustrations roused echoes in problem pupils, a learning about panic that might be turned into a better course. It followed that if panic was contagious, that is, learned, then poise too could be learned from teachers.

The study materials selected were not standard anthropological ones, for these deal largely with preliterate peoples and are intended for scholars. Instead, the materials were assembled and adapted largely from the California scene,[3] which concerned educators and welfare workers directly. The wide ethnic range in California offers opportunity for comparisons, on which anthropological methods and insights rest.

Not every area of anthropological scholarship is directly useful to educators and other practical professions. The Claremont project and the social work program stressed comparative study of the family in different cultures; study of schooling, health care, and other institutionalized activities in diverse culture settings; study of teaching and learning generally in different cultures among native born and among immigrants; and study of relationships among race, culture, and language. Educators were led to postpone asking *why* a behavior occurs until after they could answer operational questions of *how*, *when*, *where*, and through *whom* the behavior occurs, and toward *what* ends. This is because when asked initially, *why* often begs issues with stereotypes.

The cultural approach to teaching stressed the mental gifts and social inheritances of human groups above their physical or racial semblances. The attribute of "minority" was tied rigorously to socio-political status, not to race, culture, language, or population figures. A minority status isolates occupants socially from the dominant mode of life, to a greater or lesser degree, and this was shown to favor persistence or development of minority "subcultures" or of traits and deficiencies that diverge from the high-ranked practices, especially among the poor and illiterate.[4] Educators, including those of minority origins, described themselves as of dominant and middle-class status, or occasionally of upper class. Some ascribed this rank and its culture to themselves because of their profession and its salary bracket, others because of their position as public officials.

Educators came to view the culture discipline as one offering tools for the dominant group's penetration of other cultures and minorities, in a necessary war against behavior that defies schooling. Of course, interpenetration or commingling of traditions is as old as human contacts. Lord Frederick Lugard, distinguished governor of former British Nigeria, early in this century, polished his country's application of cultural knowledge to colonial administration into the philosophy he called "indirect rule"; accordingly, Lugard had tribesmen educated in British modes of government. At Claremont, methods of intercultural penetration were studied deliberately to advance teaching in desegregated and integrated schools.

Teachers took from the culture discipline broader expectations of themselves on their jobs, including obligations to the families and neighborhoods shaping pupils' lives. It was understood, however, that real effectiveness required entire school systems to join such efforts. Families and neighborhoods were recognized as root sources of life meanings for all individuals and groups—including educators.

The Claremont project shows, as does New York City's Higher Horizons program,[5] that public teaching must reckon with culture's dimensions if culturally mixed parties are to learn the required behavior and are to develop personal integrity. The project showed, on its very small scale, that a reliable sense for cultural phenomena requires supervised experience. Perhaps in the future there will be field interneships, such as Mexico has required of medical graduates, sending them to tribal hinterlands. Many folk and great traditions will yield to our mechanized age and universal literacy, as they have before to conquering civilizations, but principles of cultural existence will persist.

Notes

1. Claremont College's Education faculty, initiating the project, wrote in their draft of being "stimulated" to do so "in part by the ideas presented in" George D. Spindler (ed.), *Education and Anthropology* (Stanford: Stanford University Press, 1955). This book consists of papers and discussions from a conference of educators and anthropologists.
2. Ruth Benedict called custom the "laboratory of Culture."
3. Besides materials in the preceding pages, see the appendices.
4. In her celebrated book, *A Room of One's Own* (New York: Harcourt, Brace and Company, 1929), Virginia Woolf discusses the complete dependence of a great writing tradition on social opportunity. Addressing the women's colleges of Oxford University, she attributes the dearth of great women writers in England to Englishwomen's traditionally low positions until the twentieth century. Showing that Englishmen produced great writers through social position, she quotes, pp. 186–188, a paragraph from *The Art of Writing* by Sir Arthur Quiller-Couch, then Professor of Literature at Oxford:

   What are the great poetical names of the last hundred years or so? Coleridge, Wordsworth, Byron, Shelley, Landor, Keats, Tennyson, Browning, Arnold, Morris, Rossetti, Swinburne—we may stop there. Of these, all but Keats, Browning, Rossetti were University men; and of these three, Keats, who died young, cut off in his prime, was the only one not fairly well to do. It may seem a brutal thing to say, and it is a sad thing to say; but as a matter of hard fact, the theory that poetical genius bloweth where it listeth, and equally in poor and rich, holds little truth. As a matter of hard fact, nine out of those twelve men were University men: which means that somehow or other they procured the means to get the best education England can give. As a matter of hard fact, of the remaining three you know that Browning was well to do, and I challenge you that, if he had not been well to do, he would no more have attained to write *Saul* or *The Ring and the Book* than Ruskin would have attained to writing *Modern Painters* if his father had not dealt prosperously in business. Rossetti had a small private income; and moreover, he painted. There remains but Keats; whom Atropos slew young, as she slew John Clare in a mad-house; and James Thomson by the laudanum he took to drug disappointment. These are dreadful facts, but let us face them. It is— however dishonoring to us as a nation—certain that, by some fault in our commonwealth, the poor poet has not in these days, nor has had for 200 years, a dog's chance. Believe me—and I have spent a great part of ten years in watching some 320 elementary schools—we may prate of democracy, but actually, a poor child in England has little more hope than had the son of an Athenian slave to be emancipated into that intellectual freedom of which great writings are born.

Time magazine, November 21, 1960, quotes Dr. Horace Mann Bond's research findings that in rich suburbs 25 per cent of all pupils score an I.Q. rating of 125 and over; in poor areas only 6 per cent score so. The slum I.Q. falls with rising age because of poor exposure to books, conversation and material things.

5. See *Toward Greater Opportunity. A Progress Report* from the Superintendent of Schools to the Board of Education dealing with Implementation of Recommendations of the Commission on Integration. (New York: Board of Education of the City of New York, June 1960.)

See also *The Open Enrollment Program in the Elementary Schools. Progress Report*. School Year 1960–1961. Division of Elementary Schools. New York City: Board of Education, City of New York.)

See also (mimeographed) *Annual Report* 1960–1961, Board of Education, New York City, Central Zoning Unit.

Appendix 1

The Mexican-American Family

This appendix outlines aspects of Mexican-American life in California and the Southwest. The knowledge has been found useful by educators, social workers, public health officers, and police. The outline interprets the writer's own research, amplifying observations made earlier in the book. The bibliography given here supplements the previous references.

Social History [1]

Segregation and other unfair demonstrations of community prejudice inflict constant arbitrary punishment. The practices of any minority or segregated group include defensive and aggressive responses to this behavior. These responses are diverse—public conformity and disguise, civil rights programs, a special language, youth gangs, police violations. Otherwise, the cultural backgrounds of the great minorities vary widely. It is obvious that nothing much can be learned about, say, Jews from observing, say, Mexicans, or others of a special traditional nature. The distinct cultural heritage of each minority must be studied before we may understand how this influences relationships with the larger American community.

Mexicans possess a distinctive physical type and an ancestral culture. American federal and state legislation classifies the Mexican

291

people physically as white or Caucasian. Anthropology classifies them as a stabilized blend or subrace of varied American Indian types mixed chiefly with Spaniards and also with small proportions of other European stocks and with some Negro stocks. The culture too is a Hispanic Amerindian blend, in regional variations. The ancestral language is Spanish, but Indian tongues persist in Mexico's interior. The historic religion is Roman Catholic, incorporating elements from Mexico's and New Spain's native tribal religions, but some 10 per cent of the population is said, unofficially, to be Protestant. Mexicans consider the Southwest and California to be historic sections of their ancestral homeland, lost unfairly in the 1846–1848 war between the United States and Mexico; and so may answer prejudice with proud assertions of their deep roots in the region.

Old Mexico regards her post-1910 government as revolutionary. To her this connotes independence of Spanish rule, abolition of ecclesiastical rule (though the Catholic Church now functions openly), continual redistribution of vast landed estates, and glorification of the high Indian cultures with an accompanying mystique called *indianismo*. The glorification invokes classic grandeurs of Aztec, Maya, and lesser tribal civilizations, and accomplishments of great Indian personalities after the Spanish conquest. This does not mean that the Spanish ancestry is not venerated, though the conquerors cannot be wholly forgiven. Mexican immigrants to the United States have named one of their fraternal orders the "Sons of Anahuac," thus boasting of pre-Aztec [2] Indian origins.

The fateful revolt against Spanish rule was led by a *criollo* (colonial born of Spanish parents) priest named Miguel Hidalgo y Costilla, in the state of Guanajuato, parish of Dolores. Another shout like Paul Revere's, Father Hidalgo's *grito de Dolores* (cry of independence, at Dolores), September 16, 1810, still resounds in the Spanish-speaking world. Hidalgo led poorly armed Indian peons against the ruling Spanish vice-regents and *criollos;* and he was defeated. Mexican tradition stresses the facts that Hidalgo was Spanish, an impoverished but learned and defiant priest, and was shot to death by Spanish order. In 1821 Mexico won her independence. She continued, however, to be governed by *criollo* aristocrats of the Mexican *latifundia* (great landed estates).

In 1861–1866, Mexico again struggled for her freedom, led by a Zapotec Indian from Gualatao, Oaxaca, named Pablo Benito Juárez. Born a poor tribesman and soon orphaned, he was early educated in Roman Catholic schools, then practiced law, served in public offices, and was elected president of the nation. He headed his armed people against invading forces of Napoleon III and other European powers at the time that President Abraham Lincoln headed the Union army against the rebellious Southern Confederacy. Juárez came to be called the Lincoln of Mexico. The American Civil War ended; in February 1866 the United States issued an ultimatum to Napoleon III, advising him, in keeping with the Monroe Doctrine, to withdraw his troops from Mexico. This ended European imperialism in Mexico. Juárez was regarded as the greatest Indian since the Conquest. Yet not long before, there were unofficial American proposals, such as Horace Greeley's in his newspaper, the *New York Tribune,* to annex border Mexican territory and to enslave the tribes.

Such conflict has long attended the international border and the Rio Grande region. Exiled Mexicans, including Juárez, have found ready refuge in New Orleans, for example, but predatory Americans stopped at no violence in Texas, both before and after they took Texas from Mexico. Until about 1943, observers remarked that some maps in schools of Mexico labeled Texas an area "temporarily in the possession of the United States." In the United States and in Mexico, Mexicans and their United States-born children annually celebrate the *cinco de mayo* (May 5, 1861) defeat of Napoleon III at Puebla and they celebrate Hidalgo's September sixteenth *grito.* They also preserve bitter memories of *Yanqui* exploitations.

After Mexico lost the presently designated Southwest lands to the United States, the new Anglo-American settlers regarded the old Spanish-speaking communities as hatefully and contemptibly alien. Indian tribes also claimed possession of the region. Frontiersmen, like some contemporary Westerners, have professed to regard Mexicans as "savage Indians" and often segregated them accordingly. Carey McWilliams quotes an earlier authority that "Toward the Mexicans remaining within the limits of the [Texas] Republic . . . the feeling of the Texans was scarcely better than toward the Indians," and a contemporary authority that "Texans could not get it out of their heads that their manifest destiny was to kill Mexicans and take over Mexico." [3] Anti-Mexicanism has historic European origins in Anglo-Spanish rivalries at sea, over New World discoveries, and over papal authority. The defeat of the Spanish Armada is still an English boast and a Mexican-American boo. The Catholic Church in the United States has held aloof from the Catholic Church in Latin America.

In 1910 the Mexican citizenry violently overthrew the powerful corrupt government of President Porfirio Díaz. The memory is, as it were, enshrined in the name of Mexico's official political party, the *Partido Revolucionario Institucional.* Refugees, fleeing battlefields and general devastation, crossed over the border into the Southwest and California. Thus began a permanent flow of Mexican immigrants, entering legally and illegally for economic betterment. Since during the Second World War the United States received, in addition, train-loads of contracted Mexican laborers, or *braceros*, who worked for limited periods in agriculture and other occupations, under super-vision of both governments, and then returned home; the program ended December, 1964.

The Hispanic, loosely called Mexican, population of the American Southwest and California derives from different periods. The upper class usually emphasizes its Spanish blood and culture over American Indian components, leaving the latter to those willing to be called Mexican or Mexican-American. Otherwise, descendants of original Spanish and Spanish-Indian settlers are called in Texas *tejanos* and Latin Americans, in New Mexico, *hispanos* or Spanish Americans, in California, *californios* or Old Californians. *Hispanos* and *californios* are somewhat, or irregularly, discriminated against locally, as in New Mexico, and always less extremely when recognized to be upper class. They hold aloof from *tejanos, braceros,* and Mexican immigrants who, since 1910, have contributed the bulk of the Mexican-American popu-lation. *Hispanos* and *californios* state forcibly that they do not con-sider themselves Mexicans. The attitude cannot be reduced to simple snobbery in a situation poisoned with prejudice, for it describes their view of historic identities. Anglos often confuse Spanish and other Latin American immigrants with Mexican-Americans.

The social origins of the post-1910 immigrants are largely rural and small town; the people are poorly educated (if not illiterate), unskilled workers, traditionally Catholic; there are also small pro-portions in business, in skilled labor, in educated and professional classes; some are Protestants. In pre-1910 Mexico, all were reared by the hierarchical modes of an extreme, corrupt, decaying feudalistic system, burdened with privilege and peonage. The 1910 revolutionaries hoped to eradicate land monopolies, the class of aristocrats, and peonage. As the single largest landlord, the Catholic Church was de-prived of perquisites and authority; the hierarchy was driven to function more or less secretly, or into exile after the emigrants; and its enormous wealth was redistributed. Today the Church is back in open strength and respectability. Chronic poverty and ignorance maintain bribery, or *mordida*, throughout Mexico; this open scandal is attacked to no avail in election campaigns and presidential ad-dresses. Traditionally the people of Mexico expect to be sold out, by their own and by foreign exploiters alike; they fear and distrust all officials and all in positions of advantage, although they are trained to obey.

Yet, traditionally the people rest short-term confidence in local leadership, called *caudillismo,* in the charismatic, natural leaders called *caudillos.* These men are recognized as virile characters; such were Pancho Villa who fought in the North of Mexico during the revolution, and Emiliano Zapata who fought in the South. President Díaz and even Juárez, after they became celebrities, were not so considered. In every form, the people express the view that established *políticos* will milk them.

Caudillismo, like bullfighting, manifests the mystique of *machismo,* or stylized male bravado. This is a conviction at the heart of Spanish and Mexican life, even in Los Angeles slums. As Mexicans say, males must "dominate," quite apart from familiar codes of honor. Living up to this cultural demand, in a hierarchically organized milieu, requires skill, energy, and arrogance; but not responsibility in the individualistically perservering Anglo-American sense. On the contrary, by Anglo standards a *macho* man can behave irresponsibly and indecisively. Males outrank females, except perhaps old family matriarchs who are shown much courtesy; the male sphere is in public activities, above and separate from the domestic one of women and children. Female activity is confined, often extremely, by males and delegated chaperones, a practice supposedly influenced by Arab culture during the Arabs' seven-century control of the Iberian peninsula. Courtship is patterned to evoke *machismo.* It challenges fierce taboos of kinship (thus, the *prima* or first cousin, prohibited in romance and marriage, becomes the tragically sublime love of life and literature) and of female chastity. It tests the venality of chaperones and the double standard of sex. It relies on the inevitable forgiveness of male sinners, and stages the whole glory of *macho* men. But women who violate the limits on their sexual conduct, even in the upper class, are likely to be cast out as prostitutes.

Immigrants found that our country's advanced economy forced the unskilled into hard migratory labor. In Mexico, such unskilled had lived bitterly under peonage; in the United States they have been similarly oppressed by racist prejudice and by their own ignorance. During the Depression of the 1930's, local authorities, especially in California, "sent back to Mexico" Spanish-name families requiring public assistance; but many of these had been resident years and generations in their native United States. The Mexicans usually responded submissively or apathetically; such "obedience" did not keep deported families from returning if they could. In this atmosphere, until the 1950's, many long-resident immigrants would not learn English nor qualify for citizenship, nor would many native-born children vote.

However, the immigrants' culture underwent marked changes. It was influenced by the ambition and individualism of the Protestant atmosphere at school, recreation, and work; it was given new directions by literacy, urbanism, and the relative equalities between the sexes and generations. Men's traditionally "commanding" roles were undermined, and women's roles somewhat confused by the pervasive freedoms between sexes, generations, and classes, and by anti-Mexican discrimination. This is a characteristic hazard to lower-class immigrants of all origins because they are hurt by prejudice. Women of these groups, however, may get unskilled jobs more readily than men, as Negroes found upon migrating to Northern cities; and through their biological endowment women perpetuate life and emotional ties for their families.

During the Second World War, Mexican-Americans attended to military and economic opportunities and were rewarded. In 1947 a young veteran challenged California segregation in housing by seeking property outside the barrio. At a civil rights meeting he declared, "In the war I was not afraid to die for my country; in peace I am not afraid to live for it." At a church meeting another young veteran said that when he was offered citizenship for his army service he hesitated but he felt that now he could accept "without any reservations." In 1961 Texas and California each elected its first Mexican-American congressman while another Texas Mexican was appointed to the foreign service. Mexican-Americans are presently "in a fever," as a seasoned Mexican-American observer said, to enter schools, businesses, professions, politics. Still, there persist great handicaps of prejudice, segregation, poverty, culture conflicts, and the Mexicans' belated entrance into general American life.

The Mexican-American Family in California [4]

Disturbing to Anglo-American officials are certain features, of Mexican-American personality and conduct, which root in the traditional family life. This family is a large patriarchate, considerably protected, though inadvertently, by segregation and poverty. Though forbidden to speak Spanish at most or all public schools and at many places of employment, the Mexican-American family fosters a vociferous use of Spanish.[5] It fosters tender memories of Mexico, home of ancestors, living kinsmen, and the Mother Church. It teaches children never to forget "loyalty" to Mexico nor guilt over leaving it. In old Mexico people reciprocally accuse the immigrants and their descendants of "disloyalty" in migrating. Under general alienation from the American community by prejudice, immigrants teach their children that *gringos* always exploit the motherland.

The proprieties of being father and husband set no limits to male authority or "tyranny," as the Mexicans express it.[6] A man's heavy authority over his son progresses from teasing in infancy to open conflict as the child reaches three or four years and starts to protect his mother against father's rages. When a child of three or four demonstrates will, the father or a delegated elder demands obedience under threat. Parents show alternating severity and permissiveness that favor children's stomach upsets, called *empacho*. According to the Mexican community, *empacho* characterizes boyhood history. It appeared in clinic records of young men, where it seemed to forewarn of later neuroses. Children and adults express ambivalent feelings towards father, priests, and other males, in frank or covert words and acts; this is extended to Anglo-Americans. In Los Angeles teenagers' slang, the father is *jefe* or chief, the mother is *jefita* or little chief; in English, the father is also referred to as the "warden." Men declare that "the husband [father] is always right." Children and female kin secretly attack this. But in the absence of the patriarch, women also demand unquestioning obedience as their due of "respect." College-bred young people, catching themselves in this behavior, may say helplessly, "This is the only way we know!"

At school the Mexican habit of obeying, of enduring authority without question or overt challenge, is called by troubled educators "apathy and lack of motivation." The obligations to "obey" and "respect" and "be quiet and good" were announced in this fashion by an upper-class grandmother to her American-born grandson: "Do as I say for I am twice your mother, being your mother's mother." Fathers flaunt their authority and are feared, but the actual rearing of children is accomplished by mothers, grandmothers, aunts, elder siblings, and elder cousins.

Mexicans experience anger and frustration daily from their prejudiced situation in the western United States. Educators, social workers, and others criticize Mexican behavior that, however, should be weighed against this prejudice for proper interpretation. The behavior is described as indifference to education, to work skills, and to acquisition of wealth; as low ratings on intelligence tests; as irresponsibility; and as talk of suicide and homicide, expressing feelings of inferiority and hypochondria, and of anger directed violently against the speaker's own person.[7]

At home, emotions are often expressed noisily, swinging from violence to gentleness and sweet merriment, especially among males. To induce pending explosions that later permit some peace and penance, women and children egg on battles with words and blows. Exhibitions of temper are held to further intimacy, meaning affection, releasing the excitement generated by patterned differences of sex, generation, and other statuses. To a *gringo* critic, Mexicans observe, "What else is so interesting?" The dynamics and the outcome are of never-failing moment. This is the "constant uproar" that troubles teachers in East Los Angeles *barrios*. A school principal complained that "Adults are unreliable, especially men. Husbands don't get along with wives or children and desert so often that we've come to expect broken families. . . . What we teach about equality and teamwork makes no sense in their lives. A man doesn't have to lift a finger if he doesn't want to; the family women slave for him. They seem to think there is nothing like a man. In Mexican families, every boy, even, is a king." It is consistent for East Los Angeles Mexicans of both sexes to comment bitterly that youngsters cannot find proper male figures after whom to model conduct. The American arena ignores the *macho* drive for recognized action.

Fathers and brothers feel obliged to protect the daughter's and sister's "honor," meaning her premarital chastity. Often jealous of her male friends, they discipline her severely. Such patriarchal *machismo* struggles to control children who stay out late unsupervised or who obey rival "commands" of women teachers and probation officers, rather than of parents. The harassed father may beat his daughters or lock them out or in to show who "commands" at home. Daughters, like sons, retaliate by picking locks or running away. The wrought-up father may himself disappear, careless of the fates of wife and children. Then the eldest son takes over as "little father," often behaving as severely as "the old man." At church service, the priest scolds his flock openly, naming the sinners, including the absent fathers. When the missing father returns, he resumes his place easily against pretenders, for the wife is trained to serve and to allow compassionate latitude.

In a life broken by migration, poverty, revolution, and prejudice, the men often drink excessively, act overabusively, and run off, pursuing the *macho* will-o'-the-wisp. Even seemingly irresponsible men feel disturbed by failure to provide for their families. But wives and mothers keep the homes more or less open and forgiving.

The mother is the outstanding figure of responsibility. All bear a tender relationship toward her and flee to her in trouble. If the wife is not trapped in quarrels, she stands by like a mother. If driven to report her husband to the police for undue abuse, she generally withdraws charges at the last, "for this is a family affair," and perhaps her husband has been enacting *machismo*. A woman's strength is such "kindness" to the family, responsibly forgiving, serving, and accepting. All girls are trained accordingly.

Women, however, can also feel bitterly. An upper-class Mexican woman told her American-reared daughters that "a wife just becomes a common woman for the man's use." Lower-class Mexican girls in California express mistrust of marriage from what they have seen, yet dread the disgrace of spinsterhood. Both sexes prepare for adult domesticity in the parents' home, when sister mothers brother, he "protects" her, and both observe physical modesty.

Emotional stresses between the sexes seem eased in teen-aged groups, including playmates and youth gangs. Adolescent siblings of Los Angeles' lower class express affectionate closeness in a term, *mi carnal(a)*—which means literally, my flesh.

In the crowded homes and streets of the poor, facts of sex are known to all. Mexican custom does not taboo the knowledge, as does the Anglo-American middle class, but it taboos the wrong conduct, especially female immodesty and unchastity. The proper conduct is taught at home, often conflicting with schools' demands for undressing and bathing in open facilities.

Whatever its problems, the family should present a united front in public. Anything else is "disloyal." It is also "disloyal" to move out of the *barrio* away from *la raza*, and it is somewhat disloyal to marry a *gringo*. These are descending orders of "disloyalty"; they are judged more moderately in recent years.

The army service and other military services carry young Mexicans directly into the general American world, where also the Southwest's kind of prejudice against them is unknown or mild. The young men live in new geographical and social surroundings, acquire more education and occupational skills, grow used to time schedules, marry girls of every origin, allow some individual freedom to women and children.

Though the Americanized family of Mexican origin resorts to secular agencies that their elders regard as Protestant, like the YMCA, the people generally retain strong bonds with the Catholic Church. Parents may try to elevate family status by giving children to the Church and religious orders, especially ambitious families of poor social origins. Protestant Mexicans, said to make up perhaps 10 per cent of the population on both sides of the border, are viewed with suspicion and some hostility. Yet Americanization means that all absorb some Protestant values and habits, of the sort often called puritanical and individualistic.

In the Americanized family the balance of roles shifts but keeps within the accustomed pattern. Thus, the man remains family head and *macho*, but shares some authority and perquisites with his wife, or she takes them. Individuals can separate somewhat from the family body and its male authority, as in pursuing education, marriage, and place of residence. Parents demand obedience less extremely without becoming permissive. An emerging ideal seems to be to allow children of both sexes to fulfill themselves individually if they can also serve the family. English, except in pockets of continuing segregation, is spoken customarily and command of Spanish suffers. Most parents, however, show affection and authority with Spanish, children conciliate with a Spanish phrase, and many use some Spanish idioms playfully with intimates outside the home. The social discipline of the family continues strong.

Notes

1. Useful reading for background:
Carey McWilliams, *North from Mexico* (Philadelphia and New York: J. B. Lippincott, 1949). Hudson Strode, *Timeless Mexico* (New York: Harcourt, Brace and Co., 1944). Ralph Roeder, *Juárez and His Mexico* (New York: Viking Press, 1947), 2 vols. Munro S. Edmonson, *Los Manitos,* A Study of Institutional Values (New Orleans: Middle American Research Institute, Tulane University, 1957), Publication 25, pp. 1–72. John H. Burma, *Spanish-Speaking Groups in the U. S.* (Durham, N. C.: Duke University Press, 1954). Ralph L. Beals and Norman D. Humphrey, *No Frontier to Learning, The Mexican Student in the U. S.* (Minneapolis: University of Minnesota Press, 1957). R. L. Chambers, "The New Mexico Pattern," *Common Ground* (Summer, 1949). Ernesto Galarza, "Program for Action," *Common Ground* (Summer, 1949). The last two articles are reprinted in *The Mexican American: A National Concern* (New York: Common Council for American Unity, n.d.), pp. 20–38.
2. William H. Prescott, *History of the Conquest of Mexico* and *History of the Conquest of Peru* (New York: Modern Library, Random House, n.d.), in section *Mexico,* pp. 13–15 and n. 11.
3. Carey McWilliams, *North from Mexico*, p. 101.
4. The following discussion is based on the writer's studies among Mexican and Mexican-American neighborhoods of Southern California towns and on records of a public clinic.
5. These studies are recommended: George C. Barker, "Social Functions of Language in a Mexican-American Community," *Acta Americana* 5 (1947), 185–

202. George C. Barker, "Pachuco: An American-Spanish Argot and its Social Functions in Tucson, Arizona," *University of Arizona Bulletin*, Vol. 21, No. 1; *Social Science Bulletin*, No. 18 (Tucson: 1950)

6. The word "tyranny" is often used by Mexicans in this connection and the implications are discussed by the Mexican psychiatrist, Alfonso Millán, "El Mexicano Desnudo Frente a Sus Complejos," in *Los Mexicanos Somos Así?*, Roberto Nava Luján (ed.) (Los Angeles: P.O.B. 2686, n.d.).

7. In this connection school drop-outs should be studied. See Paul M. Sheldon, "Mexican-Americans in Urban Public Schools. An Exploration of the Drop-Out Problem," *California Journal of Educational Research*, Vol. XII, No. 1 (January, 1961), pp. 21–26.

Appendix 2

Comparative Chart of Negro Race Relationships [1]

American Negroes migrate heavily from the South to the North and West, and from rural areas to big cities. Negro populations in older centers, such as New York, Washington, and Chicago, mount strikingly. Large and small cities of California, which knew no Negroes ten and twenty years ago, meet them now in conspicuous numbers [2] and face attendant school problems of high turnover, high drop-out rate, and low achievements among pupils. Stereotyped racist thinking and discrimination hinder integration, though accustomed lifeways of Negroes change in the new freer urban surroundings.

The position of Negroes, as of any group, varies with interests of the host society. This is clear in the United States, Brazil, the Union of South Africa, and the United Kingdom, where Negroes live in a traditionally Western society dominated by ruling whites. Since the Second World War, Negro (or black) and other "colored colonials" (such as British West Indians, Lascars, Cypriots) have migrated to Britain in rising numbers until July 1, 1962, when legislation attempted to control the immigration. [3]

The following table illustrates some comparative aspects of

Negro-white relationships in the culturally akin United States and United Kingdom and shows further contrasts in Brazil's treatment of former African slaves.

United States	*United Kingdom*
Centuries of chattel slavery on the land.	Chattel slavery abroad in colonies, not in the imperial homeland.[4]
For over three centuries Negroes shared blood and history with white masters.	Slave and master races shared blood and circumstances in the colonies. After the second world war, U. S. quota restrictions accelerated migrations of colonial blacks to Britain, chiefly young males migrating before 1950s, then increasingly both sexes.
Racial intermarriage tabooed by custom and law, with some exceptions outside the South. Extra-marital, furtive cross mating frequent, especially between white males and black females but not excluding white females and black males.	Intermarriage legal in the absence of customary or legal barriers. It has occurred chiefly with working-class Britons and with rare upper- and middle-class exceptions. Until the late 1950's, there were regularly Negro males heading the Negro-British white families.
Race segregation by custom and law. The traditional South has practised upper-class white patronage of Negroes and "poor-white" hostility towards Negroes.	England's three-class structure of society forces most Negro colonials into the bottom working class when it does not exclude them as "foreign." Rare marriage of black Africans into English upper class has resulted in the couples' immediate emigration abroad.
Negro race, of American slave origin, is always a major social handicap.	"Color" is attributed widely as a social handicap to "foreigners" ranging from European Latins to East Indians, Africans and Orientals. Exceptions are made for individuals, such as a great West Indian cricketer decorated by George VI.

United States	United Kingdom
Anti-Negro discrimination is conveyed by a special racist vocabulary.	Britons tend to use the word "race" approvingly and in self-reference. Social handicaps relate to class and nationality, usually. "Negro" is not used regularly but in scientific anthropology. "Colored" can refer slightingly to all peoples except North Europeans. Nationality terms, like Jamaican or Nigerian, are used where Americans say "Negro." The British uses reflect the distances of geography and administration between (white) rulers and (black) ruled.
Negroes stress color of complexion in terms of social prestige, the lighter the skin, the more it is appreciated. "Passing" for white results from American racism.[5]	Color gradations are not defined nor is "passing" a social issue.
Various localities term certain non-Negro groups "colored" and discriminate against them by racist modes similar to those developed in relationships with Negroes. The groups include Orientals, East Indians, Amerindians, Mexicans and other Latin Americans, Puerto Ricans, Hawaiians and other Pacific peoples.	"Color" is attributed as a social handicap to most other peoples in Europe, Asia, Africa, and the Americas.
The United States is considered biracial physically, i.e., Negro and white, but shares one culture and one national Constitution guaranteeing civil rights. Local institutions guide discrimination for the races, such as the special interracial "etiquette" of the old South.[6] Negroes "belong" in the United States and are considered American in culture.	No special instruments of race discrimination exist in custom or law. The three-class system allocates all socially, either to a class (following criteria of speech, wealth, family, job, etc.) or outside the system as foreigners. People in Britain are said to be protected by "the rule of law." Colonial immigrants, like all foreigners, are expected to "return home." There is steady con-

United States	United Kingdom
	troversy over whether "colonials" belong in Britain through imperial or Commonwealth citizenship.
All descended from a Negro are "Negro" in status, if the white community is aware. Some Southern states specify the fractions of Negro blood that define Negro affiliation, despite a white appearance.	British mixed-bloods are called "half-caste" and have no clear social status. Often they are confused with West Indian "colonials" and expected to "return home."
In the old South a mixed-blood with a white parent must be Negro and is illegitimate unless legitimized by Negroes.	Mixed-blood children of British (white) women are legitimate if the parents are married.
In the old South white males have tacit customary rights over Negro females.	There are no customary sexual rights over Negroes.
Besides discrimination, the old South practices "kindness" and other *noblesse oblige* towards "good Negroes."	The United Kingdom tends to be inexplicit about civil rights and has no interracial rulings.
Men and women are trained to show the same race discriminations.	Colored "colonials" state appreciatively, and Britons state critically, that British women of lower class are friendly to the colored.
Race is a permanent indicator of social status. Violations of segregation are punished harshly, especially in the South. Racist doctrine conveys suspicions of Negro intent to rape white women; and puts white women's sexual virtue on a pedestal.	Social status is determined primarily by family origins and training within the three-class social structure. Other races are considered social unknowns and inferiors. Any race mixing is usually blamed on irresponsibility of the British (i.e., white) partners. While the colored and all foreigners are subject to ridicule for supposed high sexuality (like French and Americans), the men are never accused of rape. But British women part-

United States	United Kingdom
	ners have long been accused of being "concubines" and prostitutes of the colored with whom they associate. Scorn of colonial colored immigrants, until the 1950's, was conveyed in the charge of being "stowaways."
Liberalism about race in the North and West rests upon economic forms that developed without slavery.	The appearance of liberalism about race rests partly on the absence of a historic colored population on the land. British relationships with colored peoples rest upon overseas conquest and administration.
Negroes have developed as a significant minority in American society by evolving legal and other peaceful modes of asserting their civil rights and responsibilities. Various legislatures have passed civil rights defense measures, generically called FEPC (Fair Employment Practices Committee).	Until the late 1950's, colored immigrants felt confused by British society's "veiled discrimination," as colored leaders voiced complaints in print and oratory. They lacked precedents for civil rights procedures in the courts and have not been able to secure protective legislation from Parliament. African and West Indian colonials, however, led nationalist protests that helped create the new nations.
Federal, state, and local governments exercise responsibility for equality and fair practices in acts like the late 1862 Emancipation Proclamation, amendments to the federal Constitution, President Roosevelt's FEPC during World War II, subsequent state and municipal FEPCs, the 1954 Supreme Court decision against school segregation, other Supreme Court decisions against segregation in interstate transportation and commerce.	Responsibility for fair care of "colored colonials" has been entrusted to the British Colonial Office and to National Welfare services. Legislation has been proposed, after American models, but resisted.
American racism has stimulated great creativity among all Ameri-	Biracial conflict in Britain, the colonies and the Union of South

United States	United Kingdom
cans in every major art form (notably literature, music, sculpture, painting) and humanistic discipline (notably history, the behavioral sciences, political science and education).	Africa stimulates a new creative literature and developments in behavioral sciences by Britons, West Indians and Africans.

Contrasting with practices of the English-speaking Protestant peoples are some that flourished in Catholic Colonial Brazil and the later Brazilian empire, whose plantation and mining economy depended on a huge Negro slave force. One Brazilian practice required, as the Africans came off the slave ships and before they could be sold in the markets, that they be endowed with souls through compulsory Catholic baptism. The English and American practice instead chattelized slaves by increasingly harsh customs and legislation. Another Brazilian practice was the masters' often open acknowledgment of slave concubines and their mulatto offspring, which could give the latter family privileges of sons or godsons. Family portraits, drawn and painted in the early nineteenth century by the French artist Jean-Baptiste Débret [7] show slave kinfolk with the masters ranged behind them in slave attire. The English-speaking, however, tightened the taboo on racial intermarriage more and more.

Brazil encouraged diplomatic, trade, and cultural exchanges with West African kingdoms or chiefdoms, tolerated many African practices among the slaves and freedmen, and so allowed an Afro-Brazilian subculture to evolve; Brazilian scholars and the people generally boast of the Afro-Brazilian life. However, the English-speaking in their own colonies and states intended to destroy the slaves' African traditions, and therefore broke up tribal groups of slaves and prohibited ancestral customs. When Brazil's imperial government emancipated the slaves in 1888, the freedmen were absorbed into the class system, based on a *latifundium* or plantation economy. Thus, most blacks fell into the lowest class, along with equally impoverished whites and mixed-bloods; a few wealthy, accomplished blacks and lighter "men of color" were securely established in the upper class; ever since, growing numbers of "blacks" and "mulattoes" have helped to create a middle class. Latin influences on American slavery and race relations are evident in parts of the deep South, such as parts of Louisiana and South Carolina.[8]

Notes

1. This section is based on the writer's studies. Besides previous bibliographical references about Negroes and Negro-white relationships, and those in following footnotes of this appendix, these titles are recommended:

Michael Banton, *White and Coloured: The Behaviour of British People Towards Coloured Immigrants* (London: Jonathan Cape, 1959).

Horace R. Cayton and St. Clair Drake, *Black Metropolis* (New York: Harcourt, Brace and Company, 1945).

John Dollard, *Caste and Class in a Southern Town* (New Haven: Yale University Press, 1937).

Bertram Wilbur Doyle, *The Etiquette of Race Relations in the South* (Chicago: The University of Chicago Press, 1937).

Charles S. Johnson, *Patterns of Negro Segregation* (New York: Harper and Brothers, 1943).

————. *The Negro in American Civilization* (New York: Henry Holt and Co., 1930).

————. *Growing up in the Black Belt: Negro Youth in the Rural South* (Washington, D. C.: American Council on Education, 1941).

James Weldon Johnson, *Along this Way* (Autobiography) (New York: The Viking Press, 1933).

Kenneth L. Little, *Negroes in Britain* (London: Routledge and Kegan Paul, 1948).

Gunnar Myrdal, *An American Dilemma, The Negro Problem and American Democracy*, 2 vols. (New York: Harper and Brothers, 1944).

2. The *New York Times*, May 7, 1961, reported that Mr. Harry P. Sharp informed the Population Association of America that "in all the central cities the proportion of white has 'declined drastically' . . ." However "suburbs of the nation's 12 largest metropolitan areas have maintained a population 93 to 99 per cent white . . ." by realty restrictions against Negroes. The *Los Angeles Mirror-News*, July 1, 1961, reported the first action instituted in California, under the Unruh Civil Rights Act, "to recover damages for discrimination by persons engaged in the real estate business."

3. The *New York Times*, July 1, 1962, states that on this date the new British Commonwealth Immigrants Act became effective, obliging arrivals "to show that they have a job waiting for them and will not be a health or financial burden. The bill was approved over strong . . . charges that the Government was restricting colored immigration. Irish immigration will continue unrestricted.

"Government spokesmen argued that some control was needed to check the sharp rise in Commonwealth immigration, which rose from 43,000 persons in 1955 to 136,000 last year. This year's figures may reach 180,000 despite the [Act] . . ."

"It has been estimated that 685,000 persons from the Commonwealth and Ireland came to Britain and stayed between World War II and 1959. Half were Irish. Of the rest, half were colored." © 1962 by The New York Times Company. Reprinted by permission.

4. See K. L. Little, *Negroes in Britain*, for an account of some slaves and freedmen in England.

5. See discussion in Arna Bontemps and Jack Conroy, *They Seek a City*, Chapter IX (Garden City, New York: Doubleday, Doran and Co., 1945).

6. See C. S. Johnson, *Patterns of Negro Segregation* and B. W. Doyle, *Etiquette of Race Relations*.

7. See Jean-Baptiste Débret, *Voyage Pittoresque et Historique au Brésil, 1816–1831*, 3 vols. (Paris, 1835). Two of Débret's paintings are reproduced in Donald Pierson, *Negroes in Brazil* (Chicago: University of Chicago Press, 1942), facing pp. 76, 78.

8. A wealth of source material appears, for example, in *Gumbo Ya-Ya, A Collection of Louisiana Folk Tales*, compiled by Lyle Saxon, Edward Dreyer, and Robert Tallant (Boston: Houghton Mifflin Co., 1945). Cf. also W. E. B. DuBois, *Black Reconstruction, An Essay Toward a History of the Part Which Black Folk Played in the Attempt to Reconstruct Democracy in America, 1860–1880* (New York: Harcourt, Brace and Company, 1935).

Appendix 3

American Indians in Transition

Because of great cultural differences from American civilization, conquest by European and American powers, loss of territories and self-government, poverty, prejudice, and discrimination, American Indian children are probably more neglected by public education than any other. The recent program of relocating reservation families in great cities has not bettered their opportunities. Los Angeles school welfare and attendance officers tell of relocated Navajo families who "walk back to Arizona" from their "flea-bag" living quarters and indifferent schools in Southern California. These impoverished Indians seem to fit the negative stereotypes. There are no stereotypes that provide for the many educated Indians except the ones that assign them "back to the blanket."

As with other minority peoples, our discriminatory relationships with Indians are beset by moral obligations and a history of violated guarantees. In the Southwest, besides, teachers often mistake the Indians for Mexicans because of Spanish surnames, and often refuse to be corrected. In a similar spirit, some teachers and police criticize Mexicans for being "Indians"; however, this form of insult is widespread on both sides of the border, among both Spanish- and English-speaking. The insult is backed by stereotypes of Indians as "primitive" and "savage" though exceptions may be "noble." Film and television westerns reflect all the stereotypes and some of the realities.

In 1492 there were some two hundred tribes in North America, numbering under a million persons, speaking about three hundred languages, pursuing varied cultures, and economies that ranged from simple food gathering to elaborate gardening and hunting.[1] By the end of the last century, our civilization seemed about to extinguish the tribal populations. But in this century, Indian populations have risen to number perhaps half a million.[2] For nearly a century policies of Congress and the federal government have handicapped American Indians. Notable exceptions among policy makers were former U. S. Indian Commissioner John Collier (1933–1945) and former U. S. Assistant Indian Commissioner William Zimmerman, Jr. (1933–1950). In the past decade Congress has supported the policy called "termination" of federal responsibility for Indians on reservations, expressed in "voluntary relocations" of Indians from home reservations to distant large cities. But instead of facilitating Indians' absorption into the general population, as the Indian Bureau anticipated, termination and relocation have increased Indians' liabilities by raising new legal, cultural, and emotional problems.[3] The tribes have resorted to legal channels for resistance, and therefore, "termination proceedings have been generally halted." [4]

In 1924 all Indians were granted citizenship by Congress, though some individuals in the tribes "resent" it.[5] All Indian children are subject to school law, and attend schools on and off reservations, segregated and integrated.[6] Off-reservation pupils frequently suffer disastrous alienation from tribal life and find it difficult to strike roots in general American life.[7]

In June 1961 a unique American Indian Conference [8] assembled at Chicago to plan the course of Indian survival. The Conference drew attendance from 90 bands and tribes across the nation, as well as from off-reservation Indians in Chicago.[8] The chairman of the opening session was a Cherokee, who was a state supreme court justice; the keynote speaker was a Pueblo, a professor of anthropology.[9] The Conference delivered a formal protest to the government and the nation against the termination policy, voicing Indians' attachment to ancestral lands and cultures, the preference for developing their lands instead of relocating their persons, and the right to participate in government plans for technical assistance. The Conference also recalled America's traditional guarantees of protection. This Conference placed Indians on the national scene as another, the latest, minority mobilized to secure its civil rights.

In the public schools, reservation children appear less accessible than any other group.[10] To deal with Indians of any age and condition, educators must reckon exactly with the operations of tribal cultures in particular situations. A tribe may prohibit intimacies with a "cross cousin"—who is child of a mother's brother or father's sister—or oblige respectful duties of formal "joking" with the cross relative. The tribe's customary standards function for any aspect of life, whether mental disorder,[11] quirks of character or temperament,[12] genius or approved normality.[13] Behind the strange cultures and walls of prejudice, Indians are human beings as endowed as others on earth.

In 1915 there appeared a remarkable autobiography by a Sioux Indian named Charles A. Eastman, or Ohiyesa,[14] showing the rapidity and excellence with which this tribesman moved from "primitive" ways to those of a world society. In 1872 Ohiyesa's father had taken him "from wild life in Canada" with the exiled Santee division of Sioux [15] to study in U. S. schools for a medical degree. "Only a few years earlier . . . [my father] himself was a wild Sioux warrior"; [15] captured by the U. S. military for his part in the Minnesota Sioux uprising of the 1860's, the father had taught himself reading and writing. During about ten years at U. S. schools, Ohiyesa mastered "absolutely unknown" subjects "in a foreign language," meaning English,[16] along with other Indian men and women.[17] Eventually he practiced medicine, wrote books about race and Sioux culture, and represented his people to the American government and to world assemblies. When discussing Indian men and women distinguished in modern American life,[18] Eastman bitterly criticized race prejudice. He declared that Indians, even those already occupying permanent houses and wearing "citizens' clothing," [19] "are likely to undergo . . . considerable demoralization as soon as they mingle freely with the surrounding whites." [20]

The Second World War drafted Indians into combat units; it accepted them in war industry if, like others, but ludicrously, they could prove American birth or citizenship.[21] In the deep South, including Texas, they were segregated, sometimes with Negroes, sometimes with Mexicans, sometimes alone.[21] Individuals showed superb heroism during battle and were awarded highest honors. Upon returning home they had to face race prejudices from others and cultural hostilities from tribal fellows.

Some tribesmen employed at war industry remained in the cities after war ended, and some married whites. The writer received letters from such a man, known before the war on his tribal reservation. He had been a high-spirited, clever youth, skilled in English, machines, and also in ancestral sorcery. The sorcery had been taught him by his adored grandmother. Before the war he was teaching sorcery to his half-white, motherless son of four; in a letter he wrote at the time, he boasted, "My young hopeful is getting along swell. He's really loyal to me." After the war, the father and son both married white women in the town where war industry had taken them. In a 1958 letter, the father brooded, "I am the last Indian," for even his son would never use the hereditary medicine bundles; nor would the nearly white infant granddaughter, with fair hair and blue eyes. The letter went on, "I'm not sure what I want to do. . . . I have asked the manitou to guide my destiny." Now he fought "prejudice and discrimination" in industry. Long ago he had boasted of his "wise and powerful" grandmother; in 1958 he boasted that his Irish wife also had "power," having intervened successfully on his son's behalf, "because she is white."

A fellow tribeswoman of this sorcerer, still living on the reservation, corresponded with the writer for years, using pen, pencil, or typewriter, describing reservation events in English and in the English-lettered native tongue. When her children finished high school, they continued studying at Haskell Indian Institute, and then found jobs in government and private industry. Yet she, and her non-English-speaking mother obliged the children to learn their dwindling tribe's intricate kinship system, "so they would know how to behave [to the different generations and classifications of even remote kin] and not marry their cousins. . . . My son tells me that every time he likes a girl, I tell him, 'You can't. She's your cousin.'" Whatever the schools' opinion of "returning to the blanket," these people know the rules of chiefs' descent though the present chief-apparent is 1,500 miles away in Los Angeles. In this family all the women practiced exquisite traditional beadwork, weaving beads into sashes, headbands, and necklaces, and embroidering beads on deerhide moccasins and on Hudson's Bay blue four-point blankets. Such people maintain their traditions with conscious tenacity, deliberately choosing to live on the reservation with the conservative tribe, even after periods of time in cities.

Intermarriage of whites and Indians has always occurred. Tribesmen comment not on the concept but on the *behavior* of the white spouse. Thus, in a letter to the writer, a tribeswoman said, "My sister saw Joe's [white] wife at the funeral of Joe's father [on the reservation]. We have certain ways, my sister said [referring to the tribe's customs of mourning and burial]. Joe's wife did whatever he did [in the prescribed ritual] so that it sounds to me, she is a nice woman."

The Indian cultures' foundations of traditional morality and ambition, of male and female personality types, must alter drastically in the great metropolitan centers. Of what use there are skills of the woodlands hunter and of the deerhide tanner? What will be the prices in mental health? What of the love for ancestral memories? What indeed is life without the ancestors' past? An Indian Bureau welfare worker answered such queries from college students on a public occasion with the opinion that Indian cultures could not be protected just for academic research.

Successful acculturation, or assimilation, by American standards has occurred in many Indian lives for centuries. Many such families managed to combine tribal traditions with rural and metropolitan ones. Among the Potawatomi tribe, for example, over a hundred years ago several Potawatomi families were flourishing ranchers in frontier Kansas, competing with whites while they developed the vast reservation to which they had been moved from the east by the United States military. Other Potawatomi were successful farmers in frontier Michigan, moving west in season to join kinsmen on the annual buffalo hunt. Descendants of these families, literate, solvent Christians, supplied the writer with invaluable information about the traditional culture, whose religion, cookery, and mythology they maintained along with modern American ways. Their children and grandchildren developed respectable careers in farming, in business, and in federal service, but continued active use of various Potawatomi beliefs and techniques, even after moving as far away as Washington, D. C.

Relocated Indians today face the old need to keep alive the ancestral tribal ethos and culture. In some large cities, such as Los Angeles, intertribal social centers appear, hoping to serve the needs. They battle, however, against the indifference and ignorance of burgeoning cosmopolitan populations.

Notes

1. A classic volume of simple description is Clark Wissler, *The American Indian, An Introduction to the Anthropology of the New World* (New York: Oxford University Press, 1922).
2. A good orientation to contemporary American Indians is provided by the special issue of "American Indians and American Indian Life," *The Annals of the American Academy of Political and Social Science*, Vol. 311, Philadelphia, May, 1957. The articles include bibliographies. J. Nixon Hadley has an article on "Demography of the American Indians." See also Harold E.

Fey and D'Arcy McNickle, *Indians and Other Americans. Two Ways of Life Meet* (New York: Harper and Brothers, 1959).

3. Nancy O. Lurie, "The Voice of the American Indian: Report on the American Indian Chicago Conference," in *Current Anthropology,* December 1961 (Vol. 2, No. 5), pp. 478–500. (Chicago: University of Chicago Press.)

4. Lurie, p. 480.

5. Lurie, p. 492.

6. See James E. Officer, *Indians in Schools* (Tucson: University of Arizona Press, 1956).

7. This is expressed in various ways. Traditional is the hostile stereotype that school Indians "return to the blanket" or "revert to type," deteriorating morally and socially, upon returning home to the reservation. Oliver LaFarge's stories give subtle sympathetic insights to Indians' behavior and bitter illumination of American prejudices. Some fatal accidents result from anti-Indian prejudice and cultural injury. A social worker on the Pima tribe's reservation described the case of the Pima marine, Ira Hayes, a hero of Iwo Jima in World War II, who became alcoholic and died soon after: "Ira [was] unable to find acceptance among the Pima after the war because of his hero role and [was] unable to find acceptance among the white population because of his Pima ways." Eventually he drowned on the reservation while, drunk, he stooped to drink from a spring. See James A. Helm, manuscript, San Bernardino County (California), Department of Social Welfare.

8. Lurie, p. 489.

9. Lurie, p. 490.

10. A Child Welfare Consultant to the Bureau of Indian Affairs wrote that "In many ways, the American Indian child is . . . apart from other children." Aleta Brownlee, "The American Indian Child," in *Children,* March–April 1958 (Vol. 5, No. 2), pp. 55–60. (U. S. Government Printing Office, Washington, D. C.)

11. See Ruth Landes, "The Abnormal Among the Ojibwa," *Journal of Abnormal and Social Psychology,* January 1938 (Vol. 33), pp. 14–33.

12. As in Ruth Landes, *The Ojibwa Woman* (New York: Columbia University Press, 1938).

13. As in Ruth Landes, "The Personality of the Ojibwa," *Character and Personality,* 1937 (Vol. 6), pp. 51–60.

    Also Ruth Landes, "Dakota Warfare," *Southwestern Journal of Anthropology,* Spring 1959 (Vol. 15, No. 1), pp. 43–52.

    Also Ruth Landes, "The Ojibwa of Canada" in Margaret Mead (ed.), *Cooperation and Competition Among Primitive Peoples* (New York: McGraw-Hill Book Co., 1937). Reissued in Boston: Beacon Press, 1961.

14. Charles A. Eastman, *The Indian Today, the Past and Future of the First American* (New York: Doubleday, Page and Co., 1915).

15. Eastman, p. 100.

16. Eastman, p. 77.

17. Eastman, p. 116.

18. Eastman, pp. 155–161.

19. Eastman, p. 94.

20. Eastman, p. 97. In this connection, the *New York Times,* September 7, 1958, printed a significant report on "More U. S. Indians Going to College,"

based on information from the U. S. Department of the Interior, Commissioner of Indian Affairs. A number of tribes were listed as having scholarship programs, so that with financial aid from other sources, "the number of Indians studying beyond high school level rose from 2,300 in the 1954–1955 academic year to more than 3,800 in 1957–1958."

21. Such grievances were submitted to the President's Committee on Fair Employment Practices, Washington, D. C., 1941–1945.

Bibliography

Books

Alexander, Franz. *Psychosomatic Medicine.* New York: W. W. Norton and Co., 1950.

Amory, Cleveland. *The Proper Bostonians.* New York: E. P. Dutton and Co., 1947.

Ashton-Warner, Sylvia. *Teacher.* New York: Simon and Schuster, 1963.

Banton, Michael. *White and Coloured: The Behaviour of British People Towards Coloured Immigrants.* London: Jonathan Cape, 1959.

Barker, George C. *Pachuco: An American-Spanish Argot and Its Social Functions in Tucson, Arizona.* Tucson: *University of Arizona Bulletin,* Vol. 21, No. 1; Social Science Bulletin, No. 18, 1950.

Beals, Ralph L., and Humphrey, Norman D. *No Frontier to Learning, The Mexican Student in the U. S.* Minneapolis: University of Minnesota Press, 1957.

Bell, Norman W. and Vogel, Ezra F. (eds.). *A Modern Introduction to the Family.* Glencoe, Illinois: The Free Press, 1960.

Benedict, Ruth F. *Patterns of Culture.* Boston: Houghton Mifflin, 1934.

———— *The Chrysanthemum and the Sword: Patterns of Japanese Culture.* Boston: Houghton Mifflin, 1946.

Boas, Franz. *Changes in Bodily Form of Descendants of Immigrants.* New York: Columbia University Press, 1912.

———— and others. *General Anthropology.* New York: D. C. Heath and Co., 1938.

Boas, Franz. *Race, Language and Culture.* New York: Macmillan Co., 1940.

Cayton, Horace R. and Drake, St. Clair. *Black Metropolis: A Study of Negro Life in a Northern City.* New York: Harcourt, Brace and Company, 1946.

Chase, Stuart. *American Credos.* New York: Harper and Brothers, 1962.

Clark, Margaret. *Health in the Mexican-American Culture.* Berkeley: University of California Press, 1959.

Cohen, Nathan Edward. *Social Work in the American Tradition.* New York: The Dryden Press, 1958.

Davenport, Marcia. *The Constant Image.* New York: Charles Scribner's Sons, 1960.

Davis, Allison and Havighurst, Robert J. *Father of the Man.* Boston: Houghton Mifflin, 1947.

Débret, Jean-Baptiste. *Voyage Pittoresque et Historique au Brésil, 1816–1831,* 3 vols. Paris: 1835.

Deren, Maya. *Divine Horsemen: The Living Gods of Haiti.* London and New York: Thames and Hudson, 1953.

Dobzhansky, Theodosius. *The Biological Bases of Human Freedom.* New York: Columbia University Press, 1956.

—— *Mankind Evolving: The Evolution of the Human Species.* New Haven: Yale University Press, 1962.

Dollard, John. *Caste and Class in a Southern Town.* New Haven: Yale University Press, 1937.

Doyle, Bertram Wilbur. *The Etiquette of Race Relations in the South.* Chicago: The University of Chicago Press, 1937.

DuBois, W. E. B. *Black Reconstruction, an Essay toward a History of the Part Which Black Folk Played in the Attempt to Reconstruct Democracy in America, 1860–1880.* New York: Harcourt, Brace and Company, 1935.

Eastman, Charles A. *The Indian Today, The Past and Future of the First American.* New York: Doubleday, Page and Co., 1915.

—— *Indian Child Life.* Boston: Little, Brown and Co., 1913, 1930.

Edmonson, Munro S. *Los Manitos, a Study of Institutional Values.* New Orleans: Middle American Research Institute, Tulane University, 1957, Publication 25.

Eells, Kenneth W., Davis, Allison, and others. *Intelligence and Cultural Differences: A Study of Cultural Learning and Problem-Solving.* Chicago: University of Chicago Press, 1951.

Efron, David. *Gesture and Environment.* New York: King's Crown Press, 1941.

Fergusson, Harvey. *Rio Grande.* New York: W. Morrow and Co., 1955.

Fey, Harold E., and McNickle, D'Arcy. *Indians and Other Americans. Two Ways of Life Meet.* New York: Harper and Brothers, 1959.

Frazier, E. Franklin. *The Negro Family in the United States.* New York: Macmillan Co., 1957.

—— *Black Bourgeoisie.* Glencoe, Illinois: Free Press, 1957.

Gamio, Manuel. *The Mexican Immigrant, His Life Story.* Chicago: University of Chicago Press, 1931.

Garn, Stanley M. *Human Races.* Springfield, Illinois: Charles C Thomas, 1961.

Gordon, Albert I. *Jews in Suburbia.* Boston: Beacon Press, 1959.

Harris, Sara. *Father Divine: Holy Husband.* Garden City, New York: Permabooks, Doubleday and Co., 1954.

Huxley, Julian. *Evolution in Action.* New York: Mentor Books, 1957.

Johnson, Arlien. *School Social Work: Its Contribution to Professional Education.* New York: National Association of Social Workers, 1962.

Johnson, Charles S. *Shadow of the Plantation.* Chicago: University of Chicago Press, 1934.

—— *Patterns of Negro Segregation.* New York: Harper and Brothers, 1943.

—— *The Negro in American Civilization.* New York: Henry Holt and Co., 1930.

—— *Growing Up in the Black Belt: Negro Youth in the Rural South.* Washington, D. C.: American Council on Education, 1941.

Johnson, James Weldon. *Along This Way.* New York: Viking Press, 1933.

Kardiner, Abram and Ovesey, Lionel. *The Mark of Oppression.* New York: W. W. Norton and Co., 1951.

Klineberg, Otto. *Race Differences.* New York: Harper and Brothers, 1935.

—— *Negro Intelligence and Selective Migration.* New York: Columbia University Press, 1935.

Kroeber, Alfred L. *Configurations of Culture Growth.* Berkeley: University of California Press, 1944.

—— *Style and Civilizations.* Ithaca: Cornell University Press, 1957.

La Farge, Oliver. *All the Young Men.* Boston and New York: Houghton Mifflin, 1935.

—— *The Enemy Gods.* Boston and New York: Houghton Mifflin, 1937.

—— *Behind the Mountains.* Boston: Houghton Mifflin, 1956.

—— *A Pause in the Desert.* Boston: Houghton Mifflin, 1957.

Landes, Ruth. *The Ojibwa Woman.* New York: Columbia University Press, 1938.

—— *The City of Women.* New York: Macmillan Co., 1947.

—— *Latin-Americans of the Southwest.* St. Louis: McGraw-Hill-Webster, 1965.

Lewis, Oscar. *Five Families: The Anthropology of Poverty.* New York: Basic Books, 1959.

—— *The Children of Sánchez.* New York: Random House, 1961.

Lilly, John C. *Man and Dolphin.* New York: Doubleday and Co., 1961.

Little, Kenneth L. *Negroes in Britain.* London: Routledge and Kegan Paul, 1948.

Lynd, Helen Merrell. *On Shame and the Search for Identity.* New York: Harcourt, Brace and Company, 1958.

Macgregor, Frances C., and others. *Facial Deformities and Plastic Surgery: A Psychosocial Study.* Springfield, Illinois: Charles C Thomas, 1953.

—— *Social Science and Nursing.* New York: Russell Sage Foundation, 1960.

McWilliams, Carey. *Brothers Under the Skin.* New York: Little, Brown and Co., 1942.

—— *North From Mexico, The Spanish-Speaking People of the United States.* Philadelphia and New York: J. B. Lippincott Co., 1949.

Mead, Margaret. *Male and Female, A Study of the Sexes in a Changing World.* New York: W. Morrow and Co., 1949.

de Mille, Agnes. *To a Young Dancer. A Handbook for Dance Students, Parents and Teachers.* Boston-Toronto: Little, Brown and Co., an Atlantic Monthly Press Book, 1962.

Myrdal, Gunnar. *An American Dilemma: The Negro Problem and Modern Democracy.* 2 vols. New York: Harper and Brothers, 1944.

Nevins, Allan. *The State Universities and Democracy.* Urbana: University of Illinois Press, 1962.

Officer, James E. *Indians in Schools.* Tucson: University of Arizona Press, 1956.

Özgün, Murat and Gökçe, İhsan. *Alfabe.* Istanbul: Devlet Basimevi, 1936.

Piers, Gerhart, and Singer, Milton B. *Shame and Guilt: A Psychoanalytic and a Cultural Study.* Springfield, Illinois: Charles C Thomas, 1953.

Pierson, Donald. *Negroes in Brazil.* Chicago: University of Chicago Press, 1942.

Prescott, William H. *History of the Conquest of Mexico* and *History of the Conquest of Peru.* New York: Modern Library, Random House, n.d.

Rambusch, Nancy. *Learning How to Learn: An American Approach to Montessori.* New York: Helicon Press, Inc., 1962.

Riessman, Frank. *The Culturally Deprived Child.* New York: Harper and Brothers, 1962.

Roeder, Ralph. *Juárez and His Mexico.* 2 vols. New York: Viking Press, 1947.

Saunders, Lyle. *Cultural Difference and Medical Care: The Case of the Spanish-Speaking People of the Southwest.* New York: Russell Sage Foundation, 1954.

Saxon, Lyle, Dreyer, Edward and Tallant, Robert. *A Collection of Louisiana Folk Tales.* Boston: Houghton Mifflin Co., 1945.

Snyder, Charles R. *Alcohol and the Jews.* Glencoe, Illinois: Free Press, 1958.
Spindler, George D. (ed.). *Education and Anthropology.* Stanford: Stanford University Press, 1955.
Stonequist, Everett V. *The Marginal Man. A Study in Personality and Culture Conflict.* New York, Chicago: Charles Scribner's Sons, 1937.
Strode, Hudson. *Timeless Mexico.* New York: Harcourt, Brace and Company, 1944.
Sullivan, Harry Stack (eds., Perry, H. S., and Gawell, M. L.). *The Interpersonal Theory of Psychiatry.* New York: W. W. Norton and Co., 1953.
Symposium. *The Race Question in Modern Science.* New York: United Nations, distributed by W. Morrow, 1956.
Thomas, W. I., and Znaniecki, Florian. *The Polish Peasant in Europe and America.* New York: Alfred A. Knopf, 1927.
Tuck, Ruth D. *Not with the Fist: A Study of Mexican-Americans in a Southwest City.* New York: Harcourt, Brace and Company, 1946.
Tylor, E. B. *Primitive Culture.* London: John Murray, 1871, 2 vols. New York: 7th edition, 1924.
Waller, Willard. *The Family.* New York: Cordon, 1938.
Warner, W. Lloyd, Havighurst, Robert J., and Loeb, Martin B. *Who Shall Be Educated? The Challenge of Unequal Opportunities.* New York: Harper and Brothers, 1944.
Wilensky, Harold L., and Lebeaux, Charles N. *Industrial Society and Social Welfare.* New York: Russell Sage Foundation, 1958.
Wissler, Clark. *The American Indian, An Introduction to the Anthropology of the New World.* New York: Oxford University Press, 1922.
Woolf, Virginia. *A Room of One's Own.* New York: Harcourt, Brace and Company, 1929.
Wright, Richard. *Native Son.* New York: Harper and Brothers, 1940.
—— *Black Boy, A Record of Childhood and Youth.* New York and London: Harper and Brothers, 1937, 1945.

Articles

Alexander, Louis. "Texas Helps Her Little Latins," *The Saturday Evening Post,* August 5, 1961.
The Annals of The American Academy of Political and Social Science, "American Indians and American Indian Life," Vol. 311 (May 1957).
Barker, George C. "Social Functions of Language in a Mexican-American Community," *Acta Americana* 5 (1947).
Bienenstock, Theodore. "Social Life and Authority in the Eastern European Jewish Shtetl Community," *The Southwestern Journal of Anthropology,* Vol. 6, No. 3 (Autumn 1950).
Bliven, Bruce. "East Coast or West—Which?" *New York Times Sunday Magazine,* March 12, 1961.
Boas, Franz. "Changes in Bodily Form of Descendants of Immigrants," *American Anthropologist,* n.s., Vol. 14, pp. 530–562 (1912).
—— "Anthropology" in E. R. A. Seligman and Alvin Johnson (eds.), *Encyclopedia of the Social Sciences,* Vol. II, p. 79, New York: Macmillan Co. (1934, 1954).
—— "Race" in *op. cit.,* Vol. XIII, pp. 25–36.

Brewer, W. D. "Patterns of Gesture Among the Levantine Arabs," *American Anthropologist*, Vol. 53, No. 2 (April–June 1951).

Brownlee, Aleta. "The American Indian Child," *Children*, Vol. 5, No. 2 (March–April 1958).

Carneiro, Edison. "The Structure of African Cults in Bahia," *Journal of American Folklore*, Vol. 53, No. 210 (October–December 1940).

Chambers, R. L. "The New Mexico Pattern," *Common Ground* (Summer 1949).

Crossley, Robert P. "The Secret of Getting Into Harvard," *McCall's Magazine* (July 1961).

Dobzhansky, Theodosius. "With Comment," *Current Anthropology*, Vol. 3, No. 3, pp. 279, 281 (June 1962).

Galarza, Ernesto. "Program for Action," *Common Ground* (Summer 1949).

Garn, Stanley M. "Race and Evolution," *American Anthropologist*, Vol. 59, No. 2 (April 1957).

Hadley, J. Nixon. "Demography of the American Indians," Annals of the American Academy of Political and Social Science (entitled) "American Indians and American Indian Life," Vol. 311 (May 1957).

Huxley, Julian. "Evolution, Cultural and Biological" in W. L. Thomas, Jr. (ed.), *Current Anthropology*, Chicago: University of Chicago Press, 1956.

Kelley, William Melvin. "If You're Woke You Dig It," *New York Times Sunday Magazine*, May 20, 1962.

Klein, Philip. "Social Work, General Discussion, Social Case Work," in E. R. A. Seligman and Alvin Johnson (eds.), *Encyclopedia of the Social Sciences*, Vol. XIV, pp. 165–183, New York: Macmillan Co. (1934, 1954).

Landes, Ruth. "The Personality of the Ojibwa," *Character and Personality*, Vol. 6, pp. 51–60 (1937).

——— "The Ojibwa of Canada" in Margaret Mead (ed.), *Cooperation and Competition among Primitive Peoples*, New York: McGraw-Hill Book Co., 1937; and Boston: Beacon Press, 1961.

——— "The Abnormal Among the Ojibwa Indians," *Journal of Abnormal and Social Psychology*, Vol. 33, No. 1 (January 1938).

——— "A Cult Matriarchate and Male Homosexuality," *Journal of Abnormal and Social Psychology*, Vol. 35, No. 3 (July 1940).

——— "Fetish Worship in Brazil," *Journal of American Folklore*, Vol. 53, No. 210 (October–December 1940).

——— and Zborowski, Mark. "Hypotheses Concerning the Eastern European Jewish Family," *Psychiatry*, Vol. 13, No. 4 (November 1950).

——— "Negro Slavery and Female Status," *African Affairs*, Vol. 52, No. 206 (January 1953); and in *Les Afro-Américains* (Dakar: Mémoires de l'Institut Français d' Afrique Noire), No. 27 (1953).

——— "Biracialism in America: A Comparative View," *American Anthropologist*, Vol. 57, No. 6 (December 1955).

——— "Dakota Warfare," *Southwestern Journal of Anthropology*, Vol. 15, No. 1 (Spring 1959).

——— "Culture and Social Work," *Social Work Papers*, Vol. 9, pp. 1–8, University of Southern California, School of Social Work (1962).

——— "Culture and Education," in George F. Kneller (ed.), *Foundations of Education*, New York: John Wiley and Sons, 1963.

——— "Cultural Factors in Counseling," *Journal of General Education*, Vol. 15, No. 1 (April 1963).

—— "An Anthropologist Looks at School Counseling," *Journal of Counseling Psychology*, Vol. 10, No. 1 (Spring 1963).

Lewis, Hylan. "The Changing Negro Family," in Eli Ginzberg (ed.), *The Nation's Children*, Vol. 1, *The Family and Social Change*, New York: Columbia University Press, 1960.

Livingstone, Frank. "On the Non-Existence of Human Races," *Current Anthropology*, Vol. 3, No. 3, pp. 279–281 (June 1962).

Lurie, Nancy O. "The Voice of the American Indian: Report on the American Indian Chicago Conference," *Current Anthropology*, Vol. 2, No. 5, pp. 478–500 (December 1961).

Maslow, Will. "De Facto Public School Segregation," *Villanova Law Review*, Vol. 6, No. 3 (Spring 1961).

The Mexican-American: A National Concern, New York: Common Council for American Unity, n.d. This contains reprints of Chambers and Galarza articles, pp. 20–38.

Millán, Alfonso. "El Mexicano Desnudo Frente a Sus Complejos," in Roberto Nava Luján (ed.), *Los Mexicanos Somos Así?* Los Angeles: P.O.B. 2686, n.d.

Park, Robert E. "Migration and the Marginal Man," *American Journal of Sociology*, May 1928.

Sánchez, George I. "The Crux of the Dual Language Handicap," *New Mexico School Review* (March 1954).

Sheldon, Paul M. "Mexican-Americans in Urban Public Schools. An Exploration of the Drop-Out Problem," *California Journal of Educational Research*, Vol. XII, No. 1 (January 1961).

Spier, Leslie. "Some Central Elements in the Legacy" in Walter Goldschmidt (ed.), *The Anthropology of Franz Boas*. Memoir No. 89, American Anthropological Association, Vol. 61, No. 5, Part 2, October 1959.

Stein, Herman D., and Cloward, Richard A. (eds.), *Social Perspectives on Behavior*. Glencoe, Illinois: The Free Press, 1958. This contains articles about the family in different cultures (by Paul J. Campisi, E. Franklin Frazier, Margaret Mead, Ruth Landes and Mark Zborowski, Talcott Parsons), Ruth Benedict's on continuities and discontinuities in culture, and Allison Davis' and R. J. Havighurst's on social class and color differences in child rearing.

Tanner, J. M. "Boas' Contributions to Knowledge of Human Growth and Form," in Walter Goldschmidt (ed.), *The Anthropology of Franz Boaz*.

Wolman, Marianne. "Cultural Factors and Creativity," *Journal of Secondary Education*, December 1962, Vol. 37, No. 8, pp. 454–460.

Zborowski, Mark. "The Place of Book-Learning in Traditional Jewish Culture," *Harvard Educational Review*, Vol. 19 (1949).

—— "Cultural Components in Responses to Pain," in Stein, H. D., and Cloward, R. A. (eds.), *Social Perspectives on Behavior*.

Reports

Annual Report of the Child Welfare and Attendance Branch, Los Angeles City Schools, 1960–1961 school year.

"Guidance Roles of School Personnel," Evaluation and Research Section, Los Angeles City Schools (California), 1961.

Point of View: Educational Purposes, Policies, Practises. Los Angeles City Schools, Publication 470. 1961 Revision.

California State Department of Education. Division of State Colleges and Teacher Education, Sacramento, California, December, 1954: California State Printing Office. Article 34, General Pupil Personnel Services Credential.

Council of Chief State School Officers, 1201 — 16th Street, N.W., Washington, D. C.: Pupil Personnel Services.

Toward Greater Opportunity. A Progress Report from the Superintendent of Schools to the Board of Education dealing with Implementation of Recommendations of the Commission on Integration. New York: Board of Education of the City of New York, June 1960.

The Open Enrollment Program in the Elementary Schools. Progress Report, School year 1960–1961. Division of Elementary Schools. New York City: Board of Education, City of New York.

(mimeographed) Annual Report 1960–1961. Board of Education, New York City, Central Zoning Unit.

Maslow, Will. "School Segregation, Northern Style" (mimeographed), a report for the American Jewish Congress submitted to the House Committee on Education and Labor, March 29, 1962. (New York: Stephen Wise Congress House.)

Security First National Bank Research Department, Los Angeles Monthly Summary of July, November, December 1960 (Vol. 39, Nos. 7, 11, 12, no paging) and January 1961 (Vol. 40, No. 1).

Stewart, Lawrence H. (mimeographed). "The Counselor and the School Guidance Program: Some Considerations for a Framework." Report of a conference, University of California, Berkeley, 1961. (Department of Education.)

Unpublished Manuscripts

DuPrez, Virginia H. "A Technique for Integration of a Minority Bilingual Group." Riverside, California.

Farner, Frank. "Comparative Achievement and Bilingualism of Matched Groups of Nisei, Mexican-American and Anglo High School Students." Manuscript at Claremont Graduate School.

Maxwell, Allan. Unpublished M.A. thesis in Education, Claremont Graduate School, 1962.

Werner, Fred H. "Cultural Shock in Student Transition," paper read at Southwestern Anthropological Conference, University of California, Santa Barbara, Goleta, California, April 1, 1961.

Newspapers

Claremont Courier. March 30, 1961.
Los Angeles Herald-Examiner. August 8, 1962.
Los Angeles Mirror-News. July 1, 1961.
Los Angeles Times. July 5, 6, 1962.

New York Times. September 7, 1958. April 10, May 15, November 21, 1960. February 12, May, June 18, 1961. May 20, May 27, June 17, June 24, July 1, July 8, July 22, August 26, 1962.

Magazines

Newsweek. January 8, August 13, August 27, September 3, 1962.
Saturday Evening Post. September 8, 1962.
Time. November 21, 1960; May 12, 1961.
What's New. Winter 1960 (No. 221) and February–March 1961 (No. 222).

Public Document

Morrison, A. C. (compiler). Education Code, Vol. 1. Sacramento: State of California Documents Section, Printing Division, 1961.

Index

325

Parsons, Talcott, 90 n13

Park, Robert E., sociologist on Negroes, and "marginal man," 3–4, 7, 44, 60 n17

Piers, Gerhart, on shame and guilt, 61 n22, 319

Pierson, Donald, on Negroes in Brazil, 309 n7, 319

Prescott, William H., on Mexico, 300 n2, 319

Quiller-Couch, Sir Arthur, on creativity and opportunity, 288 n4

Rambusch, Nancy, on Montessori schools, 187 n18, 319

Record, C. Wilson, on California minorities, 89 n9

Riessman, Frank, on deprived child, 62 n26, 319

Roeder, Ralph, on Mexico, 300 n1, 319

Sánchez, George I., on schooling, 89 n5, 322

Saunders, Lyle, on Mexican culture and medicine, 90 n11, 91 n19, 319

Saxon, Lyle, on Negro folklore, 309 n8, 319

Sheldon, Paul M., on Mexican dropouts, 301 n7, 322

Singer, Milton B., on shame and guilt, 61 n22, 319

Sherman, Gene, on California Negroes, 132 n3

Sisk, J. B., on mobility, 17 n11, n12

Snyder, Charles R., on alcohol and Jews, 91 n21, 320

Social work and culture, 7–8, 139–189
applying culture knowledge to, 141–182, 186–187 n13, 188 n27
concepts, methods, techniques of, 139–141
counseling in, 145–147
and schools, 139, 140
social work research in alcoholism, 179–180; in delinquency, 180, 189 n29, n30, n31; in family cultures, 148–179; in intermarriage, 180, 189 n32; in Skid Row, 176
and women, 144, 147–148, 188 n27

Spier, Leslie, on Boas, 58 n9, 322

Spindler, George D., 135 n8, 288 n1, 320

Stein, Herman D., 90 n13, 91 n19

Stewart, Lawrence H., on school counseling, 184–185 n12, 323

Stonequist, Everett V., on "marginal man" concept, 59 n17, 320

Stromberger, Mrs. Herman G., on teaching, 282 n2
see also Soledad S. C. Coronel

Strode, Hudson, on Mexico, 300 n1, 320

Supreme Court Decision against school segregation, 9, 28, 40, 42

Sullivan, Harry Stack, psychiatrist, 5–6, 52, 320

Tallant, Robert, 309 n8, 319

Tanner, J. M., on Boas, 58 n8, 322

Teachers' queries, 18–34
diverse origins of, 48
and dominant group, 23, 31–34
and "frustration," 16, 20, 48, 259, and throughout *passim*
and integration, 22
and minorities, 22–31, 34, 54
and separateness, 20–21
and special language, 16, 20–23, 50

Teachers' research in culture, 190–282
research goals and methods, 190–193
research subjects, the aged, 196
children of many origins, 205–235
children's poems, 227–235
communication, 235–238
community and minorities, 200–205
family, 205–216
family cultures, 259–280 (including Anglo-American, 262–263, 266–269, 277–280; French-American, 269–271; French-Canadian, 265; German-American, 275; Greek-American, 275–277; Hungarian-American, 263–264; Jewish, 261–262; Mormon, 265–266; Russo-German-American, 273–275; Scandinavian-American, 271–272)
foreign students, 198–200
foreign students abroad, 196–198